汉水流域（十堰段）旅游资源国际推广项目（编号：2018A06）成果
湖北省高校人文社会科学重点研究基地汉水文化研究基地资助出版

Charming Hanjiang River —Show the International Tourists Around Shiyan

魅力汉江之带老外逛十堰

祝东江　祝丰萍　著

·北京·

内 容 提 要

十堰，作为汉江上一颗璀璨的明珠，其地处鄂西生态文化旅游圈的核心位置，山水文化旅游资源丰富。为了让更多的国际友人了解汉江，亲临十堰，感受其独特魅力，提升汉江旅游产业软实力，实现其健康、快速、可持续发展，从事汉江文化研究的专家学者们共同开展汉水流域（十堰段）旅游资源译介工作，撰写、译著完成了本书。

本书包括四个部分，分别为：第一部分：全景十堰（General View of Shiyan City）；第二部分：问道武当（Visiting Wudang Mountains）；第三部分：探秘神农（Exploring Shennongjia Forest）；第四部分：十堰周边（Shiyan Suburbs）。

图书在版编目（ＣＩＰ）数据

魅力汉江之带老外逛十堰 ： 汉文、英文 / 祝东江，祝丰萍著. -- 北京 ： 中国水利水电出版社，2021.9
ISBN 978-7-5170-9944-4

Ⅰ. ①魅… Ⅱ. ①祝… ②祝… Ⅲ. ①旅游指南—十堰—汉、英 Ⅳ. ①K928.963.4

中国版本图书馆CIP数据核字(2021)第187403号

责任编辑：鞠向超　　　封面设计：梁　艳

书　　名	魅力汉江之带老外逛十堰 MEILI HAN JIANG ZHI DAI LAOWAI GUANG SHIYAN
作　　者	祝东江　祝丰萍　著
出版发行	中国水利水电出版社 （北京市海淀区玉渊潭南路 1 号 D 座　100038） 网址：www.waterpub.com.cn E-mail：mchannel@263.net（万水） sales@waterpub.com.cn 电话：（010）68367658（营销中心）、82562819（万水）
经　　售	全国各地新华书店和相关出版物销售网点
排　　版	北京万水电子信息有限公司
印　　刷	三河市华晨印务有限公司
规　　格	184mm×260mm　16 开本　21.75 印张　584 千字
版　　次	2021 年 9 月第 1 版　2021 年 9 月第 1 次印刷
定　　价	128.00 元

汉水文化书系编委会

序

在东西方世界中都有一条银河，而且，令人不胜惊异的是她们都与“乳汁”密不可分。在古希腊的神话中，主神宙斯背着夫人赫拉生养了一个私生子。宙斯期盼这个儿子能够长生不老，便偷偷地把婴儿放在熟睡的夫人赫拉身旁，让他吮吸赫拉的乳汁，不料孩子把赫拉惊醒，一看吃奶的孩子并不是自己的亲生儿子，赫拉便一把推开，孩子含在口中的乳汁溅洒在空中。神奇的乳汁滑过浩瀚的太空，星光闪闪、波光粼粼，立刻在宇宙之间铺开一条乳白色的大河，这便是银河在西方传说中的起源。而在中国的古老传说中，银河也叫云汉、银汉，是牛郎和织女相会的地方，而且，这条天河实际上与大地相连，《诗经》中有云，“维天有汉”，唯一与银河相接的地上河流便是汉江。汉水又叫沔水。沔、孊古音同声转注，沔可读为孊（mi），孊即“咪咪”，“咪咪”就是“妈妈儿”的意思，而“妈妈儿”在汉水流域指的就是乳房，故沔水即奶水，意即沔水浇灌哺育一方苍生。沧海桑田，万古如斯。汉水行诗走歌、流金淌银，不仅是一条绿色生态之河、商旅黄金之河、文化大河、历史大河和魅力大河，更是华夏文明的重要发源地和中华民族的母亲河，被世界文化学家誉为东方的“莱茵河”。

汉水是中国最古老的大河，比长江黄河还要早七亿多年，堪称中国的“祖母河”。在战国《禹贡》一书中的“九州导山导水示意图”和北宋沈括的《禹迹图》中，黄河与长江的流向都与如今所见并不相同，中途几经改道，唯有汉江，在这两幅地图上描绘得与今天的地图几乎一样。这就是说，人类在2500年前就认识了汉江，在1137年前认识了黄河，在400年前还不知道长江源头在青海省境内。人类对于汉江的认识，要早于长江与黄河，直至春秋时期，汉江都保持着古中国第一大水的地位。

汉水流域既是地球上古老生命的发祥地之一，更是人类的重要发祥地。这里既是世界上规模最大、数量最多、分布最广，龙蛋共生的恐龙蛋化石群，其距今大约6500万年；又是东方从距今200万年到5万年的古人类演变完整链条化石群的所在地。这里出土的郧县人化石大致距今80万年至200万年之间，梅铺猿人牙齿化石距今75万年，白龙洞猿人距今10万－20万年，而黄龙洞猿人则距今5万年。汉水流域古人类演变完整链条化石群的发现，彻底改写了人类起源于非洲的历史，使汉水流域升格为人类的老家，成为人类当之无愧的摇篮。

汉水流域是中华民族和中华文明的重要发祥地。在地球的版图上，有一条神秘的北纬30度线，许多古老的河流文明正是沿着这条纬线，开始了自己跨越千年的文明旅程。公元前3000年，两河流域出现了十几个城邦，由此进入了早期的国家状态；尼罗河三角洲一带，也因为土地肥沃，人口密集，成为古代“地中海沿岸的粮仓”，也是古埃及文明的发源地。汉江，正好处在这条黄金般的北纬30°文明线之上。据吕思勉和钱穆的观点看，古代民族的得名往往是他们居住的地区。古老的华夏民族主干最早就是生活在汉水流域。他们认为，华夏族就是生活在华山以南、夏水两岸的民族。而古代华山就是现在的河南嵩山，夏水就是今天的汉水。这说明，汉水流域是中华民族最古老族源的发祥地。也正因为如此，汉江还是中国唯一一条被国外（韩国）系统复制迁移了名称、风俗文化和流域地名的大江。

2003年前后，武汉大学考古学家王然教授带领自己的学生来到了汉水之滨的郧县柳陂镇。这里是南水北调的淹没区。他们的任务是抢救性发掘即将被淹没的文物。在一个叫辽瓦梁子的地方，他们被发掘地点的奇异景象惊呆了。此处的文物从明清开始依次纵深掘进，1米到2米不等，就代表一个朝代的文物层，层层叠压，一个朝代压着一个朝代，中间从未间断，连续开挖竟然挖出了夏商时代的文物。这是在世界文物考古发掘史上都少见的奇观。它雄辩地说明，汉江流域的古老文明一脉长流，历经悠悠五千年从未断绝。因此，他们理直气壮地将遗址所在地辽瓦梁子命名为“中华文明通史遗址”。与之相得益彰的，这里不仅留下了伏羲画八卦、女娲补天、神农尝百草的神话，牛郎织女、嫦娥奔月、汉水女神、大禹治水等传奇也在这里诞生。在钟祥发现了中国最早的稻作遗址，在汉口发现了中国最早的盘龙城，在随州发现了春秋时代世界上最先进的乐器编钟……

作为兴龙之地，从汉水走出了西汉和东汉两朝的开国帝王刘邦和刘秀。汉帝国的兴起，使汉水与汉朝、汉人、汉语、汉字、汉族、汉服、汉学等等有着密不可分的直接联系，使汉水流域成为华夏文明的发祥地之一，也成为世界各地华夏子孙和汉民族祖居之圣地。

自古以来，汉水流域缔造出伟大的文明。据现代学者考证，在远古，汉水流域生活的是炎帝的子孙——主要是巴族、苗族和后来的楚族。著名的“西土八国”不仅在当时掌握了先进生产力、作为助周倒商的强大军事劲旅，而且代表了春秋以前神州大地大西南和华南的最高文明。中国文学的两大源头《诗经》和《楚辞》均发源交汇于汉水流域，《诗经·汉广》描写的汉水女神是中国文学史上最早的江河女神形象。诗祖尹吉甫在这里创造了中国最早的个人署名诗篇，并且采编了中国诗歌元典《诗经》。爱国诗人屈原是中国最伟大的浪漫主义诗人之一，也是我国已知最早的著名诗人和伟大的政治家。他创立了“楚辞”这种文体，也开创了“香草美人”的传统。《离骚》和《诗经》开创了中国文学现实主义和浪漫主义的伟大先河和光辉传统，成为中国文学的渊薮。

出土自曾侯乙墓中的二十八宿天象图，拉开了中国最早天文学之序幕，而《甘石星经》的作者之一甘德是楚人，其发现彗星远远早于印度，更比伽利略早1300多年。张衡诞生于南阳郡汉水流域白河之畔的西鄂县（今河南南阳市石桥镇），是我国东汉时期伟大的天文学家、地震学家和发明家。他提出浑天说，改进浑天仪，升级了我国航天遥测技术；他探索地震起因，发明了世界上最早的地动仪。

西汉时期的外交家张骞从汉水边的城固踏出了第一条通向世界的丝绸之路；东汉的蔡伦封侯于汉水边的龙亭铺，发明了造纸术。“医圣”张仲景是东汉南郡涅阳县（今河南省南阳县）人，是我国古代伟大的医学家，因其仁心仁德，后人尊称他为“医宗之圣”或“医圣”。他所著述的《伤寒杂病论》是我国最早的理论联系实际的临床诊疗专书，是继《黄帝内经》之后最有影响的一部医学典籍，被后世医家誉为“万世宝典”。“千古良相”诸葛亮“鞠躬尽瘁，死而后已”的献身精神，择才擅用、任人唯贤的用人之道，忠诚无私的高尚品格，开拓创新的进取意识，千百年来一直为人们所敬仰、称道和怀念。其手摇羽扇，运筹帷幄的潇洒形象，千百年来已成为人们心中“智慧”的代名词。习凿齿是东晋史学家，他所著作的《襄阳耆旧记》是中国最早的人物志之一。“宰相之杰”张居正，世人称其为“张江陵”，他是中国历史上最优秀的内阁首辅之一，明代最伟大的政治家、改革家。“茶圣”陆羽擅长品茗，对中国茶业和世界茶业发展作出了卓越贡献，被誉为“茶仙”，尊为“茶圣”，祀为“茶神”。

汉水流域物华天宝，人杰地灵。这里不仅文化伟人英雄辈出，撼动天下、扛鼎历史，而且更富跨代绝响、超世贡献。在政治历史、经济社会、农业医药、科学技术、军事外交、文学艺术、语言文字等方面，都在不同历史时期，谱写了中华文明不同发展阶段的绝顶奇迹，对人类文明做出了巨大贡献，留下了不可磨灭的丰功伟绩，泽被千秋，影响深远，为古今中外的文化历史学家所景仰、赞叹。

汉水流域拥有丰富璀璨的著名文化品牌。汉水流域不仅享有古人类、中华民族、中华文明三大发祥地之誉，更是一座国内少有、世界罕见的文化资源宝库。这里有世界独一无二的野考基地神农架，有世界文化遗产武当山和明显陵，有世界最大的流放地古房陵，有世界民间故事村伍家沟村，还占有中国七大历史文化名城和二十大国家级文化品牌，他们分别是三皇品牌、汉民族史诗《黑暗传》、汉民族第一民歌村吕家河、中华文明的第四源头古巴域、中国最古老的大江汉水、中国第一诗人和第一诗人的故乡尹吉甫和房陵、中国郧县人、中国楚文化的发祥地、中国孝文化的摇篮孝感、中国最古老的城堡盘龙城、中国古代最先进的乐器曾侯乙墓古编钟、拥有最宽的人工护城河和最完备古城的中华第一城池襄阳城、中国最有影响的布衣山水田园诗人孟浩然的故居所在地和隐居地鹿门山、中国智圣诸葛亮的隐居地与耕读地古隆中、在宋元之战号称铁打的襄阳、沿用时间最长的私家园林鼻祖和郊野园林典范习家池、“牛郎织女”与七夕节起源地、被誉为古代土木工程的第三大奇迹的褒斜石门古隧道、太极湖和中国最早的楚长城。此外，这里聚集了 68 处国家文化遗产保护单位、49 处国家非物质文化遗产，还有大量的文化遗址正在论证、申报之中，至于省级文化保护单位和非物质文化遗产则比比皆是，初步统计已达 1100 余处。这些宝贵的文化资源，有的填补了人类文化的空白，有的代表了中华文明该历史时代发展的高峰，有的昭示了人类无法揣度、永无止境的高贵智慧，有的则是取之不尽、用之不竭的精神宝藏。他们闪烁着中华文明的璀璨光华，散发着强烈的东方智慧和神奇魅力，是中华民族骄傲、自豪和无上光荣之所在，也是汉水流域永续发展的信心和福祉所在！

汉水文化是中国传统文化中的重要题材与主题。汉水流域是人类的古老发祥地之一，是以华夏民族为主干的汉民族重要发祥地，更是古老、伟大中华文明的重要发祥地。600 年前，因为明朝北修故宫、南修武当使汉水武当与北京建立起神秘的连接而异军突起，一跃而为圣山、仙山，600 年后的今天，随着南水北调工程的实施和完成，汉水与汉水文化又将再一次与北京缔结神秘的联系，将会成为横空出世、举世瞩目的圣河和文化宝藏。

在这个意义上，如果说，大唐文化在西安，大宋文化在开封，那么，我们也有充分的理由说，大汉文化、汉文化就在汉水！汉水文化不仅属于汉水、汉水流域、汉民族，而且更属于神州大地，属于中华民族，属于人类和世界。而汉水文化内含的价值和高度，不仅具有流域文化的地标性，更富于民族特性和国家高度，是我们伟大民族和伟大国家应该倍加珍惜和保护、大力弘扬和传承、科学发掘和开发的无上宝藏。

习近平总书记指出，历史和现实都证明，中华民族有着强大的文化创造力。每到重大历史关头，文化都能感国运之变化、立时代之潮头、发时代之先声，为亿万人民、为伟大祖国鼓与呼。没有中华文化繁荣兴盛，就没有中华民族伟大复兴。中华优秀传统文化是中华民族的突出优势，中华民族伟大复兴需要以中华文化发展繁荣为条件，必须大力弘扬中华优秀传统文化。要对传统文化进行创造性转化、创新性发展，让收藏在禁宫里的文物、陈列在广阔大地上的遗产、书写在古籍里的文字都活起来。正是基于这种认识，汉江师范学院立足于文化历史学、文化社会学、文化哲学和文化地理学等学科背景，着眼于历史性、时代性、全面性、典型性、学术性和普及性等学术定位，运用现代学术规范，从全流域的角度，系统地梳理了汉江流域经济社会、历史文化发展的辉煌历程，汉水文化的形成和发展的古今概貌，揭示了汉水文化的基本内涵和特征，全面地描绘了汉水流域具有典型意义、五彩纷呈的文化事象和民风民俗，形成了“汉水文化研究书系”这部独具特色的地域文化研究、流域与河流文化研究的系列丛书。丛书的出版，既是汉水流域文化研究的喜事、盛事和要事，也是汉江师范学院学科建设、教育教学改革转型发展的重要成果，更是地方高校践行政产学研企融合、努力传承发展地方历史文化、强力服务地方经济社会发展的突出表现，值得社会各界的点赞和欢迎。

汉水是古代“江河淮汉”四大名渎之一，在中国流域文化中，其文化的兼容性、开放性、固执性和创新性都非常典型。汉水文化是特异型的流域文化。汉水流域历史上基本形成了整体性的文化系统和文化结构，构成了相对独立的文化区；汉水流域的历史发展和文化变迁是中华文明历史演变的一个缩影。汉水流域以两大平原（江汉平原和伊洛平原）和三大盆地（汉中盆地、南阳盆地和襄阳盆地）为地理环境条件，以四大流域文化（秦陇文化、巴蜀文化、荆楚文化和中原文化）为人文语境条件，形成上游、中游、下游三个区系，它是甘、陕、鄂、豫、川、渝交界地区，是承东启西、连接南北的枢纽地带，形成内陆性的文化走廊和黄金文化带。作为特异型的流域文化，汉水文化在自身的历史进程中处于南北文化激荡交锋的锋面，融合黄河文化和长江文化的优长，具有兼容会通的特色，独树一帜，别具一格，是得天独厚、不可代替的流域文化范型。对汉水文化的观照和审视，从某种意义上说，就是对中华文化的重心和关节点的观照和审视。我坚信，随着《汉水文化研究书系》的问世，关于汉水文化赋存资源现代转型的研究和开发，对于中西部地区的先进文化建设与和谐文化建设，对于流域文化、城市文化和文化学的学科建设，对于进一步振兴中华民族传统文化，具有重要的理论意义和现实意义；对于全流域地区的文化资源优势转化为文化产业优势，对于推进文化强省建设和文化产业跨越式发展，对于南水北调中线工程实施和文化生态保护，具有重要的促进和推动作用。我们期望，随着《汉水文化研究书系》的出版，一个更大范围、更大力度的保护和传承、研究和发展汉水文化的高潮会尽快到来。

是为序。

张维国

（原中共十堰市委书记、人大常委会主任）

2017 年 5 月

前 言

随着世界的和平稳定、经济的发展与人民生活水平的提高，旅游逐渐成为现代人类生活中不可或缺的重要内容。旅游业已经成为世界上规模最大和发展势头最强劲的产业，许多国家和地区都纷纷把它作为经济发展的重点产业和先导产业。中国独特的山水名胜、人文景观吸引着全球旅游爱好者，使得旅游业在国民经济中的地位越发重要。欧睿国际在2018世界旅游交易会（World Travel Market）上表示，到2030年，中国将取代法国成为全球头号旅游目的地（the leading destination worldwide）。中国国务院《关于加快旅游业发展的意见》明确指出，“要把旅游业培育成为国民经济的战略性支柱产业和人民群众更加满意的现代化服务业。”全国上下积极开展对外旅游宣传，推动旅游业国际化发展。

汉江，又称汉水，与长江、黄河、淮河一道并称“江河淮汉”，是长江的最大支流。汉江流域是湖北省资源要素最为密集的地区之一：自然资源丰富、经济基础雄厚、生态条件优越、文化底蕴深厚、沿线城市文化特色鲜明（道教文化、三国文化、石家河文化、曹禺文化等），是连接武汉城市圈和鄂西生态文化旅游圈的重要轴线、连接鄂西北与江汉平原的重要纽带，具有“融合两圈、连接一带、贯通南北、承东启西”的功能，在湖北省经济社会发展格局中具有重要的战略地位和突出的带动作用。

湖北省委省政府指出“要加快推进鄂西北生态文化旅游圈建设，实现湖北由资源大省向旅游经济强省的跨越”。十堰市委市政府也明确指出，“要把十堰建设成国际知名生态文化旅游区、国际知名旅游目的地和鄂西生态文化旅游圈的核心板块和重要支撑。”2018年10月8日国务院批复《汉江生态经济带发展规划》，要求河南、湖北、陕西省人民政府、国家发展改革委全面贯彻党的十九大和十九届二中、三中全会精神，以习近平新时代中国特色社会主义思想为指导，落实党中央、国务院决策部署，主动融入“一带一路”建设、京津冀协同发展、长江经济带发展等国家重大战略，围绕改善提升汉江流域生态环境，打造美丽、畅通、创新、幸福、开放、活力的生态经济带。

十堰市位于湖北省西北部，地处鄂、豫、渝、陕交界地带，是美丽的山城、新兴的现代车城、内陆山区唯一的国家级园林城市、“中国优秀旅游城市”、“2017年度最佳文化旅游目的地”。十堰山川秀美，历史悠久，自然、人文景观交相辉映，旅游资源丰富密集、品位很高，拥有世界自然与文化遗产武当山（“中国道教圣地”、太极拳的发祥地、全国武术之乡、国家5A级风景名胜区、“中国世界纪录协会中国道教第一山”“欧洲人最喜爱的中国十大景区”）、世界闻名的商用车生产基地和举世瞩目的南水北调中线工程核心水源区，是名副其实的旅游资源大市，主要旅游景点有：武当山风景区、丹江口水库、赛武当自然保护区、青龙山恐龙蛋化石群国家级自然保护区、五龙河旅游风景区、女娲山天池、野人谷野人洞等。周边有“华中屋脊”神农架，群山巍峨、森林苍茫、石林诡秘多姿、风光四时各异，是我国南北东西珍稀物种交会地，誉为“华中天然动物园、东方物种基因库”；野人之谜、白化动物更为其平添了几分奇幻色彩。

按照鄂西生态文化旅游圈核心旅游板块的定位，十堰市正发挥山水文化旅游资源综合优势，全面提升旅游产业实力，积极建设以大山大水大人文为特色的中国优秀旅游目的地城市和带动鄂西北、辐射渝陕豫周边地区的区域旅游中心城市。十堰上下，尤其是政府部门和学术界都在认真分析反省，积极开展联合营销、总体宣传，营造鲜明的区域旅游形象，让大十堰走向全国、走向全世界。地方高校更应责无旁贷地开展汉水流域旅游资源研究，提高旅游翻译质量，以朴实客观、结构紧凑、简洁明了、规范地道的译文和良好和谐的语言文化氛围有效传播汉水文化和旅游资源，让更多的国际友人了解汉江，亲临十堰，感受其独特魅力，提升汉江旅游产业软实力，实现其健康、快速、可持续发展。

为此，在汉江师范学院、湖北省高校人文社科重点研究基地汉水文化研究基地大力支持和资助下，长期从事地方旅游文化翻译研究与实践的祝东江副教授联合陈梅副教授、祝丰萍讲师（武汉文理学院）、彭小燕副教授、何建友博士副教授、周娟副教授、张希萌讲师、朱卫志讲师等专家学者一起开展汉水流域（十堰段）旅游资源译介工作。在本书的编译过程中，参阅了众多专家学者的著作论文和相关旅游景点网站介绍，得到了中国水利水电出版社、汉江师范学院领导同事的指导和帮助，在此表示由衷的谢意。本书由祝东江负责总策划、撰稿、翻译、审稿、并完成第二、第三部分书稿，陈梅负责景点协调选择和全书审稿，祝丰萍负责完成中文资料收集及第一、第四部分书稿，彭小燕、何建友、周娟、张希萌、朱卫志等人参与了部分章节内容的编译工作。

衷心希望本书能为您的学习和工作提供便利和帮助，能为汉江流域文化旅游、尤其十堰市国际化推广做出贡献，同时也希望您不吝赐教，批评指正，使本书更加完善。谢谢！

此致！

作 者

2021年8月湖北十堰

目　　录

Part 01
全景十堰
General View of Shiyan City

Part 02
问道武当
Visiting Wudang Mountains

Part 03

探秘神农

Exploring Shennongjia Forest

Part 04

十堰周边

Shiyan Suburbs

Appendix

问道十堰 逐梦茅箭

Appreciate Taoism in Shiyan and Realize Dreams in Maojian

Part 01 全景十堰

General View of Shiyan City

Chapter 1 Shiyan 十堰

十堰因车而建，因车而兴，她既是“东风车”的故乡，号称“东方底特律”的汽车城，也是一座灵山秀水环抱、四季景色诱人的山城、旅游城、生态园林城。十堰是旅游胜地，是“长江三峡—神农架—古隆中—武当山—丹江口水库—古城西安”黄金旅游线上的一颗璀璨明珠，境内有列入世界文化遗产名录并获得5A级旅游区称号的道教圣地武当山，有号称亚洲第一大人工湖的丹江口水库，有轰动中外的郧县猿人遗址，有恐龙蛋化石群和恐龙骨骼化石，是世界罕见的恐龙故乡。有温泉、瀑布、天池、峡谷、溶洞，有原始森林，有现代汽车都市。十堰这个地方，冬季无严寒、夏季无酷暑……十堰作为地名存在，其来历有种说法：相传古人在这里修了十条堰，故今称十堰。

十堰是闻名全国的汽车工业基地，十堰是享誉中外的旅游胜地，十堰是物产富饶的资源大市。真诚欢迎四方游客前来旅游观光。

Shiyan City has been set up and thrived because of the automobile industry. Well-known as “the Oriental Detroit”, the birthplace of the Dongfeng Automobile, Shiyan City is also a mountainous city, tourist city, and ecological garden city with the surrounding charming mountains and rivers, full of changing scenery in the four seasons. Tourists pour into this mountainous city for its beautiful scenes all year round. The rich tourist resources help Shiyan become the “Ecological Garden City” as one of the most attractive places of interest, just like a brilliant pearl shining on the golden travel route “the Three Gorges of Changjiang River-Shennongjia Forest-Ancient Longzhong-Wudang Mountains-Danjiangkou Reservoir-historic Xi'an City”. The 5A-Level tourist attraction, “Wudang Mountains”, known as the holy land of China Taoism, is located here and been listed as the World Cultural Heritage Site by the UNESCO. Other equally famous scenic spots worthy of visiting are the biggest man-made lake in Asia-Danjiangkou Reservoir, world-renowned relics of ape man and the rarest fossils of pre-historic dinosaurs in Yunyang District. Hot springs, waterfalls, valleys, karst caves and primitive forests all abound in this modern Automobile City. The mild climate here makes it devoid of intense heat in summer or severe cold and in winter. A legend goes that the ancient residents used to build ten weirs around the city, hence the name “Shiyan” (ten weirs in Chinese).

Shiyan, rich in natural resources, now gets worldwide acknowledgment as one of the key national automobile industry bases and one of the most charming resorts. We sincerely welcome all the visitors and friends coming from a far.

Chapter 2 Shiyan, a City of Taoism, Praised by All 十堰，一个人人称“道”的地方

在神奇的北纬 30° 线上，在中国版图的几何中心，在鄂西北母亲河汉江温婉的臂弯里，一座山水生态之城，以其特有的体温，温暖着我的梦境，她就是我的家乡——十堰。

我想念着家乡武当山的道骨仙风。天之道，道法自然；地之道，在乎和美；人之道，贵为厚德。

600 年前，明成祖朱棣敕令北建故宫，南修武当，遣 30 万工匠，历 13 个寒暑，铸就了八百里武当山，33 处道教宫观建筑群的旷世恢弘，承载起一个王朝的太和之梦。

金顶、南岩、紫霄宫、太子坡，每一石、每一柱、每一阙，那蕴含人生玄机的古建筑，连同那玄妙飘灵的武当功夫、深邃高远的道教文化，无不透映出世界文化遗产和国家地质公园的神秘、神奇与神圣！

真人张三丰当年预言：“此山异日必大兴”。鲁迅断言：中国文化的根祇全在道教。上善若水，抱朴含真，天人合一，“道”滋养着我们的性灵，也修炼出城市的千年太和道德，万般灵秀山水！

我思念着家乡碧水的烟波浩渺。十堰，是南水北调中线工程核心水源区。2014 年 12 月 12 日，蓄秀涌翠的汉水从这里跨越千山万水，一路北去三千里，润泽着京、津、冀、豫干涸的大地。600 年前，神权与皇权呼应；600 年后，水都与首都一衣带水，血脉相通！

我自豪，我来自“东风”车的故乡。她，因车而建，因车而兴，她是东风汽车的摇篮，是名副其实的“中国卡车之都”。

我想再听听家乡神秘的传说。抟土造人的女娲为何在这里采石补天？牛郎织女七夕是如何在这里牵手鹊桥的？真武得道成仙、神农搭架采药、“野人”不期而遇……多少人儿时的梦想被这些传说一次次刷新！

我沉迷于 100 万年前的“郧县人”的挖掘发现，它向世界宣称：汉江是汉文化的摇篮、“郧县人”是汉民族的祖先！在这里，我依稀听到了恐龙的咆哮，嗅出了古楚长城上的硝烟。

我憧憬回到这个诗意山水之地，流连于那秀美的十八里长峡、幽深的野人谷，徜徉在这座国家级园林城里，陶醉于生态城满目青翠中。

缠绕我舌尖的，总是鲜香的竹溪蒸盆、酸辣的郧阳三合汤、房县滑韧的小香菇、丹江口水库细嫩的翘嘴鲌的味道，那是家乡的味道。如果再来一壶荡气回肠的房县黄酒，我会沉醉在家乡的怀抱里。

十堰，我魂牵梦萦的家乡，她就像一杯被光阴的流水浸泡的武当道茶，沁人心脾，回味悠长。如果说，今生要来一次说走就走的旅行，你一定要来这里看看，我陪你，用心路抵达！

In the magical line of North Latitude 32°, in the geometric center of China, in the tender arms of the Hanjiang River, the mother river of northwest Hubei Province, an Ecological City of Mountain and Water, warms my dreams with her unique body temperature, She is my hometown—Shiyan City.

I miss Taoism in Wudang Mountains. Way of Heaven, follows the Nature; Way of Earth, pursues harmony; Way of Man, respects morality.

600 years ago, Zhu Di, Emperor Cheng of the Ming Dynasty (1368—1644) ordered to build the Forbidden City in the North, Wudang Taoist Palaces in the South, and sent 300,000 workers and artisans through 13 years, made Wudang Mountains of four hundred kilometers, 33 magnificent Taoist palaces and halls, bearing the Taihe (Supreme Harmony) Dream of the Ming Dynasty.

Jinding (Golden Top), Nanyan (South Cliff), Zixiao Palace (Purple Cloud Palace), and TaiziSlope (Prince Slope), every stone, column, and watchtower, the ancient buildings containing the life mystery and mysterious Wudang Gongfu and profound Taoist Culture, all made World Culture Heritage Site, National Geopark mysterious, magical and sacred.

Zhang Sanfeng, master of Taichi once predicted, Wudang Mountains will be prosperous in the future. Lu Xun, one of the great Chinese Writer said, Chinese Culture is totally rooted in Taoism. The greatest benevolence is like water, embracing simplicity and contain truth, and unifying human and Nature. “Taoism” has nourished our minds and the City of thousand-year supreme harmony and graceful, mysterious mountain and water.

I miss the vast clear water in my hometown. Shiyan is the core water resource area of South-to-North Water Diversion. On December 12, 2014, clean and clear water of the Hanjiang River flowed across thousands of mountains and rivers and through fifteen hundred kilometers northward, moistening the dry lands in Beijing, Tianjin, Hebei, and Henan. 600 years ago, theocratic authority and imperial power echoed, 600 years later, Shiyan and Beijing connected by water, drinking the water from the same river.

I am proud because I’m from the Home of “Dongfeng” Automotive. She was built and become prosperous by “Dongfeng” Automotive, She is the cradle of Dongfeng Motor, the home of Chinese Truck.

I would like to enjoy the mysterious legends in my hometown once more, such as Nüwa made man by earth here, the Cowherd and the Weaving Maid meeting in the Magpie Bridge, Emperor Zhenwu became immortal, Shennong picked herbs by putting up frames, and Wild Man in Shennongjia... Many childhood dreams have been refreshed again and again.

I’m interested in the discovery of “Yunxian Man” one-million-year ago, which declared to the world, the Hanjiang River is the cradle of Chinese Culture and “Yunxian Man” is the ancestor of the Han People. It’s here where I could hear dinosaurs’ thundering roar and smell the smoke of war on the ancient wall of Chu Kingdom.

I long for going back to the poetic landscape, lingering in the charming Eighteen-Li Long Gorge, Deep Wild-manValley and strolling in the national garden city, being enchanted by the green in the Eco-city here and there.

Enjoy the aftertaste of delicious Steaming Bowl, Zhuxi County, hot and sour soup, Yunyang District, fresh little mushrooms, Fangxian County, and delicate culter alburnus from Danjiangkou Reservoir, which are the taste of my home. And more with a glass of Yellow Wine, Fangxian

County, I will be intoxicated in the arms of my hometown.

Shiyan, my hometown, I miss her very much. She is like a glass of Wudang Tea soaked by the water of time, refreshing and after-tasting. If you want to have a trip without delay, you are advised to come here please. Enjoy the charming landscape and excellent people here with your happy heart and my tender accompany.

Chapter 3 Charming and Miraculous Shiyan 神奇十堰

神奇十堰，山灵水秀

天下第一仙山，亘古无双圣境。武当山山水川谷远取其势，近取其质；七十二峰接天青，二十四涧水常鸣。宫观庙祠，适形而止。一柱十二梁、九曲黄河墙。“挂在悬崖上的故宫”，虽为人造，宛若天成，不仅问鼎中国艺术和建筑的最高水准，更成为“天人合一”的真实化身。

六百年大兴，武当山由皇室宗庙折桂世界文化遗产。三月三庙会、九月九祈福法会、撞钟迎春等道教节庆，世界各地的道教名流、善男信女都云集十堰，登武当问道，祈天下太和。

山水形胜入画来，一起来赏吧！

太极峡浑然天成，天然形成的经典太极图使得道教文化在这里永恒。

青龙山龙蛋共生，国家级地质公园守护着最完整的亿万年前恐龙化石群落，世界罕见。

沧浪山秀外慧中，国家级森林公园尽显原始天然氧吧的妩媚与神秘。

十八里长峡，崖陡石怪，山与水、刚与柔的角力，解密造物的超然与神奇。

千里汉水蓄秀涌翠。亚洲第一大人工淡水湖烟波浩渺，清冽甘甜。太极湖风生水起，嫁接山水，养生人文。湖光山色间，动，可一日千里；静，则心无落尘。

时空穿越，风云际会。600 年前，明永乐皇帝北建故宫、南修武当，十堰的神山与皇权呼应；600 年后，南水北调，十堰 30 万亩良田沉入江底，30 万百姓饱含眷恋举家外迁，这条生命之河挟裹着楚汉魂魄的深情厚谊，千里北上，十堰的圣水与华北京津大地共饮。

汉江两岸，山峦起伏、植被葱郁，山泉小溪随处可见，游鱼细石清澈透明。

赏水之秀，八百里堵河清纯俊美，纯洁无瑕；五龙河五龙捧圣，珠玉飞溅；九龙瀑千迭瀑布，虎啸龙吟。

品水之性，黄龙滩水库随波踏浪，“食水鲜、居水岸、娱水面”，情趣盎然；堵河漂流，体验探险之乐；韩家洲戏水，人与汉水亲密无间。

神奇十堰，人杰地灵

或许是生命的始祖将这方热土点染，更或是秦山汉水的灵气让这里生机无限。

一百万年前，“郧县人”择居汉水，这片土壤从此有了人类的炊烟。

迈瓦店子遗址，发掘了跨越五千年的不断代历史遗存，成为中国绝无仅有的地下通史。

“汉之广矣，不可泳思。江之永矣，不可方思”，《诗经》中留下了诗祖尹吉甫，当年采风汉水江畔的身影。

自秦以来，（魏王李泰、燕王李忠、唐中宗李显、后梁惠王朱友能等）三十余位帝王将相（万余名达官贵族）先后流放十堰，（宫廷习俗）皇室隐居文化，成为这片土地上的另一道风景。

世界上第一位与野人搏斗的老人，至今仍在此守候，昔日的伤痕和野人的毛发清晰为证。数十年来，无数探秘野人的足迹遍布“华中屋脊”神农架。野人洞、野人谷，声名远播。

人类始祖女娲在竹山炼石补天，遗落五彩石——绿松石，质地高雅，品冠全球，天下推崇。

牛郎织女，十堰天河鹊桥相会，爱情故事，千古传诵，沁人心脾。

厚重的历史积淀，让这方土地人文蔚起。

非物质文化遗产凤凰灯舞、汉调山二黄，新琴古韵，历久弥新；“中国民间文化活化石”伍家沟故事，“中国汉民族民歌第一村”吕家河民歌，口口相传，震古烁今！

汉水文化厚重灵动，博大精深。

秦音豫律，蜀声楚音，京腔越调等地域文化并存，远古文化、武当文化、郧阳文化、移民文化，和谐共生，十堰堪称文化生态的热带雨林，多元多样，移步换景。

神奇十堰，天外来城

秦巴腹地，方园千里之水，在十堰汇集；西高东低，面向东方，朝阳朝气，把十堰沐浴；大山阻隔，沃野千里，聚气藏风，十堰人杰地灵；武当山，华夏精神高地，皇家崇尚，百姓敬仰，曾系（既）江山社稷；郧阳抚治威震一方，辖八府九州六十五县，二百零五年，关乎家国安宁。

从皇家辉煌建筑到生物多样性，从人文生态到世纪工程，十堰总能在国家战略中彰显地位。

强国之梦，十堰从偏安一隅的山间小镇，到鄂、豫、陕、渝毗邻地区中心城市，这座被誉为“构架在车轮上的城市”，四十余年的成长史，挥就中外城市建设的奇迹。

因车而建，因车而兴。东风商用车研发、制造、销售，100 万辆汽车产能，中国第一，世界前三，中国卡车之都，闻名遐迩。

秦巴医疗中心、商业中心、教育中心、文化中心，流光溢彩，车流如织，城市氛围现代、时尚、高雅，充满滋味、韵味。

城在山中，房在林中，人在园中，百里花园城，生态园林城，颐养人生。

南北交汇，食在十堰，别具一格的地方小吃：丹江翘嘴白，郧西马头羊，郧县白羽乌鸡、三合汤，房县黄酒、黑木耳，竹溪蒸盆、魔芋，竹山腊肉、懒豆腐，尽享舌尖上的十堰。

仙山、秀水、汽车城，三张惊世名片赋予十堰无限张力。武当国际旅游节、世界传统武术节、武当太极拳国际联谊大会、房县诗经文化节、郧西天河七夕文化节，系列重大节庆此起彼伏；金庸、成龙、李连杰等武当问道，《神秘中国》《问道武当》《天下太极》影视剧组蜂拥而至。现代文化，让十堰更加迷人、更加精彩。

连接重庆、西安、郑州、武汉黄金旅游圈，打造国际商用车之都、国际旅游目的地、国家生态文明示范区，建设区域性交通枢纽、区域性现代服务中心，绿色生态农产品供给基地。大力发展以武当山为龙头、以太极湖为引擎、以“三区三线三圈”为中心的山水一体大旅游新格局。

四十六家 A 级景区，旅游配套，现代超前，上百家星级酒店，星罗棋布，遍布城乡的休闲农家，购物娱乐，应有尽有。城区交通，快捷畅达，一个机场、两个码头、三条铁路、四条高速，立体交通让十堰达江通海，向世界敞开胸怀。

山水十堰，自然神奇；人文十堰，历史神奇；车城十堰，当代神奇；未来十堰，辉煌神奇。

——神奇十堰欢迎您

Miraculous and Charming Shiyan

Million years ago, mountain building movement brought up miraculous mountains and waters of Shiyan City.

North Latitude 30° boasts of the world wonder here, enjoying the same popularity with Maya ancient buildings, Egypt pyramids, and Bermuda Triangle.

Here is the Home of Dinosaur and Wild Man, the cradle of humans, the base of Dongfeng Automobile Company, and the source of the Mid-line Project of South-to-North Water Diversion.

Now, follow me to enjoy the charm of Shiyan City, please!

Charming Landscape

Wudang Mountains is the holy land of China Taoism; here are seventy-two peaks and twenty-four streams, and Taoist palaces and temples. Here, one pillar with twelve beams, Nine-turning Yellow River Wall, and other wonders, seemed as formed naturally instead of being made by humans, renowned as the Imperial Palace on the Cliff.

Through six hundred years' development, the imperial palaces and temples in Wudang Mountains have been listed as the World Cultural Heritage Site by the UNESCO. On March Third Temple Fair, September Ninth Blessing Ceremony, Striking Bell to Welcome Spring, outstanding Taoists and pious followers all come to Shiyan City to discuss Taoism and pray for world peace in Wudang Mountains.

Charming and attractive mountains and waters.

In Taiji/ Taichi Gorge, god-made Taiji /Taichi Diagram interpreted Taoism perfectly.

In Qinglong Mountain, state-level Geo-park preserved eggs of Dinosaurs of millions years ago.

In Canglang Mountain, state-level forest park is an original oxygen bar.

In Eighteen-li Gorge, cliffs, stones, waters interpreted the miracle of the Nature.

The Hanjiang River is over one-thousand miles long. Here are the first biggest man-made freshwater lake, Danjiangkou Reservoir, and the Taiji Lake connecting water and mountain, good to preserve health.

Back to 600 years ago, Emperor Yongle of the Ming Dynasty (1368—1644) ordered to build the Imperial Palace in the North and Wudang Palaces in the South, so that Wudang Mountains were closely connected with the royal power; 600 years later, South-to-North Water Diversion, lead to 300,000 acres fertile lands were drowned in water and 300,000 people left for other places. The Hanjiang River, full of friendship and contribution of Hubei people, has been flowing north to moisten the North China, especially, Beijing and Tianjin cities.

On the banks of the Hanjiang River, here are peaks and ridges, trees and grasses, springs and streams, fish and fine stones.

To enjoy the charm of waters, here are Eight-hundred-mile Duhe River, Five-Dragon River, Nine-Dragon Waterfall, and Yellow Dragon Reservoir, we can live by the water, play in the water and taste the fish.

Great People

The origin of life, or the mountains and waters here have made here full of life.

One million years ago, Yunxian Man lived by the Hanjiang River; the wisps of smoke rose up firstly from the chimneys on this earth.

Liaowadianzi Ruins dig up the history of over five thousand years ago has become the general history of China under the earth.

Yin Jifu, the ancestor of Chinese poems, recorded the charm of the Hanjiang River region in *the Book of Songs*.

Since the Qin Dynasty, over thirty emperors and generals were exiled here. Royal hermit culture formed another feature.

The first old man who fought against Wild Man in the world is still alive here with former scars and hairs. During several decades, lots of explorers have been to Shennongjia Mountains, the ridge of Central China, leading to the popularity of Wild Man Cave and Valley.

Nüwa, the ancestor of human, smelt and mend the sky in Zhushan County. Her lost colour stones, calaits, first-rate quality, are loved by the World.

The Cowherd and Weaver Maiden met on the Magpies Bridge of Tianhe River of Yunxi County, Shiyan City, whose love story is deep in minds of the people all over the world.

Intangible cultural heritages, phoenix lantern dance, Shan'erhuang folk song, take a new charm; here are the living fossil of China folk culture, Wujiagou Folk Story, and Lüjiahe Folk Song, best known.

The Hanjiang River Culture is rich in and profound with many kinds of regional cultures, such as, Shaanxi Province, Henan Province, Sichuan Province, Hubei Province, Chongqing City, Beijing City, and ancient cultures, Wudang culture, Yunyang culture, migrate culture harmoniously coexist. Hence Shiyan City is the tropical forest of culture ecology.

Dongfeng Automobile Company Headquarter

Qinba Ridges has provided Shiyan City with great mountains and rich waters so that here have brought up many outstanding people, and Wudang Mountains have been respected and worshiped by the former royal families and current common people. Shiyan City, the former Yunyang Yamen, ruled 65 counties and 205 years.

Shiyan City is outstanding in the state strategy, for example, the imperial palace, ecological diversity, humanities and century project.

The dream of Strong Country has made Shiyan City change from a small country town into the central city of neighboring regions of Hubei, Henan, Shaanxi, Sichuan provinces and Chongqing City. Now, Shiyan, the city on the wheels is creating the miracles of urban construction.

Shiyan City proper has been set up and become prosperous by automobiles. Dongfeng Commercial Vehicles Company, researches and develops, produces and sells one million cars a year, the first of China and the third of the world, hence the world-famous Home of China Trucks.

Shiyan City, the center of Qinba medicare, commerce, education, and culture, is full of modern life, fashion and elegance.

In Shiyan, the City is in the mountains, house in the forests, and people in the parks so that it got the name—City of Garden, City of Ecological Forest, and the paradise of preserving health.

Shiyan City, the joining zone of the South and the North, is rich in local cuisines, Danjiangkou fish, Yunxi goat, Yunxian silkie and sour hot soup, Fangxian yellow rice wine and black agarics, Zhuxi steaming bowl and konjak, and Zhushan long-preserved meat and toufu, you can enjoy the bite of Shiyan.

Wudang Mountains, Danjiangkou Reservoir, and Vehicle City, the three top brands have provided Shiyan City with more and more strength. Wudang International Travel Festival, World Traditional Wushu Championship, Wudang Taiji Boxing International Competition, Fangxian Culture Festival of *the Book of Songs*, and Yunxi Tianhe Culture Festival of China Lovers' Day provide delicious culture cuisines. Jin Yong, Cheng Long, Li Lianjie and other celebrities' promotion and many TVs and films, such as, Miraculous China, Wudang Taoism, Taiji in the World, have made Wudang Mountains, Shiyan City known to more and more people.

Modern culture has made Shiyan City more charming and colorful.

Shiyan City, connecting Chongqing, Xi'an, Zhengzhou, Wuhan golden travel circles, is continuing to build the capital of international commercial vehicle, the home of international tourists, the model zone of state ecological civilization, the regional communication hub, the regional center of modern service, and the base of green farm products.

Now Shiyan City is doubling effort in building a new setup of mountains and waters travel with Wudang Mountains as the flagship, Taichi Lake as the engine, and three zones, three lines and three circles as the core.

Here are 46 Class-A scenic spots with complete supporting facilities, over one hundred star-level hotels, big supermarket and shopping centers and lots of rural restaurants, so that the tourists will feel at home in Shiyan City. The communication of Shiyan City is convenient with one airport, two ports, three railways and four expressways.

To Shiyan City you will enjoy the landscape, the culture, the history, the modern life and also the bright future here.

Welcome to Shiyan City!

Shiyan is waiting for you all the time!

Be there, or be square!

Chapter 4 Tourist guide words of Shiyan City 十堰导游词

Version I

Shiyan City, seated in the northwestern part of Hubei Province, borders Xiangyang City to the east, Ankang City of Shaanxi Province to the west, Shennongjia Forest Region to the south, Chongqing City to the southwest, and Nanyang City of Henan Province to the north. It covers an area of 23,698 square kilometers and has a population of 3.36 million. It has a subtropical monsoon climate with four distinct seasons.

Wudang Mountains, a famous Taoism mountain, is located in Shiyan City. The ancient building complex of Wudang Mountains has been included in the list of World Cultural and Natural Heritage Sites by the UNESCO. Shiyan City is a famous auto production base in China because Dongfeng Motor, is headquartered in the City.

Shiyan is rich in natural resources. Over 2,700 species of Chinese medicinal herbs and over 50 kinds of mineral resources, such as gold, silver and rare earth elements, have been discovered in the region. The transportation infrastructure is well established. The Xiangyang -Chongqing Railway runs through the city, connecting it with Beijing, Shanghai, Wuhan, Zhengzhou and other cities. State highway 209 and State Highway 316 intersect in the city. Wudangshan Airport is located very near to the city proper.

Shiyan is an old civilized land. The 1,570km long Hanjiang River has nurtured the unique civilization of Shiyan. The discovery of "Yunyang Man" shook the theory that man originated in the Africa. The excavation of the fossil of dinosaur's eggs and bones in Yunyang District ended the history that there were dinosaur's bones but no eggs. The Wujiagou Village in Danjiangkou city was entitled as "The First Story Village of China".

Shiyan City is also a young land. Forty years ago, Shiyan was a small town and you can't find its position on the map of China; but forty years later, Shiyan has become one of the national largest automobile producing bases. The Dongfeng Automobile Company is in the hinterland of Shiyan City. It was called "the automobile city" in China and "China's Detroit" in the world.

Shiyan is a rich land. The reserves of coal, gold and silver are the richest in Hubei Province. The hydroelectric resources are also very rich, there are more than 5,000 rivers flowing across this piece of land. Danjiangkou Reservoir, the biggest man-made freshwater lake in Asia, is the source of the central line of South-to-North Water Diversion. The green foods such as black edible fungus, yellow ginger, Tung oil and mushroom are well-known in the world, especially the output of black edible fungus in Fangxian County is the highest in China.

Other major industries in Shiyan include pharmaceuticals, textile, metallurgy, chemicals, electricity production and supply. Hubei Wudangshan Bio-Pharmaceuticals and Shiyan Kangdi Pharmaceuticals of Wuhan Jianmin Pharmaceutical Group are the leading pharmaceutical producers in Shiyan. Tourism is a pillar industry of the service sector in Shiyan.

Shiyan enjoys splendid cultures and a profound history. The Neolithic Ruins discovered in Yunxian County of Shiyan in 1975 showed that Longshan Culture, Yangshao Culture and Qujialing Culture, all of which are part of Han Chinese culture, are blended in the region.

The City got its current name during the Ming Dynasty. Shiyan, whose name means ten dams in Chinese, derives its name from the ten dams built in Yunxian County.

Shiyan is surrounded by diverse historical sites and beautiful natural scenery. Wudang

Mountains Scenic Spot consists of many ancient buildings, most of which can be traced back to the Tang Dynasty and the Yuan Dynasty. Travelers should also go to see Shennongjia Forest Region, the Hot Springs in Fangxian County, Danjiangkou Dam in Dangjiangkou, the Great Wall of Chu Kingdom, the Dinosaur Fossils and Fulong Mountain Nature Reserve.

The local dishes in Shiyan are also popular among the tourists. Wild Mushroom Soup, Spicy Shrimp Balls, Grilled Fish and Zhuxi Steamed Dishes (stewed ham, chicken, mushrooms, poached eggs, sliced bean-curd and other ingredients) are the most characteristic local dishes in Shiyan.

With the implementing of the strategy for developing west China, today's Shiyan has become a new modern industry city. The beautiful automobile city—Shiyan, is attracting more and more tourists to visit.

Version II

Located in the northwest of Hubei Province, the upper and middle reaches of the Hanjiang River, Shiyan is the only regional central city among Hubei, He'nan, Shaanxi, Chongqing and their adjacent areas. The city has a total land area of 23,680 square kilometers, with jurisdiction of Maojian District, Zhangwan District, Yunyang District, Yunxi County, Zhushan County, Zhuxi County, Fangxian County, and Danjiangkou City, Wudang Mountains Tourism Special Economic Zone, and Shiyan Economic Development Zone, with a total population of 350 million.

Shiyan is an automobile city, built up with the development of automobile industry. It is the hometown of "Dongfeng Motor", known as "Oriental Detroit", a city that boasts of greenery mountain, tourism and well-protected ecology.

With a long history and splendid culture, Shiyan is an important birthplace of Chinese nation. In 1991, two intact skull fossils explored by archaeologists at the Quyuan River of Yunxian County, were named "Yunxian Man". The archaeologists believed that this discovery filled in the vacancy of the development of Asian human "roller chain". It was ranked as the top of "Ten Great Discoveries of Archaeological Studies of the World" of that year. The current name "Shiyan" of the urban area, originated from the ten dams built in the Qing Dynasty, on the Baier River and Jiang River for irritation. Shiyan is the origin of Taoism and Wudang Martial Arts. Wudang Taoism has already had a history of thousands of years. Wudang ancient architectural complex has been listed in the world heritage by the UNESCO.

Shiyan accounts for 1/8 of Hubei Province in area, featured with abundant water and mineral resources. The mineral deposit that is already verified now amounts more than 50 kinds as turquoise, gold, silver, coal, iron, tin, vanadium, marble, etc., whose potential value is above 400 billion RMB Yuan. The hydro-power resource reserves reach 5 million kw theoretically, 340kw expected to be utilized, annual average flowing up to 10 billion square meters and 28 billion square meters in transition; special native products won good reputation; Fangxian County, abundant in tea and edible fungus with high output, is crowned as "the Township of Jew's Ear"; among 235 varieties of medicinal material listed in country's most-important-category, 2,700 kinds are produced, praised as "Natural Medicinal Material Storehouse".

Shiyan is a nationwide automobile city, one of the automobile industrial bases with largest scale in China, known as "Oriental Detroit". Shiyan is the cradle of Dongfeng Motor Company, with numerous influential automobile fitting enterprises and most competitive automobile technology research institutes as well as automobile fittings trade market. Automobile manufacturer, associated spare part enterprises are up to more than 200 in the whole city, with which has more than 200,000 auto industry assets, annual capacity of automobiles in various types up to 300,000. The strategic cooperation between Dongfeng Company and Nissan Company, the greatest joint venture project in China's automobile industry circle, started comprehensively in 2003. Shiyan, is one of the main commercial car production bases.

Shiyan is a popular resort. It is a shining pearl on the golden tourism route going across the Three Gorges of the Changjiang River, Longzhong, Wudang Mountains, Danjiangkou Reservoir and Xi'an City. Within the border, Shiyan has been noted for its tourism attractions, such as Wudang Mountains, holy land of Taoism, listed in the world cultural heritage and titled as Five-A grade tourism zone, Danjiangkou Reservoir, crowned as the first largest man-made lake in Asia, is the homeland of dinosaur with concentrated dinosaur eggs and skeletons fossil. And the site of ape in Yunxian, holds hot spring, waterfall, gorge, and cave. The integration of virgin forest and modern city shows a poetic and picturesque scenery, with either hot summer or cold winter. Shiyan is an ideal place that makes people reluctant to leave.

Shiyan is the water source of "South-to-North Water Diversion" Project. The border of Danjiangkou Reservoir and Shiyan is the water source of the middle line of the Project. The implementation of the project will supply water to four provinces and cities including Beijing, Tianjin, Hebei and He'nan. With the construction of the project, Shiyan has been provided more new opportunities.

Shiyan is an ecological barrier. Thanks to the joint of Qinling Mountains and Ba mountains, forming up a geographical climate boundary, preventing the occurrence of sand storm as well as acid rain from South to North. Therefore, Shiyan is an ecological conditioner.

Since the establishment of Shiyan forty years ago, especially the implementation of reforming and opening up to the world four decades ago, "Two Civilizations" (spiritual and material civilization) have made fruitful achievements, grew up from a poor town to a relatively regional major city with scale and competitiveness.

The spiritual civilization yield fruitful results, such as the honors, "National Hygienic City", "National Advanced Tourism City" and "National Top Ten Afforesting Administration" etc. Currently, the leading industries such as automobile, water and electricity have been formed into scale to some extent, and the construction of economy is to be perfect. Science, education and culture are booming. The urban management has been promoted and the social economy is developing in harmony.

The next economic development strategy is to construct a traffic passage that links up the Eastern with Western part of China, building Shiyan into a metropolitan automobile industry base and establishing the Hanjiang River- the Du River hydropower Industrial Zone. And Shiyan is expecting to set up a golden tourism circle that connects Northwest with Southwest of the Country and develop into a key district of western ecological economy of Hubei Province so as to drive Shiyan to become an important growth pole with distinctive characteristics.

Part 02

问道武当

Visiting Wudang Mountains

Chapter 1 Wudang Mountains Special Zone of Tourism and Economy 武当山旅游经济特区

Wudang Mountains Special Zone of Tourism and Economy is located in Shiyan City, Hubei Province, China, having the following neighbors: the ancient city Xiangyang in the east, the primitive forest of Shennongjia Mountains in the south, the Shiyan City proper in the west, and Danjiangkou Reservoir in the north, the biggest man-made lake in Asia.

There are full of attractive places of interest in Wudang Mountains Special Zone of Tourism and Economy, as charming as the rainbow in the sky; especially Wudang Mountain, the famous Taoism Mountain which has combined quietness, wonder, beauty, and elegance into one, has these following famous scenic spots, such as, seventy-two peaks, thirty-six cliffs, twenty-four valleys, eleven caves, three pools, nine springs, ten lakes, nine wells, ten stones, and nine pavilions. There are four distinct seasons with their own features, the mountains are green and full of flowers in the spring; there are wind, thunder, and rainstorm with cloud and fog twisting the mountains in the summer; the forest are in gold yellow and the laurels send fragrance in the autumn; and all the mountains is covered by the white snow in the winter.

Wudang Mountains is the cradle of Wudang Taoism and Wudang Boxing, whose Taoist buildings may be raced back to the seventh century. There are many palaces and temples built in the caves or valleys, wonderful in arrangement, magnificent in size, superb in skills, which collectively demonstrated the architecture art achievements of Taoism buildings in the Yuan (1271—1368), Ming (1368—1644), and Qing (1636—1912) dynasties, represented the highest level of Chinese ancient buildings.

Wudang Mountains is attracting visitors home and abroad with its special charm and taste, today as prosperous as before. These centuries old Taoist palaces and temples, melodious Taoist musics, miraculous Wudang martial arts, abundant myth legends, and these pious believers all give off the sense of Chinese ancient culture.

Wudang Mountains Special Zone of Tourism and Economy has set up the grand object to create world-famous scenic spot and the city of landscape and garden of China in the region. In order to realize the object, create a tourist and living place so as to make the visitors easy and comfortable, the investors reassured and prosperous, and the citizens happy and secure, the special zone government has, at the past years, made a scientific arrangement for the Zone's surrounding, protection and building, planted trees and grass along the highway and around the scenic spots, repaired and bettered the travel routes and supporting facilities. Such infrastructure buildings as Wudang Shopping Precinct, Wudang Mountains Bus Station, Five-star Holiday Hotels, Folk Culture Village Project, Wudang Culture Square, Wudang Museum, and Wudang Art-performing Center are under construction or completely finished.

Wudang Mountains Special Zone of Tourism and Economy has a better and newer appearance than before, with the rapidly-developing urban infrastructure buildings, ever-improving service functions, complete systems of culture, education, health, sports, scientific and technological education, and the ever-strengthening awareness of scenic spot, civilization and tourism.

In Wudang Mountains Special Zone of Tourism and Economy, the transportation is very convenient: the railway from Wuhan to Chengdu, the railway from Xiangyang to Chengdu, the railway from Wuhan to Shiyan, the highway from Wuhan to Shiyan all pass through the Zone; Wudangshan Airport and Xiangyang Airport are nearby; with the acceleration of trains and the construction of new airports, the transportation here will be improved further. As to post and communications, the Zone, having realized transferring by fibre communications and making a long distance call automatically, is able to communicate with more than 160 countries and regions by direct telephone.

So far, Wudang Mountains Special Zone of Tourism and Economy is the Five-A Tourist Spot of China, national place of history interest, the openning area of China's important religion activities, the home of China martial art. In 1994, United Nations Educational, Scientific and Cultural Organization and World Legacy Committee enlisted Wudang Mountains into The List of World Cultural Legacy.

Wudang Mountains, the world-famous China Taoism holy land, is welcoming all visitors and investors all over the world, with her special charming and heartfelt warmth.

Chapter 2 About Zhang Sanfeng 张三丰传奇

Zhang Sanfeng, the founder of Wudang Boxing, was a legendary character. In accordance with history books and folk tales, he was born in the Yuan Dynasty and died in the Ming Dynasty, having a life of over 200 years. He was always kind-hearted to oppose the evil and help the weak, and also humorous and easy to communicate, so the people liked and respected him very much. He had made many proposals for the government, including building Wudang Mountains; with the power of Emperor Zhenwu, he had frightened and controlled those sons and grandsons of the emperors who wanted to rebel against the reign of the Ming Dynasty, making Emperor

Yongle be able to pacify the frontiers and maintain national unity so as to set Chinese domain for the later generations.

He, broad-minded, had proposed to combine Confucius, Buddhism, and Taoism into one, which made Wudang Taoism develop very quickly, and then became the No.1 religion in China. Especially, he, on the base of Taoist theories, such as the naturalness of Taoist theories, keeping in a humble position and so on, had combined Taoist Inner Exercise, guarding skills of regimen, boxing acts of martial art, military sciences of militarists into one, then created Wudang Boxing, which is with the Inner Exercise as the body, attacking as the purpose, regimen as the first important thing, self-protection as the main principle, and to defeat the tough by a tender act, charge the active by the still movement, attack the opponent with his own force, strike only after the opponent has struck. For hundreds of years, Wudang Boxing, with Zhang Sanfeng as the banner, has developed vigorously into many schools and has had millions of students, which is famous in the world and does good to the human beings.

For his outstanding contributions, he has been respected by the people. When he was alive, Emperor Yongle had ordered to build Meeting God Palace for him, in which his statue is worshiped and offered sacrifices to him, treated as the emperor. Nowadays, Zhang Sanfeng's copper statue still demonstrates his charm as an amiable man of virtue, and the founder of Wudang Boxing.

Having consulted many history books, we have gotten to know the whole life of Zhang Sanfeng, which is the following:

1. Saved by a profound Taoist

On the midnight of April 9, 1247, in Scholar Zhang Juren's home, (Taziyin Village, Yi County, Liaoning Province) Ms. Zhang, who was in her family way, was awaken by a dream, then she woke her husband, Zhang Juren, and told him that she dreamed a swan flied from the East Sea to landed on their roof.

He touched her wife's big belly and smiled that it was a good sign that their new baby would be born. With his words, his wife's belly began to ache; a moment later, a baby boy came into the world. According to the legend, a swan circled around Zhang's home three times, had a shout, then flied up into the high sky. All his family members and servants ran out of the home to look at the swan, happy and excited.

Hugging the boy in the arms, Zhang found that his son had a special form with big ears and round eyes, knowing that he was not a usual man. So he named him Quanyi, hoping that he would be an intact man; then he gave Junshi to him, meaning that an honor man should be honest, hoping that he would become a perfect man of honor.

Zhang Quanyi was very clever so that he could read books at the age of three; recite hundreds of poems of the Tang Dynasty. Zhang Juren, born in a family of letters, was knowledgeable and once given an official position in the Yuan Dynasty, but he preferred an easy country life to the government work, so he stayed at home with his wife to lead a simple but happy life.

The parents hoped that Zhang Quanyi could study hard at Confucius and get a position in the government, so that gave honor to his family. Unfortunately, at the age of five, he got eyes trouble; the illness became worse and worse, in the danger of losing his sight.

Just when the parents felt nervous and uneasy, a traveling Taoist named Zhang Yun'an appeared. He said that he was familiar with Yin and Yang and could forecast the future, also could read curse to pray for fortune and get rid of disasters. So Zhang Juren invited him to have a look at the boy's eyes trouble. After watching a moment, Zhang Yun'an became surprised and then said, "The boy is uncommon, is special. He will have many fortunes and long life than I can say." Heard the words, Zhang Juren asked the uninvited gust to cure the eyes of his son.

Comforting his beards for a moment, the Taoist said solemnly, "Your son's eyes are harmed by the devil of the mortal world. Only he makes me teacher and study from me can he keep away from the mortal world and cure the eyes." Finding that there were some difficult feelings in Zhang Juren's face, he laughed, "Don't worry, I will take good care of your son when he is with me. I will send him back when the eyes trouble is cured. I know he will be working in government for several scores of years, and ask him study Confucius when his eyes are recovered."

Heard that the Taoist would take the son away to study Taoism, the mother cried sadly and held the son in her arms tightly, not letting him go. Seeing this, the Taoist smiled and said, "That the parents love the children is human nature. But his eyes must be cured. The eyes are on him, so we should know what he will decide." Then Zhang Quanyi looked up in his mother's arms and said, "Mom, do you want a blind son to be with you, or a healthy son to lead a successful life?" All the audiences were frightened, for a common child of five could not speak like that. The parents just looked at him quietly and listened what he said, "Mom, when master cures my eyes, I will work hard at studying, pass the Imperial Examination as my father and help the government run the country." So the mother let the Taoist take the son away.

Who knew that there was not any message about him after they left, so Zhang Juren thought that the Taoist had cheated the son out of him, missing and worrying about his son, then he was ill in bed. Ms. Zhang was the worse, just crying and looking forward to his son's returning at the door all the days. Seven years later, young Zhang Quanyi returned home at last.

Formerly, the Taoist took Zhang Quanyi from Liaoning Province to Hebei Province, then lived in Zhenwu Temple, in Qingyuan County, Hebei Province. There he cured Zhang's eyes for half a year, and then the eyes recovered. So he taught him Taoism. Zhang was very intelligent that he could remember what he read by just once reading. He also read books of Confucianism and Buddhism when he had some free time. During the seven years, he had read all the important books of Taoism, Confucianism, and Buddhism, and had understood the gist of them…

2. Worked honestly and industriously in the government

When he returned home, his father then invited outstanding scholars to teach him

Confucianism. In 1260, thirteen-year-old Zhang Quanyi passed the county examination, but later he failed in many examinations, not because that his essay was bad, but then politics situation was unfair. When the Mongols established the Yuan Dynasty, they divided the whole nation into four degrees: the first was Mongol, the second the minorities in the west of China, the third the Han nationality, the fourth the Han nationality of the South Song Dynasty. Zhang was a Han people, in the third degree, so accordingly he could not have a fair treat in examination and matriculation. He was not depressed, just kept on studying, not only Confucianism, but also Taoism and Buddhism.

He had begun to study Taoism and practice cultivation and swordplay, so he was not only profound in learning, but also healthy and strong in body. He had made up his mind that he would never marry until he succeeded in the government. The parents agreed with him, so he worked harder than before.

When he was 45, his father got a serious illness and could not be cured. When dying, the father sent for the son to his bed and encouraged him to work harder to be an important official in the government so as to make up for his own pity. He said that Zhang Quanyi was just in his forties, which was the best time to make a success. Excited, he knelled down before his father and vowed that he would go to Beijing, have a fine performance in the Imperial Examination, and to be a successful official, not idle away the life.

Just after his father's death, his mother died too. He was staying at home mourning his parents and studying. Ten years later, he passed the Imperial Examination; not bribed the relevant officials, he was ordered to be the Magistrate of Qingyuan County.

The first thing he did when he took the post was to visit his teacher Zhang Yun'an, who was very old with long white beards, but quite energetic. They had a long talk overnight. The teacher said to him, "There are three kinds of officials: honest officials, evil officials, and greedy officials. Honest officials help the people; evil officials cheated the people; and greedy officials harm the people. Honest officials develop the country; evil officials delay the development; and greedy officials make the country die. So that honest officials have a good fame remembered by people for a very long time; greedy officials have a bad fame remembered by people for a very long time; and evil officials have been laughed at by all the people. I hope that you will be an honest official and make a good contributions to the country and the people." Zhang Quanyi agreed with his teacher in many nods. Then the teacher continued, "It is dangerous to be a greedy official; easy to be an evil official; difficult to be an honest official. If you want to be an honest official, you should be determined to go through many hardships." He, in front of the teacher, vowed that he would be an honest official no matter how difficult it would be, never be an evil official or a greedy official.

During the Yuan Dynasty, there had a custom to trade people. At the beginning, the soldiers sold the captives from the battlefield as slaves; then they caught the students of the South Song Dynasty and traded them as slaves; at last, they robbed and traded innocent women as slaves, which became a custom. In the man markets all over the country, most of the goods were women. In Qingyuan County there was a big market where people traded horses, oxen, goats, pigs, and donkeys on the left side of the road; traded students, adults, women, children on the right side of the road. So that there were very dirty and noisy, unbearable to man.

One day he inspected the man market privately, where he found many men kneeling there with a grass sign on their head, all in rages, thin and sad. He made up his mind that he must change the situation to treat humans as animals. There he met a raged old man had to sell his own daughter, for he had no money to cure his seriously sick wife in bed. Very sad, he gave the old man money and let them go home, without telling a word of himself.

Once he returned to the County Court, he began to write a memorial to the throne, in which he pointed out many serious shortcomings of man market and applied the Emperor to cancel man trade in the whole nation. Later, the Emperor did set order to prohibit man trade. The government did prohibit man trade, but the Mongol aristocrats want only robbed lands in the central of China, made lot of peasants leave from their lands and travel to other places for life. They had no other choice to make a living but selling their children, so that slave trading could not be prohibited. Under this circumstance, a landlord in Qingyuan County came to ask for help from Zhang Quanyi.

The landlord, named Lin Shaokun, who had a fifteen-year-old daughter, had a steady friendship with Zhang Yun'an, the teacher of Zhang Quanyi. Heard that the government would look for unmarried women all over the country and then give them to Mongol aristocrat as slaves, so he came to Zhang Yun'an for an advice. Zhang thought for a moment and said, "Maybe your daughter have predestined relationship with my student. He made up his mind not to marry until he pass the Imperial Examination and have a position in the government. Now he has just begun his official duty, having not married yet." Zhang told him that it was the County Magistrate of Qingyuan County, Zhang Quanyi. He was very glad to marry his daughter to the County Magistrate, but he wondered whether the County Magistrate would accept her or not; so he asked Zhang Yun'an to write a letter to Zhang Quanyi, for the purpose of making the match.

So Zhang Quanyi married Lin's daughter and they had a happy and sweet marriage. Several years later, they had a clever daughter who could read books at three, recite poems of the Tang Dynasty and verses of the Song Dynasty. Having a daughter when he was very old, Zhang loved her very much and treated her as the apple of his eye.

3. Left the government for Taoism

Qingyuan County was short of water supply, so that there were wind and sand in the spring and dry and red earth in the summer and autumn, the people there had no harvest and led a very hard life accordingly. Zhang Quanyi sent some men to look for water and led the people to build water projects. They had dug scores of dams and channels to transfer water to water the lands, so that the people began to have a heavy harvest.

In accordance with the official system of the Yuan Dynasty, an official could retire from the government when he was over seventy. But when Zhang was over seventy, he failed in many times to retire from the government, for his contributions of building water projects were to the liking of the government; Qingyuan County is very near to Beijing, so the prosperity and stability of Qingyuan County was quite good to Beijing, the rein of the Yuan Dynasty.

But Emperor Shun worked hard to run the country at the beginning, later he indulged in wine and beauties. He often set orders to look for beauties all over the country; Qingyuan County was near to Beijing, so the beauty looking began there first. It was very common to look for beauties in the feudal societies, so Zhang had no other thought about it. His daughter was very charming and clever, so that she was taken away. Later, he was invited to Beijing to have a meal with the Emperor, for his outstanding contributions; there he found out that the Emperor was evil and wicked. Emperor Shun ordered the officials to have sexual relations with the beauties in Jinlan Hall where the government discussed the state affairs, while he sat aside and enjoyed watching the farce. When Zhang found that his dear daughter was there, he got fainted; while his daughter could not stand the shame and bumped at the pillar and died.

When Zhang returned from Beijing, he got a serious illness that he could not deal with government affairs for three months.

The government was so evil and wicked that many people rebelled, such as Liu Futong, Han Shantong, and Chen Youqiong. In order to stop peasants' uprisings, the government held a Wushu competifion, so as to get rid of all the men who were good at Wushu. When the Emperor set orders to hold a Wushu competifion, Wushu experts in the country all went to Beijing to take part in the competifion. Zhu Yuanzhang, a Wushu expert of Anhui Province, led his several friends to go for Beijing. When they went by Qingyuan County, Zhang Quanyi gave them a warm welcome and told them that the Emperor had an evil intention. Knowing the Emperor's evil intention, they watched out for the Emperor's deeds; later they saw through the evil plan and rebelled. After they left Beijing, they had several days' rest in Qingyuan County and declared their rebellion when they returned to Anhui Province.

Later, that Zhang Quanyi took in the insurrectionists was known by the government, so the Emperor sent soldiers to catch him. Zhang already saw through the evilness of the Yuan Dynasty and thought that it was doomed to be overthrown, so he had no interest for the government. He left his official stamp in the County Court, packed up baggage and sent his wife to her mother's home overnight. After saw off his wife, he walked to Zhenwu Temple under the moon.

The leader of Zhenwu Temple, Zhang Yun'an, over one hundred years, was not surprised at Zhang Quanyi' coming. He smiled and nodded, "I know you will come to me, for it is time for you to practice Taoism. But you have lived and worked in the mortal world for many years, the government will look for you again and again." Zhang Quanyi felt very sad, for he didn't realize his parents' expectation. The leader comforted him, "what you can do is already determined by nature. Since you have left the government, you should concentrate on Taoism." With the words, he undressed his own hairpin and combed Zhang Quanyi's hair with the pin, then continued, "Zhenwu Temple is not a safe place for you, which is so near to Beijing, so the Emperor's men will find you very easily. I have a classmate who is the leader of Jintai Temple in Baoji County, Shaanxi Province, you can go there."

After rested in Zhenwu Temple for several days, Zhang Quanyi was about to go for Jintai Temple. When departing, Zhang Yun'an gave him a Taoist name, Sanfeng. He understood the intention of his teacher; Sanfeng meant that the nature, the earth, and the people were all prosperous, which referred to his outstanding contributions as an official. The teacher smiled, "You have been an honest official, making the people have a happy life and the government happy at your work; so you are true to Sanfeng. As to your future life, I have already known that you will have a big fortune and long life than I can say. You will be a founder with millions of students and followers. So it is reasonable to name you Sanfeng."

Thanked and said good-bye to his teacher, Zhang Sanfeng began his travel. After traveled through Hebei Province, across the Yellow River and over Qinling Mountain, he got to Jintai Temple at last. The leader of Jintai Temple, Wang Yunhe, the descendant of Wang Chongyang, the founder of Quanzhen Taoism, was quite knowledgeable, especially in the Eight Diagrams. Under his tutor, Zhang Sanfeng had learned a lot.

When he was young, Zhang had learned Static Qigong from Zhang Yun'an, so he combined Static Qigong with Eight Diagrams, with a purpose to create a new Wushu. However, it was not easy to create a new one, he could not combine Static Qigong with Eight Diagrams together. One day when he was practicing, a Taoist in rages went by him and laughed, "All things are coming from the chances, determined by the chances. If the chance is coming, you can make something very easily, or very difficultly." Surprised, he looked the Taoist, not handsome, but have profound philosophy in his words. So he stopped practicing at once and asked the Taoist for some advice. But the Taoist just put one hand in front of the stomach and the other behind the back, and then walked away quickly. Zhang understood the sign that there were many profound experts in the word and that he could not just stay at one place to practice Taoism; instead, he should travel out for more experiences and learning. So with the permission of Wang, he began his traveling again, to visit more famous experts and learn more knowledge.

When he traveled to Zhongnan Mountain in Shaanxi Province, he found a temple in the dense forest. Looked carefully, he found the name of the temple, Fire Dragon Temple, where came out of smoke and reading voice. So he walked towards it and met by a yellow-haired and yellow-bearded Taoist. Then he recognized that he was the Taoist that he met in Jintai Temple. The Taoist, Fire Dragon Immortal, had cultivated here for over ninety years and would die in three years, so he wanted very much to accept the last student. After traveling over the country, he didn't found a qualified student; when he met Zhang, young and intelligent, he decided to take him as the last student.

After Fire Dragon Immortal took Zhang as student, he gave him another Taoist name, Xuan-xuan, meaning Mystery, and taught him The Gist of Virtue, to help him understand the secret of Taoism.

As to *The Tao and Teh* by Lao zi, he had read for many times, but he could understand new things when Fire Dragon Immortal taught it. Fire Dragon Immortal said, "When the humans respect the nature and the earth, the nature will have a good climate, the earth will have a good harvest; when the humans disrespect the nature and the earth, the nature will wind and rain unlimitedly, the earth will have nothing on, for the nature and the humans are united and change between the cause and the result, influencing each other." Zhang nodded, "I understand that. Now the humans are evil and fighting with each other so that the people have a hard life, so the nature became angry and bring many disasters to the world." Fire Dragon Immortal sighed with emotion, "The troubled world makes the heroes. Some certain man will come out to deal with the troubles so as to make the nature, the earth, and the humans coexist together harmoniously." Zhang asked, "Sir, who is the hero?" Fire Dragon Immortal answered, "He who is conforming to the nature and the people's minds is the hero." Zhang did not ask any more, but remembered the nature and the people's minds in the heart, and decided to travel around to visit heroes and help them.

After learning Taoism in Zhongnan Mountain for four years, he decided to leave there and travel around the country. On the way, he found the government was worse and the people had a harder life than before. When he returned to Qingyuan County, he found the people there all complained about the evil government. Thought of his wife in her mother's home, so he went there to have a look quietly. There he found just a ruin on the place of his parents-in-law's home. Villagers nearby told him that when he left the government, the government soldiers got to know the location of his wife and came to kill all the family except his wife who had went to Zhenwu Temple to be a nun the day before, and then they fired the house down.

Thought of that he had brought so much disasters to the father-in-laws, he could not help crying with tears flowing around the eyes. He went to Zhenwu Temple to visit his former wife for the last time, and then returned to Jintai Temple and continued his cultivation.

Later, the leader of Jintai Temple died. When he was dying, he asked Zhang Sanfeng to be the new leader. It was not for two years since he became the leader of Jintai Temple, one thing happened unexpectedly. Sun Jingde, another student of Wang Yunhe, who longed for becoming the leader for many years, became very angry and hated Zhang very much, for Zhang had taken away what he wanted. When Sun heard that Zhang was the former County Magistrate of Qingyuan County, an escaped criminal circularly arrested by the government, so he went to the government nearby and told him on.

When he heard that Sun had told him on, he was in a dilemma: if he goes away, which will bring bad reputation to Jintai Temple; if not, the government soldiers will come to catch him, which will make Jintai Temple worse in reputation. He thought that his own death was less important than the fame of Jintai Temple, so he had an idea. The next day, he pretended that he had died, which made the temple see through the disaster. He wrote on a paper "There is death in the life, the life in the death; there is soberness in drunkenness, drunkenness in soberness; there is the wrong in the right, the right in the wrong; and there is the curve in the straight, the straight in the curve." Then he order vice-leader of the temple, "Put the paper on the Grand Hall.

Anyone who understands the meaning of the letter can be the new leader." With the words, he laughed and left Jintai Temple.

4. Created Wudang Boxing and taught students

When Zhang Sanfeng came to Wudang County, he found that there were many buildings distributing here and there among the high mountains, with crossed streets, wood of trees, and crowded people and vehicles, so he thought that here was not a usual place.

When he came to Wudang County Court (Yuxu Palace now), he found that the Grand Hall rising high in the 8-shaped walls, backing the green mountains and facing the busy street, full of magnificent atmosphere. On one of the walls, he met a notice with his photo on to arrest him, which said that Qingyuan County Magistrate Zhang Quanyi had colluded with the insurrectionist Zhu Yuanzhang and wanted to rebel against the government, then escaped to Jintai Temple to be a Taoist and pretend death, living a bare coffin there, so all the counties should work hard to arrest him.

This made Zhang think a lot, he never thought that the evil government had not let him go till that time and that the government would follow Sun Jingde to open his grave, which made him more determined to overthrow the reign of the Yuan Dynasty.

Had just come to Wudang Mountains and been chased by the government, he thought it unsuitable to live in temples as a traveling Taoist; so he went to find a cave at the foot of Phoenixes Mountain, which was dirty but safe to hide him. He collected some dry grass and spread them in the cave, sat there practicing Static Qigong. Static Qigong, also named Inner Medicine Exercise, can be achieved after the practicer has gotten the medicine. The dark and wet cave is the best place to practice Static Qigong. He practiced from Static Qigong to stopping eating any food when he could live without a grain for half a month, then when he stopped practicing, he could eat up several kilograms of rice.

He had practiced in the cave for three years and then he succeeded in get the medicine, meaning that he had succeeded in practicing Static Qigong. Now his clothes were dirty and worn out; his hairs and beards were long and disorderly; his face and body were black and full of disgusting odor. So the people nearby called him Dirty Taoist, or Dirty Zhang.

After he had practiced the Inner Medicine Exercise, he left the cave for Nine-Dragon Mountain to the east of the county, where there were full of mountains, streams, and green trees, which was a good place to cultivate. So he built a hut under the mountain, named Meeting Gods Temple. There he practiced Static Qigong at night, Dynamic Qigong at day, with the purpose to combine the two into one, but failed for many times.

One morning just when he came to the yard in front of the hut and began to practice, he suddenly heard a pie crying urgently behind the hut, so he went there to see what had happened. There he found an interesting story. A pie made a nest in the phoenixes tree, but a snake wanted to eat the pie' eggs, so they began a fight. The pie flied here and there to attack the snake, but the snake twisted on the tree with his tail and tried his best to avoid the attack and make some counter-attack too, so the pie had to fly away again. They fought for a very long time, but could not come to a conclusion. Watching the fight, Zhang understood suddenly that he should practice Dynamic Qigong like the pie and the snake, in the way of round Taiji.

Enlightened by the fight, he understood the gist of Taoist Dynamic Qigong, then combined Taiji, the Eight Diagrams, Inner Medicine, boxing acts of martial art, military sciences of militarists together and created a new boxing, which is as quiet as a virgin, as active as a flying hair, as soft as a snake, and as tough as a powerful tiger. This new boxing is standing in the pace of seven stars, waving curve and turning around, to control the active acts by the still ones, overcome the tough acts with the gentle ones, attack the opponent by use of his own force, and strike only after the opponent has struck. That time Zhang Sanfeng just created thirteen acts, so the later generations named it the Thirteen-Act of Sanfeng Taiji Boxing, which is Wudang Inner Boxing created by Zhang Sanfeng for the first time since the world came into being, also the mother boxing of Inner Boxing. The later generations, on the base of Zhang's Taiji Boxing, have studied, developed and made it form a complete Wudang Boxing system with many schools and genres, widespread in China and famous all over the world. After several years' practicing, Zhang Sanfeng had exercised the Thirteen-Act of Sanfeng Taiji Boxing perfectly.

One day when he was practicing, a young Taoist suddenly came to watch his practicing, who was surprised and could not believe what he was seeing. The Taoist, named Sun Biyun, came to be a Taoist instead of one landlord in Yuxu Temple when he was very young. He often met Dirty Zhang before and thought that he was a crazy Taoist. Unexpectedly, when he met Dirty Zhang under Nine-Dragon Mountain that day, he came to know that Zhang was a profound Taoist with very high gongfu. So when Zhang finished exercising boxing, he came up and asked Zhang to be his teacher.

Sun Biyun was Zhang Sanfeng's first student, so Zhang taught him very seriously; he taught him cultures of Taoism, Confucianism, and Buddhism, and Taiji Boxing. Sun was very clever that he made many progress in learning Taoism. Zhang had took Sun as student, so many more people came to know the real visage of Dirty Zhang, several more profound Taoists came to study Taoism and Taiji Boxing under Zhang' s tutor, among which, Li Suxi was very famous. For he had followed Zhang's advice to offer betelnut to Emperor Yongle, which moved Emperor Yongle to build Wudang Mountains in a large scale.

5. Destroyed the evil and helped the weak and the kind

Found that his students were more and more, Zhang Sanfeng decided to leave his Meeting Gods Temple to Sun Biyun, and he began his traveling again.

The first destination of his traveling was Changchun Temple in Wuchang, one district of Wuhan City, the Capital of Hubei Province, which was built for the purpose of remembering Qiu Changchun, the leader of the seven men of Quanzhen School. That year Qiu Changchun was invited to travel eastward to see Genghis khan, the first Emperor of the Yuan Dynasty. When Genghis khan asked him how to rule the country successively and how to enjoy a long life, Qiu answered, "You should respect the nature and love the people, and also be short of desires." "If you want to unify all the country, you should not indulge in killing people." So Genghis khan made him God, and stopped killing people. Qiu Changchun's one advice "not to kill people" helped millions of people survive from being killed, which taught Zhang Sanfeng many things during his visit in Changchun Temple. Who would be qualified to rule the country when many heroes rebelled against the reign of the Yuan Dynasty and fought against each other? Zhang Sanfeng decided to find a true hero who respects the nature, loves the people and dislikes killing the people and help him succeed in unifying the country.

When he heard that Zhu Yuanzhang, whom he had saved as he was Qingyuan County Magistrate, had many soldiers and horses and had taken over Jinling City, he traveled eastward by boat. Jinling City, also named Stone City in history, was very small. A scholar named Zhu Sheng gave Zhu Yuanzhang nine words to help him unify the country, which said like this: to build the city walls high, lay aside grains more, and become king late.

That time many leaders of uprising armies had become kings, for instance, Chen Youqiong named King Han, Zhang Shicheng named King Wu, and so on. The generals of Zhu Yuanzhang all asked him to become king, but he took Zhu Sheng's advice, not to become king so early that becomes the target of other kings, but to do something useful to make him strong in power. The first thing he wanted to do was to build city walls high and extend and strengthen Jinling City; but the project was so large that he should have lots of money, where could he get lots of money?

When Zhang Sanfeng came to Jinling City, he heard that the people there spoke highly of Zhu Yuanzhang to the effect that he ruled the army very strictly, not to kill the innocent, but work hard at improving people's livings. He felt happy that he had saved the right person.

The first richest man in Jinling City, Shen Wansan had lots of money and boasted, "If he will be poor, the sea will be dry and the dragons will cry." When he was very old, his wife gave birth to a clever and handsome boy, so he loved him very much. But the boy had a strange trouble, easy to cry; once he began crying, he would cry for several days at a stretch, no matter how hard you worked to stop him. Once when he heard someone destroy china and tear silk cloth, he would stop crying, which made all china and silk clothes in his home destroyed.

When Zhang Sanfeng heard the strange story, he paid a visit to Shen Wansan. Strangely enough, when the boy saw Zhang Sanfeng, he did not cry but begin to laugh. Shen Wansan was surprised that the Taoist was so strong and great and that he could stop the boy's crying; so he asked Zhang why. Zhang smiled, "Time flies fast and life is short. Money is easy to go like wind and dirt; however, fame is lasting forever like the moon, the sun and the stars. Why the boy cry is that you love money more than fame." Considered it reasonable, Shen asked Zhang to teach him how to do this. Zhang said, "Now Zhu Yuanzhang, in order to save the people from fire and sword and unify the country, followed Zhu Shen's nine-word advice. He wanted to build Jinling City walls high, but short of money. This is the right time for you to become famous in the world forever." Shen asked, "You mean that I offer money to build city walls?" Zhang kept his fingers crossed and smiled, "Yes. If you offer money and help build city walls, Zhu Yuanzhang will be easy to unify the country and bring fortunes to the people. In this way, you will make a big contribution and be remembered by the following generations." Enlightened and appreciated, Shen invited Zhang to have a dinner. When they departed, Shen asked Zhang to tell his name; Zhang said, "I am Wudang Taoist Zhang Sanfeng," and then he left.

Later, Shen offered lots of money to help Zhu Yuanzhang build city walls and said that he was enlightened by Wudang Taoist Zhang Sanfeng. So Zhu asked him to invite Zhang, Shen said that Zhang had been gone.

Zhang Sanfeng left Jinling City, took a boat in the Changjiang River to travel upward. When he came to the Boyang Lake, he found that King Han Chen Youqiong was building large warships and drilling naval armies, which the people there complained against it very much. After watching by the lake for several days, he went back to Jinling City. Here Zhu Yuanzhang heard a message that Chen Youqiong would lead his naval armies to attack Jinling City, so he gathered all his generals to discuss how to cope with it; a soldier came into and offered a letter to him and told him that the letter was from Shen Wansan. Opened the letter, Zhu found a piece of yellow paper on which written "Set fire to Chen Youqiong when there is a wind and God Zhenwu will be with you." That time, Chen's warships locked together were large and powerful, but Zhu's warships were small and weak; Chen had more than six hundred thousand of soldiers, but Zhu just had ten hundred thousand. In this unfavorable situation, how could he defeat the enemies? Zhu was very worried; now the word "Fire" had enlightened him.

Later, they had a furious fight in Boyang Lake; Zhu defeated Chen by using of fire, which made Chen lose better half of his soldiers. Then Zhu used fire again to attack Chen, made Chen lose all of his armies; as to himself, was shot to death too.

Zhang Sanfeng was traveling in the south reaches of the Changjiang River then, when he heard the news, he came to Shen Wansan's home to say good-bye, "Now the whole situation has set, we should go back to Wudang Mountains." Shen asked, "Now there are many heroes uprising and only Chen Youqiong was defeated. Why could you say that the situation is set?" Zhang answered, "Now, the government of the Yuan Dynasty was dying and beyond medicines. Among the uprising heroes, only Chen Youqiong was able to compete with Zhu Yuanzhang. Now that Chen died, who else can fight for the ruling of the country with Zhu Yuanzhang?" Shen wanted to learn Taoism and boxing from Zhang, so he invited Zhang to stay there for more days and wait for Zhu Yuanzhang. Zhang laughed, "I have been used to traveling around to my heart. It is better for me not to see Zhu Yuanzhang," with the words, he left.

6. Spread Taoism and Wudang Boxing

When Zhang returned back to Wudang Mountains, he began to teach his students Taoism and Wudang Boxing. Now the real visage of Dirty Zhang was revealed to the public, lots of Taoists came to study under his tutor. Meeting Gods Temple was too small to hold so many people, so they built some huts nearby.

At the very beginning, he taught the students to exercise stake work. He said, "Stake work is the base of gongfu; only having a steady base can we make a progress in gongfu. Taoist stake work has two kind, Taiji Stake and Wuji Stake. It can not say that we succeed in exercising stake work until we stand there steadily as the tree sprouts roots into the earth." Then he taught them Wudang Taiji Boxing, Wudang Swordplay, Wudang Light Exercise, Wudang Inner Medicine Exercise, Wudang Vital Point-Hitting Exercise, and Wudang Sleeves Exercise.

Besides teaching the students Wushu, Zhang also wrote many poems, especially the Twenty-Four Poems of Wuji Root, to explain Taoist cultivation and boxing exercising, which influenced the later generations a lot.

In order to teach the students gongfu better, he ordered them to plant many posts in the shape of a club in the yard in front of Meeting Gods Temple and then he practiced and taught Taiji Boxing on these posts. One newcomer saw Zhang practiced Taiji boxing in a very tender way, which seemed as if there was no strength in, so he said, "Sir, what you practice is nice, but not useful, not worth learning." Zhang jumped down the post and said, "I will practice Taiji Boxing, you can hit me with your full strength." The big and strong newcomer thought that he could hit Zhang down to earth by one attack, so he made a violent attack towards Zhang's stomach when Zhang was practice Taiji Boxing casually. Zhang turned around a bit and then met his attack with his left hand, made a tender palm towards his stomach, which made him backed up for several paces and sat on the earth. Not to accept defeat, he jumped up his feet and gave another violent attack to Zhang; Zhang avoided away and got hold of his wrist and gave a tender attack on the back with his right hand, which made him spring forward about ten meters and fell down. He stood up, wiped out the dirt on the face and said, "Sir, you just use a miracle way to defeat me, which is not enough to make the opponent convinced."

Zhang smiled, "Young man, I just used less that one of my strength to fight against you, or I will hurt you. If you want to see the power of Taiji Boxing, I can show it to you." With the words, he began practicing Taiji Boxing slowly, and then suddenly gave a palm to one of club post, which made the bowl-thick post break into two parts. Becoming excited, he kicked up a large blue stone and then gave a palm, making the stone into pieces. Convinced, the newcomer knelt down before Zhang and said, "Sir, Taiji Boxing is so powerful that I am convinced now." Zhang stopped his practicing and smiled, "Young man, Taiji Boxing is seemingly soft but very tough in reality. When soft, as soft as swimming silk, can twist the opponent's hand, which stops him from escaping; when tough, as tough as iron and steel, can break logs and open stones, which makes the opponent bad injured or lose his life. Taiji Boxing is the first-rate one among all the boxing in the world."

Suddenly, a man shouted "Very good" out of the yard; when Zhang looked towards the voice, he found a monk standing on the road, who was fat and tall, with a thick iron truncheon loaded his luggage on the shoulder. He went forward to the yard and put his truncheon into the earth, which dropped into the earth more than one foot deep. When he heard that Zhang Sanfeng had created Wudang Boxing, so he wanted to complete with him. He said that Zhang could create his own school only when he could defeat him. He was very impolite to Zhang and hurt some students of Zhang, which made Zhang determined to teach him a lesson, so he said, "OK, let us have a competition. I will stand here still, you can hit me first."

Zhang stood there with a Wuji stake, the monk gave a violent boxing to Zhang's stomach; but Zhang was there still without any movement, while the monk was sprung three meters away, nearly fell down. He made forward again, jumped up to kick Zhang's face, the latter just put out one hand and poked away his foot, which made the monk turn two somersaults in the air and fell down to the earth. He jumped to his feet once again and stroke Zhang violently with his own head. Zhang was still there without any movement, but the monk's head was stuck so tightly that he could not take it away, no mater how hard he would try. The monk had no choice but to ask for mercy, "Sir, I am wrong. Please forgive me!" Zhang let up his belly and said "Go away," the monk was sprung away more than three meters away and fallen down to the earth. Red-faced, the monk said, "We will meet in the future", and then went away with his iron truncheon.

Saw off the monk and thought of something, Zhang gathered all his students and said, "Wudang Boxing is profound, but we should not keep it indoors, but spread it widely. When you have grasped Wudang Boxing, you may created a school and become a founder." Heard this, all the students knelt down and said, "We will never forget or betray you." Zhang continued, "I have combined most of things of gongfu, Guarding skills and Inner Medicine Exercise, then created Wudang Boxing. In the future, if you want to create a new school, you must put Wudang before your school." These students did remember Zhang's order and created many schools, which made Wudang Boxing widespread in the world.

After the reign of the Yuan Dynasty was overthrown, the new Junzhou County Magistrate escorted the Imperial Envoy of the Ming Dynasty to Wudang Mountain to visit Zhang Sanfeng, with the Emperor, Zhu Yuanzhang's order to give Zhang a government position and court clothes. When they came to the entrance of Meeting Gods Temple, they asked Qiu Yuanjing, one of Zhang's students to report.

On hearing that the Imperial Envoy came to Wudang Mountains and wanted to see him, Zhang understood their intention, but he decided not to meet them. So he ordered some Taoists to get him his dirty clothes, hemp shoes, broken cap made of bamboos, and an iron rule. He seldom wore this set of costumes, only when he went out for a travel. After put them on and told something to Sun Biyun, he took a broom in the corner and went out to sweep the yard. He went on sweeping till to the entrance where the Imperial Envoy met him and asked, "Sir, could you tell me Zhang Sanfeng is in or not?" Zhang just pointed to Meeting Gods Temple and continued his sweeping.

The Imperial Envoy and his suit hurried into Meeting Gods Temple, where Sun Biyun gave them a warm welcome. The Imperial Envoy asked, "Where is Zhang Sanfeng?" Sun answered, "You had a talk with Zhang Sanfeng just now." Till now the Imperial Envoy understood that the Taoist sweeping the floor was Zhang Sanfeng, so he hurried out to look for him; but there was only a broom left, Zhang was gone.

7. Offered advice at the proper time

Zhang Sanfeng traveled around for several years with the dirty clothes on. When he saw the Imperial Order and court clothes, he smiled and asked Sun Biyun to lay them aside. Sun wondered, "Since you do not like to accept the offer, why not return them back?" Zhang said, "No. Zhu Yuanzhang is determined to invite me to work in government, so it is useless to return them back. You can use them when you work in the government in the future." Sun smiled, "You make a joke on me." Zhang said seriously, "In order to develop and strengthen Wudang, you need to work in Government."

The next day, Zhang led Sun to climb up to Gold Top. On the way, they felt very sad when they saw many palaces and temples destroyed by fire and war. Zhang said, "During the changing of the dynasties, the battles did not bring troubles to the humans but also to Gods." Sun asked, "Gods can help the people from troubles, why not help themselves?" Zhang laughed, "You asked a right question! It seems that you have learned something of Taoism." Sun said, "Please teach Taoism in details." Zhang said, "Taoism should be understood, not by teaching. You'd better think it over and you will understand the gist of Taoism."

After several months, they visited all round Wudang Mountains. So Zhang asked Sun, "What have you found these days?" "The ruined phenomenon of Wudang Mountains." "You should also find the prosperity of Wudang Mountains." "Most of palaces and temples were destroyed, just with broken bricks and tiles. Where can I find the prosperity?" "Something is coming from nothing. Nowadays ruins and relics will be palaces and halls in the future."

One day when they passed through Canglang Island, they walked directly towards a mountain in front of them, on which they could have a clear view of the Hanjiang River, Junzhou City, and Wudang Mountains. Zhang asked Sun again, "Here, what do you find?" "I find the wonder of lots of mountains worshiping Wudang Mountains and that Junzhou City, surrounded by water and mountains, has a lucky vision." Zhang commented, "You just find the external things, not the internal ones. Wudang Mountains is really a god sitting there, with Heavenly Pillar peak as the head, Golden Top as the cap, which was worn out, but we can change a new one. Purple Cloud Peak is his stomach, Five-Dragon Peak and South Cliff the left arm, Five-Senior Peak and Qiongtai the right arm, and the lower part of Crown Prince's Slope the legs and feet." Sun understood suddenly, "Sir, you mean that Wudang Mountains is the form of Emperor Xuan, Emperor Xuan is the spirit of Wudang Mountains." "How clever you are! Only that the clothes of Emperor Xuan are worn out now, in the need of changing a new one. You see Junzhou City once again, waters and mountains are spreading forward straightly to Golden Top, just like a straight line, which is the root of Wudang Mountains." Sun was really clever, he was enlightened once again, "Sir, I know why you take me to visit Wudang, you are going to build Wudang Mountains at a large scale." Zhang Sanfeng waved his hands, "It is a secret, do not let out!"

In 1399, the founder of the Ming Dynasty, Zhu Yuanzhang died. Because that the prince Zhu Biao had died before, Zhu Yunwen, grandson of Zhu Yuanzhang took the throne and became Emperor Jianwen. He began to weaken the power of these princes so as to strengthen the central authority, which caused Prince Yan, Zhu Di led his soldiers to rebel against him.

In 1402, Zhu Di took over Nanjing City and the throne, naming himself Emperor Yongle. That Zhu Di defeated Zhu Yunwen, the rightful emperor and made himself emperor was against the throne succeeding system, so the princes else and the people were not obedient. Zhu Di used blood and iron to rule the country and killed the officials who did not obey him, or all their offspring.

Zhu Di's high-pressure policy did not wipe out the political crisis, instead, caused worse danger. More than twenty princes colluded together and was going to attack Zhu Di at the same time; aristocrats in the west, Mongol, Northeast, and other places also rebelled and named themselves Kings. Emperor Yongle was confronting with the three big difficulties: officials and people were disobedient, brothers rebelled against him, and the frontiers were not in peace, which made him worried and busy all the days.

Zhang Sanfeng, as the founder of Wudang Boxing and profound Taoist, was concerning about the state affairs. He visited Nanjing and the ChangJiang River reaches, so he knew Zhu Di's difficult situation very well. When he returned to Wudang Mountains, he thought it over and again, then had a way to solve these difficulties. He gathered several reliable students and told them his plan, then set off to Sichuan Province. The next day in Wudang Mountains there spread a saying "Wudang Mountains will be prosperous and important in the near future."

When he got to Sichuan province, Zhang Sanfeng told King Shu, Zhu Chun of his strategy "Building Wudang Mountains to rule the country with the help of gods." He said that since long time before, men created gods and gods ruled men. China was named God Country because that China was the world of gods. So emperors of every dynasty declared that their rights to rule the country was given by gods. If Zhu Di wanted to rule the country and compose these kings, he must rely on the help of gods. Zhu Chun told the strategy to Zhu Di, who decided to pay a visit to Zhang Sanfeng by himself.

After several days' preparation, Zhu Di led Zhu Chun and some escorts to begin their travel privately, came to Wudang Mountains. When they went by a big mountain, they suddenly found an old woman fainted on the earth. One adult carried the woman on the back to Meeting Gods Temple and shouted to a family nearby, "Black Ox (the nickname of one man in the family), come here quickly!" Zhu Di asked him why not send for a doctor, the man said, "the grandma has no body illness, or mental problems, why send for a doctor?" "How do you know that she is not sick?" "When we examine a man, we should examine his breath and face. If he has a body trouble, his body color is black; if he has some worries in the heart, his body color is red. Now that her body color is not black or red, so I can say she has no illness." "If she is healthy, why did she fall faint?" "Since there is saliva in her mouth, she must be fainted by hunger." Really, when Black Ox fed her some meals, she came back to herself slowly.

Watched the man carefully, wearing a net headband, short clothes and trousers, thick eyebrows and big eyes, thick hands and large feet, black face with full of beards and moustache on, completely a peasant in the countryside, but he could examine the illness, Zhu Di was very surprised. He had not thought that there was this kind of strange man in the wild mountain, so he invited the man to give him an examination. Just a look, the man said to Zhu Di, "You body color is red, you have something worried in mind." Very surprised in heart, Zhu thought the man had a sharp sight, so bowed and asked him to give some advice. The man said slowly, "Men are different from each, hearts too, so their mind problems are different from each other too. Some worry about their homes and families, some worry about the country and its people. The former is small mind problems, the latter big ones."

Zhu asked in surprise, "Can you tell me which kind of mind problem I have, small or big?" The man smiled, "You are a big man with a big heart, so you have a big mind problem." Found that the man was not common, so Zhu bowed again, "Can you help me?" The man brought out a small bag and passed it to him, "I have a prescription here, maybe it will do some help to you." Opened the bag, Zhu found a piece of white cloth on which written, "When Wudang Mountains is prosperous, the country is peaceful" and four sentences, "To build Wudang Mountains to protect the frontiers, to pacify the central land, to gain the people's support, for Emperor Xuan will be with you." The following were two sentences as opening medicine, "A rage of wind in Poyang Lake, and a piece of cloud over Baigou River."

Watching these, Zhu felt puzzled, was the man to enlighten him ordered by Zhang Sanfeng? He wanted to require the man, but when he turned round, the man had been gone. So he asked Black Ox, "Do you know where Zhang Sanfeng is now?" "You just had a long talk with Zhang Sanfeng." Had a careful look at the prescription, Zhu understood at once, excited and full of hope, so his worries were all wiped out. He ordered his followers, "Do remember to build a palace here to commemorate my meeting with Zhang Sanfeng and name it Meeting God Palace (Yuzhen Palace)".

8. Built Wudang Mountain at a large scale

Emperor Yongle followed Zhang Sanfeng's strategy of "Building Wudang Mountains at a large scale and ruling the country with the help of gods". It was the high time to make Wudang Mountains prosperous, so Zhang Sanfeng told Sun Biyun to draw a set of pictures of Wudang Taoist palaces and temples, which was offered to Emperor Yongle at a proper time. Found that the pictures were grand and magnificent, the palaces and temples proper in locations, all just like a large park of real mountains and waters, Zhu Di felt very happy. But he had one thing puzzled, "Why must we build Taoist palaces and temples in Wudang Mountains, not any mountain else?"

Sun Biyun pointed to the pictures and explained, "My tutor Zhang Sanfeng is good at chronometer and geography. He said to me that Wudang Mountains, linking sky hinge and earth axis, is the best place to build palaces for Emperor Xuan. Linking shy hinge and earth axis, so Wudang Mountains can control the whole country. The Song and Yuan dynasties all built palaces for Emperor Xuan in Wudang Mountains as royal ancestral temple, with the purpose to control the frontiers and pacify the country." Zhu Di was convinced by Sun's explanation, so he offered an important position in government to be in charge of China Taoism. Then he set orders to send three hundred thousand folk people and soldiers to build Wudang Mountains in accordance with the pictures devised by Zhang Sanfeng.

In the pictures devised by Zhang Sanfeng, there was no Meeting God Palace, so Emperor Yongle changed Xuantian Palace near Meeting Gods Temple into Meeting God Palace, and then changed the hall to worship Emperor Xuan into Real God Hall to worship Zhang Sanfeng. Here was a palace for Zhang Sanfeng, so Dragon and Tiger Hall and Parents' Hall were omitted. There is a big yard inside the Mountain Gate, for the students of Zhang to exercise boxing. Behind the yard, there are Worshiping Hall, Grand Hall with a copper statue of Zhang Sanfeng worshiped on the shrine, and Right and Left Side Halls.

Zhang Sanfeng was very moved when he heard that Emperor Yongle built palaces and statue for him, so he led his students to protect these imperial envoys Zhang Xin, Guo jin, Yu Moxin, others officials and workers and soldiers who were building Wudang Mountains with their gongfu during the ten years' building period.

The monk, who had been defeated by Zhang Sanfeng that year, was now very profound in Gongfu after scores of years' being taught by tutors and cultivation, and named himself "Lighting Rabbi". Directed by the fugitive Emperor Jianwen, he came to Wudang Mountains to kill these imperial envoys Zhang Xin, Guo jin, and Yu Moxin.

One afternoon, he took his students to Meeting Gods Temple and declared a fight with Zhang Sanfeng. Heard that two martial art experts would have a fight, the students of Zhang and the builders on the construction fields all came to have a look. Zhang Sanfeng, observing Taoist principle "Reducing disputes and spreading kindness", wanted to enlighten, instead of defeating Lighting Rabbi in the fight. So kept escaping from violent attacks of Lighting Rabbi, not did any harm to him. However, the monk thought that Zhang could not defeat him, so he was playing with him on purpose, so felt ashamed and became angry, making more violent attacks to Zhang. Suddenly he was stumbled by a large stone and almost fell down, so Zhang shouted, "Stop", both of them all stopped fighting.

Zhang Sanfeng bowed down and carried up the large stone by one hand, "The stone was stumbling you, so I should put it away!" With the words, he gave a violent palm to the stone with the other hand, which made the stone break into pieces. Lighting Rabbi understood at once, Zhang Sanfeng was not inferior to him, but giving a mercy to him, for he could break the large stone into pieces, let down his body of blood and fresh. Ashamed, he went away with his students.

Zhang Sanfeng reduced disputes, destroyed the evils and spread kindness, which protected the safety of these officials, workers and soldiers, making the project carry on smoothly. The nine palaces and nine temples devised by Zhang Sanfeng were finished soon. The former Wudang County Court was also changed into Yuxu Palace, the leader of the nine palaces.

Emperor Yongle was very concerning about the building of Wudang Mountains, especially the foundry of Golden Hall and the statue of Emperor Zhenwu. He examined the blueprints till he felt satisfied. He also ordered to found these in Beijing and ordered an important official He Jun to carry these to Wudang Mountains. It was said that statue had the body of Zhenwu and the face of Emperor Yongle. The face of Emperor Zhenwu statue in Golden Hall was really as same as Emperor Yongle's picture. There involved many blood and toil of the workers and the intention of Emperor Yongle in the founding of the statue.

In accordance with the rules of the Ming Dynasty, all the brothers of Yongle should come to worship Wudang Mountains and pray when Golden Hall was set up. In order to offer convenience to these princes when they worship Wudang Mountains, Zhang Sanfeng had devised thirty-six temples as their living places at the same time he devised nine palaces and nine temples.

These temples, sponsored by these princes, were different in size according to their offers. When these princes climbed on Golden Top and saw Emperor Zhenwu, they were all surprised: Emperor Zhenwu was identical with Emperor Yongle. They thought to themselves, the reason for Emperor Zhenwu protected and helped Emperor Yongle was that Emperor Yongle was Emperor Zhenwu. Some of them, who had thought of rebelling against Emperor Yongle, hurried to bow before Emperor Zhenwu for mercy and then gave themselves to Emperor Yongle.

From then on, all the princes were obedient, without any other thought to rebel against Emperor Yongle. That Emperor Yongle was Emperor Zhenwu was widely spread in China, so all the country became obedient and peaceful. When stabilized the political situation, Emperor Yongle began to deal with the frontiers' troubles. After five years' hard work, he stabilized the frontiers and laid a steady foundation for fixing up Chinese territory.

Postscript

Found that the large royal building group of nine palaces, nine temples, thirty-six temples, seventy-two cliffs and temples was finished, Meeting God Palace for him built by Emperor Yongle where his statue was enjoying the offers, his students were wide spread in palaces and temples in Wudang Mountains, and the hope of making Wudang Mountains prosperous and important was realized, Zhang Sanfeng thought satisfied and began his travel again.

Zhang Sanfeng, profound in Wushu and medicines, taught many students, wiped out the evil and helped the innocent, and cured the folk people of their illness during his scores of years' traveling. There are many folk stories that speak very highly of him all over the country.

In 1459, Emperor Tianshun of the Ming Dynasty, in order to command Zhang Sanfeng's contributions, named him Tongwei-Xuanhua Immortal and built a copper stele for him on which carved Zhang's picture and inscribed the Imperial Orders to name him. This stele, preserved in Wudang Mountains, left for the later generations a real vision of Zhang Sanfeng.

During the past 500 years, Wudang Boxing created by Zhang Sanfeng has developed into a complete Wudang Boxing system same to Shaolin Boxing, with millions of students all over the world.

Zhang Sanfeng had made lots of contributions in helping Emperor Yongle manage the country, stabilize the political situation, pacify the frontiers, and unify the country. He had created Wudang Boxing to teach people how to exercise the body and cultivate the character, keep strong and healthy, and prolong the lifespan, which did a great good to human beings. Zhang Sanfeng was qualified to be a founder of Wudang Boxing, the emperor of martial art.

Chapter 3 Wudang Taoism Culture 武当道教文化

Wudang Mountains, one of the famous scenic spots in China, whose perimeter is over 800km, full of picturesque hills and intense forests, was praised as the meeting place of heaven and earth. For its enchanting scenery and the legendary home of gods, many Taoists and hermits came to cultivate themselves here, so Wudang Mountains was regarded as the origin place of China Taoism.

It is said that Emperor Zhenwu had been cultivating himself here for over 40 years and became god.

During the Song Dynasty, Wudang Taoism had developed into some certain size, forming its own organizational form, and also had set up many Taoist buildings. On the days of Zhenwu's birthday and becoming god, lots of pious people would come here to worship Wudang Mountains from all directions. Emperor Zhenwu, came to Wudang Mountains when he was very young and cultivated here for 42 years in spite of all kinds of dangers and difficulties; then lived in Wudang Mountains to perish devils and protect the people, was regarded as the God of Fortune.

Wudang Taoism came to the most prosperous stage in the Ming Dynasty. Emperor Cheng, Zhu Di ordered to support and develop Wudang Taoism after he became the Emperor. He wrote all the orders by himself, from reconnaissance and devise of Taoist buildings, sending qualified officials to overlook the project, to the ways for Taoists to cultivate. There were all high buildings on the both sides of the 140km ancient road to the Golden Top.

After thousands years' development, there produced proud and profound Wudang Culture in Wudang Taoism: nature-upholding Taoist buildings, mysterious Wudang Boxing, Wudang Ways to keep healthy, talking-with-god religion service, court-like Taoist music, unrivalled carvings, China traditional medicine and herbs, all are the crystal of Chinese national cleverness.

Taoism has played an important role in ancient politics, economy, culture, and ideology of China. Taoism, with Chinese characteristics and nearly 2,000-year history, is still influencing Chinese life.

Taoism thinks that all the creatures in the world are controlled by other thing, the god, who has supernatural power, so worships many kinds of gods. Joss worshiped by Wudang Taoism, can't be counted and beautiful in shape and extract in craftsmanship, are national treasures.

Wudang Taoism is the important part of China Taoism. That lots of famous Taoists and hermits cultivated here has left some rare records in the history of Wudang Taoism.

Taoist service, also called Jiao, is full of strong religious atmosphere. Taoism thinks that it is a rite to talk with gods and pray for good fortune and prolong the lifespan so as to became god and so on, which can not be fulfilled by mortal power.

Taoism is strong against all the behaviors and acts that are looked down upon by the civilized society. There are more than 1,000 rules and disciplines, the main tenet of which is to ask all the Taoists to engage oneself and actively cultivate themselves so as to become successful; otherwise, will be given relative severe punishment.

1. Gods in Wudang Taoism 武当神仙

Supreme God of Originality 元始天尊

"Supreme God" is a title for the most distinguished heavenly Gods in Taoism. There are not so many gods can be bestowed the title "Supreme God". While the three Qings/ Cleanness, i.e., Yuqing Supreme God of Originality, Shangqing Linbao Supreme God and Taiqing Supreme God of Morality, are among the group. The celestial residences of the three gods are called Yuqing, Shangqing and Taiqing Territory.

Among the three Qings/ Cleanness, Supreme God of Originality has the highest official rank, for he is the forefather of all the Gods in the Taoism. The Word originality is a term to describe the source or root of the universe. Later according to this word the Taoists transfer it to an image as the most distinguished God. In Taoist books, Supreme God of Originality is said to live on the thirty-sixth layer of Heaven. And He has existed before all the things are created, never vanished and will be eternal. He will descend from Heaven to teach people and transmit knowledge to human beings when a new world is set up.

Supreme God of Originality is generally worshiped in the middle of the statues of the three gods. Over his head mysterious light broods. Body in the robe, he wears an upright coronet. His left hand is seemingly grabbing something while the right hand is upward and half-opened. The gestures symbolize the state of chaotic and unformed universe.

Supreme God of Holy Mist 灵宝老君

Supreme God of Holy Mist is the next to Supreme God of Originality, also called Taishang Taoist. According to Taoist documents, he was born from the elementary materials before the world was set up. It is said that he originated from the light and nutrition of the sun and moon, smoke and mist of the universe, and was born after he stayed in the belly of the universe for 3,700 years. He has been living in the mysterious jade mansion in the Shangqing Territory, escorted by 30,000 virginal boys and girls respectively. He has saved uncountable sinful people from the hellish situation. He is said to be able to exist in 36 different states and 72 sub-states. In fact, he is almost omni-present.

In the temple, his statue is usually put on the left hand to that of Supreme God of Originality. In his hand there is a Taiji Chart or a Jade Ruyi that symbolizes auspiciousness.

Supreme God of Morality 道德天尊

Among the Three Qings/ Cleanness, Supreme God of Morality is the most well known. At the beginning, Supreme God of Morality is also called Taishang Laojun, an honorable title for Lao zi, Li Er, the founder of the school of Taoism before the Qin Dynasty. Because he was born with complete white hairs, so people gave him a name Lao zi, means an old man.

In accordance with Taoist scripts, it was Lao zi who spread the essence of Taoism, which exists before the existence of world, can function as the root of the royal family and the guidebook for cultivating immortals. He employed his unusual wisdom to write down the 5,000 words *Tao and Teh*. In the process of the history, all walks of people, such as militarist, law researcher, diplomatist, boxer and astrologist, etc. have sought the inspiration and encouragement, sources and principals of their theories and regulations from the Book. While Taoism has taken *The Tao and Teh* as the holy scripts, given great amount of illustrations from the perspectives of the conception of laws and virtue and formed their unique principals of theology. And on the basis of the principles, Taoism has formed their own doctrines and creeds by derivation and deduction. By apotheosis and added explanations of generations, Lao zi has already been canonized as a Supreme God of opening a new era.

He has white hairs, an affable smile and a divine fan in his hand.

Jade Emperor 玉帝

He is the supervisor of all the Gods and the creator of the World. The Chinese Yu refers to the word "Imperial" which is exclusive for the emperor.

In Taoism, Jade Emperor, the highest emperor in heaven, is in charge of heaven, the earth and the waters, all the affairs in all the four directions and all the lives.

The prototype of Jade Emperor originated from the ancient adoration to heavenly emperor. In the primitive societies, the people venerated the natural Gods of the Sun, the Earth, the Thunder and the Lightning; therefore, omnipotent heavenly emperor, who takes charge of the other gods, appeared. Later canonized by the rulers of all dynasties, that emperor became the most distinguished almighty Jade Emperor in charge of the universe and all creatures.

Emperor of the North Pole 北极仙翁

Emperor of the North Pole is the god who assists Jade Emperor to be in charge of the latitude and longitude of the earth, constellations and weather and seasons of the earth. The image of this god originated from the worshiping for the stars. Ancient people matched the stars with the kings and top officials. The North Pole here refers to the Polaris and that the god was called Emperor of the North Pole is thought to be the suzerain of all the gods of constellations. So the Polaris is also named King Star.

In Taoist scripts, Emperor of the North Pole governs all the gods of stars and celestial figure of mountains. And he is the launcher of ail natural phenomena. He can make order the gods of thunder, lightning and ghosts.

Emperor of Heaven 天官

He is in charge of the north and south poles, all the living things and the military affairs of human beings. It is said that he is a brother of Emperor of the North Pole who was born by Lady Purple Light in the Zhou Dynasty.

Emperor of Mother Ground 地官

This goddess has another name, Queen of Mother Ground. She is in charge of the transformations of different elements, the bearing of creatures, the physical appearance of all beings and the beauty of all lands, mountains and rivers, so she is called Ground Mother as a counterpart title to another title Heaven Father for Jade Emperor.

The creed on the goddess rooted in the veneration to lands. Ancient people prayed the god of land for proper weather, crops harvest and auspicious life. The title "Mother Ground" began to be used during the Spring and Autumn Period. As for the reason of using this word, various sayings exist at present. One of the explanations is as the following: in the patriarchal society, the word "Mother" referred to the great grand mother treated as the chief and authoritative figure; while the word "Ground" referred to the mother of all creatures, that is, the land. So the title in fact means Mother of the Land.

Emperor Zhenwu 真武大帝

Zhenwu is named Emperor Zhenwu, the Founder or the Grand dad in Heaven. This supreme god is evolved from the image of the ancient northern god, Xuanwu. In Taoist legends, it is said that Zhenwu, made up of the universal essential material of gas, is a copy version of Taiji. He was born in Jingle Kingdom by the Queen on March 3, in the first year of Emperor Huang. Intelligent, valorous, uninterested in the world affairs but keen on cultivation, he left his parents at 15 and came to Wudang Mountains with a purpose of acquiring the true meaning of Taoism. After forty-two years' cultivation, he ascended to heaven on September 9, in the fifty-seventh year of Emperor Huang, escorted by five dragons.

Zhenwu has a big bulk and an affable countenance. He may be bare-footed and hanging-haired while wearing a Taoist robe or armor. He may wear coronet and richly manufactured imperial robe with a stately air with the company of General Tortoise and General Snake. Sometimes he may stand on the backs of tortoise and snake watching heaven, the earth and waters, with a sword in hand.

Mother of Cynosure 西王母

She is the goddess of wisdom worshiped in Taoism, mother of all the stars in the cynosure.

In Taoist Books, She, one princess of Jade Emperor of the Zhou Dynasty, had another name Lady Purple Light. She had nine sons, the eldest Emperor Heaven, the second Emperor of the North Pole. The other seven sons are respectively the seven stars in the cynosure.

The goddess has four heads and eight arms. The eight arms are equivalent to the Eight Diagrams. She always holds bow, halberd, or weapons with a shape of the sun or the moon in her hands.

Purple Gas Immortal 紫气大仙

It is said that he was the teacher for Zhenwu's cultivation. When Zhenwu was born as the prince of Jingle Kingdom, he was not willing to succeed the throne but intended to learn Taoism so as to serve God and help the common people. Purple Gas Immortal was deeply moved, so under his careful and cautious guide, Zhenwu finally became an immortal after a cultivation of 42 years.

With a chignon on the hair, an iron pestle in one hand and a loose robe on the body, he was affable and plump and smoothed-skinned in countenance.

Flag-Holding God 执旗官

Flag-Holding God, also called the Tiangang, is Zhenwu's subordinate god for holding his flag. Tiangang is an official title for the god who is in charge of the Seven Stars in the spoon-like cynosure, staying in the handle position.

He has sword-like eyebrows and double eyelids. Old-fashioned cap on head, armor on body, his clothes and girdle fluttering in the wind, he looks so valorous and stately, with a huge flag in one hand.

Sword-Handing God 捧剑官

Sword-Handing God, also called Taiyi, is another Zhenwu's subordinated god for holding his sword. In accordance with Verse on Astrology and Astrological Phenomena, Taiyi, a subject of Zhenwu, can yoke sixteen dragons and foretell the weather, war affairs, and the arrival of starvation and illness. In the mortal world, he is a supreme god who can predict the rain, wind, draught, war, starvation and disasters.

An upright cap for martial arts learners on head, armor on body, clothes and girdles waving in the wind, he looks valorous and stately, with the two hands holding a sword.

Golden Boy 金童

Golden Boy, also called Jade Boy, is the god who is in charge of etiquette and recording the affairs about the goodness, wickedness, achievements and errors.

He is standing on the left hand of Emperor Zhenwu, with a volume of records in his both hands and eyes gazing at something, elegant, cautious and sedate.

Jade Girl 玉女

Jade Girl, Lady Peach Blossom, is the goddess who is in charge of etiquette and recording the affairs about the goodness, wickedness, achievements and errors.

She is standing on the right hand of Emperor Zhenwu, with both hands holding the brush pen, ink and inkstone and two eyes gazing at something, mild, calm, coy and obedient.

The Six Generals 六大将军

The six generals are the generals of Emperor Zhenwu. It is said that they are made in accordance with the arranging principle of traditional date recording method. In Taoism, these men can drive wind and thunder, control certain minor ghost and divine beings.

Thunder God 雷神

He is in charge of thunder. This belief is derived from the creed on the natural thunder and lightening and other phenomena of the ancient people. The original image of Thunder God was a beast, then half beast and half man, at last evolved into the present humanized god.

It is said that the residence of Emperor Zhenwu is called the capital of Thunder, for God

Thunder, with other gods such as Lightning God, Wind God, Rain God, Dragon God and River God, lives there as a dependent God to Emperor Zhenwu.

The image of Thunder God is enshrined and worshiped in Wudang Mountains. With three eyes, claws of bird, feet of human beings, face of monkey, mouth of hawk, helmet of animal on his body and two wings on his shoulder, he looks so particular, valorous and frightening.

Official Wang　王判官

He is thought to be the God to keep these mountain gates of palaces and temples in Wudang Mountains in Taoism. His hatred to evil doings, uprightness and unselfishness are so much canonized by civic people.

He wears armor, a scarlet face, three eyes and a ferocious countenance, with a golden whip in his hand, having an appearance to punish anyone sternly that dare to behave wickedly, which makes everyone frightened.

Lady Xuan of the Ninth Heaven　九天玄女

She is also called Lady Origin. The Ninth Heaven refers to the highest position in Heaven, which means that the goddess has a very high official rank. So she is called Lady Xuan of the Ninth Heaven.

Her earliest image was an immortal bird called Bird Xuan. It was said that Emperor Xuan ordered her to fall into the earth and gave birth to a baby whose name was Qi who established the Shang Dynasty. Therefore, she was respected as the ancestor of Shang Clan. Later, her image became a celestial bird with a head of mankind. Eventually, she becomes a goddess who is one of the most beautiful and the highest divine goddess. In the following times, by using her name, some people wrote a book named *Book of Lady Xuan* narrating the skills of sexual intercourse, pregnancy of delivering and ways to preserve one's health, so the folk also called her Mother of Bringing Babies. In the family of the Chinese celestial beings, her position is next to Nüwa and the Western Queen.

Gods of the North Pole　北极诸神

The belief in cynosure originated from the worshiping to the constellations. In Taoist books, Mother of Cynosure has nine sons totally called Lords of Cynosure, or Gods of Cynosure. In accordance with the astrological book, it is said, "in the key position of the middle sky, all the gods in charge of the stars in the Cynosure can control all the people on the earth, the distribution of fortune, official position life and death. If people pray sincerely, all the wishes can be achieved."

Gods of Taoism-Protecting　道教保护神

The four Gods of Taoism-Protecting, also called Four Celestial Generals, are among the divine 36 generals of Emperor Zhenwu.

They wear armors and helmets, stately and valorous.

Emperor of Three Elements　三元神

Three Chargers also called Three Elements, is the whole term for Charger of sky, Charger of ground and Charger of water, which are the earliest gods worshiped by Taoists. This kind of belief derived from the natural oblation to sky, ground and water.

Taoism thinks that the Three Chargers can offer happiness to people, forgive the sin, and wipe out the trouble; in other words, the Charger of Sky can offer happiness to people, the Charger of ground can absolve people from guilt and the charger of water can release people from the unlucky situation. The various rulers had always cried up the belief on the Three Chargers so that the temples for the Three Chargers were set up everywhere. Even the governments set up the taboo for sacrificing the Three Chargers. For example, in the Tang Dynasty, during the fete there must be no animal killing, nor fishing, nor hunting. In the Song Dynasty, in the ceremony of memorizing the three chargers, the officials can neither cross-examine nor execute the death-doomed criminals.

Supreme God of Misery-Curing　救苦天尊

This God has many titles. The most commonly accepted are Taiyi Supreme God of Misery-curing, Voice-Tracing Supreme God of Misery-curing, and All-Direction Supreme God of Misery-curing and so like. He is a god rich in transformations.

In accordance with Taoist books, he is extremely kind, powerful and full of miracles. If meeting people suffering from trouble or misery, he would chant the script of Taoism to save people from apprehension or endangered situation. Among Taoists and the folk, he is not only a god to save people from the misery and disaster but also a god to save suffering and wronged ghosts in the hell.

2. Taoist Festivals　道教节日

March 3 Temple Fair　三月三庙会

March 3 of each year in the lunar calendar is one of Taoist traditional festivals. It is said that the God of Taoism, Emperor Zhenwu, was born on that day, so Taoism followers celebrate the day in a great style.

In accordance with the history, Wudang Taoism has held religion services on the day every year from the Song Dynasty; folk believers also came to Wudang Mountains to worship Emperor Zhenwu. So the religion service has become the March 3 Temple Fair.

March 3 Temple Fair is a folk cultural activity with a strong participation, among which Taoist culture, Wudang gongfu, folk customs are combining together. During the fair, Wudang Taoism holds many religious activities of strong Taoist characteristics, such as religion service of Fasting and Jiao, offering Dragon-Head Incense, baptizing keepsakes, hitting Fortune Clock and so on. There are also Wudang gongfu performances, Wudang Tea performances, Shadow Boxing plays, folk songs and other acrobatics and lamp fair, which fully show the folk customs of Wudang mountains.

All Taoists, Taoism followers, and traveling teams, including these from Taiwan, Macao, Hong Kong, come to Wudang Mountains to worship Emperor Zhenwu. On the day, there are full of visitors and happy tones in Wudang Mountains.

September 9 Praying Service 九月九祈福法会

September 9 of each year in the lunar calendar is one of Taoist traditional festivals. It is said that on the day Emperor Zhenwu succeeded in cultivation and became a god after forty-two years' cultivation, so Taoists and Taoism followers celebrate the day in a great style.

September 9 of each year, all the halls and temples in Wudang Mountains are all decorated up and full of Taoist music, for Wudang Taoism are holding the September 9 Praying Service. Taoism followers from the world come to Golden Top of Wudang Mountains to worship Emperor Zhenwu.

During the service, there are also many religious activities of strong Taoist characteristics, such as the performances of Wudang gongfu, offering Dragon-Head Incense, baptizing keepsakes, hitting Fortune Clock, Praying for better fortune, and so on.

3. Taoist Religion Service 道教法事

In the Taoist halls or temples, people often see the Taoists singing some ancient songs and dancing in the mandala with colorful clothes and some kinds of religion service wares in hand, which is the Taoist service rite, Taoist Rite, or attending the religion service to the letter of rules.

"Fast" refers to that the attendant should have a bath and change clothes, not eat meat or drink wine, not sleep with one's better half before the rite, to show one's piousness. Taoism absorbed this for the purpose of clearing the mind by eating vegetables and cleaning the body by having a bath, in other words, fasting. Doing good things to get rid of the evil thought, conforming to god as to keep healthy, and then cultivating, are the three stages of fasting. Taoism has paid more attention to fasting and set a series of rules to direct fasting process.

Jiao was a sacrifice, an old Taoist rite. Taoism has absorbed and developed this meaning of sacrifice, by which to communicate with gods. Jiao also has many rules in the process and rite. Jiao has many other names, for people pray for what, there will be some relative kind of Jiao, for example, a Jiao to pray for rain. At first, the rules of fasting were different from that of Jiao, but after several dynasties' development and combination, fasting and Jiao were combined into one, the pronoun of Taoist rites.

Fasting and Jiao rules refer to the rules and regulations that Taoist religion service should observe. The following are some services that the Taoists often attend:

(1) Morning and Evening Lesson in the Mandala, is a must for all the Taoists living in the temple, whose purpose is to exercise body and cultivate mind, to pray for good fortune, to stabilize one's mind to be a Taoist, to release souls from purgatory, and to demonstrate the management of the temples.

(2) Welcoming ceremony for the founder is to welcome Emperor Zhenwu ascend the mandala, to demonstrate his great power to the effect of protecting scriptures, Taoism, and temples and halls, so as to keep the Taoist temples and halls quiet forever.

(3) Fete for the singles is a rite done in the evening lesson, to sacrifice the single ghosts and release souls from purgatory for them.

(4) Birthday ceremony is the rite to celebrate the birthday of the founder of Taoism, Zhang Sanfeng.

(5) Celebration ceremony is also the rite to celebrate the birthday of the founder of Taoism, Zhang Sanfeng, which is done at day.

(6) Meeting the emperor rite is used in the morning, the midnight point, on 25th of the twelfth month of the lunar calendar, to meet the Jade Emperor of Heaven, by which to ask the emperor to descend to the mortal world and bring good fortune to humans and keep them healthy and living longer.

(7) Big-Turning Rite is to demonstrate the power of Taoism, to get rid of all evils and release all creatures in the world, which is at the end of service.

(8) Sending Letter (melting letter, or burning application) Rite, is a very important rite in the fasting and Jiao, widely used in all kinds of big service, by which, Taoists send their application letters to Jade Emperor, to invite all gods to descending to the mandala and bringing fortune and preserving humans' life and releasing souls for the dead.

(9) Water-and-Fire Tempering Rite is a common rite to release souls for the dead.

(10) Lamp Rite is also a commonly performed rite done in the evening after the sun has set, with lamp as the religion service ware, by which to light the world and perish the darkness.

4. Taoist Rules and Regulations 清规戒律

There had the biggest Taoist organization all over the country in Wudang Mountains during the Ming Dynasty. In accordance with the words of Yang Jinmin, the Magistrate of Yunyang Prefecture, there were more than 10,000 Taoists in this region. We can imagine that it was impossible to rule these Taoists without laws. In Taoism, these laws are called Taoist rules and regulations.

The most authoritative rule in Wudang Mountains was the Imperial Order set by Emperor Cheng, Zhu Di of the Ming Dynasty. In all halls and temples in Wudang Mountains, there had a stele pavilion in which inscribed this order, saying "All Taoists in Wudang Mountains must have happy spirit and everlasting simplicity... Any Taoist that does not well cultivate and does bad things to affect others' cultivation or Taoist reputation should be exiled out of the Mountains, or even tell on the Government."

The Imperial Order made Wudang Taoism have independent right of justice. Yuanhe Temple in Wudang Mountains was one judicatory institution, called Taoist prison.

Taoist rules and regulations in South Cliff Palace of Wudang Mountains had stated that the State has laws while the mountain has 108 rules, from firing the face or toasting the eyebrows or making medicines or being exiled out of Taoism, to punishing by sticks or by making to carrying medicines, and to making to worship gods with offerings, different punishments to different violations.

Taoist rules and regulations in Purple Cloud Palace also stated that all these rules and regulations are the yardstick of gods' behaviors and actions, gods should not neglect, so the humans can't violate them, or should be punished heavily.

There are more than 1,000 rules and regulations in Taoism, whose purpose is to make Taoists self-controlled, to the effect of concentrating on Taoism.

All those behaviors and actions that violate Taoist rules and regulations are looked down upon in the civilized society, also strong opposed by Taoism. Any violation has a correspondent punishment.

Imperial Order　皇帝圣旨

All Taoists in Wudang Mountains must have happy spirit and everlasting simplicity. You should concentrate on cultivating only and have a simple life, without any thought on other human things, just keep on cultivating without a short-time stop. All the visitors except for those are clever and earnest in studying Taoism mustn't make troubles to disturb Taoist cultivation or religion service, otherwise they would be punished severely. Any Taoist that dose not well cultivate or does bad things to affect others' cultivation or Taoist reputation should be exiled out of the Mountains, or even tell on the Government.

Emperor Yongle

Rules in South Cliff Palace　南岩宫规条

The State has laws while the Mountains has 108 rules, from firing the face, toasting the eyebrows, making medicines, being exiled out of Taoism, to punishing by sticks or by making to carrying medicines, and to making to worship gods with offerings, different punishments to different violations. Now we set the 33 rules as the following:

(1) Anyone who rapes, steals, does bad deeds should be punished by toasting the eyebrows, or ordering to making medicines, or being exiled out of Taoism.

(2) Anyone who gambles should be punished by sticks.

(3) Anyone who makes rumors to puzzle others should be punished by sticks.

(4) Anyone who becomes the leader by force should be punished by sticks.

(5) Anyone who misinforms the long-term inhabitants should be punished by sticks.

(6) Anyone who smokes should be punished by sticks.

(7) Anyone who gathers people to make troubles should be punished by sticks.

(8) Anyone who cheats others into Taoism by tricks should be punished by sticks.

(9) Anyone who want only talks about the state affairs should be punished by sticks.

(10) Anyone who has meat and/ or drink should be punished by sticks.

(11) Anyone who has disorder in mind and the habit of oversleeping should be punished by sticks.

(12) Anyone who does bad things to others without respect for Taoism should be punished by sticks.

(13) Anyone who collects money for one's own benefit without handing it in the temple should be punished by sticks.

(14) Anyone who allies with others without respect for Taoism should be punished by sticks.

(15) Anyone who steals Taoist or visitors' property should be punished by sticks.

(16) Anyone who teases or hurts the weaker should be punished by sticks.

(17) Anyone who plays as royal official and disorders Taoism should be punished by sticks.

(18) Anyone who makes disputes to hurt the harmony among Taoists should be ordered to carry medicines.

(19) Anyone who is jealous of others and does harm to the efficient should be ordered to carry medicines.

(20) Anyone who privately accommodates visiting Taoists should be ordered to carry medicines.

(21) Anyone who leaves the mountain secretly without asking for leave should be ordered to kneel to worship gods and offer offerings.

(22) Anyone who pays less attention to his words and speaks dirty words should be ordered to kneel to worship gods and offer offerings.

(23) Anyone who is late for service should be ordered to kneel to worship gods and offer offerings; the senior, the sick and the one on business are to the exception.

(24) Anyone who privately makes food for oneself without consideration for others should be ordered to kneel to worship gods and offer offerings; the senior, the sick and the one on business are to the exception.

(25) Anyone who doesn't observe his duty but interfere with others' business should be ordered to kneel to worship gods and offer offerings.

(26) Anyone who doesn't come to the hall when the statues of gods are invited to the hall should be ordered to kneel to worship gods and offer offerings.

(27) Anyone who doesn't take off the light when the set time comes should be ordered to kneel to worship gods and offer offerings.

(28) Anyone who doesn't follow when the ban is lift should be ordered to kneel to worship gods and offer offerings; the senior and the weak are to the exception.

(29) Anyone who plays before the statues of gods should be ordered to kneel to worship gods and offer offerings.

(30) Anyone who makes a noise in serious situation should be ordered to kneel to worship gods and offer offerings.

(31) Anyone who makes a quarrel with others but not take advice should be ordered to kneel to worship gods and offer offerings.

(32) Anyone who hurt others' property should be repaid in accordance with the actual value.

(33) Anyone who goes out nakedly or with untidy clothes on should be ordered to kneel to worship gods and offer offerings.

Taoist Rules and Regulations in Palace of Harmony 太和宫清规榜

The purpose to publicize Taoist rules and regulations is to make all Taoists understand that all things they do should be for the benefit of the leader and most of the Taoists and that they should observe these rules and regulations to the letter, or should be punished in accordance with the rules and regulations.

(1) Anyone who has disorder in mind and the habit of oversleeping or makes a noise in

serious situation should be ordered to kneel to worship gods and offer offerings.

(2) Anyone who heavily violates Taoist rules and regulations and does not take the sentence by right of his strength should be punished by sticks.

(3) Anyone who steals the money in the hall for one's own purpose should be exiled out of Taoism publicly.

(4) Anyone who is against Taoist rules and regulations and doesn't observe the restriction should be exiled out of Taoism.

(5) Anyone who collects money for oneself and cheats long-term inhabitants should be exiled out of Taoism.

(6) Anyone who rapes the women, steals others' property, or does great harm to others should be destroyed the face by fire.

All the above is to help Taoism develop stronger and spread wider. All Taoists have the obligation to observe them, or should be punished heavily.

Taoist Rules and Regulations in Purple Cloud Palace　紫霄宫清规榜

Palaces, halls, and temples are the sacred places for Taoists to cultivate their minds and characters where has no harassment from the immortal world but the morning clock, evening drum, and the reading both in the morning and evening to make it possible for you to get rid of all other thoughts, just concentrate on cultivation. Once you come into Taoism, you should perform Taoist service and observe Taoist rules and regulations. In order to protect the holiness and power of Taoism, twelve rules and regulations are set. Here are the following:

The leaders in all levels should not neglect his duty, or should be ordered to carry medicines.

The leaders in all levels should work harmoniously and help each other, or should be ordered to carry medicines.

(1) Anyone who is interested in doing bad things and travels privately in the folk world, should be destroyed the face by fire.

(2) Anyone who doesn't respect a worthy person but praising the evil for the purpose of outstanding oneself should be exiled out of Taoism.

(3) Anyone who exploits the public property to enrich oneself should be exiled out of Taoism.

(4) Anyone who makes friends with the evil or accommodate visitors privately should be punished by sticks.

(5) Anyone who speaks evilly of others and does great harm to others should be punished by sticks.

(6) Anyone who plays improperly before gods and destroys the temples should be punished by sticks.

(7) Anyone who frames a case against others and breaks the harmony among Taoists should be exiled out of Taoism.

(8) Anyone who has meat and/ or drink to bother the temples should be punished by sticks.

(9) Anyone who steals the property when carrying them and privately makes meal for oneself should be punished by sticks.

(10) Anyone who publicly believes other belief and makes excuses for it should be exiled out of Taoism.

All these rules and regulations should be strictly observed; any violation should be punished accordingly, no matter you are old or young, relative or not; but the senior, the sick, the one on business, and the one who is excited to break them involuntarily are to the exception.

5. Zhang Sanfeng and Other Outstanding Taoists 张三丰及其他知名道士

Zhang Sanfeng was the famous Wudang Taoist during the late years of the Yuan Dynasty (1271—1368) and the beginning years of the Ming Dynasty (1368—1644).

It was said that Zhang Sanfeng, originally named Zhang Quanyi, nicknamed Sanfeng, born in Yizhou City, Liaoning Province, was tall and strong, with tortoise shape and swan bone, big ears and round eyes, hard beards and moustache. He always wore a coir raincoat and a pair of grass shoes, no matter summer or winter, lived in the lonely deep mountain or traveled in the crowded city. He could remember what he read just by one look, talked nothing but moral, kindness, faith and filial piety. He could talk with the gods and understand Taoism, so he could forecast the future and solve all the difficulties in the world. He could live without a meal for five days, even for two or three months; he could penetrate the mountain and drive the stones when he was happy; he lived in the snow when he was tired; he traveled here and there without any information, so all the people then were surprised at him and thought him as one of gods.

Wudang Taoist Medicine Cultivation has a long history, especially the Inner Medicine, which is to cultivate the breath into medicine so as to make one strong, keep one healthy, and prolong the lifespan by way of breathing. Zhang Sanfeng had a profound cultivation in Inner Medicine, he said in *Ode to Big Road*, "To cultivate the mood before cultivating the medicine; to cultivate big medicine before cultivate the mind; when the mind is steady, the medicine will come by itself; when the mood and character have cultivated, the big medicine will be in reach.", which figuratively explained the progress of medicine cultivation. He had written many books on medicine, such as, *The Gist of Gold Medicine*, *The Secrecy of Gold Medicine*, *A Song of Inner Medicine*, *Twenty-four Principles of Rootless Trees*, and *Taoist Song of Earth Element and Real Immortal*, which had been published in the Ming Dynasty. Later, the later people had compiled them into *A Full Collection of* Zhang Sanfeng's *Works*, with eight volumes.

Zhang Sanfeng was not only profound in medicine cultivation but also in martial art, especially good at boxing and swordplay. He, on the base of Taoist theories, such as the naturalness of Taoist theories, keeping in a humble position and so on, had combined Taoist Inner Exercise, guarding skills of regimen, boxing acts of martial art, military sciences of militarists into one, then created Wudang Boxing with the Inner Exercise as the body, attacking as the purpose, regimen as the first important thing, self-protection as the main principle, to defeat the tough by a tender act, charge the active by the still movement, attack the opponent with his own force, and strike only after the opponent has struck. From the Ming Dynasty, martial art world have respected Zhang Sanfeng as the founder of Wudang Inner Boxing and Taiji Boxing. Wudang Martial Art, through many generations' succeeding and development, has become one important school among China martial art, spread among the folk people, with a long and profound influence.

During the beginning years of the Ming Dynasty, Zhang Sanfeng came to Wudang Mountains, worshiped Emperor Zhenwu on Heavenly Pillar Peak, and built a hut to the north of Flag-Stretching Peak in which offered incense to Emperor Zhenwu. Then he built a hut in another place, named Meeting Gods Temple. He once said to the seniors in the mountains that Wudang Mountains would be different from that day. Later, the second emperor of the Ming Dynasty did order to build Wudang Mountains at a large scale and made Wudang Mountains the head of the Five Famous Mountains in China, naming the Biggest Mountain.

In the 21nd year of Emperor Hongwu of the Ming Dynasty, he left Wudang Mountains without any information. When the King of Hunan Province, Zhu Bai worshiped Wudang Mountains and could not find him, Zhu Bai wrote a poem to him, *A Poem to Eulogize* Zhang Sanfeng, which said to the effect, "Zhang Sanfeng loves gods. He drinks the water from the clean river in the morning, sleeps under South Cliff in the evening. He has cultivated Taoism in Wudang Mountains for many years, paying no attention to the changes of seasons and landscapes. When I could not find him in the bare mountains, how sad I am! There is only an empty hut left, an old Taoist sleeps under the pine tree."

In the 24th year of Emperor Hongwu, Zhu Yuanzhang, the founder of the Ming Dynasty, sent profound Taoists to put in order all Taoism in China. For that Zhang Sanfeng was so famous, he specially ordered them: "If you meet Zhang Sanfeng, invite him to me." But they could not find Zhang Sanfeng.

Yin Xi

Yin Xi, a doctor in 1067—1042 BC, was good at astrology. Once when he was watching the astronomical phenomenon, he found a group of purple cloud floating westward and predicted that a profound Taoist would pass through Hangu Pass. In order to make known with the Taoist, he decided to become official of Hangu Pass. Later, actually a profound Taoist, Lao zi coming near to Hangu Pass on a green ox, so he went to meet him with his students and asked Lao zi teach him Taoism. Then Lao zi stayed there and wrote two books to him, *Book of Dao* and *Book of De*, which is the famous *Tao and Teh.*

After he got the book, he pretended to being ill and stopped being the official and went to Wudang Mountains to cultivate in a cliff, Yin Xi Cliff. When Lao zi heard this, he came to Wudang Mountains on the green ox to visit Yin Xi, and the two started their traveling without any more information. Later, the mountain visited by Lao zi was named Green Goat Mountain; the stream passed by Lao zi the Manger Stream.

Ma Mingsheng

It is said that when Ma Mingsheng was young, he was hurt to dying by the robbers and was saved by a god's medicine. So he left home to learn Taoism from An Qisheng.

An Qisheng, a god in Taoist history, enjoyed a very long life, so was name One-Thousand-Year Man. He often traveled to sell medicines and made friends with Yingzheng, the first Emperor of the Qin Dynasty (221BC—207BC). He gave his *Book of Taiqing Medicine* to Ma, and Ma went to Wudang Mountains made medicines with his wife. When his medicine was made, he first took half and became an immortal god in the mortal world and took his students to travel all over the country; when he then took the other half, he became a god in Heaven.

Zhu Geliang

Zhu Geliang, a clever man in Three Kingdoms (220—280), living in Wolong Valley, Longzhong Prefecture, Sichuan Province, read all the famous persons' books in the corner of plantings in the field. He was good at making friends with famous men of letters and modest to learn from others. After learned from many famous men and studied military books and Taoism, he became a man full of knowledge in Taoism, politics, and military affairs.

After he became knowledgeable, he was made prime minister of Sichuan by Liu Bei, one of the three emperors in the Three Kingdoms, and demonstrated his cleverness in many things, which were recorded in many stories, such as Three visits to the Hut.

There were four schools of Taoists, leaving the world, living in the world, hiding in the world, and ruling the world. Zhu Geliang was the example of living in and ruling the world. In all his life, he had learned many things in Taoism, among which were politics, military affairs, astrology, calendar laws, and medicines, magical arts, which had played an important role in his life with Liu Bei.

Yao Jian

Yao Jian, born in Sui Dynasty (581—618), was made Junzhou Official to govern Wudang Area by Li Shimin, the second emperor of the Tang Dynasty (618—907), after he helped the latter become emperor.

During the years between 627 and 648, there broke drought and disaster of grasshopper in China. Li ordered Yao Jian to pray for rain in Wudang Mountains. Yao heard that there were five dragons cultivating in Wudang Mountains and that when asking for rain in the year of drought, there would be a heavy rain, so he accept the order and succeeded in praying for rain in Wudang Mountains. Therefore, Li ordered to build Five-Dragon Temple to worship the five dragons.

After succeeded in praying for rain, Yao got tired of being an official in the government and wanted to learn Taoism. When he got a permission, he took his family to Five-Dragon Temple and then became god. Emperor Xuan sent him to protect Wudang Area and save the country out of the disaster of drought and grasshopper several times, so the government of the Song Dynasty (960—1279) ordered to build Mighty Temple in the Purple Cloud Palace for him.

Lü Chunyang

Lü Chunyang, or Lü Dongbin, a famous Taoist in the Tang Dynasty, was one of the Eight Immortals in legend. In accordance with the history, his father, whose surname was Li, was the offspring of the royal family of the Tang Dynasty; his mother had surname Lü. Lü Dongbin, formerly named after his father, and passed the imperial examination to become Zhuangyuan, the First Winner in the Imperial Examination. But later Wu Zetian robbed the sovereignty and cruelly persecuted the offspring of the royal family of the Tang Dynasty, so Lü Dongbin changed to name after his mother and began a hermit life in deep mountains. First, he cultivated in Mount Hua, Shaanxi Province, and succeeded in gaining the power of three elements (the heaven, the earth, and the man). Because he worked hard to help humans, so Jade Emperor named him God Zhuangyuan, the founder of religion. He often visited Wudang Mountains and cultivated there, so he was very familiar with Taoist history. There is a cliff named Dongbin Cliff, which may be the place for him to cultivate.

Sun Simiao

SunSimiao, born in 581, lived 102 years. In accordance with the history, he was born clever and could recite more than one thousand poems at the age of seven. When he grew up, he specialized in the theories of Lao zi and Zhuang zi; and then he cultivated in Changbai Mountain, to research the knowledge to rule the country and help the man, being good at astrology, calendar laws, magical arts, and medicines.

He once cultivated in Lingxu Cliff, Five-Dragon Hill, Wudang Mountains. He had written thirty kinds of books, such as *Medicine Book of One Thousand Prescriptions*, *A Book on Nutrition-Absorbing*, and *Gist of Taiqing Medicines* and other Taoist books, was regarded as Chinese famous Taoist philosopher, and Medicine Master.

In 682, after he had a bath and fast, he sat there and died. It is said that when the people put him into the coffin, there just clothes left, his body had gone to become god.

Chen Tuan

Chen Tuan, born in 871, lived 118 years. He was very clever and easy to learn any thing, but could not passed the Imperial Examination; so lost hope in being an official in the government and began to visit scenic spots and places of interest. Influenced by many Taoists with whom he had made friends, he began learn Taoism and cultivated in Wudang Mountains for 30 years. Taught Sleeping Skill by the five dragons, he created his own Sleeping Gongfu, the first mystery in the world. There were two Chinese characters "Fortune" and "Longevity" in the wall of South Cliff Hall, the moral of his Sleeping Gongfu, which were well protected. Five-Dragon Palace, Pavilion to Read Scriptures, White Cloud Cliff, and Nine-room Cliff were all his places to cultivate. He had made great success in Taiji Diagram, and greatly influenced the Song Dynasty, Taoism and Confucianism. He had written some important books, such as, *A Discussion on Mystery*, *Moral of the Three Hills*, *Collections of Gaoyang*, and *Collections of Fishing Pool*.

He died on July 22. After he died, his body kept warm for seven days and there were colorful clouds floating in and outside his room for over a month.

Zhang Shixun

ZhangShixun was born poor in Junzhou County, at the foot of Wudang Mountains. When he was reading in Taoist Children Hall in Wudang Mountains, some Taoists asked him to learn Taoism from them, he didn't agree; but kept on study Confucianism and became Prime Minister of Emperor Kangxi in the Qing Dynasty (1636—1912).

Later, influenced by Taoism and Taoist's prediction, and the evil conditions in the government made him leave government for Taoism. So he cultivated in Wudang Mountains and succeeded in becoming god.

Sun Jiran

SunJiran was a Wudang Taoist in the early years of South Song Dynasty (1127—1276). In accordance with the history, he left home to cultivate in Supreme-Clean Temple on Mount Mao in the late years of North Song Dynasty (960—1127), taught by the Taoists there, he had learned special skills in making medicines. In 1141, he took his students to Wudang Mountains where the halls and temples were destroyed by swords and wars, nearly became a ruin, and he decided to rebuild Wudang Mountains. In order to collect money for rebuilding the halls and temples, he went around to heal disease for the folk. That time the country was under a plague, so he went around and put his medicine into the well. After taking the well water, the people recovered, so many people believed him and gave more money to him. With several years' working, he rebuilt all halls and temples in the Five-Dragon Palace. Then he led his students and followers build roads to sacrifice offerings, which made Wudang Taoism famous again in China.

He lived over 100 years, and died of no illness.

Ye Yunlai

Ye Yunlai, a Wudang Taoist in the Yuan Dynasty, born on March 5, 1251, was in the family of Ye Fashan, the national master of Taoism in the Tang Dynasty.

Taoists in the South believed in Taoism, but not left home to cultivate in mountains, just stayed in their homes, was named Home-living Taoists. Taught Yin-Yang augury, nutrition-absorbing skills, Ye Yunlai was interested in Taoism when young and learned Qingwei Taoism. During the period between the late years of the Song Dynasty and the early years of the Yuan Dynasty, for escaping the wars, he came to Wudang Mountains to learn Xiantian Taoism from Huang Dongyuan, the famous Taoist in Wudang, with Zhang Daogui and Liu Daoming, and then became a famous Taoist in Five-Dragon Palace. In 1285, he was invited to Beijing to demonstrate the skills of stopping wind and cloud, quieting thunder and lightning, praying for rain and snow, and healing illness, was highly praised by the government, so was ordered to manage all the Taoists in Beijing and other important temples. Then he returned to Wudang Mountains and lived as a hermit and died.

Li Mingliang

Li Mingliang, a Wudang Taoist in the Yuan Dynasty, was born in 1286 in a rich and influential family, and very clever as a child. After grew up, he was not fond of home fellow and business, but of traveling and Taoism; so in 1297, he went to Wudang Mountains to learn Taoism from Lin Daofu. After learned Taoism, he cultivated and studied Taoism in a grass hut for 15 years. When he was the leader of Five-Dragon Palace, he worked hard to collect money and succeeded in building the Main Hall of Five-Dragon Palace, Jade Statue Pavilion, Huayang Cliff and other buildings. He thought more for Taoism and the public, little for himself, so many people respected him and learned from him.

He was also good at writings and paintings. There is a painting statue of him made by himself in 1345, vividly as living. He also had written a self-praising poem for the painting statue.

Zhang Shouqing

Zhang Shouqing, a Taoist in the years of the Yuan and the Ming Dynasties, but more famous in the Yuan Dynasty, was born in 1266. He began cultivating in Wudang Mountains at the age of 39, learned the methods to make medicines and gist of Qingwei Taoism. Then he continued studying from Ye Yunlai, Liu Daoming, and Zhang Daogui. He worked hard and wasted no effort in building the roads and temples, planting trees, and worshiping gods.

He was the important man to connect the proceeding and the following in Taoist history. He learned all schools of Taoism in Wudang Taoism, started in the real sense Wudang Taoist style of absorbing and merging all the schools of Taoism, and formed new and complete Wudang Taoism. He widely collected and taught students to the effect that made Wudang Taoism stronger in Taoist organization; he also ordered his students to compile many Taoist books to the effect that widened the influence of Wudang Taoism in the whole society.

He, after doing these things, went the back mountain of Qingwei Palace, in the Heavenly Pillar Peak of Wudang Mountains to study Taoism and then died.

Li Suxi

Li Suxi was one of the famous Taoists in the Ming Dynasty. In accordance with the history, he left home for Taoism in Wudang Mountains in the late years of the Yuan Dynasty. He learned Taoism from Shan Dao'an, who was the student of Zhang Shouqing. He became the leader of Five-Dragon Palace in the early years of Emperor Hongwu of the Ming Dynasty, then cultivated in his Nature Hut to study *Zhouyi*, good at Taoist sciences. Emperor Zhu Di was fond of him, so ordered to build halls and temples in Wudang Mountains.

In 1421, after advocated his students that Taoism had been prosperous and all of them should work hard at Taoism, he died. It was surprising that his bones and teeth were all green after being burned. His remains and cap and sword were buried in Black Tiger Stream.

Qiu Xuanqing

QiuXuanqing was born in 1327. He left home to learn Taoism from Zhang Sanfeng at his young age. For his hard work in the starting of Wudang Offerings led by Zhang Sanfeng, he was promoted the leader of Five-Dragon Palace.

Very generous and knowledgeable, he was respected and liked by Zhu Yuanzhang, the first Emperor of the Ming Dynasty, and was ordered to manage Taoism in China. He was well up in *Book of Yellow Hall* and *Tao and Teh*. Besides reading and worshiping gods, he often sat there thinking deeply. One evening, he said to his colleagues, "I will die tomorrow." The next day, after having a bath and changing his clothes, he sat there and died, enjoyed a life of 67 years.

Sun Biyun

Sun Biyun was born in the middle years of the Yuan Dynasty, clever in the young age and felt interested in Taoism. Therefore, he left home and learned *Book of Yellow Hall* and *Zhouyi*, then studied all theories of Confuses, and became famous in Taoism. In the early years of Emperor Hongwu, he went to Wudang Mountains and studied Taoism and Wushu from Zhang Sanfeng. Later, he created in South Cliff Palace a widely going around school of Wushu, Betelnut School, an important division of Taiji Boxing. For this school of boxing was based on the theory of Taiji Yin-yang Fish, and the boxing movement was like a fish swimming, so was changed to Fish Boxing of Betelnut School.

In 1412, Emperor Yongle Zhu Di ordered that Sun could travel all over the country at his will. The next year, ordered to build Wudang Mountains, and charged him to be responsible for the sites-selecting and general devises of Meeting Real God Palace, Five-Dragon Palace, South Cliff Palace, Purple Cloud Palace, and Yuxu Palace. And then he was permitted to cultivate in South Cliff Palace and be the leader.

By the end of 1417, most of buildings in Wudang Mountains were finished. One day, after having a bath, changing the clothes and worshiping gods, he sat there died, enjoyed a life of more than 80 years. Later, Wudang Taoist Tai Yizi collected his works and compiled a book *Collections of Green Cloud*.

Ren Ziyuan

Ren Ziyuan was a famous Wudang Taoist in the Ming Dynasty. In accordance with the history, he had predestined relationship with Taoism even when was very young, he had read all the Six Books and also had some certain research works. Then he left home for cultivating for over 20 years and understood the gist of Taoism; and he was also good at Taiji Boxing, so he became more and more famous.

He was ordered by the emperor to compile many books, such as *The Annual of Yongle*, *Taoist Book*, and *The Annual of Wudang Mountains*. In 1428, he was ordered to manage all the Taoism in China. He died in the sixth year of Emperor Xuande.

Yang Laiwang

YangLaiwang was a famous Taoist in the late year of the Qing Dynasty. He, formerly an official in the government, left his office for learning Taoism in Wudang Mountains in 1862, as a student of He Yangchun, the leader of Dragon Gate School. Then he made his mind to repair all halls and temples in Wudang Mountains, so he took his students and colleagues to collect money. After their ten years' effort, they succeeded in repairing 3,000 rooms of halls and temples. At the same time, he taught and spread Taoism in Purple Cloud Palace, South Cliff Palace, and Clean Happiness Palace, and received over 50 students.

He died on April 8, 1909, enjoyed a life 70 years.

Xu Benshan

Xu Benshan, born in 1860, learned Confucianism at his young age, and then went to Wudang Mountains to learn Taoism, as one of the 15th generation students. For he was wise and hard working, honest and tolerant, the Taoists there all liked him and taught him Wudang Boxing during the spare time of cultivation. After ten years' exercise, he succeeded in gaining profound Gongfu, living up to his teachers' expectations.

He had learned a lot in the causes of repairing the halls and temples and developing Wudang Taoism with his teachers, so he made his mind to work hard to make Wudang Taoism prosperous again. Profound in morality, Taoism, and Gongfu, he was made Leader-General of Wudang Mountains. From then on, he began to deal with Taoist affairs, set Taoist rules, propose to manage Taoism by disciplines, and encourage Taoists to do good deeds for the people; on the other hand, he collected money to found a school, build temples to make medicines, compile scriptures and eight volumes of *The Continuation of Wudang Mountain Annual*; which made the dying Wudang Taoism prosperous again.

He was killed by the bandits in 1932, enjoyed a life of 72 years.

6. Taoist Music 道教音乐

Taoist music is the music used by Taoists when they hold the Fasting and Jiao ceremonies, celebrate the birthdays of gods, pray for good fortune, subdue and get rid of Old Nicks, and release souls from purgatory and other religious activities. Taoist music is the indispensable part during the process of Taoist Fasting and Jiao ceremonies, for it can foil and romance religious atmosphere, and strengthen the believers' admiration for holy land and respect for gods and psyche.

Taoist music, as one of the ancient religion musics, contains the basic religion belief and aesthetic theory both in music pattern and rhyme, forming their own special characteristics.

The aesthetic theory of Taoist music reflects Taoist desire for a long life and quietness and inactiveness. The rhyme is solemn and peaceful, to show the majestic vigor of collecting and ordering gods and generals, the force and determination to subdue and get rid of the evils, the happiness and buoyancy of praying for fortune and holding a celebration, the beauty and peace of praising the gods, and the magic illusion of praying and cultivation. With the foiling and romancing of music, Taoist religion activities become more solemn, more divine, and more mysterious. All kinds of gods' images will be lively shown in the music, which take humans' sensibility into mysterious immortal world.

Taoist music is made up of two parts, vocalization and instrumental music, with many kinds of performances, such as solo, chorus, and so on. The vocalization is the main part of Taoist music for religion service, whose melody is very concrete, expressing the hope and prayer of the man who attends the service, such as asking for help from gods, and praising gods. The harmonious unification of melody and lyric and the reasonable cooperation of all kinds of music patterns, make up the whole religion activity.

The instruments of Taoist music almost include all the instruments of Han nationality, such as clock, drum, pan, bell, wood-fish, pipe, flute, violin and the like.

7. Lao zi and *Tao and Teh* 老子与《道德经》

Lao zi, Li Er, was an intelligent and famous man of Chu Kingdom of Spring and Autumn Period. It was said that he was born white-haired, so he was named Lao zi, meaning old man in Chinese.

He had been the history official of the Zhou Dynasty, then he left the government and led a hermit life, planting and teaching students Taoism. He, knowledgeable, was one of the famous philosophers, thinkers in China history, whose theories was mainly about self-hermit and being inactive. He had written with great wisdom the masterpiece *Tao and Teh*.

Tao and Teh, consisted of two parts, Book of Tao and Book of Teh, of about five thousand words, so was also called *Lao zi Five-thousand Article*. In *Tao and Teh*, he first produced the notion of Tao. He thought that Tao is the origin material; virtue is the personification, idealization, and ethicality of Tao. In *Tao and Teh*, he, with profound wisdom, discussed many important problems, such as, the formation of universe, the laws of nature, the running of a country, and the cultivation of one's body and mood, and produced these famous philosophical notions of Tao, Nature, Inactiveness, containing profound dialectic and giving people unlimited thinking enlightenment.

Tao and Teh, with 81 chapters, was simple in word but profound in meaning, and wide in scope but deep in spirit. His poem-like words, delicate thought, special features, plump ardor, are qualified to make the reader excited, enlightened and give them wisdom.

Just because that his theories covered the universe, the society and the life and that his philosophy is profound and mysterious; in the history, militarist, legist, orator, expert of martial art, fortune-teller, all looked for their root and cause in *Tao and Teh* and found their theoretical base and behavior rules. Taoism has done in this aspect most completely, having regarded *The Tao and Teh* as their holy book since the founding of Taoism, having explained the notions of Tao and Virtue from the perspective of religion, having formed their own theology theory, and on which derived and deducted Taoist theories. With Taoists' long-time apotheosization of all aspects, Lao zi, finally became the supreme god who created the world from a common man, philosopher.

Lao zi has been the historical figure of world influence during the past 2,000 years. *Tao and Teh*, a monument of Chinese culture history, also a pearl of wisdom of humans' civilization treasure, has been translated into many languages, having great influence upon the world.

Chapter 4 The Legends in Wudang Mountains 武当神话传说

1. The Legend of Emperor Zhenwu 真武大帝的传说

Unusual birth

Wudang Mountains is the holy land where Emperor Zhenwu cultivated himself and succeeded in becoming a god. But here was not his birthplace; he was born in the west of the sky, the other side of the Pacific Ocean. In ancient times, there was a Country/Kingdom called Jingle, in which the Emperor was upright and strict, the Queen beautiful and kind; they ran the country so successfully that the people led a peaceful and joyful life.

One day, the weather was quite fine and the Queen was in a happy mood too; so she went out for a walk in the Imperial Garden. Suddenly, she saw a group of color clouds with a lot of gods on. One god bought a red sun and threw it down to the earth. When approaching the Queen, the sun turned into a red fruit and moved in her mouth and slid in the body. So she began to be pregnant.

The Queen had been pregnant for almost fourteen months. On March 3 of the next year, she felt a heavy pain in the belly, knowing that the child was going to come out. At that time, groups of color clouds flied over the palace and groups of birds sang happily over the palace, and there was full of fragrance in the palace. She gave birth to a white and fat baby. All the country talked about the birth of the prince.

In order to memorize the birth of the prince, people built a palace named Jingle Palace near Wudang Mountains. Wudang Taoism has set the birthday of Emperor Zhenwu, March 3 in the lunar calendar, a great festival on which they hold various solemn activities every year.

Studying life

The Prince was born intelligent. He was fond of reading and could memorize what he saw at the first sight. The Emperor, the Queen and the officials in the court all paid more expectations on him, hoping that he would become a qualified and respectful emperor, so often taught him the strategies of running a country.

However, the Prince didn't want to be an emperor. Instead, he dreamed of being an immortal to perish all the evil and help all the humans. He often secretly visited some famous intellectuals and learned many things from them. At the age of fifteen, he had learned a lot of knowledge and excellent Martial Arts.

But how to realize his dream? This made him very puzzled. One day when he was thinking hard in the Imperial Garden, a nun in purple appeared from the flowers and advised him, "If you want to succeed in cultivation and becoming a god, you'd better leave the mortal world. Go across the sea and eastward on, and then you'll find a mountain called Wudang Mountains, which is the best place for cultivation..." With the words, she disappeared. She was an immortal who was moved by the Prince's determination and faith to Taoism and came to enlighten him. The Prince understood at once and decided to go to cultivate him in Wudang Mountains.

That Emperor Zhenwu studied hard at youth and brew great ambition set a good example. So people built a palace called The Prince's Reading Palace in Wudang Mountains, for the purpose of encouraging the following generations.

Leaving home for cultivation

The Prince decided to leave home to cultivate himself in Wudang Mountains. All the people, including the Emperor, the Queen, and the officials came to prevent him from going there. Especially, the Queen, so worried about her son, burst into tears to persuade him not to leave them. But the Prince was so determined that he said good-bye to his parents and set off alone that day.

As the Chinese proverb "The mother worries about the son when he is away" goes, the Queen was so worried that she couldn't fall asleep and she didn't want to eat anything after the prince left home. So she went to run after the Prince together with 500 soldiers.

After 81 days' chasing, she caught up with the Prince at the foot of Wudang Mountains. When met each other, the Queen and the Prince all burst into tears, especially the Queen shed so much tears that there appeared a lake of tears. Later the people called it Shedding Tears Lake. The Queen cried and caught the Prince's clothes to persuade him to go back home with her. The Prince loved his mother and didn't want to make her feel sorrow; but he thought that cultivation was more important and he should not change his mind. So he brought his sword and cut the part of clothes caught by his mother. The part of clothes flied into the sky and then dropped in the Hanjiang River and turned into mountains, which were named Big Dress Mountain and Small Dress Mountain.

After cutting the clothes, the Prince went on with his journey. The queen ran after him again. In a dilemma, so the Prince cut his sword behind and there appeared a river at once, which separated the mother and the son. Later, the people named the river Sword River and built a bridge across it, Sword River Bridge.

The Queen had no idea but return home. On the way back, she cried "My dear son" at every step, so did the prince. They called each other 18 times on the way. So today there are the Upper Eighteen Steps and the Lower Eighteen Steps, which are thought to be the parting place of the Queen and the Prince.

In the ancient times, there were full of dense forests and steep cliffs in Wudang Mountains, so the Prince lost his way, even the directions. When he was quite anxious, there appeared a crow circling over his head. He said to it, "If you can understand my words, please lead a way for me. I want to look for a perfect place to cultivate myself." Luckily, the crow understood his words and led the way for him.

There were full of dense trees the mountain among which many wild animals lived there. Although the Prince could protect himself from the attack of animals with his excellent martial arts and sword, he could not quiet his mind to cultivate, so he felt distressed. One day when he was sitting under a cliff, a black tiger appeared to attack him. He jumped up and gave a palm to the tiger and made it lie on the ground and could not move any more. When he was about to kill it, he found that the tiger lying there obediently like a cat, so he left it be for mercy. But the tiger had something of a man, grateful for his kindness, voluntarily protected the Prince day and night.

The Prince cultivated himself in a cave named The Prince's cave. Living in a place where the summer was hot and the winter was cold, just the crow and black tiger accompanying him, he felt very lonely and distressed, he wanted to give up and return home. One day, he left the crow and the tiger for Jingle Country/ Kingdom.

On his way home, he met a white hair granny rubbing a pontil. Puzzled, he asked what the granny was doing. The granny answered that she wanted to rub it into a needle. He said surprisingly, "When will you rub such a big pontil into a small needle?" The old granny said, "If you work hard, you can rub a pontil into a needle." Enlightened by her words, He decided to go back and continue his cultivation.

Actually, the old granny was a god in Heaven who came to give the prince some inspiration. Later, a palace called Needle-Rubbing Well was built there to commemorate this story.

Strenuous cultivation

On the way back to Wudang Mountains, the Prince broke a branch of plum and input it into a betelnut tree and vowed, "If I can succeed in cultivation, you live and blossom on the tree." Later, when he succeeded in becoming a god, the branch did live and blossom and have fruits on the tree.

He found a cave in South Cliff and stayed there practicing for years. It is a very beautiful and enjoyable place where he could see Heavenly Pillar Peak, the highest mountain in Wudang Mountains.

He was so preoccupied with his cultivation that even the birds stayed on his head and gave birth to babies, a lot of vines grew around his body, for he paid no attention to what happened around him. He just cultivated without food and water, so the guts and the stomach could not stand the hunger and complained against in his belly. So angry, he used his sword to open the belly, cut down the guts and the stomach and threw them into the valley down the cliff. Later the guts turned into a snake, the stomach a tortoise, which then cultivated together with the Prince and became The General of Tortoise and The General Snake.

After 42 years of strenuous cultivation, the prince succeeded in cultivation and became a god in Taoism.

Five dragons holding the saint

On September 9 of that year in the lunar calendar, when the Prince was cultivating in the morning, he suddenly had a special feeling about himself, realizing that he would succeed in cultivation and become a god. The time was coming!

So he stood up to stretch his body. At that time a charming girl came, with a cup of tea in hand. She tried to seduce the Prince by helping him with dressing his hair and clothes. The Prince refused her favor and told her to behave herself, not to do such unsuitable things, which irritated the girl. She angrily said that the Prince misunderstood her and she would jump into the valley to die. He persuaded her, "It does not matter that you have evil thought, if you can change for better, that is OK. You should treasure your life, which is the most valuable thing in the world." But she paid no attention to his word, still jumped into the deep valley.

This made the Prince in a dilemma: if he jumped off to save her, he would die and all the effort of years would come to nothing; if he didn't save her, it would be against the doctrine of a god. Thought this, he jumped into the valley to save the girl. Suddenly five dragons appeared and held him up into the sky.

Actually, the girl was the god who had enlightened the prince, who came to see whether the Prince had gotten rid of mortal thoughts or not. Now there is a steep peak in the South Cliff Valley named Flying Peak, on which a big stone named Heart Touchstone. It is said that the Prince did jump off from that stone.

Perishing the evil

After the Prince flied into Heaven, the Heaven was in chaos. Some evils came to Heaven and fought there everyday, which made the God of Origin very angry, so he ordered Jade Emperor to get rid of all the evil. Jade Emperor then ordered the Prince to eradicate the evils. With the help of the Generals and soldiers in Heaven, he destroyed the evils overnight.

But some of the evils slid into mortal world and made many troubles on the earth, making the people live a hard life. So the Prince was ordered again to come to the earth and destroy them. After numerous fights, he finally killed all the evils. Besides, he called Rain God and Thunder God to help people. From then on, people had harvest years and led a peaceful and comfortable life.

For his fighting to kill the evils, he was respected as the God of War; and also for his kindness to help the people have a happy life, he was respected as the God of Fortune.

Governing Wudang Mountains

The Prince eradicated all the evils after experiencing a lot of hardships, which was a big contribution. So the God of Origin was quite satisfied with his work and made him Emperor Zhenwu, changed Harmony Mountain into Wudang Mountains, which meant that only Emperor Zhenwu was qualified to govern Wudang Mountains.

The God of Origin also ordered Jade Emperor to go to Wudang Mountains to award the Prince; so that all the gods and humans could know the power of the Prince. That day many Gods came to attend the ceremony: some flied here on clouds, some on fog, some rode here on a white deer, some on an immortal crane.

From then on, Emperor Zhenwu governed Wudang Mountains; he led the generals and soldiers of Heaven to protect the world, so people led a happy and peaceful life. In order to pay tribute to him, people came to Wudang Mountains to worship him every year, which lasted for thousands of years without any break. Later, a palace of gold was built at the highest peak of Wudang Mountains, which is the most famous ancient building in Wudang Mountains, Golden Palace.

2. The Legends about Laoying Scenic Spot 老营景区传说

Golden Flower Tree 金花树

There was a mountain valley on the eastern side of Xuanyue Mountain Gate, Wudang Mountains. In the valley, a prosperous landlord lived there. Although he lived a luxurious life, the landlord wanted to be an immortal so as to enjoy the happy life forever.

Therefore, he invited the crafty workers to build a big temple in the valley and planted two cypresses. He usually got down on his knees under the tree when he prayed for himself. In two years the cypresses grew quickly and the shadow covered the whole yard.

One day, he was chanting the holy script when a Taoist, riding on the white cloud, suddenly descended from the sky and stopped on the top of one of the cypress. At once the landlord threw himself on his knees and kowtowed at the feet of the Taoist. Then he arranged a big feast to welcome the divine Taoist.

The Taoist felt quite at home and began to enjoy the delicious food and liquor. Of course, he didn't forget the pious landlord. So when taking the food and liquor, he told the landlord a piece of good news, i.e. the Supreme God, Jade Emperor would like him to be an immortal in the heaven to live a quiet and homely life, for he found that the landlord was a pious worshipper. And the Taoist would help him ascend to the heaven right away.

Heard this, all the family members of the landlord came around him. The landlord begged for the way to ride clouds. The Taoist took out of a celestial peach for the landlord and said to him: "finish the peach, then you can ride clouds to fly to Heaven." The landlord accepted the peach and he smelt the delicate scent. When he had a try, he found that it was as sweet as honey. After he ate up the whole peach, a flake of cloud appeared under his feet, the body of the landlord was as light as cotton and rose slowly from the ground. In a short while, the landlord had already ascended to the air.

All his family members who were watching the ascending began to wail. One of the concubines who, as beautiful as a divine flower, closely attached to the landlord started to endlessly weep and wail while rolling on the ground. The landlord couldn't bear and felt attached to the woman. He was hesitated to go to the heaven. So he pressed his belly and the peach was pushed out of his stomach. The landlord fell back on to the ground and would never be immortal.

The peach gushed out by the landlord fell on the cypress. Soon it transformed into masses of golden flowers on the tree, which could be seen and the fragrance could be smelt in tens of miles.

A Gigantic Tortoise with the Imperial Edict Stele 龟驮碑

Among all the big temples and palaces, there are 12 gigantic tortoises on which a huge stone stele is set. The cap of the stele was vividly carved with two dragons that are playing with a peal-like ball. On the board of the stele the imperial edict are engraved. So people address it Gigantic Tortoise with the Imperial Edict Stele or Gigantic Tortoise Carrying Stele. Among all the steles, the biggest one has a height of 9.9 meters and a weight of 120 tons.

When seeing these steles, people can't help asking why the emperor built these staffs.

It was said that Zhu Yuanzhang, the first Emperor of the Ming Dynasty, in order to consolidate his state, made about 20 sons of his the subsidiary kings of the central government. His purpose was empty when he died, because all his sons occupied different provinces and showed their disobedience to the new Emperor who was the grandson of the first Emperor. The new Emperor decided to recollect most of their power. However, he took the radical means to implement his purpose. This way aroused one of his uncles' protesting and the king in the northern provinces launched a war against the central government. So the war began and caused great injuries and death to both sides. Once the king lost a battle and had to run away for life. When he climbed mountains, all his soldiers and war horses were so exhausted to move a step. But a big river was before them and the opposite troops were approaching. When all the men were in despair, the water was suddenly rolling. In the middle of the river appeared a vortex and the spoon-drift splashed. With a fit of strong sound of billows, a huge tortoise arose from the water stretched out its neck, and said to them:"Come on, jump and stand on my back, I will carry you across the river." The King was thus rescued and took to the opposite side. Looking back on the other side, the enemy was worrying how to pass the river. The King took a deep breath and felt he should reward that tortoise. The tortoise, shaking its head and tail, said: "No. But please offer me a position in your court when you ascend the throne. That will be enough." After said that, it sank back into the river.

Later, the King always won in the war and eventually became the Emperor of the Ming Dynasty. He offered all kinds of positions for his kin members that followed him except the tortoise. When he thought of the event that the tortoise had saved him, there was no proper position for the tortoise. Therefore, he ordered: "the celestial tortoise had saved my life, so it has the greatest achievement. I will bestow it the greatest honor, i.e. it will carry imperial edict for me, for it has endless might, and it is as steady as the biggest mountain, Mount Tai. To use it as the one to carry imperial edict symbolize the consolidation and immortality of my state."

From then on, the tortoise accepted the task and carried the imperial edict to the Wudang Mountains, who thought that Wudang Mountains was a wonderful spot to live in, to be accompanied by lovely birds and fragrant flowers. So it never left this place. The emperor saved by the tortoise consider that it could be hurt by rain, snow or strong sunlight, thus he ordered the artisans to build the pavilion for it in the place where it stays.

Yuanhe Temple 元和观

In Yuanhe Temple, people may find the iron shoes, beds or pillars. Generally, in a temple, one may find the Bodhisattva (the God in the Buddhism) or the founders of the school. So why? In fact, this was a jail for those Taoists who offended the laws of the Wudang School.

It was said that at the beginning there was no Yuanhe Temple when all the buildings on Wudang Mountains were set up. At that time, there was a temple named Baxian Temple where a gang of Taoists lived. Because they thought they were rich and powerful, they usually did very bad things there. The civilians who followed them would be rich and saved. If not, they would be unlucky.

One day a brother and his sister came back from the Golden Top Palace after they worshiped the founder of Wudang Taoism. They went to the Baxian Temple to worship the deities. The senior Taoist grasped the sister because she was very good-looking and jailed the sister in a secret room while put the bound brother into a water dungeon. The water dungeon was set in a cavity behind the Temple. On the top of water dungeon there were sharp nails while on the ground deep water covering the waist. Therefore, people in it can neither stand nor sit. They had to half stand or half stoop when tired. The heavily tortured brother didn't know how many days he had stayed there until one day he heard the slight sound near the mouth of the hole. Then the brother gazed for a while then he found an old white-haired man weeding. The brother cried for help with a very voice. When the old man knew the experience of the brother, he saved the young man. Then the young lad decided to accuse the senior Taoist of his bad doings. The official was a man in charge of religious affairs. He thought it impossible that the Taoist would do like that because their profession allowed no sexual intercourse with women. However, he decided to check what the lad told them.

The next day the official disguised as an itinerant peddler to secretly inspect the Baxian Temple. Those junior Taoists bought the rouge and cosmetic powder for women. The official believed what the young lad said then. So he ordered to scour the Temple and found tens of young girls.

From that time on, the regulations and laws were also made. They made a use of the name "Yuandi Yuanhe Qianxiao Fu" to bestow a new title for the Baxian Temple. So the Temple was called Yuanhe Temple. And there was jail in the Temple and there were 500 soldiers guiding the prison. The prison was for the Taoist who didn't attend to his proper work and duties. That is to say, if a Taoist didn't attend to chanting their holy script or were maliciously did immoral things; they would be cruelly treated by the way of burning. They were forced to lie on the burning hot iron bed, wear the extremely hot iron shoes, or hug the hot pole until they were scalded to death.

The Number One Mountains 第一山

One day during the Song Dynasty (960—1127 A.D.), a very famous calligrapher named Mi Fu visited Wudang Mountains and was deeply attracted by the beautiful scenes. So he wrote three Chinese Characters "Di Yi Shan" (which meant "the most beautiful mountain") on the rock cliff. No sooner had he just finished up the writing than a middle aged woman with a bamboo basket passed by, therefore asked the lady what she thought of his pen craft. The woman sneered at his handwriting and said: "what a pity! They can not breathe!" In the following day the calligrapher thought over on what that lady meant. On the third day he eventually worked out the implication. She meant Mi's calligraphy could not create imagination! From that day on, he carried on practicing. It seemed that woman's cute hairstyle always appeared in his mind. So he thought it perfect that his handwriting would be like the lovely hairstyle.

One evening he strolled about near a small river, because he felt very tired. He saw a mix-colored snake swimming in the river. The snake, shaking its head and wringing its tail, seemed quite at ease. Mi thought: "May I shake my brush like that!"

In some midnight, Mi was enjoying watching the moon. When passing through the window of one old Taoist, he saw that man, who was crossing his legs on a bed, cultivating so comfortably and at ease. He said to himself: "if I can write as comfortably as that, how happy will I be!"

So Mi began to patiently practice. After uncountable days, he went to Wudang Mountains again. He wrote "Di Yi Shan" on the rock cliff again. Co-incidentally, that woman with a basket passed there again. However, she compassed her lips to smile to show her approval just as Mi started to write and bashfully left bending her head down, because the first character was just like her beautiful hair style.

People then comments on the three characters as the following:

"Di/ No." is as imaginable as a beautiful maid's coiling hair without hairpin.

"Yi/ One" is as picturesque as a dragon in water;

"Shan/ Mountain" is as vivid as a deity sits crossing his legs on the bed.

The Chinese character "Yi" is really like a snake swimming in the water while "Shan" is sitting as firmly as a cultivating Taoist.

3. The Legends about Crown Prince Slope 太子坡传说

Rubbing a Pontil into a Needle 铁棒磨针

Emperor Zhenwu had cultivated in Wudang Mountains for many years, but he could not have become a god. So he became depressed and left Wudang Mountains for home.

On the way home, he met an old grandma, who was rubbing a large pontil near a well. Puzzled, he came up and asked what she was going to do; the grandma said that she was going to rub a sewing needle for her daughter.

Very surprised, he cried out: "My God! How large the pontil is! How small a needle is! When will you succeed in rubbing the pontil into a needle?" "Perseverance makes success/ Persistence is success; if I insist on rubbing, I will succeed."

Left the grandma and began his travel again, he thought about the grandma's words; suddenly he came to understand: "What I am cultivating is just same to rubbing a pontil into a needle. Perseverance makes success; if I insist on cultivating, I will succeed, too. Now the years that I cultivated are not enough, so I have not succeeded in becoming a god." Understood this, he turned back and returned to Wudang Mountains to cultivate again.

In South Cliff, he just went on cultivating, without any other thought. He just sat there, without any food, water, move, or sleep, even the bamboo shoot penetrated through his feet and grew into a big bamboo, the vines twisted around him and grew into a big net of vines, the birds made nests on his head and left the night soil on his face. He cultivated like this one year and one year again, at last he succeeded in becoming a god, the main god to guard Wudang Mountains.

Sword River 剑河

Wudang Mountains is the holy land where Emperor Zhenwu cultivated himself and succeeded in becoming a god. When Zhenwu decided to leave home to cultivate himself in Wudang Mountains, the queen, so worried about him, burst into tears to persuade him not to leave them. But Zhenwu was so determined that he said good-bye to his parents and set off alone that day. The queen ran after him again and again. So Zhenwu cut his sword behind and there appeared a river, which separated mother and son. Later, the people named the river Sword River and built a bridge across it, Sword River Bridge.

Dragon Spring Temple 龙泉观

One night, Emperor Yongle of the Ming Dynasty had a nightmare: an old dragon was waving in the river, ordering the other three small dragons to cross the river and take over the country. So frightened, he woke up and had a cold sweat. The next morning, just when he got up, he heard the soldiers outside sing "On February 2, the dragon raises the head, the snake moves out of the den, the small plant comes out of the earth…"

This song made him think a lot: that the dragon raises the head, just realizes what he dreamed last night that three dragons wanted to take over the country. Emperor Jianwen, the real emperor, is recruiting soldiers and horses to take over the reign again? No, he can't. I must press this dragon down. Thought this, Emperor Yongle took soldiers with 300 dans of lime and 300 dans of Chinese tong oil to the river, waiting for the dragon.

That day, there died a man in the opposite village; three sons of the dead wore white clothes on body and white towel on head and came to the river to report the death. Emperor Yongle thought that they were the three dragons, so ordered his soldiers shoot them to death.

This bad thing made the dragon in the river very angry, so he led his soldiers and generals to kill the evil emperor, for the revenge of the three innocent men. When the dragon is going to jump out the water, he will first aspirate a breath, just like the fish; so there are full of bubbles and waves in the river. Saw the bubbles and waves, Emperor Yongle ordered to pour tong Chinese oil into the river; when the dragon and fish inhaled the water of tong oil, they began to sick up, without strength. Emperor Yongle then ordered to pour lime into the river, which made the dragon blind.

Dared not live in the river any more, the dragon ran secretly to Wudang Mountains and hid in a spring near Sword River, which later was named Dragon Spring. The folk thought that the dragon was so kind to get rid of the evil emperor for the people, so they built a temple near Sword River to worship the dragon. So the temple was named Dragon Spring Temple.

Bone-drying Mountain 晒骨岭

It was said that the queen's soldiers wanted to catch zhenwu, however, Zhenwu brought his Seven-Star Sword and gave a blow behind him. Suddenly there was a thunder in the sky and appeared a big river behind him, which drawn them to death.

Time flies, the bodies of soldiers in the river became rotten and fishy, the people nearby fished them out and laid them on a mountain, which was named Bone-Drying Mountain from then on.

4. The Legends about Purple Cloud Palace 紫霄景区传说

The Highest Gods 神上神

On the ridge of the Grand Hall of Purple Cloud Palace in Wudang Mountains there is a pearl bottle, which is connected with by four silver threads in the four directions and there are four children holding the silver threads, so the bottle can stand there steady against the wind and rain. The four children are not the common children, are the highest gods.

In accordance with the legend, when Purple Cloud Palace was built up, the whole project would finished if the pearl bottle on the ridge was put there steady right. Only the bottle stands there right, without any leaning, can it make the country peaceful and prosperous. The builders tried many ways to make the bottle stand steady right, but did not succeed; so they became wrought-up.

Just then Jiang Ziya came to Wudang Mountains to name gods. When he came to Purple Cloud Palace and named gods, there appeared four children, the four sons of him, crying for being gods. Though loved his sons very much, he was very strict with them, he did not give them permission. They cried and jumped, made a big stir; so other people came up to ask Jiang Ziya to name them lower gods. They were very young, but they were ambitious, unwilling to be lower gods, but the highest gods.

When Jiang Ziya was in a dilemma, he suddenly saw the bottle on the ridge of Grand Hall of Purple Cloud Palace, so he came up an idea to let them hold the bottle. He said to them: "Don't cry any more, you all go up to the Grand Hall and hold the bottle steady right. You stand at the place that is higher than Jade Emperor and Emperor Zhenwu. Are not you the highest gods?"

They looked to his direction and saw the great Purple Cloud Palace standing on the red flat roof, the birds and the animals on the ridge and eaves are vivid and magnificent, so they felt happy and flied onto the ridge and held the bottle steady right. Thought that they were the highest gods, higher than Emperor Zhenwu and Jade Emperor, they were quite satisfied. But soon later, they had tasted the bitter; the rainstorm and cold wind made them very weak and dying. So they tried many ways to ask the father to discharge their duty, but not succeeded; they wanted to run away. Jiang Ziya just gave them a point, which made them stand there still, can't move any more. Then he puffed a breath out, which changed into four silver threads and connected the bottle and the four children.

From then on, the four children stand on the four directions and hold the bottle standing steady right on the ridge of Grand Hall of Purple Cloud Palace, day and night. The people named the four children pitiful children, also the highest gods.

Gold Frog 宝金蛙

There is a divine road made up of stone slates in front of the Grand Hall of Purple Cloud Palace in Wudang Mountains. If the visitors stamp on one of the slates in the road, there has a sound beneath the slate, the more stamps, the more sounds. It is said that there is a gold frog under the road.

In the ancient time, the gold frog was worshiped on the shrine of Purple Cloud Palace, as big as a big bowel, shining gold lights day and night. If it wrinkled its big eyes, the country would be in fortune; if it sang a sound to a direction, the direction would be in peace; if it waved its tail, there would be a gold egg. It was said that the frog was the birthday present sent to Emperor Zhenwu by Goddess of Mother Ground, he loved it very much, so placed it on the shrine, letting the folk people have a chance to have a look at it.

When a greedy County Magistrate visited Purple Cloud Palace, he took away the gold frog to his home. For fearing that the frog would run away, he tightened the tail with iron thread for many times and locked it into a box.

The frog could not have a breath in the closed box, so it tried its best to creep toward the light when there was a light through the gap of the box. The more it crept, the shorter the front legs became, the longer the hind legs became, which is the reason why the frogs nowadays have short front legs but long hind legs. Worked very hard, it finally crept to the gap and opened big the eyes to look outside, so big that its eyeball were almost falling down, but it could not escape from the box, which is the reason why the frogs nowadays have the big eyeballs. Very angry and sad, it opened its mouth and began to cry without a stop, the more it cried, the bigger its mouth became, which is the reason why all frogs have big mouths nowadays.

Made uneasy by the cry, the Magistrate opened the box to know why; but when he opened the box, the frog broke the tail and changed into a gold light and flied to Purple Cloud Palace, left the tail in the box. From then on, the frogs have no tails any more. For fear that the tail would run away too, the Magistrate wrapped the tail with red silk cloth over and over again and hid in a safe place.

Not give up, the Magistrate wanted to catch the frog again. He led many men to Purple Cloud Palace pretending to offer incense and worship gods, to look for the frog. When he heard the frog sing under the road, he hurriedly ordered them open the slates to catch the frog. They opened and recovered the slates many times, but they did not find the frog. Then a servant came to him and told: “The tail changed into a big fire and burnt your home.” The Magistrate became very angry, crying and stamping his feet. The frog sang happily under the road, laughing at the Magistrate.

From then on, the gold frog never appeared, just hid under the slates. If you stamp on the slates, the frog will give a sound, but you can’t find it.

Pearl Peak 宝珠峰

The mountains in front of Purple Cloud Palace in Wudang Mountains are very strange; two peaks stand there, one big and one small, just like two pearls, very miraculous. The mountains in the two directions zigzagging away, just like two flying dragons playing with the pearls.

In accordance with the legend, there was just a sea of water, without any earth in the world. When humans were made out of soil, they had no earth to plant, so had a very hard life. Emperor Yu was kind and powerful, with two magical weapons, mountain-driving whip and treasure-digging hoe. If he waved his whip, all the mountains would obey his order and go where he ordered; if he waved his hoe, the digging can dig a hole deep enough to connect the sea. Emperor Yu took troubles to do good things for humans, making the water all flow into the sea; so the earth nowadays appeared.

When he passed Flag-Stretching Peak of Wudang Mountains, Emperor Yu felt very thirsty; but he had driven all waters into the sea, where could he find water to drink? Suddenly he thought of his treasure-digging hoe, so he dug out a big pool that connects with the sea, full of sweet cool water. After drank some water from the pool, he felt satisfied. Saw the people had no water, he ordered Yellow Dragon and Green Dragon stay there and make clouds and rains, so as to make the people to have a happy and prosperous life. In order to remember Emperor Yu, the people there named the pool Emperor Yu Pool.

Yellow Dragon and Green Dragon worked very hard to make clouds and rains; they would have a bath in the pool after working everyday. After ten thousand years, their sweats coagulated into a large stone in the pool, smooth and shining. One day, the stone suddenly moved around and jumped, then changed into a pearl, flied to the hands of Yellow Dragon first, then to the hands of Green Dragon, into the pool, then up into the sky. Yellow Dragon and Green Dragon both jumped to catch it, almost fought with each other.

Here, the pearl began to speak: "Don't quarrel, don't fight, go to sleep quickly! Tonight I will bring in a small one, so you each will have one pearl!" Agreed with his words, they waved their tails and went to sleep. The next day, they found that the pearl did have a small one, which was smaller than the former, but more charming, more smooth, and lighter.

From then on, they needn't work hard to make clouds and rains. If someplace was in need of water, they just brought the pearl and showed it over the place, there would be a good season. The pearls became bigger and bigger; at last, they became two peaks, named Big Pearl Peak and Small Pearl Peak. Yellow Dragon and Green Dragon, respected by the people, turned into two long and zigzagging mountains and often flied into the sky, just like two flying dragons playing with the pearls.

Sun Lake and Five-Color Fish 日池和五色鱼

In front of the Grand Hall of Purple Cloud Palace in Wudang Mountains, there is a round lake, made of green stone and enclosed with flower-carved stone rails, clean and charming, just like the moon on Mid-Autumn Festival, named Sun Lake. In the lake there is a kind of small fish, which can change its colors with the changes of time and climate, named Five-Color Fish.

In accordance with the legend, Sun Lake and Five-Color Fish were holy things.

On March 3 of that year, the birthday of Emperor Zhenwu, all the gods came to celebrate his birthday with their treasures. Only Vega came the last with nothing; she came up to Emperor

Zhenwu to celebrate his birthday: "The gods and immortals have brought all the treasures in the sky, on the earth and in the sea, so I will weave a picture for you."

Vega was clever and smart and what she weaved is more valuable than anything else. Emperor Zhenwu felt very happy to hear this, and told to himself that he must make her show her stunt and make out a treasure that can't be found in the world. He said to Vega: "please weave me a picture in which the blue sky spreads on the earth, color clouds float on the earth, all the birds fly in the water and all the mountains fall to one direction."

She agreed and strolled out of the Grand Hall and then sat on the rail. After looked up and down, she put out her hands to take the rainbow as the embroider workshop, tore a piece of blue sky to cover the workshop, snatched a group of clouds and rubbed into embroider threads, and picked up a falling star as his embroider needle, then she began her embroidering. A moment later, she embroidered out a wonderful picture in which there were full of green mountains, clean water, flowers, birds and fishes.

All the gods clapped their hands to celebrate her wonderful work. Emperor Zhenwu also nodded, "Very wonderful, thank you very much! But if you can make these things in the picture move, which is better." Vega smiled and came to the yard, put the workshop down to the stone slates, the embroider workshop suddenly changed into a round lake in which the blue sky spreads on the earth, color clouds float on the earth, all the birds fly in the water and all the mountains fall to one direction, just as what Emperor Zhenwu wanted. Vega smiled again and threw her embroider needle into the lake, the needle changed into a fish at once, which changed his color from black, green, red, yellow, to white and swam among the clouds and mountains. They are Sun Lake and Five-Color Fish nowadays.

5. The Legends about Five-Dragon Scenic Spot 五龙景区传说

Parents' Bridge 父母桥

If you climb up Wudang Mountains by the way of the West Divine Road, you will find a bridge of about 100 meters long near a swag in the valley. It can't be imagined that an old couple built this bridge in such dangerous terrain. How could they do this? Here is a long story.

The old couple once lived here. At that time, people had travel in waters and stones to worship Wudang Mountains. Seeing this, the old couple made up their mind to build a bridge in the valley. However, they had no daughter or son and couldn't even feed themselves up. But they began to carve stones and make bricks, after several years' hard work, they fell on bed with illness. One day a girl surnamed Bai came to look after them willingly. Because she had no parents, the old couple took her as their daughter.

Miss Bai was good-tempered. But it was puzzling that she always spit some spittle secretly to the bowls of the old couple. Gradually, the old couple recovered. That day there was a play in the temple nearby, so she took the couple to watch the play.

A landowner who lived at the foot of the Mountains often bullied the poor. When he saw beautiful Miss Bai on the temple fair, he ordered his hatchet men to rob her. The old couple was almost beaten to death while protecting Miss Bai. Finally, Maid Bai agreed to marry him on a condition that he should offer a glorious ceremony and a great deal of betrothal. The landowner agreed. When she returned home, she comforted the old couple, "Do not worry me, I will take good care of me. These wealth can help you live a better life and build the bridge."

On the wedding day, the landowner fulfilled all the things and took Miss Bai to his home. Just when he opened the coach, Miss Bai turned into a big white dragon. She played tricks to rush the landowner and his halls away with water. Then the big white dragon turned into a small one flew into the swag behind the couple's shed. From then on, Miss Bai never appeared. People call the swag White Dragon Swag.

It was the couple's work to build the bridge that moved the white dragon. So the white dragon turned into a maid to help them. The old couple remembered her words and completed the bridge, which was later called Parents' Bridge.

Hermit Cliff 隐仙岩

In Wudang Mountains, there is a cliff named Hermit Cliff, for some person had met Immortals here.

Once here was a landowner, who treated his cattle boy unkindly and even refused to offer a lunch. So the poor cattle boy had to feed himself just on peaches picked up from mountains. One day he found a big peach tree that was full of big, red, and sweet peaches. He did not want to eat them up, so he put some in a cave. But he couldn't find any when he returned at night. That lasted for several days. Who stole the peaches in such a desolate mountains? He was so confused. Later he found out that it was an old man who ate his peaches. He caught the old man who gave his a hat in return. The old man said that he could go anywhere with the hat on and then disappeared.

The cattle boy fell in love with the landowner's daughter on the first day. But he was afraid to tell her because of his humble situation. Wearing the hat, he flied to her bedroom at once. Seeing that he was handsome, she also fell in love with him and secretly hid him in her bedroom. From then on, she ordered her servants to bring two bowls and two pairs of chopsticks to her, which later gave away the secret.

Her mother cheated the cattle boy out and caught him, as well as robbed the supernatural hat. The cattle boy was beaten to death. The maid was so sorry that she put the hat on him and buried them together. Ten months later, she gave birth to a boy. In order to save face, her mother brought up the baby, who later called her mother while called the maid (his real mother) elder sister.

Eighteen years later, the boy passed the Imperial Examination and was awarded the first prize. When returned home, he knew the story of his birth, so asked to see his father. When the coffin was opened, his father, the cattle boy was alive again with the protection of the hat.

The family got reunified. The cattle boy asked his son to built a temple at the place where he met the immortal, in order to pay tribute to him. From then on, people called the place Hermit Cliff.

Fenghe Bridge 丰和桥

In Wudang Mountains, there is an exquisite bridge named Fenghe Bridge, which connected an interesting story.

Long time ago, there was a school in Wudang Mountains where two students, whose names were Zhang Feng and Li He respectively, became good friends. Several years later, Li He lost his grandpa and then his father. In order to make a living, he and his mother left Wudang Mountains and begged on the way to their relatives in Shaanxi Province.

On the other hand, Zhang Feng made a fortune and became an important official. He was going to marry a beautiful maid from a big family. At the luxurious ceremony, he invited many relatives and sent somebody riding horse for Li He who was in Shaanxi Province.

Li He was in a dilemma: if he did not make a gift, he would be sorry for his best friend; but if he made a gift, what he had could be a gift? He thought it over and decided to bring the present, the only goose in his family. He begged on the way to his friend's home. Unfortunately it snowed one day when he was in a desolate place. He then sheltered himself in a cave. He was so cold and hungry that he ate the goose. What were left were only some feathers of the goose. So he wrapped the feathers of the goose as a gift. When he arrived, the keeper, who saw his shabby clothes and assumed he was a beggar, excluded him from Zhang Feng's house. Quite angry and upset, he wrote two poems on the wall and left.

Just after Li He left, Zhang Feng found the poems on the wall and knew Li had come; so he rid a horse to run after him. Finally, he caught up with Li who was too hungry to walk further and rested on a stone bridge. Although Zhang made repeated apology to him, he still sat there without a word or move. Zhang then ordered to prepare a banquet on the bridge to welcome him. When he introduced Li to his guests, he said, "This is my friend Li He. He is so sincere that he brought the goose feathers as a gift to me from Shaanxi Province on foot, which is more valuable than gold. I love the gift very much."

From then on, there was a saying in Wudang Mountains: Feathers of goose from a far is light in value while heavy in friendship. The later People spoke highly of their friendship, and named the bridge where they met after their names, Fenghe Bridge.

Weilie Temple/ Benevolence and Reverence Temple 威烈观

There is a temple named Weilie Temple, or Benevolence and Reverence Temple in Wudang Mountains, where there is a sculpture of Yao Jian, an former Magistrate of Junzhou County during the Tang Dynasty. Here is a story about him.

Yao Jian was so honest and responsible that he administrated his county quite well, all the civilians led a happy life. So people here appreciated him very much.

One year there was a drought that dried all the fields and withered all trees and crops. With no harvest for two years, people had to beg out of hometown with their families. Yao was so upset to face this that he wanted to do something. When he heard that there were five hot-tempered dragons that could make rain and wind lived in Five-Dragon Pool, he went to ask them to make a rain alone.

On the way he encountered a lot of hardship and met five old men who tried to persuade him back, but he continued his climbing. Finally he arrived at the foot of Five-Dragon Hill after experienced many difficulties. There he found that the five old men were waiting for him. They smiled to him:"You are so kind to all the folks and never think of your safety. We have told the dragons to make a rain. It'll rain tomorrow. Please go back." Then they disappeared and Yao came to know that they are immortals.

Who were they? They were the five dragons who were moved by Yao and decided to do good deeds for the humans. It did have a heavy rain the next day. All the people began to lead a normal and happy life. In order to pay his tribute to the five dragons, Yao built Five-Dragon Temple at the foot of Five-Dragon Hill. The place where Yao met the five old men was later named Five-Senior Hill.

When Li Shimin, the Second Emperor of the Tang Dynasty, knew the story, he honored Yao Jian the King of Benevolence and Reverence, and built Benevolence and Reverence Temple for him.

6. The Legends about South Cliff Scenic Spot 南岩景区传说

Thunder God Hole 雷神洞

On the Flag Peak of Wudang Mountains, there is a hole called Thunder God Hole, where Thunder God lived. Under the Candle Peak, there is another hole lived a fox seductress, which was controlled by the former, connected with an attractive story.

Once, at the foot of Pearl Peak, there was a squire who employed a young cattle boy, who should graze the cattle on the slope and cut a big bunch of grasses in the day; feed the cattle and clean the stable at the night, busy all the day. That year was very dry, so the river, the well and the spring had no water at all. Hence no enough grass for the cows. But the squire just ordered the young boy feed his cows well, paid no attention to whether he had ability to do this or not. If the boy had no grass, he would whip him heavily, so the young boy was very sad, crying day after day.

He had no choice but trying his best to look for grass everywhere around Wudang Mountains. One day, when he suddenly found a big stone that was like a chair, in which, green grass was growing vigorously. He cut them off, and soon there was grass growing out again, so that he collected a large pile of grass. From then on, he just came here to get grass, not worrying about the shortage of grass. When his mother found that he was not beaten any more, she felt puzzled and asked him why, so he told her the truth. She therefore told him to carry a hoe to find what under the place.

Then next day, he came there and found an earth salver, so he took it home. When he put a piece of rice in it, there came a salver of rice; a coin, there came a salver of coins. They knew that salver was a treasure, so hid it secretly; their life became easy without working for the squire.

But after the salver had been moved away, there was a heavy black cloud in Wudang Mountains. The fox seductress knew that the salver had been carried to the boy's house, she wanted to get it. So she changed into a beautiful young lady, went towards the boy's house. When she passed the Crown Prince's Hall, God Zhenwu found her, so ordered Thunder God to live the hole nearby to prevent the fox seductress from doing bad things. From then on the hole has been called Thunder God Hole.

When the seductress got to the boy's house, she stole the salver away in the dark. When she wanted to set fire to the house, Thunder God stopped her by a thunder and made her change back to a fox. In order to control the fox seductress, God Zhenwu put her into the hole under the Candle Peak, and blocked a big stone at the door, so the fox seductress couldn't come out anymore. From then on, this hole has been called Stone-door Hole.

Betelnut Temple 榔梅祠

Long time ago, God Zhenwu was practicing in Wudang Mountains. One day, when he was having a rest under a big areca tree, he found a big plum tree not far away, which was full of flowers. He loved the flowers so much and he couldn't help cutting one branch and inserting it on the areca, praying "If one day I can be successful, please make the flowers bloom, if I can't, please let them die with me."

He was practicing year after year, while the plum branch was growing year after year. At last, when he succeeded, the plum branch in areca tree really became a big tree and had many fruits. From then on, people called it betelnut tree. The fruits in it were big and sweet, shining and shedding sweet fragrance, which could be sensed far away. The ill in the poor families would soon be well after eating the fruits; the weak would soon be strong after taking them; the young soon became the adult; the old soon became the young again.

One year when the fruits were ripping, the Queen got ill, but no one could cure her. So the Emperor set an order that he would award heavily the man who could cure the Queen. When heard that, a Wudang Taoist took the fruits to the Emperor; soon, she recovered. Very happy, the Emperor named the Taoist The True Man of Betelnut. The Emperor knew that the fruits were valuable, so ordered Wudang Taoists to shed it from the poor, The True Man of Betelnut to look after it, and built Betelnut Temple for him. Strangely enough, from then on, there was no fruit at any more and nor was the flower. The tree died away. There is only Betelnut Temple, no betelnut tree.

Dragon Head Incense 龙头香

In the South Cliff of Wudang Mountains, there is a stone dragon protruding out from the mountain, whose head on which lays a incense stove is hanging in the air far away from the earth. Many pious tourist believers climbed there to offer incenses for the sake of piety, but most of them dropped from it and lost their lives.

It was said that there was a river near Wudang Mountains. Near the river, there was a mountain called Dragon Mountain in which appeared an evil dragon. The evil dragon often made troubles, turning over the boats in the river and eating the sailors dropped off from the boats. The people there hated the dragon very much and wanted to deal with him, so they asked God Zhenwu to help them. God Zhenwu helped them catch the dragon and confined him under the Dragon Mountain, and asked people to build a pagoda on the mountain so as to suppress it. Some days later, God Zhenwu went to see whether the dragon had changed better or not. The dragon cried and promised that he would never do bad things from then on. Seeing that he was serious and honest, God Zhenwu believed him and set him free. But he made more troubles to the people after God Zhenwu left.

So once again, the people went to invite God Zhenwu, who caught the dragon and took it back to Wudang Mountains. When they were passing South Cliff, God Zhenwu thought there was a little far distance from there to Golden Top. So he ordered the dragon to change into a bridge to connect South Cliff and Golden Top. But the dragon felt it too long and afraid that people's steps would break his waist; so he just stretched out his first part of body and stopped. God Zhenwu then ordered him just to stay there, and got a stove on his head. Therefore people could offer incenses by stepping on his back. But he was not obedient, he would move his head and body to drop them off and down into the deep valley when people were stepping on his back. Seeing that, God Zhenwu felt very outrageous, and shouted "change" to the evil dragon, which was changed into a stone dragon and couldn't move anymore.

Heart Touchstone 试心石

To the west of South Cliff, there is a steep peak called Flying Cliff, on which there is a large stone platform called Flying Platform. There is a large stone named Heart Touchstone protruding out the cliff. Long time ago, there were twins. They looked quite the same. But the elder was an honest person who just did good things; while the younger was lazy and greedy, always did bad things. So the elder was often scolded by mistake, but he thought that it was nothing if he could help his younger brother get back. It was a pity that the younger never followed his brother's words and still did bad things every day.

Once the younger went to steal his neighbors, but was caught and hurt the left eye. The older felt sympathy toward him, and asked him to change. The younger was moved and followed his words. The older then asked him to go to worship gods in Wudang Mountains with him. On the way, they met an old man carrying a big bag who told the twins that he once was a robber, now he decided get back as a noble man, so he would send the bag of gold to God Zhenwu. The story moved the younger brother and made him do something for the gold.

It was strange that the old man chose a narrow road instead of the big way. The elder tried his best to help the old man while the younger was thinking how to get the gold from the old man. When they got to Flying Cliff, the old man was so exhausted that he put down the bag and wanted to have some water. So the elder brother helped him look for water. The younger caught the chance, pushed the old man down from the cliff. When the elder came back, he found the old man had been gone, so asked his younger brother what had happened. Knowing the fact, he felt angry and ashamed, and then he dived from the cliff. At that time there floated a group of white cloud, caught him and took him high into the sky.

Seeing that the elder brother had jumped off the cliff, the younger felt happy, for he got the gold alone. But when he went to get the bag, the bag suddenly changed into a large stone and he heard the laughter of the old man. Looking up, he found that the old man and his elder brother were standing on the cloud. The old man pointed to the stone and said, "It's not a bag of gold, but a heart touchstone to test your heart." From then on, Heart Touchstone in South Cliff was famous near and far.

Crown Prince Sleeping in the Dragon-Bed 太子睡龙床

In the Stone Hall of South Cliff in Wudang Mountains, there is a dragon-bed in which Crown Prince of Jingle is sleeping sound. Seeing this, the viewer can't help asking why the powerful dragon let Crown Prince sleep on his body. Here is a story.

Long time ago, there was a poor village near Wudang Mountains. The people there were living a hard life. Later, there appeared a special young child who came from the earth and walked around the village for 3 times; thereafter the village began to have a harvest. So all the people there were very grateful to the young child and bowed to him when met him. But good days were so limited; the young child disappeared suddenly. People there were poor again. They looked for the child here and there. On a slope they found a big dragon hitting the stones, they knew that the dragon had eaten the child and couldn't digest the child. So they all went to hit it and caught it at last.

When they came back, they met a young intellectual sleeping in the wet grass to have a rest. After asking, they knew that he was the Crown Prince of Jingle who came to Wudang Mountains for cultivation. Thought that he was so determined and was faithful that he would succeed in becoming a god, they dropped on the dragon, "He who does bad things will have no good return; he who does good things will have a good return that. If you can change into a bed for the Crown Prince, he will take you to Wudang Mountains. When he becomes a god, you will also have a good future." The dragon did as the people taught and took Crown Prince to South Cliff. 42 years later, the Crown Prince did become a god, God Zhenwu, and the dragon became a god, too.

In order to remember the story, the people there named the place where they caught the dragon the Entrance for Catching the Dragon.

7. The Legends about Golden Top Scenic Spot 金顶景区传说

Golden Boy Peak and Jade Girl Peak 金童玉女峰

In front of Golden Palace, there stand two steep and graceful peaks: one looks like a slim and charming girl, called Jade Girl Peak; the other a strongly-built handsome boy, called Golden Boy Peak. A high mountain ridge, looking like a heaven screen, separates the two peaks.

The golden boy and the jade girl used to be the personal servants of Jade Emperor; why did they become two peaks in Wudang Mountains? Here is a widely-spread beautiful legend.

In order to rule the gods in heaven, Jade Emperor had made many rules and regulations for them; their food, clothing, shelter and transport were rigidly restricted; their behaviors should not be lax in discipline; men and women should not play jokes, let alone falling in love with each other. Those who dared violate the rules and regulations, for a slight mistake would be forced to come down to earth and for a big one would be punished strictly in accordance with the laws of heaven. Therefore, the Celestial Cloud Palace looked very magnificent, but was gruesome and cold just like an ice-house.

When golden boy and jade girl stood day-by-day on the left and right of Jade Emperor, they dared not talk or laugh or move. Although they were dressed in silk and satin and wore gold, silver and pearl ornaments, they suffered untold misery and hardships. They couldn't show them out and what's more, they had to pretend to smile with great respect before Jade Emperor.

Time flied, golden boy and jade girl fell in love with each other. Though they always made eyes to each other and understood each other, they dared not come out with what was on their minds.

One day when Jade Emperor came out to inspect the world with his officials and officers, they spoke out their love towards each other finally. They were so happy that they talked, laughed and danced freely. However, suddenly they knocked over Jade Emperor's Imperial Table accidentally. The incense burner, the candle-holder and the imperial writing brushes all rolled out of heaven and fell down in Wudang Mountains, becoming the Incense Burner Peak, the Candle-holder Peak, the Big Writing Brush Peak and the Small Writing Brush Peak in Wudang Mountains.

Just at that time, Jade Emperor came back and became so furious that he decided to punish them strictly. The Queen of Jade Emperor (a legendary figure in Taoist mythology), thinking of their honesty and diligence, asked Jade Emperor to be tolerant. Then he threw them out to serve God Zhenwu in Wudang Mountains.

But when they came to Wudang Mountains, they still loved each other and met secretly. When Jade Emperor knew this, he bawled so angrily that he picked up a board used as the token of authority and threw it toward them violently. With an earsplitting sound, the board landed on before Heavenly Pillar Peak and became a high and steep mountain that separated golden boy from jade girl completely. Later this mountain is called "the Ridge Separating Golden Boy from Jade Girl."

From then on golden boy and jade girl couldn't meet each other. But they were so deeply loved that they gazing eagerly at the mountain day and night, but they caught no sign of each other and their tears streamed down their cheeks' every day. They became more and more determined to love each other but they became thinner at the same time. The more they got thinner, the taller they found themselves to be. At last they became two graceful peaks: the Golden Boy Peak and the Jade Girl Peak in Wudang Mountains.

The Goddess of Wind was so moved by their love story that she always run between them to send word for each other and let them share their innermost feelings. When she ran fast, there was strong wind; when she ran slowly, there was breeze. Therefore it's always windy in

Wudang Mountains all over the year just because golden boy and jade girl have so much to tell each other that the Goddess of Wind is busy with conveying their words forever.

Sunrise on Wudang Mountain 武当日出

In ancient times, there were ten suns in the sky. With so many suns the rivers and lakes run dry, the trees and the plants withered and people were hot to death. Then people persuaded Hou yi, a legendary figure who was powerful and good at shooting, to subdue the suns. Hou yi was very strong and had a horse which could run ten thousands miles a day and a magical arrow which could shoot with great accuracy. When asked he readily agreed, then he drew back the bow and shot ten times toward the sky. Nine suns fell into the sea; the last was hurt and rolled down into big mountains. No sun appeared in the sky, so it was totally dark on the earth. People couldn't see anything and became very terrified.

In order to redeem his error, Hou yi decided to chase the sun back and let it go back to the sky. He rode on his horse, running after the wounded sun. At last he rode to Wudang Mountains. The horse was so tired that it staggered and died. Later it became a beautiful peak named "Heaven Horse Peak" by the later generation. Hou yi was very sad to see the horse's death and he cried a lot. Then he went on chasing the wounded sun regardless of his exhaustion. He looked for it for a very long time. He was so worried that he didn't even remember his exhaustion and hunger. Finally under the cliff near the Sword River, he found the wounded sun, seeing there was still an arrow in the body of the sun and the sun was red all over as a result of excessive loss of blood. Hou yi regretted a lot for not knowing that the sun was still useful and nearly killing all of them. Immediately he went to hug the sun, pulled out the arrow and touched gently its wound so that there left a black scar on the surface of the sun. Then, with the arrow holding the sun, he drew back the bow fully and shot the sun slowly into the sky. This is the sunrise on the earth.

Up to now the sun rises earlier on Wudang Mountains than that in other place. Every morning it rises gently and slowly, totally red with a black scar. Later in order to commemorate the sun, people build a temple under the cliff it ever lived where the sun is worshiped and the cliff is called "the Cliff of Sun".

The History of Golden Palace 金殿的来历

The Golden Palace on the top of Heavenly Pillar Peak of Wudang Mountains is beautiful in shape with superb craft, famous at all times and in all over the world. There is also a legend about the history of Golden Palace.

Zhu Yuanzhang, the first Emperor of the Ming Dynasty, seized state power from the Yuan Dynasty by armed force. Once his army fought a battle with that of the Yuan Dynasty and was defeated in complete annihilation. He was also in a most distressed position: exhausted, thirsty, hungry and nearly captured. Just as he was in near despair, Zhang Dahu, his sworn brother, struggled with the enemy fiercely and fought his way out of the heavy encirclement with Zhu on his back and took their flight. When they were chased to the foot of Wudang Mountains and was nearly captured, suddenly a fierce wind rose, whirling up sands and stones, and darkening the sky and the earth. The pursuing troops had no sense of direction and got lost.

Zhu and Zhang run for a long time, suddenly they saw in front of them a big cypress besides which there was a thatched hut and an old Taoist, with hair disheveled and feet bare and sitting with rapt attention, was muttering the scripture. They had no place to hide themselves, so they got down their knees and pleaded with the Taoist to help them. The Taoist opened his eyes a little and said: "I would like to help you, but I'm afraid when succeed, you will forget the brothers who have gone through fire and water together." "No, I won't!" he swore, "Those who demolish the bridge as soon as the river's crossed won't die in bed. I won't be such an ungrateful person!" "But what if I save you and the pursuing troops set fire to my thatched hut, then where should I live?"

Zhu Yuanzhang was anxious to survive, so he promised that as long as the Taoist saved him, he would build a golden palace for him if his hut were burnt down. Then the Taoist did a hiding magic to save Zhu and Zhang. When the pursuing troops arrived and found nothing, they thought it must be the Taoist who had hidden them, so they set fire to the thatched hut. Later when Zhu and Zhang saw the hut was destroyed, but the Taoist disappeared, even his dead body couldn't be found, then they realized that it was God Zhenwu who showed his power and saved them. Then they got down on their knees and thanked God Zhenwu.

Later, Zhu Yuanzhang recruited men and bought horses everywhere, rallied his forces and overthrew the rule of the Yuan Dynasty. He became the first Emperor of the Ming Dynasty. The moment Zhu Yuanzhang became the Emperor, he forgot to thank his brothers, but feared that they might scramble for his power someday for they had rendered outstanding service and wielded tremendous power, he became unreasonably suspicious every day; once he heard anything sounded unpleasant or saw anyone as an eyesore, he would put them in prison or killed them. Even this couldn't satisfy him, and then a venomous scheme came to his mind.

He declared that in order to thank and commend the persons who had rendered outstanding services to establish the Ming Dynasty, he specially built a multi-storied building to celebrate the victory. As soon as the building was competed, he invited those who had made great contributions to attend the banquet. When the wine had been drunk three times, those men were a bit tipsy. While all the men were dazed, Zhu Yuanzhang sneaked away and ordered his favorites to set fire to this building. All the men died in the fire except Zhang Dahu. Seeing Zhu was so venomous, Zhang said angrily, "You are just the person who demolishes the bridge as soon as the river's crossed. You ever swore before God Zhenwu, how can forget it totally?" Zhu Yuanzhang became both ashamed and angry. He hated that Zhang Dahu knew everything about him and was afraid that he might tell them to others, so he killed Zhang who ever saved his life personally.

Later, thinking that he ever killed so many people, Zhu Yuanzhang became more and more suspicious, because he felt that the living were unreliable and the dead would revenge themselves on him. He was filled with anxiety and fear and looked absent-minded day and night.

Although treated by the doctors in and outside the palace, his condition was deteriorating day by day. One day Zhu's heart contracted in pain as if stabbed by a knife, and fell into a coma. Just at time he heard God Zhenwu said angrily, "Since you have hoodwinked Gods above and deluded the men below, you have committed a serious crime and can't be forgiven." Then he pointed to Zhu, "Return my thatched hut!" Zhu Yuanzhang was shaken to the depths of his soul, waking up after a long time, then he called immediately the ministers and his descendants and urged: "be quick, be quick to pay for God Zhenwu's thatched hut and build a golden palace for him!" After that he died.

Later Emperor Zhu Di, the fourth son of Zhu Yuanzhang, built the splendid Golden Palace on the top of Heavenly Pillar Peak in Wudang Mountains.

General Tortoise and General Snake 龟蛇二将

Behind Purple Clouds Palace in Wudang Mountains, there are the sculptures of General Tortoise and General Snake made of blue stone. Here you can find that General Snake, as wide as a bowl, twines tightly round General Tortoise who is as big as a wicker basket; however, General Tortoise puts his head aside and cranes his neck spitting water, which is clean and sweet, so has been called Fairy Water.

It's said that when Zhenwu gave himself up to austere religious discipline in Wudang Mountains, he took off his socks and shoes, putting them aside, and sat cross-legged quietly day and night without eating or drinking. This caused the stomach and the intestines suffering, so they complained against and quarreled with each other all the time, which made Zhenwu on pins and needles and not inclined to going into religious self-cultivation. Zhenwu was so furious that he cut open his belly, took out the stomach and the intestines and threw them away into the thick growth of grass behind him. Staying in the grass, the stomach and the intestines listened to Zhenwu reciting Taoist scriptures day and night. As the years went by, they were possessed by Taoist magical art, so they began to have a glib tongue, were able to fly and run quickly, and could fly in the sky and swim in the sea. They were so infinitely resourceful that they could not only change into rare species of birds and strange animals but also different kinds of personages. But they couldn't change their original shapes, so they wanted to become more beautiful.

One day when they saw Zhenwu in a sound sleep, they sneaked out of the grass. The intestines got into the socks, rolled on the ground for three times and became a huge snake covered with scales all over. The stomach covered Zhenwu's shoes on his back, also rolled on the ground for three times and became a big tortoise.

From then on, Zhenwu had no socks and shoes and was bare-footed. Till now, the sculptures of God Zhenwu in Wudang Mountains are bare-footed. When Zhenwu walked, he had to use the tortoise and the snake to be his shoes, so the tortoise and the snake became Zhenwu's personal mount. Later when they became more powerful, they always sneaked out of Wudang Mountains and ate the civilians' pigs, sheep, oxen and horses. Sometimes they even ate people. That time, Zhenwu succeeded in becoming a god, seeing they made so many troubles, he went to subdue them with his sword.

Although the tortoise and the snake changed from God Zhenwu's stomach and intestines, they had become demons, so they wouldn't obey to him. God Zhenwu angrily brandished his sword and chopped four times on the tortoise' back; however, the tortoise didn't feel any pain at all. Instead, beautiful decorative patterns existed on its back. From then on, there were decorative patterns on all the tortoises' backs.

The snake dashed at God Zhenwu, and twined him tightly. Then God Zhenwu brandished again his sword. With a thunderous sound, five pillars of the sky fell down and then the sky collapsed and flattened the tortoise. At the same time, the pillars became ropes and trussed up the snake more and more tightly, so from then on, the snake became slender and long.

The tortoise turned around only to find that it was not the sky but the bare foot of God Zhenwu that pressed his back; the snake turned his head only to find that it was not the ropes changed from the pillars but God Zhenwu's hand that bundled him up. Then they begged God Zhenwu to forgive them. Seeing that the tortoise and the snake changed from his stomach and intestines, good at martial skills and subdued, God Zhenwu accepted them to be his personal mount and designated them as General Tortoise and General Snake. However, General tortoise still had evil idea, performing honest but doing bad things secretly. Every time when God Zhenwu was reposing, he stole the fairy food and fruit, or changed into a playboy and slipped out to go dining, wining, whoring and gambling, led a life of dissipation. He did so many evil things that the civilians complained about him to God Zhenwu.

God Zhenwu was not quite convinced, so he asked General Tortoise to tell the truth. Seeing that God Zhenwu didn't get any evidence, he quibbled desperately. Then God Zhenwu observed carefully, hoping to find out the fact. Once when God Zhenwu was reposing with his eyes closed and pretended to fall asleep. Thinking that God Zhenwu had been in a sound sleep, General Tortoise changed into a handsome dandy and sneaked out of the palace, went dining, wining, whoring, and gambling and enjoyed himself very much. He changed back when returned to the palace, finding offering fairy fruits on the celestial table; he ate up a big one. What the tortoise had done was seen clearly by God Zhenwu, so he stepped on the tortoise right now, and the fruit rolled out of General Tortoise' belly. God Zhenwu ordered General Tortoise to confess all the bad things he had done, but General Tortoise was scared into a cold sweat and couldn't say anything.

General Tortoise violated the laws of heaven and couldn't be forgiven, so God Zhenwu brandished his sword and cut off General Tortoise's head. Then immediately he kicked off the tortoise's head and the rest body behind Purple Cloud Palace. Then he ordered General Snake to twine round General Tortoise and forced him to speak everything out, or his head would not be fixed again. From then on, the tortoise behind Purple Cloud Palace had no head any more and flew out water from his neck. Because the tortoise didn't want to tell everything out, so the water can never flow out, and he can never regain his head any more.

The Wind-Calming Fairy Pearl 定风仙珠

Among the seventy-two peaks in Wudang Mountains, Heavenly Pillar Peak stands majestically. The unrivalled Golden Palace is just on the top of Heavenly Pillar Peak where the strong wind is blowing all the time, making the hills topple, the earth quake, the sun and the moon less shining and sometimes even rooting out the trees, which are so big that it takes several people to embrace them with outstretched arms. However, to one's surprise, the lamp in the hall never sways but always flames in such a gale. How does this come? They say that it's because there is a fairy pearl in the palace that can calm the wind, which stops the wind from coming in and makes the lamp always flaming. The fairy pearl calming the wind, as big as a football, is hanged under the caisson ceiling of Golden Palace by golden chains.

It's said that during the ruling years of Emperor Yongle of the Ming Dynasty, the Emperor ordered 300,000 armies and civilians to build 33 splendid palaces and temples in Wudang Mountains. It took them 13 years to make Wudang Mountains just like the paradise on earth. But the Emperor was still unsatisfied, and then he assembled excellent artisans to build another palace, which could not be found either in heaven or on earth.

The leader of the artisans was clever and deft. He consulted with the other artisans again and again. With their concerted efforts, the most ingenious design and the superb craft, they built quickly a golden palace and then they invited the emperor to have a look. Along the divine road as steep as the scaling-ladder, the Emperor climbed up to the top of Heavenly Pillar Peak. Looking up, he found the blue sky was so near as if the sun and the moon were just around him; looking down, in the boundless sea of clouds 72 peaks manifested themselves, each being as beautiful as jade and gem, surrounding Heavenly Pillar Peak. He went round the jade railings to visit the newly-built palace which was plated with gold all over and with full equipment, and had the characters cut in relieves were very graceful and the rare birds and animals carved vivaciously. The Emperor was very satisfied.

When the Emperor entered the palace, he found on the shrine before Zhenwu Copper Image was a three-meter-high oil lamp made of gold, with oil and wick, and ready for him to light. The Emperor prayed God Zhenwu silently to bless his country as secure as Golden Palace and as prosperous as the holy lamp. However, the wind was too strong for him to light the lamp. The Emperor thought this was an ill omen, so he became furious and reproved the artisans. He ordered them to light the lamp within three days.

The artisans couldn't think out how to light the lamp. The leader was very worried. He spent three day and nights visiting Heavenly Pillar Peak only to find that it was hard to kindle the lamp while the gale howling. The deadline was coming but they still couldn't work out the method, so Lu Ban, the master carpenter of the Spring and Autumn Period changed into an old man to enlighten them. When the old man knew the entire problem, he didn't answer the question directly and only said: "Nothing in the world is difficult for one who sets his mind on it. Don't worry. Let me smoke a pipe first." The leader said, "How can you light the pipe in such a strong wind?" The old man just smiled, and then he took out the steel for flint, with several screeches, sparks flied off in all directions, and the spill was burning. He cupped his hands in the form of a fenugreek, then he blew the spill and the flame sparkled in his palms. He smoked the pipe and smiled: "You see, the pipe is lighted."

The leader became delighted at once, but when he turned to thank the old man, only to find that the old man went away on the clouds and disappeared in the horizon. Then he suddenly realized the old man must be Master Lu Ban, the founding father of their trade. He was very delighted and said to others: "Master Lu Ban's spill could be lighted against the wind because the fenugreek-like form of palms was full of wind and no wind could blow in any more. If we weld all the windows and chinks and leave only one door, which is also in the fenugreek-like form, then can't the holy light be flaming all the time?" When they heard this, the artisans all thought it was a perfect idea.

Just at daybreak of the fourth day, the general Taoist in charge of the Golden Palace found that all the artisans went away with only the strong wind blowing. He thought that the artisans must be afraid of death and escaped. However, when he came into Golden palace, to his surprise, he found that the lamp was flaming and on the golden table there was a piece of paper left by the artisans on which it said, "We built Golden Palace not for fame or wealth, but for a masterpiece noble like the sun and the moon." When he saw this, a scheme came to his mind. So he put the paper in his pocket and hanged a golden pearl in the middle of the palace.

When the Emperor climbed up to Heavenly Pillar Peak and was going to light the lamp, the general Taoist met him immediately and reported that, "Your Majesty, you built Wudang Mountains, Golden Palace, and presented the lamp, which moved God Zhenwu, so last night a Wind-Calming Pearl fell in to keep the lamp flaming forever against the wind." The Emperor accepted it as true and offered rich rewards to the general Taoist, but the artisans' painstaking efforts were neglected.

Now when visitors come to Golden Palace, they do not believe the legend of the Wind-Calming Pearl, but highly praise the masters' superb skills and creative abilities.

Chapter 5 Tourism in Wudang Mountains 武当旅游

Wudang Mountains, situated in Shiyan City, Hubei Province, China, where there are many high mountains, green forests, everlasting springs and ancient building complex, has been called the No. One Celestial Mountain in China.

Throughout history, the federal emperors of every dynasty paid increasing attention to the creation of buildings in Wudang Mountains, and in the Ming Dynasty, Wudang Mountains was the center of China Taoism. The ancient buildings in Wudang Mountains, great in size and beautiful in artistic design, built on steep hills or in sharp cliffs to achieve a harmonious unity between buildings and nature, have been praised as the ultimate showcase of China's ancient buildings and approved World Cultural Legacy. Thousands of beautiful ancient relics, the visual manifestation of Taoism, contribute the most enchanting views in Wudang Mountains.

Wudang Gongfu, the crystal of Wudang Taoism in the process of exploring life sciences, takes as its principle keeping healthy and prolonging the lifespan. It is characterized by defeating a tough rival through a soft approach and winning by striking only after the enemy has struck. As the saying goes, "Shaolin Wushu in the north s powerful, while in the south is Wudang Gongfu", Wudang Gongfu, as one of the important schools of Chinese Martial Arts, is famous all over the world.

Wudang Taoist music, beautiful and enchanting, is an emanation from heaven. Wudang Taoist service, miraculous and mysterious, is tantamount to talking with the gods in heaven. UNESCO officials, after having visited, said, "There are ancient ingenuity, historical buildings and natural views in harmony in Wudang Mountains… the great history of China lies in Wudang Mountains."

1. Laoying Scenic Spot 老营景区

Laoying is the location of Wudang Mountains Special Economic Zone of Tourism. When Wudang Mountains was built in the Ming Dynasty, here were the distribution center of all kinds of building materials, the inhabiting place of the 30,000 workers, and the headquarters of officials to rule Wudang Mountains sent by the emperors. It was worthy of the name of supreme headquarter, so was called Laoying (Chinese meaning is headquarter, or base).

Now, Laoying, a city proper, both ancient and modern, is the gate to Wudang Mountain Scenic Spot, the beginning spot for visitors home and abroad to visit Wudang Mountains. Here has charming scenery, warm-hearted folk people, high-level hotels, and convenient transportation, which make you feel at home.

Here we can visit the biggest palace in Wudang Mountains, Yuxu Palace; the former Taoist prison, Yuanhe Temple; the palace built for the founder of Wudang Gongfu, Meeting God Temple; the best carved stone torii, Xuanyue Gate; and the biggest man-made lake of Asia, Danjiangkou Reservoir as well. All these make you feel the mystery and grandeur of Wudang Mountains at the entrance.

Chongxu Nunnery 冲虚庵

Chongxu Nunnery is situated one kilometer to the north of Xuanyue Gate, the first mountain gate of Wudang Mountains, in a basin formed by surrounding hills. Chongxu Nunnery, facing Danjiangkou Reservoir and backing on the Last South Mountain, is very quiet and pleasant in every season.

In the former years, there were 36 temples and nunneries in Wudang Mountains, among which Chongxu Nunnery is better protected. It is said that Chongxu Nunnery, built in Tang and Song dynasties, is one of the earliest architects in Wudang Mountains. After many times of rebuilding, it has developed to nowadays' size. There are some sculptures of Ming and Qing dynasties and some buildings as the Palace of the Founder of Taoism, Hall of Imperial Scriptures, Lü Dongbin's Hall, Three God Hall.

A cypress flourishes next to the well in front of Chongxu Nunnery. It is said that it was Lü

Dongbin, one of the Eight Immortals who planted it. There is a story about the cypress: once an insane Taoist spread rice on the tree, which turned into golden flowers. From then on, the cypress flourishes with golden flowers, named Golden Flower Tree, which is one of famous scenic spots in Wudang Mountains.

Xuanyue Gate 玄岳门

Xuanyue Gate, the first gate to Wudang Mountains, is called the first barrier of the fairyland. So there is a saying goes that "entering into Xuanyue Gate, one's life is mastered by God" , in the other words, when you enter into Xuanyue Gate and climb Wudang Mountains, you can not grasp your fate, just ask for the mercy of god.

Xuanyue Gate, also called Stone Torii in China, was built in 1551 and made of giant stones. The ancient workmen carved many pictures, such as, crane, cloud, dragon, wishes, the Eight Immortals and so on, out of large blue stones, which are quite splendid and overwhelmingly surprising. Those pictures, achieved the highest level of stone-carving arts during that time, are thought to be the treasures of Chinese stone-sculpture arts.

There are four big Chinese characters "Zhi Shi Xuan Yue" written on the middle of the torii, whose meaning is that kings should govern the country by using Wudang Taoism and the influence of Emperor Zhenwu, the former king cultivated and became god here. From this we can understand that the king of that time had emphasized Wudang Mountains and Emperor Zhenwu out of political purpose and that Wudang Mountains had a unique important status then.

Yuxu Palace 玉虚宫

Yuxu Palace, with a full name "Upper Heaven Yuxu Palace", was built in 1413 and greatly enlarged during the ruling of Emperor Jiajing of the Ming Dynasty. Then three walls were located in it; they are Outside Happiness Wall, Inside Happiness Wall, and Purple Gold Wall. Yuxu Palace, with smaller walls in it, could be compared with the Imperial Palace at that time. There were more than 2,200 rooms, which were luxurious and grand. Looking ahead, one couldn't see the end of it. Yuxu Palace suffered a lot of fires and floods, and many buildings were destroyed in the wars. From today's Cloud Hall, Palace Gate, Parents' Hall, Steles Pavilion, one can imagine its grand size and charm in the past.

Yuxu Palace is one of the grandest buildings in size in Wudang Mountains. In the Ming Dynasty, a lot of royal activities to pray for good nature and harvest were held here. Now on every March 3 of the lunar calendar, a grand "March 3 Temple Fair" is held here. On that day, people crowd here to celebrate this fair in many ways that makes the fair busy and festive.

Yuzhen Palace/ The Palace of Meeting Real God 遇真宫

The Palace of Meeting Real God, built from 1412 to 1417, with many other buildings in it, such as, Eight-character Palace Gate, East and West Side Halls, Hall of Tiger and Dragon, Hall of Real God, is a quiet and secluded place.

The Palace of Meeting Real God was built by the Emperor for Zhang Sanfeng, a famous Taoist. He, a legendary character in Taoism and Martial Arts, full of knowledge and good at martial arts to move away quickly and invisibly, travelled all around China's famous mountains to spread Taoism and was called “Real God” by the people.

In the early years of Emperor Hongwu of the Ming Dynasty, Zhang came to Wudang Mountains for learning Taoism and martial arts. Wudang Boxing, created by him has been well known and developed by the descendants into one of the most affecting schools. Zhang was called the ancestor of Wudang Martial Arts, so the descendants of later dynasties respect Yuzhen Palace, and study and practise martial arts here.

Zhang once said, “Wudang Mountains will flourish in some day.” Really, ten years later, Emperor Cheng of the Ming Dynasty spent large sum of money building Wudang Mountains. Later, Zhang left Wudang Mountains without any information. Zhu Yuanzhang, the first Emperor of the Ming Dynasty, and Emperor Cheng sent for Zhang; Emperor Cheng had written a letter to him to the effect that Zhang had higher morality and greater knowledge than others, even the Emperor himself can't compare with, so the Emperor wanted to see and learn from him. But none was lucky enough to meet Zhang Sanfeng, who was mysterious and honourable in people's mind. In order to show his sincerity, Emperor Cheng ordered to build The Palace of Meeting Real God and Zhang's sculpture for the people to worship.

The fact that the sovereign emperor built a palace for a Taoist and his sculpture and sent officials to keep them clean is quite scarce. So Yuzhen Palace has played a great important role in Wudang Taoism.

Yuanhe Temple 元和观

Yuanhe Temple, the first temple on the ancient road to climb Wudang Mountains after entering Xuanyue Gate, was named after Emperor Zhenwu who was in charge of Yuanhe Hall in the heaven. In fact, it is the Justice Agency to punish those Taoists who break the rules of Taoism. Emperor Cheng once ordered that one should be restraint and mustn't disturb others in Wudang Mountains; otherwise, he would be seriously punished. This order gave Wudang Taoism some relatively independent justice power to punish those Taoists who break the rules of Taoism. So at the same time Yuanhe Temple became the prison of Wudang Taoism.

The buildings in Yuanhe Hall were compactly designed with a dignified, forbidden and isolated atmosphere. Many gods' sculptures are put in it, which are guardian officials of Emperor Zhenwu. In the middle sat red-faced and three-eyed Guardian Official Wang, the Judging God both in fairyland and real world.

More than 1,000 commandments are to punish the Taoists who break the rules of Taoism here, whose punishing means ranging from kneeing, whipping, extrusion, brow baking, to putting to death with fire. As the agency of enforcing law, Yuanhe Hall has played an important role in the development of Wudang Taoism.

Huayang Cliff 华阳岩

Huayang Cliff, a natural cave, is located to the east of the Five Dragon Palace, back to a high cliff and facing a deep valley. It is a comfortable place for self-cultivation, as the trees flourish in front and falling vines look like green curtain. According to the legend, a Taoist called Yang Huayang cultivated in this cave and lived for more than 100 years, so the cave was named

Huayang Cliff after the Taoist.

Huayang Cliff has a long history. Many Taoists and hermits cultivated and set up a lot of small buildings in Wudang Mountains, one of which was Huayang Cliff.

A self-made sculpture of Li Mingliang, a famous Taoist in the Yuan Dynasty is preserved here. Li was famous for his contribution to the construction of the Five Dragon Palace in the middle-late Yuan Dynasty. His sculpture was built in 1345 and valuable for the study of history and culture.

It is said in *The Story of Huayang Cliff* that Wudang Mountains has a long history and can remove calamity to bring good luck for people. There are numerous cliffs and caves that can be residences, among which Huayang Cliff is the most beautiful one.

Lingxu Cliff 凌虚岩

Lingxu Cliff, very famous among the 36 cliffs in Wudang Mountains, is situated on Peach Wood Hill, to the east of the Five-Dragon Palace. Looking around, the entire world is green; the springs ring in the valley as if the voice of sea or thunder. As isolated from the outside world, it's an ideal place to self-cultivate. You can't help being surprised by the stable belief and lasting willpower of the former Taoists and hermits. One stone palace is located in Lingxu Cliff, with lots of sculptures of Origin God, Emperor Zhenwu, and officials in heaven, in it. Looking through the dense wood, you'll find a blue-stone building, which was the famous Pavilion to Read Scriptures.

As the famous Taoism scholar, Change researcher as well as poet Chen Tuan once cultivated himself and wrote book here, Lingxu Cliff was quite renowned in Taoism history. According to historical book, he lived more than 100 years (about 108 years). When he was young, he read many books and showed outstanding intelligence. At fifty, he left home and went to learn something on god and to live long in Wudang Mountains. He lived in Wudang for many years and developed a famous sleeping way—the Five Dragon Sleeping Way. It is said he could sleep for about 100 days without awaking. He said his sleeping was different from common people's material and physical enjoyment and awake several times without any quietness, although they snore loudly. His sleeping way became a unique way of health care. He was given the names Qingxu Scholar, White Cloud Hermit, and Xiyi Scholar by the emperors of several dynasties. He had lived in Wudang Mountains for more than 20 years and then moved to Mount Hua, for he was tired of others' visits.

2. Crown Prince's Slope Scenic Spot 太子坡景区

Crown Prince's Slope 太子坡

The Crown Prince's Slope Scenic Spot includes Dragon-Returning Temple, Needle-Rubbing Well (Pure Sunshine Palace), Old Monarch's Hall, The Eight Immortals Temple, and so on. Though the route is relatively long, most of them cling tightly to the road up to the mountain; the transportation is very convenient.

The ancient buildings on the Crown Prince's Slope were elaborately built in accordance with the story of Emperor Zhenwu's cultivation. Ancient architects made full use of the topography and built up double-layered walls, the Nine-Winding Yellow River Walls. When you pass two mountain gates, a spacious courtyard will come into your sight. Walking on casually along the path, you will see quietly overlapped and secluded courtyards. In front, there was a building called Five-Cloud Building attaching to the rock; in the middle, the Halls to Store Royal Scriptures; and at the back, the Crown Prince's Palace on the dais. The layout here is irregular from left to right and dotted with each other from higher to lower places, harmonious and perfect, ingenious and full of mystery. Standing on the top of the Fuzhen Temple and looking down the deep abyss, you will see the green rivers winding away; looking at the mountains, you will find thousands of elegant and beautiful mountains. When the sun sets down in the west, you can see the wonderful sight of "Cutting Shadow".

The main places of interest here include the exquisite gloriette of Needle-Rubbing Well, the invertebrates of Paleozoic Era, right angle rock, the paintings of Zhenwu's Cultivation, the Waterfall of Heaven Pool, the Tears-Dropping Pool, one pillar with twelve girders, osmanthus trees and Nine-Winding Yellow River Walls. Besides, here are ancient road of belt-like 18-Turning, unique rocks in Nine-Passing Gully and steep Yuxu Rock, etc.

The Needle-Rubbing Well 磨针井

The buildings of the Needle-Rubbing Well were located at a high spot. In accordance with Wudang Taoism, it was right here that receives the first beam of pure positive sunshine when the sun rises every day, so it is also called Pure Sunshine Palace. The Needle-Rubbing Well is a typical exquisite building in Wudang Mountains, whose overall arrangement is very smart and beautiful, and telling about the story of Zhenwu's cultivation.

It is said that Zhenwu, Crown Prince of Jingle Kingdom, came to Wudang Mountains to cultivate at the age of 15. After cultivated in the deep forest for several decades but achieved nothing, he was totally depressed and decided to secularize; but when he came here and met God of Zi qi, in the form of an old woman, rubbing a ferrous pestle to get a needle, which made him realize that "Perseverance will prevail/ Persistence is success"; so he came back to the deep forest to go on with his cultivation and finally became god.

Entering the gate, you will see a group of smart and exquisite buildings, without symmetrical arrangement, but with a unique style and layout, which make you easily distinguish the primary and secondary ones.

On the fastigium of the Hall, there are eight frescos, simple and unsophisticated, elegant and full of imagination and innovation. These frescos are important cultural relics in Wudang Mountains. The vivid and exquisite strokes presented the whole legend of Emperor Zhenwu from his birth to his cultivation in the Mountains and then to his becoming god. The profound philosophy of the beautiful folklore about "rubbing a ferrous pestle to get a needle" endowed it with permanent vitality, thus it has been widely eulogized during the past thousand years and has become treasure of Wudang Culture.

The Prince's Study Hall 太子读书殿

The Crown Prince's Palace, built in the Ming Dynasty, is on the highest point of Fuzhen

Temple buildings. Though small and exquisite, it has the verve of royal buildings. The collocation in the Crown Prince's Study Hall is ingenuity, whose wall paintings, stone cases, brush pens and ink and ancient books have created an atmosphere to help imagine the young Zhenwu's diligent study and make people visualize Crown Prince's learning hardships, confidence and perseverance during his youth age. The Crown Prince's Reading Statue worshiped in the hall has been regarded as the only place for people to pray for good study and good fortune in Wudang Mountains. Carefully observing the expression of the Crown Prince's Reading Statue, appreciating the Crown Prince's attentive study, visitors can get some new inspiration for study.

Building the Crown Prince's Reading Hall was aimed at emphasizing the deeds of the young Zhenwu's conscientious study. It is said that coming here to look at it with reverence can make the learner's study fruitful. Countless young people came here to build up perseverance and confidence of their study. Now, a lot of parents, longing to help their children succeed in life, often come here to pray for good luck for their children.

Five-Cloud Building 五云楼

Five-Cloud Building with 15.8 meters high, also named Five-Storied Building, is the existing tallest wooden building in Wudang Mountains. The ancient builders, totally according to the topography of the mountain, built it without excavating it and made it perfectly unitary and practical.

Five-Cloud Building adopted traditional architectural technology so its walls, doors and windows were all wooden and the inner rooms were built in accordance with their own conditions and different from each other. The most famous place in Five-Cloud Building is the pillar with twelve girders on its top floor, i.e. above the pillar, the principle part, there are twelve overlapped and carefully arranged girders. This architectural skeleton was the masterpiece of ancient wooden buildings and has been highly praised from then on, thus has become an important sight in Fuzhen Temple.

Laojun Cave 老君岩

The Laojun Cave is the oldest and only grotto discovered in Wudang Mountains. In accordance with the record, Taixuan Monastery was built here in the ninth year of Emperor Tiansheng in the Song Dynasty, but destroyed in the later year of the Song Dynasty and then rebuilt in the Yuan Dynasty, which included Mountain-Gate Temple. Till the tenth year of Emperor Yongle of the Ming Dynasty, there built royal gate, corridor and 23 Taoist rooms, but all the constructions out of the cave had been damaged in the Qing Dynasty and now only a semicircle cave survived.

Laojun's Statue, sitting steadily and practicing Taoism, was cut in the middle of the rocky cave. Laojun, named Li Er, was a famous Chinese philosopher. His 5,000-word works, *Tao and Teh*, has been looked on as canon of Taoism, and Li Er the primogenitor of Taoism.

The existing relics of Laojun Cave occupy about 2,000 square meters, where the three most respectable Taoism gods, God of Origin, God of Pray-Realizing, and God of Morality had ever lived, also called Three-Illustration Place, so the furnishings here were very exquisite at that time. Ren Zigeng, the first official by the Emperor of the Ming Dynasty showed his great admiration to this place and lived here for a long time. He also compiled and published a book named *Wudang Mountain Annals*.

On the left of Laojun Cave, there are a group of stone sculptures, on which carved statues of the Crown Prince's First Arrival at Wudang Mountains and the Nine Immortals of the Penglai Island. These large rocky caves and sculptures and the ancient religious sacred records in Wudang Mountains are hard-to-get tangible items for researching the religion and history of Wudang Mountains.

The Dragon and Tiger Hall 龙虎殿

The Dragon and Tiger Hall in Fuzhen Temple is, the first gate on the axis of the whole building group, the entrance to the main divines' area.

There is an altar before the Dragon and Tiger Hall, which was set up for the sacrificial activities. When Wudang Taoism was prevalent, the governments, Taoists and folks offered sacrifices all the year round. The altar was first built in the early years of the Ming Dynasty and has been kept intact till today. The whole body of the altar is chiseled with stone and is the only well-preserved altar in the mountain.

There are Dragon and Tiger Halls in all-important palaces and temples in Wudang Mountains, sacrificing the statues of Green Dragon and White Tiger, which are full of morals. The powerful white tiger was molded very kind, while the pliable green dragon with ferocious expressions. If they can be attributed to their natures, one's positive and negative energies can adjust and nourish too, which shows Taoism morality of cultivating oneself, i.e. adjusting the Qi of the lung and the liver.

In addition, there are censers, tortoise tablet and jade tablet, etc. in front of the Dragon and Tiger Hall of Fuzhen Temple. Among them, the jade tablet, more than two meters high, made of white marble was built in the tenth year of Emperor Xianfeng of the Qing Dynasty. Its epigraphy is important historical material to study the governmental and public thoughts of the Qing Dynasty.

The Nine-Winding Yellow River Walls 九曲黄河墙

Walking into the Mountain Gate of Fuzhen Temple, you will see the 71-meter long red-jacketed walls, the Nine-Winding Yellow River Walls rising and falling on the ancient road along the mountain. The overall arrangement and purpose of the Nine-Winding Yellow River Walls are very ingenious. The smoothly curved walls with outstanding vigor, look like wave rises and falls; The lofty crooked red walls are undoubtedly a test for the new pious pilgrim's sincerity.

The Nine-Winding Yellow River Walls, 1.5 meters thick and 2.5 meters high, are perfectly round and smooth, with smooth and pleasing curves; matched with such green glazed tiles, look like two huge dragons, hovering and flying, no matter from what angle's appreciation, embody the manner of imperial building to person with sense of beauty and luxuriance.

Different people have different views about the name's origin of the Nine-Winding Yellow River Walls. Taoist theory thinks that people, who donate to the temples the clothing, scriptures, statues, buildings, musical instruments, lamps and candles, clock and single sonorous stone, food for fast, and papers made to resemble money and burned as an offering to the dead, be called "the nine kinds of charitable and pious deeds". The Nine-Winding Yellow River Walls are also a kind of building which reflects the thought of Taoism.

The Main Hall of the Revelation Temple　复真观大殿

The Main Hall of the Revelation Temple, also the Founder's Hall, is the main part of the buildings of divinities, also the highest one in the whole building complex. With the foil of Nine-Turning Yellow River Walls, the Screen Wall and the Dragon and Tiger Palace, in the second courtyard intrudes a high terrace on which the Revelation Temple stands. It looks very mighty and splendid and imbues people with a feeling of piety.

In the tenth year of Emperor Yongle's rule in the Ming Dynasty, the Revelation Temple was built and was extended in the ruling of Emperor Jiajing. At the end of the Ming Dynasty it was largely destroyed. Then, in the 25th year of Emperor Kangxi's rule in the Qing Dynasty, local officers and pious people donated some money to repair it. Though the royal atmosphere could never be regained, many folk practices of building were added to the Main Hall. So from the hall you can find the architectural skills and arts of the Ming and Qing dynasties.

In this palace, the statues of Zhenwu and his retinues, Golden Boy and Jade Girl, are worshipped. These statues are the biggest wooden sculptures decorated with coloured drawings; which, after 600 years, are still as bright and beautiful as they originally were.

The Royal Scriptures Temple　皇经堂

The Royal Scriptures Temple is the place for Taoists to read the scriptures and worship the deities. Every morning and evening, Taoists gather in a rally to read scriptures and worship the deities without exception. In every great temple of Wudang Mountains there is a Royal Scriptures Hall, clean and enchanting, secluded and sacred, where no one can enter unless permitted. The Royal Scriptures Temple was built in the Ming Dynasty and was renovated in the Qing Dynasty, so it has many architectural crafts of the two dynasties and a lot of historical and research interest.

In the shrine of the Royal Scriptures Temple the statue of God of Vanquishing Evils is worshiped. This is another image of Emperor Zhenwu, representing the civilians' wishes of punishing all villains and encouraging people to do good. In front of the Royal Scriptures Temple stands an osmanthus tree that is 400 years old. Every October, the golden osmanthus flowers send forth a delicate fragrance into the entire valley that can be smelled several hundred miles away. This is the special natural view-site of Revelation Temple.

The Head-Turning Temple　回龙观

The Head-Turning Temple is located on the Expansive Slope whose terrain is very high and on whose mountain there are wells and spring-fed streams. The Expansive Slope zigzags like a long dragon in which a peak protrudes as if a dragon turns back. The Head-Turning Temple was built on the head of the dragon, which demonstrates the wisdom of the ancient.

The Head-Turning Temple was built according to one of the plots in the legends of Emperor Zhenwu. It's said that when Emperor Zhenwu first came to cultivate himself in Wudang

Mountains, his determination wavered and he decided to go back. On the way back he saw an old granny disguised by God of Purple Qi, grinding a pestle into a needle. At first he was very puzzled. It was not until he came there that he totally understood. Then he went back to continue cultivating himself and eventually succeeded. In the Ming Dynasty a poet described this legend, saying that Emperor Zhenwu was so bright that he could understand the meaning of the god and returned to cultivate himself.

3. South Cliff Scenic Spot 南岩景区

The South Cliff 南岩

The South Cliff, also called Purple Cloud Cliff, was given the name since it faces south. With magnificent mountains and dense forests, here are the most perfectly collaborated building complex by both artificial and natural scenery among the 36 cliffs in Wudang Mountains.

The buildings of South Cliff had broken the rule that traditional buildings should symmetrize in composition and layout, achieved a high degree of harmony with the surroundings around. Ancient craftsmen made good use of its physiognomy, making the building group very imposing and grand.

The scenery in South Cliff is quite distinctive and with a lot of changes. There are Flying Cliff with the peak rising to the sky, the ancient Stone Palace built on dangerous cliff and so on. So South Cliff has become one of the main view-sites in Wudang Mountains and won many praises from the tourists.

The Hall of South Cliff Palace 南岩宫大殿

When you enter the Dragon and Tiger Palace, you'll hear the beautiful sound by opening or closing the thick and big wooden doors, as if the golden roster or phoenix sings, which is one of the famous scenic spots in South Cliff.

After going through the Dragon and Tiger Palace, you will come into the Taoist Temple yard padded with square stones. In the yard, there's a deep well, whose water is very sweet and never dry and also can cure diseases in the legendary.

Climbing upstairs, the remains of South Cliff Palace is in front of you. From the 36 delicately sculptured stone pillars, you can imagine its grand size in history. On the remains of South Cliff Palace, you will have a quite open vision. The Tiger Fall below is so deep that you can't see its bottom; to the left, Duyang Cliff is incredibly grand; to the right Flying Cliff points to the sky; in the front Skyscraper Hills cluster together; all together make you feel like an immortal in heaven.

Flying Cliff 飞身岩

The mountains here are precipitous. There is only one marrow path getting to the peak of Flying Cliff, the first fairyland in Wudang Mountains, where you can see the wonderful scenery.

Flying Cliff is the place where Emperor Zhenwu cultivated and ascended to Heaven. It was said that Emperor Zhenwu was practicing cultivation here when he was young. Facing the cliff for 10 year, but he was as quiet as well, as still as a pine. On the day of March 3 that year in lunar calendar, Emperor Zhenwu would achieve the success; his master, the God of Purple

Cloud wanted to know whether he was qualified enough to go up to Heaven, so he went to help Emperor Zhenwu comb in the form of a beauty. But Emperor Zhenwu kept away from her and at last escaped on a cliff, the beauty felt ashamed and dived from the cliff, then he also dived to save the beauty at once. At that time, five dragons appeared and helped Emperor Zhenwu go up to Heaven.

A Dressing Table on Flying Cliff was built according to this story. Outside the spot of Dressing Table, there is a large stone named touchstone. It was said that Emperor Zhenwu just from the stone dived and then flew to Heaven. Below the touchstone, there is a deep abyss. When visiting here, please be careful, get away from the touchstone.

Betelnut Temple 榔梅祠

Betelnut Temple, on the road from Crow Hill to the Golden Top, built in the tenth year of Emperor Yongle of the Ming Dynasty, is the biggest one among the 16 temples in Wudang Mountains. Now there reserved the Grand Hall, Side Hall, Wing-Rooms, Mountain Gate, and Palace Walls.

There is a close relationship between Betelnut Temple and the story of Emperor Zhenwu's practicing cultivation. People said that when Emperor Zhenwu was practicing cultivation, he wanted to give up and get away from the mountain. On the half of way he met an old lady changed from the God of Purple Cloud, who told him that perseverance spells success, and inspired him. He came back to continue his practice, when he passed here, he broke off one plum branch and stuck into a betelnut tree, said, "If I can achieved the success, please blossom." Later, when he succeed, and there were flowers truly and then fruits on the plum branch.

Betelnut tree, the rare plant in Wudang Mountains, had a very high reputation in the Ming Dynasty. During the years of Emperor Yongle, the Taoist Li Suxi butted them to the Imperial Count and was awarded by the emperor. Then the Emperor ordered to build Betelnut Temple. It was said that the fruits were not only delicious but also useful to heal diseases and prolong the lifespan. So the Emperor ordered to protect the fruits and make them offerings to the imperial family, also used them to award his outstanding officials who looked on a betelnut as a political credit and were happy at it in all their lives. But later, betelnut trees died away, becoming a mystery for the comers to resolve. Now, there are statues of Emperor Zhenwu, Jade Emperor and other officials.

Thunder God Hole 雷神洞

According to the history, Thunder God Hole, built in the Ming Dynasty, was the place of Zhang Shouqing, a famous Wudang Taoist, to exercise Qingwei Law of Thunder and to pray for rain.

Thunder God Hole is the only place to worship Thunder God, also named God Deng. In the stone hall, there is a statue of Thunder God, the biggest one in Wudang Mountains, which has a bird face in a man body, a glade mouth, two snipe eyes, two man feet, and ten glade toes, which exhibited the graceful bearing of Thunder God of China in the 15th century. The belief of Thunder

God has derived from ancient people's subconscious adoration to thunder and lightning. It was said in history that Thunder God has only one foot and looks like a cow, when he comes out, there must be rain and wind, and strong noise.

Taoism believes that the thunderclap can stand for Heaven, "It is in change of living beings and humans and can bring you fortune and misfortune." So in Wudang Mountains, there are many celestial beings having different expressions on their faces, holding their own tools that show their different duties.

Behind the Hole, there is a natural spring, streaming all the year, cool in summer, warm in winter and having a sweet taste, so is also called Supernatural Spring.

Two Bearings Hall 两仪殿

In the South Cliff, there is a hall called Two Bearings Hall. Here two bearings refer to father and mother, heaven and earth, or Yin and Yang. The main character of Taoism is loyalty and filial piety. Behind the Grand Hall of every palace and temple there built Parents' Hall to worship Emperor Zhenwu's real father and mother, by which to teach all the visitors to be filial pious to their parents, and which is the code of conduct in Taoism. All these showed that Chinese theory of faith, piety, and ethic had combined into Wudang Taoist doctrine.

In the hall, there are some statues of other gods, best devised and elaborately made, some of which have been confirmed as the first-rate cultural relics under the state protection.

Dragon-Head Incense 龙头香

In South Cliff, there is a stone sculpture spreading forward which has been the topic of the town, which is Dragon-Head Stone, or Dragon-Head Incense as people often mentioned. Dragon-head Incense faces to the Golden Top, just as playing religious homage. It's 3 meters long, 0.55 meter wide; in fact, it is two dragons carved together by the ancient workers in all kinds of techniques. On the head of the dragon, there is incense burner; under which is a deep valley; which demonstrates super skills and high scientific nature. It is said that these two huge dragons were the rider of Emperor Zhenwu, on which he often traveled here and there.

Because of its mysterious character and special status, in the past, many people wanted to show their devoutness, and tried to burn the incense on the head of the dragon. That you must move on the narrow back of the dragons by kneeling position and then move back by retreating is very dangerous. A little carelessness will kil you, because you will suddenly drop from it and dive into the gorge. There were thousands of people died because of this. So Emperor Kangxi of the Qing Dynasty sent an order to forbid this action and to set fence around the Dragon-Head.

South Heaven Gate 南天门

South Heaven Gate, inlaying in the rolling hills, is one of the masterpieces that made full use of the space environment cleverly. It, built in the years of Emperor Yongle of the Ming Dynasty, is the only road to South Cliff Palace and connects Pavilion to Pray for Rain, Taichang Temple and Thunder God Hole as well.

Though small and unique in size, it has made clever use of the topography to fully demonstrate the style of imperial architecture. Near the Mountain Gate is the large Imperial Stele

Pavilion, the special building in Wudang Mountains in the Ming Dynasty, and presenting the palace's status. In the pavilion, there is an imperial stele on the back of a tortoise showing the meaning of reserving it forever, and also demonstrating that only the large tortoise is qualified to deliver important orders to humans.

In the architectures of Wudang Taoism, the Mountain Gates of palace and temples are quite important, for once getting into the gate, it means you step in the Wonderland. It was said that South Heaven Gate is the first gate you must pass if you want to go to Heaven. So building it here, they wanted to create an ambit of fairyland.

The Taichang Temple 泰常观

The Taichang Temple, always surrounded by cloud and fog, has always been called The Temple of Cloud and Fog. It's said that a Taoist named Taichang with consummate medical skills, always lived in Wudang Mountains. Once he cured the Emperor's mother and refused to accept any reward. Then the Emperor ordered a temple to be built in Wudang Mountains in the name of this Taoist so as that he would be remembered by the later generations. It's also said that Taichang is one of the twelve gods and the Taichang Temple is the place to offer sacrifices to gods, so the Statue of Laojun is worshiped here.

The statue of Laojun, 1.96 meters high, covered with gold foil and colored drawing, serious and affectionate, appears to be delivering the sermons, and also looks as though it is thinking deeply. This statue is on a high level, for it shows perfectly the ancient culture's level of understanding in the thought of Lao zi either from its shape or from its expression, and displays vividly the world outlook of living in seclusion and doing nothing. It's not only a precious relic but also an elegant work of art. When appreciating this statue, we are often filled with great admiration for the superb skills of ancient artisans.

In the Taichang Temple the Goddess of the Big Dipper's Mother is also worshiped here. It has three eyes, four heads, and four arms on each side, with the weapons of the sun, the moon, the bow and the arrow in her hands. The statue, silk padded and covered with colored drawing, is priceless.

Tianyi Zhenqing Palace 天乙真庆宫

In South Cliff scenic spot, the most famous architecture is a stone palace named Tianyi Zhenqing Palace. It's said that after Emperor Zhenwu ascended to heaven, he lived in a palace called Tianyi Zhenqing Palace. Obviously the followers of Emperor Zhenwu on the earth built the palace. This stone palace is the one of the masterpieces of ancient Chinese architecture and is a representative of ancient Chinese stone buildings.

Tianyi Zhenqing Palace is made of wood-like stones. The roof beams, pillars, square timbers, windows, doors, joints and decorations of animal sculptures on the roof ridges, were carved from green stones and then combined together. The whole Palace, accurately designed, delicately structured, and exquisitely carved, is a masterpiece of the large Chinese stone carvings. The difficulties of building this palace on the steep cliff stretch our imagination to the limit.

Tianyi Zhenqing Palace was built by a famous Taoist Zhang Shouqing at the beginning of the Yuan Dynasty and was finished 27 years later. Zhang went to Wudang Mountains at the age of 30 and led his thousands of disciples to reclaim wasteland, plant the land and cut the cliff and then left this marvelous spectacle for the later generations.

4. Purple-Clouds Scenic Spot 紫霄景区

At the foot of Stretching Flag Peak sits magnificent and boundless Purple Cloud Palace. Here, with the cluster of hills guarding the peaks, the wood of pine and green cypress deep and remote, and the surroundings elegant and weather comfortable, the place is thought the Blessed Place in Purple Cloud Palace Scenic Spot.

Purple Cloud Palace is an apotheosis of construction by employing the particular physiognomy that is cragged in length while wide and plain on breadth. All the buildings are arrayed along the axis. On the axis lie the Green Dragon and White Tiger Palace, Imperial Stele Pavilion, Shifang Hall, the Grand Hall of Purple Cloud Palace and Parents' Palace from the bottom to the top. The altitude of these buildings gradually rises and the axis symmetries the wing houses of each construction. And through the way of stacking tall side steps, the Purple Cloud Palace is divided into three sections of yard, so as to form a kind of group of constructions in which one row is upon the other and the primary buildings are more distinctive than the secondary ones. From a far distance, the Palace has the airs of imperial worshiping rites.

Historically, Purple Cloud Palace, because of taking the responsibilities of praying for royal families, had a solemn overall arrangement and exquisite furnishings. Inside each various palace, the worshiped deities and celestial beings are ablated. Together with the divine tables, obliging apparatuses and omniscient instruments, consist of a mysterious and metaphysical world. The images created by Taoist legends are so vivid by design and various on airs. Here, people may differ them from their status, divine responsibilities, specified occupations, dispositions and thoughts.

The Emperors of the Song, Yuan, Ming and Qing dynasties often issued their orders to set up altar so as to praise and pray for good fortune, or plead deities to bless the peace of their state and the plain people or the harvest of crops. In fact, this was a ritual of communicating with Gods, for Taoism thought through that way Gods would help the prayers, bless them to be away from the disasters and prolong their lifespan.

At present, the Purple Cloud Palace is not only the best choice to visit, but also the location of the Taoism Association of Wudang Mountains, the destination of experts from all over the world. Furthermore, it is the very source for Taoism researchers to search the origin of Taoism.

Sword-River Bridge 剑河桥

Sword-River Bridge, also named Tianjin Bridge, is the main path to Wudang Mountains during the ancient times. Though located at the wilderness of remote mountains, the old tall trees, clear rivers, Dragon Spring Temple and Pingfeng/ Screen here make you feel in the family yard.

During the ruling years of Emperor Yongle of the Ming Dynasty, the Dragon Spring Temple was built on one side of Tianjin Bridge and Pingfeng/ Screen on the other side, standing against the dragon head-like mountain. The bridge, with three holes, among which, the middle holes crosses 9.6 meters and the side ones 6.7 meters, was first built in the Yuan Dynasty. It is still safe and sound after many years' strike of blood.

Besides, there is a beautiful folklore connected with Sword-River Bridge. It is said that when young Emperor Zhenwu went to Wudang Mountains to cultivate, his mother, Empress Shansheng led 500 soldiers here, asking him to return to the palace. Seeing Emperor Zhenwu was reluctant to return, the mother grasped his robe to force him to return. But Emperor Zhenwu took out his sword, cut off his robe, then lacerated a stroke on the ground, a sword-river gushed immediately, thus the river separated the mother and the son. The mother and the son broke up with tears. Emperor Zhenwu walked 18 steps upwards, which is now the Upper 18-Turning of the Wudang Mountains. The mother walked 18 steps downwards, the Lower 18-Turning.

Now, walking on the ancient road of these 36 turnings, and looking at the flowing sword river on the ancient bridge, visitors will be moved by this beautiful legend and speak highly of the ancients' wisdom for building such wonderful things.

The Parents' Hall 父母殿

The Parents' Hall was built on the lofty platform at the back of Purple-Clouds Palace. Here are full of tall ancient trees, green mountains, thus it is one of the best sights in Wudang Mountains. The Parents' Hall of Purple-Clouds Palace, a three-storied building, was built with wood and bricks. There were three shrines inside the hall and the statues of Emperor Zhenwu's parents, Emperor Mingzhen and Queen Shansheng, who were called St. Father and St. Mother by the Taoists, were worshiped in the middle shrine.

In accordance with the textual research, the Parents' Hall was first built during the ruling years of Emperor Yongle in the Ming Dynasty, but destroyed later and the existing one was rebuilt in the Qing Dynasty, bearing the architectural features of the Qing Dynasty. There were Parents' Halls in all large Temples in Wudang Mountains and that was one of the significant characteristics of royal temples in Wudang Mountains. It also reflected the religious features advocated by Wudang Taoism, which claimed the three religions (Confucianism, Buddhism and Taoism) were originally synergetic.

In the Ming Dynasty, the emperor divided Taoism into two factions, i.e. Quanzhen and Zhengyi: those whose main activities were cultivating and making pills of immortality belonged to the former, while those whose main activities were uttering and writing invocations belonged to the latter. Since Quanzhen Taoism advocated that the three religions were originally synergetic, and its votaries all abide by this principle of their primogenitor Wang Chongyang and promoted the standards of filial piety, which changed the old principle that monks or nuns should refuse to have anything to do with all kin and friends. Therefore the Parents' Hall was a hall used to worship parents and moralize the public. So Wudang Taoism also has the saying that "the three religions (Confucianism, Buddhism and Taoism) were originally synergetic".

The Green Dragon and White Tiger Hall 青龙白虎殿

Walking across Golden Water Bridge, then along the stone steps, people may see The Green Dragon and White Tiger Hall. Overlooking the mountains, the green colored glaze palace with the structure of brick and wood, stands on the large platform. The outside wall, decorated with graphs of glazed jade flower, peacocks and so forth, has a shape of Chinese Character "八/ba" (eight). Inside the palace, the image of stern, armored Official Wang with a whip in the hands (the most filial son before) is put in the center of the hall, accompanied by the clay sculptures of green dragon and white tiger on each side. The dragon and the tiger are depicted loftily, mightily, awesomely, and vividly. It is researched that these two sculptures following the style of Liu Yuanyi, whose way was well-known during the Yuan Dynasty (1206—1368 A.D.) are the most precious rare artwork of clay sculpture.

Among all the major temples and palaces, The Green Dragon and White Tiger Hall are built. In the hall the dragon and the tiger are ablated in order to protrude the solemnity of the ceremony for worshiping Emperor Zhenwu. Moreover, in the traditional culture of Taoism, green dragon and white tiger are closely connected with the method of cultivating the heart and nature. Between the positive and negative elements, the green dragon and white tiger belong to these categories respectively. Combining the dragon with the tiger in the same hall metaphorically maintains Taoist ideas of cultivation: the two basic elements are mutually complementary. In other words, if properly transformed, one of the elements can be genital to another. Therefore, appropriate employment from the positive element in the liver may be fairly helpful to the recovery of the lung; which cannot only adequately make use of one element transfuse energy into the weak element, but also it can remove too much unnecessary harmful or fatal opposite element.

The Mountain Gate 山门

Among all the group constructions of the old days in Wudang Mountains, the sidewall for the entry gate of big palaces and halls has the design of Chinese Character "八/ Ba"(eight) in shape and uses glazed tile as a way to present the grade of the imperial building. This kind of design does not only reflects the stateliness, sobriety and impressive manner of the imperial power, but also the expressive form of the belief and the concept of the taste in those days.

The "Ba" shaped walls of the entry gate consists of basic bottom named Xu-Mi, the body part of the walls and tiles on the top of the walls. In the middle part and rim of the wall are carved vivid jade flowers, rare auspicious birds by pottery and colored glazed of basso-relievo. All these pottery staff is the exactly delicate artwork and embodies the advanced level of pottery at those days.

The Shifang Hall 十方殿

On the third group of stone steps after entering Purple Cloud Palace, people will meet the second Hall of Purple Cloud Palace, i.e. Worshiping Hall. Worshiping Hall is also called Shifang Hall, because formerly the location was inhabited by a thick jungle (Shifang Conglin in Chinese, Shifang meaning all directions) and a boarding and lodging place for all Taoists from a far distance. It is said that during the Ming Dynasty (1368—1644 A.D.) the pilgrims and the pious believers could only worship Emperor Zhenwu in the hall, while The Great Hall of Purple Cloud Palace was exclusively for the emperor to pray and sacrifice. That is why this Hall is called Worshiping Hall. Another outstanding function of the Hall was to treat the travelingTaoists from the outside world, that is to say, to accommodate the Taoist from Shifang (everywhere; all directions).

The Shifang Hall was built in the tenth year of the third Emperor of the Ming Dynasty (1412 A.D.). The sidewall of the Hall is like a "Ba" in shape. On the wall jade flowers and rare precious birds are decorated. Under the wall the basic glazed bottom is set. Inside the Halls a brass gold-plating casting image is ablated in the middle part of the hall.

It is recorded that Wudang Mountains became the center of the Taoism during the Ming Dynasty. There were many Taoists continuously accommodating in Wudang Mountains. Therefore, the Shifang Hall was set up in order to treat the traveling Taoists. Historically, Quanzhen School had made the principle, that is, "Taoist from a far distance are exempt from the paying for food supplies and firewood." That is to say, if accepted by the local Taoists' organization, traveling Taoists can eat and sleep for a long term in the Shifang Hall. But the process of being accepted was very strict, for regulations and the habits concerning how to walk, salute and talk, even the content of talking would be checked. This checking was just like the modern examination to distinguish fake Taoist.

In front of the Shifang Hall, people may overlook Imperial Stele Pavilion, the Green Dragon and the White Tiger Hall, the Pearl Peak and the Imperially Bestowed Sword Platform. People looking around, the old cypress, plank road built along the cliff, running water and green mountains are an admired picture. The verve and omniscience of imperial architecture create an atmosphere of the piety from the bottom of your heart.

Crown Prince's Cave　太子洞

Behind Purple Cloud Palace lies Flag Stretching Peak where erect green cypress and joyful beautiful scenery people can see. At the end of the ancient stone steps, an entry gate, Crown Prince's Cliff is enclosed by the green shadows.

Crown Prince's Cliff was built during the early years of the Yuan Dynasty (1206—1368 A.D.). It is a good place for cultivation and inspirations with a condition of tranquil, deep and remote surroundings, climate of amenity, and aloofness to the earthly affairs. At present, the relics are mainly Three-Cleaning Cliff, Seven-Star Cliff and Medicine-Making Cliff remained by ancient hermits.

Through the entry gate, then up the steps, and cross Crown Prince's Pavilion, you will come to Crown Prince's Cave, a natural den, the cultivating spot on Wudang Mountains for young Zhenwu, the prince of the Jingle Kingdom.

At the entrance of Crown Prince's Cave, there is a stone palace in pseudo wooden structure. Inside the palace a stone inscription "Taizi Yan"(Crown Prince's Cliff) of 1290 is the proof to figure out the exact age of excavation.

Yuxu Cliff 玉虚岩

Yuxu Cliff is the most cragged as well as the most splendid in scale among all the 36 cliff temples. The temple locating on the steep perpendicular cut-like cliff is a massive grotto of 2,000 cubic meters with an utmost height of 18 meters and the width of 11.5 meters. Mountain Gate, Fasting Hall, Taoist Study and the Grand Hall all were built in the cave. So were the relics of buildings, stone inscriptions, clay sculptures and colored drawings of the image of the Gods in Taoism, which are various, vivid and lifelike in design.

Before the Tang Dynasty (618—907A.D.), lots of hermits were found in the Wudang Mountains. Those hermits chose Wudang Mountains because it was so far away from the crowded world that the sound of the earthly affairs couldn't be fallen on them. Yuxu Cliff was surely an ideal place for exiling.

It is said that the temple inside of the Cliff was built in the Song Dynasty (960—1279 A.D.) and had been rebuilt in the first year of Emperor Yuantai, the Yuan Dynasty (1206—1368A.D.). In 1412, the Emperor ordered a third time renewal. It is said that the title of the temple was named after Emperor Zhenwu, who had been there for cultivation, for his Taoist name was Yuxu Prime Minister.

The way to the Yuxu Cliff is in the canyon indeed. People need paddle the crook, pass the hanging bridge and the plank road built along the cliff, and then climb up the stone steps. The thick green shadows in the canyon and joyful scenery is more than beautiful. Walking through the canyon, people even may feel completely absorbed in the nature.

Imperial Stele Pavilion 御碑亭

Inside Purple Cloud Palace symmetrically lift two Imperial Stele Pavilions royally built in 1412, on the large platform. The whole shape is square and each side of the pavilion has an arch. In the pavilion, the Imperial Stele on the back of the huge tortoise was chiseled from one intact green stone. Crafty in chisel, vivid in design, and perfect in figure, the stone carving is a precious artwork in the world.

Imperial Stele Pavilion was one of the compulsory constructions in each big temple and palace, for the stele had to be set in. Of the two steles set in the kiosk, one was the regulation made by the third Emperor to govern Wudang Mountains; the other one recorded the reason why the Emperor decided to build Wudang Mountains and the process of constructing.

Imperial Stele Pavilion was the special construction in the Ming Dynasty in Wudang Mountains, which was the symbol of important palace. In accordance with the history records, the carving on the stele represents one of the outstanding periods of Northern Zhou Kirgdom. The carving of stele on the tortoise derives from the records of the ancient Northern Zhou Kirgdom. Ancient people thought only huge tortoise can qualify for the task to send the royal orders to all the civic people.

The Grand Hall of Purple Cloud Palace 紫霄大殿

The core construction of Purple Cloud Palace, The Grand Hall is the only left double-eaved, leaning-to-hill, and wooden building. As one of the quite rare building of uplifting wooden crossbeam construction in the history of the Taoist architecture, the Grand Hall is scientific and rational in structure and overall arrangement, harmonious and coherent in artistic style, united with the surroundings as a whole, and unique in taste and features among all the building in Wudang Mountains. Meanwhile, the Grand Hall, having absorbed the techniques of various times' artisans, demonstrated great achievements of architectures in the Ming and Qing dynasties, therefore, worthy of visiting and researching.

The inner part of the Grand Hall is dazing and full of praise from travelers. Carefully painted and well carved, the Hall is magnificent in vigour, crafty in idea, smooth and natural in sculpting, unsophisticated and gracious in decoration, and solemn and exquisite in displaying. In the Hall, five shrines are set there. Around the tabernacles hundreds of rare antiques are ablated. Most of the precious antiques, dynamic, vivid, and wonderful to see, were the images of Gods by clay sculpture and wares for worshiping during the Yuan, Ming, and Qing dynasties.

In the middle of the Shrine is ablated the image of Emperor Zhenwu. With a height of 4.8 meters, the image is the biggest clay sculpture. Another divine image made by paper and covered with pseudo golden leaves is the best preserved and most ancient paper image which comprehensively displays the marrow on craftwork of paper pasting, sculpting, gilding, colored drawing, and antisepticising, and has great value in researching ancient paper pasting.

The fastigium of the Grand Hall consists of six flying colored glaze dragons. An Aquarius is surrounded by the dragons that are painted in three different colors. Due to the heaviness and highness, the Aquarius has to be drawn by four iron chains. Each end of the chain is attached to the hand of a divine kid, it is said that the four kids of deity has stuck to their positions in order to keep the Aquarius steady no matter it is chilly, scorching, rainy, windy and thundering. Because their spacial positions are even higher than the Supreme God, the four kids are also called Supreme Gods. While the plain people address them wretched kiddies.

After the rebuilding in 1412 A.D., the Grand Hall had been repaired about ten times in different times. Therefore, it can maintain its basic features. In 1994, the experts on world relics from UN inspected Wudang Mountains and said, "Here, we witness the sample of traditional remedial means to the ancient buildings".

5. Five-Dragon Scenic Spot 五龙景区

The Five-Dragon Palace Scenic Spot is of great importance in the development of Wudang Taoism, which was called the palace of efficacy in history. The famous ancient Taoists such as Yin Xi, Yin Gui, Ma Mingsheng, and Chen Tuan all succeeded in cultivating themselves. In accordance with *the Annals of Wudang Mountains,* during the beginning of 7th century B.C, there was a heavy drought, so the Emperor Li Shimin ordered Yao Jian, the Magistrate of Junzhou Prefecture to pray for rain. Yao Jian succeeded in praying for rain and dispelled the drought. So the Emperor issued an imperial edict to build Taoist temples, which was the starting point for royal families to build temples in Wudang Mountains. In this scenic spot, there are a lot of remains of the Temples, halls and palaces along the ancient road, from which you can sense their broad scope and great significance from that time.

There are many things of historical interest in this scenic spot, such as the Five-Dragon Palace, Huayang Cliff, Hermit Cliff, Pray-Realizing Cliff, Lingxu Cliff, Temple of Kindness and Stateliness, and also the biggest clay statue and bronze statue of Emperor Zhenwu. There is also a national forest reserve here, therefore it's a place well worth touring.

Shangyuan 上元

On the ancient road, from the Five-Dragon Palace to the South Cliff Palace, three Taoist buildings, Shangyuan/ the Upper, Zhongyuan/ the Middle, and Xiayuan/ the Lower, were built in the Yuan and Ming dynasties. Now the palaces in front of the cave have been ruined, so we have to imagine what they were like.

In China, the parlance of Sanyuan/ Three Elements is widely used and has many explanations. They referred to the three things: the sky, the earth and man; or the sky, the earth and the water; or the sun, the moon and the star; or the head, the abdomen and the feet; or the head, the heart and the kidney and so on. The three things are completely displayed in the form of buildings on the ancient road. What does this mean? Some experts think it indicates two things: one is to show the process of Emperor Zhenwu's cultivation; the other is for the need of Taoism to make sacrifices to gods.

In the ancient buildings of Shangyuan, there are two delicately engraved stone dragon heads, facing upwards, which indicate the splendor and the high degree of the ancient buildings of Shangyuan. In fact they are just the exits of the drainage, however it represents history and arts and tells us vividly that even these unattractive drainage have been well-designed and have created a pleasing aspect, which is a sign of the strictness and craftsmanship of the builders.

The Five-Dragon Palace 五龙宫

The Five-Dragon Palace is the earliest building in Wudang Mountains. Alchemists came here to live in seclusion in the Han Dynasty, and thereafter more and more people settled. So it is now regarded as the birthplace of Taoism and the site of pray-realizing.

In Taoism, this place is where supernatural beings and dragons lived, so in the past there stood a tablet on which was carved "Gods' residence near, be quiet", which instructed people to keep quiet so as not to upset the gods because this place is between heaven and the abode of gods. At present Five-Dragon Palace seems rather bleak and desolate, however, when you approach, you can sense her former grandeur and profundity.

Emperor Zhenwu's Image of copper, 1.95 meter high, is the biggest copper image of the Emperor Zhenwu in Wudang Mountains. In Five-Dragon Palace remain the biggest clay figures, colorful clay statues of Green Dragon and White Tiger, which are 5 meters high and seem very solemn in appearance. It's said that they were built by Liu Chuxuan, the foremost student of the famous sculptor Liu Yuanyi of the Yuan Dynasty.

The Five-Dragon Well is another great feature of the Five-Dragon Palace. If water in one well is drawn, water in other wells will be affected. Although this is not difficult to explain, it does contribute to the unique scenery of the Five-Dragon Palace.

Originally, Li Shimin, the Second Emperor of the Tang Dynasty ordered a temple to be built here. Then the temple had been rebuilt again and over, to the size of Five-Dragon Palace. The recognition of emperors of the succeeding dynasties, and the hard working of Wudang Taoists, had made Five-Dragon Palace come to resplendence for several times; however sword and fire caused it great harm.

Emperor Zhen of the Song Dynasty had ordered the repairing and rebuilding of Five-Dragon Palace, making the buildings complete, but they were destroyed by frequent wars during the South Song Dynasty. In the Yuan Dynasty, a Taoist became the chief of Five-Dragon Palace, and rebuilt it to its former effect, making it the center of Wudang Taoism, yet again it was ruined by wars in the latter part of the Yuan Dynasty. In the tenth year of Emperor Yongle's rule, in the Ming Dynasty, Emperor Cheng, Zhu Di had rebuilt Wudang Mountains to a great size, added more buildings to Five-Dragon Palace and written "Prosperous Five-Dragon Palace". During the ruling of Emperor Jiajing in the Ming Dynasty, there were 850 rooms, occupying 250,000m^2. Unfortunately, all the buildings were again destroyed by wars except the present Five-Dragon Palace.

Xiayuan 下元

On the ancient road, from the Five-Dragon Palace to the South Cliff Palace, three Taoism buildings, Shangyuan, Zhongyuan, Xiayuan, were built in the Yuan and Ming dynasties. Now the palaces in front of the cave have been ruined, so we have to imagine what they were like.

The Hermit Cliff 隐仙岩

The Hermit Cliff is one big cave among the 36 cliffs in Wudang Mountains. In the 10th year of Emperor Yongle's rule in the Ming Dynasty (1413 A.D.), three temples were built to worship Emperor Zhenwu, God Deng and Lü Dongbin (gods of Taoism).

In Accordance with the historical data, there were many hermits who attained the highest state of spiritual enlightenment in the ancient times. A Taoist called Fang Changxu planted trees on the mountain all the year round no matter how terrible the weather was. One day when he woke up, he found himself fully bearded, and from then on he was invisible. It was said that he had become a god by the wish of the people. Hence, Taoist said that it's not difficult to become god, if you do good deeds all your life, you will be considered a god by the people.

In the stone palace of Hermit Cliff, there are stone statues. The figures look very desolate and their clothes very distinctive. As a result of archive research, it was discovered that the two statues are God of Sun and God of Moon, which Taoism worships. In Taoism, there are the Emperor of the Sun and the Emperor of the Moon. In the ancient culture, legends about the sun and the moon and their applications were widespread, which is an important cultural phenomenon. That the Emperor of the Sun and the Emperor of the Moon appeared in the Hermit Cliff at the same time is reason enough to warrant further study of their cultural backgrounds and significance.

Zhongyuan 中元

At the site of Zhongyuan, a special statue, Black Tiger Marshal, is worshiped. In the ancient times Crow Temple and Black Tiger Temple were built in accordance with the legends of Emperor Zhenwu's self-cultivation. It's said that when the prince of Jingle Kingdom came to practice Taoism in Wudang Mountains for the first time, it was the crow that led the way and the black tiger that was on patrol duty for him. Then they became his personal imperial bodyguard. Any time a wild beast approached, the crow would tip him off and the black tiger would subdue them, which made it possible for Emperor Zhenwu to practice Taoism safely in the vast forest. After Emperor Zhenwu became god and ascended to heaven, he promoted the crow to be Divine Crow and the black tiger to be Marshal of Patrolling the Mountain. These have been worshiped by successive adherents.

The Eight-Immortal Temple 八仙观

The Eight-Immortal Temple is located on the road to the Central Temple where it is very deep and spacious, warm in winter and cold in summer. It's said that this temple was built because the eight immortals including Lü Dongbin always gathered here.

In accordance with the historical data, the temple was first built here in the Yuan Dynasty; then in the 10th year of Emperor Yongle's rule of the Ming Dynasty (1413 A.D.), Emperor Xuan Palace, Mountain Gate, corridors, the abbots' rooms, fasting halls and store houses were built and thereafter rebuilt in the Qing Dynasty. The first was the Dragon and Tiger Palace; and then a yard, on either side of which were side rooms and in the middle is the Main Hall where the statues of Emperor Zhenwu and the Eight Immortals were ever worshiped, but now they are gone.

The Eight-Immortal Temple, the Mammon Temple, GuanYu (a general in *The Romance of Three Kingdoms*) Temple, and Mount Tai Temple show the compatible and comprehensive characteristics of the royal temples in Wudang Mountains. In the Ming Dynasty, when the royal families made sacrifices in Wudang Mountains, they also built temples to all the gods who were influential in Taoism and in the lives of the civilians, by having satisfied the wishes of pious men and women. In this sense, there are especial values in the study of Taoist Culture contained in the ancient buildings in Wudang Mountains.

Lingying Cliff/ Pray-Realizing Cliff 灵应岩

Pray-Realizing Cliff, also called the Five Dragon Cliff, was a place where the magistrates of Junzhou Prefecture prayed for raining in the Tang Dynasty. So it played an important role in the development of Wudang Taoism.

In accordance with *The biography of Wudang Mountains*, there was a very dry year without any rain in the Tang Dynasty, the magistrate of Junzhou County, Yao Jian came here to pray for rain, and succeeded in having a big rain. Li Shimin, the second emperor of the Tang Dynasty, ordered to build Five-Dragon Palace, which opened the prelude of the imperial families to set up buildings in Wudang Mountains.

It is said Pray-Realizing Cliff was quite effective to pray for rain here from then to the Song, Yuan, Ming and Qing dynasties. There is a well-preserved stone hall, at the back of which a spring runs all the years. There are two ways to pray for rain: one is in a mild way, just praying which brings a tender rain; the other is in a violent way, firing guns or casting dirty things which brings a heavy rain.

6. The Golden Top/ Jinding Scenic Spot 金顶景区

The Golden Palace of on the top of Heavenly Pillar Peak is the essence and symbol of Wudang Mountains, the sign of Wudang Taoism coming to the highest peak under the support of the imperial power.

The Golden Palace Scenic Spot includes Zhongguan Temple, Yellow Dragon Cave, Sky Entrance Palace, the First Sky Entrance, the Second Sky Entrance, the Third Sky Entrance and the Golden Hall of the Palace of Harmony, Imperial Scriptures Hall, Purple Gold Wall, Worshiping Hall, and some ancient buildings built in the Yuan Dynasty. Inside of these buildings, there are many precious historical relics, which not only present China's ancient high architecture skills and magnificent melting technology, but also represent Chinese national intelligence and scientific achievements.

Standing in front of Golden Palace, you can have a panoramic view of the beautiful scene of Wudang Mountains, as far as 400 kilometers away. All the peaks are stopping at the static moment, just like raged waves, which wonderfully advertises the holy prestige and lofty imperial power. Meanwhile, you can also view many fantastic natural astronomical phenomena and learn many widespread fairy tales.

We can say that Golden Palace of Wudang Mountains has a strong attraction to visitors and pilgrims. With the development of Wudang tourism, the visitors coming to Wudang Mountains will increase progressively every year. Standing in the Golden Palace, all the views will imbue you with a sense of surprise and piety.

The Palace of Harmony 太和宫

The Palace of Harmony, or the Golden Top/ Jinding, lies in the top of Skyscraper Hill, the highest hill of Wudang Mountains. Skyscraper Hill, with a height of 1613 meters, penetrating into the clouds, was regarded as a pole to support the sky and the highest view-site in Wudang Mountains. You have not come to Wudang Mountains in a real sense until you have climbed onto the peak and entered the Palace of Harmony; no matter you are Taoist, pilgrim, visitor, or man of letters.

600 years ago, one emperor of the Ming Dynasty, Zhu Di ordered to build the Palace of Harmony. Four years later, the great construction of the Palace of Harmony was finished on the steep and dangerous peak. He also named the mountain the First Biggest Mountain of Harmony, so that Wudang Mountains was put to the head of the other four biggest mountains in China. During the rule of Emperor Jiajing, the Palace of Harmony was enlarged that there were more than 520 rooms.

The constructions of the Palace of Harmony, on the dangerous peak, making full use of the natural rise and fall of the mountain ranges, achieved an artistic effect of solemnity and grandeur and showed a meaning that God is the most powerful and can't be trespassed on.

The construction had achieved harmonious unification of natural and artificial view-sites, had materialized the cleverness of Chinese to the full. After visiting, experts in world legacy, space science, and construction all felt surprised and thought the construction of the Palace of Harmony can't be rivaled.

The Middle Hall 中观

In accordance with the history, the ancient Emperor Zhenwu cultivated as a Taoist in Wudang Mountains and then became a god, was appointed the King of North Pole by the King of Heaven, Jade Emperor in Qiong Pavilion. So Wudang Taoism show great respect for Qiong Pavilion.

Qiong Pavilion, large in construction size and miraculous in construction structure, with three units of the Upper Hall, the Middle Hall, and the Lower Hall, is one of the largest among the 36 halls in Wudang Mountains. In the old history, 24 temples between which were connected by roof-covered bridges were built between the Three Halls with the ranges of mountains. So there was a saying "going out, you can't see the sky; raining hard, you won't wet the shoes."

Now the Middle Hall is the only one that has been best protected in Qiong Pavilion, with West Side Hall, Tiger and Dragon Hall, East Side Hall, Entrance Hall and Tao Temple.

The Palace of Loneness 清微宫

The Palace of Loneness, one of the nine palaces built in the Ming Dynasty, has played an important role in the ancient constructions of Wudang Mountains. The Palace of Loneness, lying in the west of the Golden Top with about a distance of 1.5 km, lying in the side of sun shining, being surrounded by hills, is a clean and quiet place where there are cool in summer and warm in winter.

The Palace of Loneness, as the place for Taoism to give lectures and the place for visiting Taoist and privileged Taoists in the Palace of Harmony to cultivate, has played an important part in the history of Wudang Taoism. During the Yuan Dynasty, here is the cradle of Qingwei Theory of Taoism. At that time, Taoists in Wudang Mountains had a higher literature attainment, they compiled and published many books to disseminate Qingwei Theory of Taoism, with a result to spread the influence of Wudang Taoism.

In accordance with the textual research, the rudiment of the Palace of Loneness was first built in the Tang Dynasty and was developed to a great scale in the Yuan Dynasty. During the Ming Dynasty, the palace was ordered to rebuild by the emperors, temples and halls were more than 300 pieces. But later, some buildings were destroyed by some and other reasons. Now we can imagine the grandeur of that time by the relics whose acreage is near to 1,000 acres.

The Hall of Fate-Turning 转运殿

On the top of the Golden Peak, there is a small hill which is as charming as a lotus, so was given a name Little Lotus Hill.

On the top of Little Lotus Hill lies a Copper Hall, which was founded in the early 14th century and was the earliest one protected in China. The Copper Hall, also named Hall of Gold, former lied on the top of Skyscraper Hill during the Yuan Dynasty. A bigger hall of god was founded in the Ming Dynasty, the Copper Hall was transported to Little Lotus Hill and protected by another hall of bricks and stones. Since it was transported from Skyscraper Hill to Little Lotus Hill, so it was renamed the Hall of Fate-Turning.

In accordance with Chinese culture, "zhuanyun" has a sense of "having a change of luck" or "turning for a better fate", so the Golden Peak has one more view-site full of mystery. All the visitors would like to have a round walk between the Copper Hall and the hall of bricks and stones, in the hope of having a change of luck and turning to a bright and prosperous future.

The Copper Hall, large in space, complicated in structure, fine in craftwork, primitive in sculpture, is the important material data to study and research the constructions of Wudang Mountains built in the Yuan Dynasty.

Gate of Pilgrimage 朝圣门

After your hard journey of the first, second, third sky-gate on the ancient road, the Purple Golden Palace on the top of the Golden Top is to greet you. Meanwhile, majestic and magnificent Gate of Pilgrimage spans before you.

The three Sky-gates and the Gate of Pilgrimage, standing erectly among thousands of stone flights, were constructed constitutionally on the site of the Yuan Dynasty in the 10th year of Emperor Yongle, the Ming Dynasty. The constructions were planned and built with such originality and skills, as if done by god. The builders applied theory of space and religion, created an environmental atmosphere to rapidly change visitors' feeling, which is the embodiment of our forefathers' great intelligence.

The loftiness of Sky-Gates acts as a foil to the holiness and grandness of heaven. When climbing up, those who make a pilgrimage will be more and more solemn and respectful. During the hard mountain-climbing to the Golden Top, especially when they meet the Sky-gate suddenly, there will be an outburst of enthusiasm and strength in the heart of visitors, which is the sublimation of aesthetics. When close to the sky-gate, Taoism believers will hail and shout, to express their happiness and joy, along with the prolonged echoing of thousands of mountains.

Heavenward Palace 朝天宫

On the way to the Golden Top, you will climb higher and higher after past Yellow Dragon Cave. The mountain climbing is very hard, although the scenery is peculiar. But later a building of red walls and emerald tiles shaded by green trees is close at hand, which is Heavenward Palace built on the route of the ancient god road.

In accordance with the legend, Heavenward Palace is the dividing line between the Heaven and the mortal world. During the ancient time, those who paid respect to Emperor Zhenwu, would think that they had got into the Heaven, must worship here and then continued mountain-climbing. It is said in Taoism that here is the supreme state for the ordinary people to attain.

The statues of Jade Emperor and Emperor Zhenwu are enshrined in the Heaven Palace. At present, there is an exhibition of decrees and inscriptions by emperors of successive dynasties to Wudang mountains, lively reproducing the development history of Taoism with the support of emperors. When resting, the tourists can know its history and the status in each dynasty.

In addition, there are East Side Hall and West Side Hall and Taoist temples where the other deities statues are enshrined.

Worship Hall 朝拜殿

The Grand Hall of Palace of Harmony, on whose stele "Palace of Harmony" was inscribed, was called Worship Hall in the Ming Dynasty. In front of the hall lies a pavilion with carved beams and painted ridgepoles to an effect of elegance and magnificence. On the two sides of the hall is Bell Tower and Drum-Tower, in which is a gigantic bronze clock made in the 13th year of Emperor Yongle, the Ming Dynasty. The bronze clock, 1.57 meters in height and 1.435 meters in caliber, is the largest and the most beautiful in Wudang Mountains. Once being struck, it produces thundering voice, with prolonging echo.

The hall was made of stones, bricks, and glazed tiles, the lower part of whose wall was carving stones. In which are statue of Emperor Zhenwu, and those of Golden Boy and Jade Maiden (servants of the Emperor), some of which are in the Ming Dynasty and some of which in the Qing Dynasty, which is the artful assembl age of the Ming and Qing dynasties.

Worship Hall was built in the 14th year of Yongle, the Ming Dynasty, and was then named the Grand Hall of the Palace of Harmony in the year of Emperor Kangxi, one of famous emperors in the Qing Dynasty.

During the Ming Dynasty, ordinary people who made a pilgrimage to Wudang Mountains only could pay their respect to Emperor Zhenwu in the Worship Hall rather than entering the high-and-mighty Golden Palace, which just could be looked with reverence at a distance, reflecting rigid hierarchy and sacred imperial authority.

Hall of Imperial Scriptures 皇经堂

The Hall of Imperial Scriptures, elegantly and magnificently decorated, was first built in the year of Emperor Yongle in the Ming Dynasty and rebuilt in the 29th year of Emperor Daoguang in the Qing Dynasty.

The Hall of Imperial Scriptures, also known as the Hall of Scriptures-reading, is the place where the Taoists to read scriptures and to attend the service. Reading Taoist Scriptures for one hour each in the morning and at dusk everyday, by means of which the Taoist priests can edify themselves and be pious to Taoism, is the exercise of priests' self-cultivating, and regarded as the ladder to Elysium.

In the center of the Hall of Imperial Scriptures hung a golden tablet, on which "Born in the Heaven and Standing in the World" were written, bestowed by the Emperor Daoguang of the Qing Dynasty. Many characters, tales and rare animals related to Taoism are inscribed exquisitely on the railings and wooden partition boards, which reflects the social life, religious belief and aesthetics in the Qing Dynasty.

In the Hall are established the shrines, where the statues of Emperor Zhenwu, the three famous emperors of the Qing Dynasty, Jade Emperor, the King of Heaven and so on are enshrined.

Yellow Dragon Cave 黄龙洞

Yellow Dragon Cave is situated on the ancient road to the Golden Peak. In Wudang Mountains, Yellow Dragon Cave is connected with the Taoist medicines, such as Yellow Dragon Cave Eye Ointment and other medicines, which were renowned in the history. On the upper side of Yellow Dragon Cave are four tablets, on two of which "Great Fame" were written, showing the medicines made in Wudang Mountains were world-renown. On the other two tablets are the information of the famous medicines uses and the remediable diseases.

Taoists take advantage of the Cave to cure diseases. A rope to which a small basket is fastened is connected with the pavilion below Yellow Dragon Cave. Those who buy the medicine can put money in the basket and then ring the bell. Thus, the basket will be pulled up by the Taoists in the Cave and lowered with medicine later.

The most outstanding feature of the Cave is that there are many smaller caves in the cave. In the Cave, the spring is everlastingly flowing, cool and sweet. In accordance with the legend, one yellow dragon cultivated here and ascended to Elysium. For expressing its appreciation to the Cave, it left a panacea in the spring to cure all the diseases. The palace and statue were constructed to show people's admiration and thanks for yellow dragon.

Yellow Dragon Cave is actually a natural scenery having tens of thousands of magnificent mountains and valleys, peaceful and pleasantly cool during the whole year. And the air here is delightful. It is recorded that here were many Taoists cultivating themselves before the Song Dynasty. In ancient times, men who made a pilgrimage to Wudang Mountains firmly believed that entering Yellow Dragon Cave meant that they had had the lot for many years' cultivation.

After the progressive building of Taoists of successive dynasties, there appeared Yellow Dragon Palace, Zhenwu Pavilion, Palace of Medicine King, God Spring Pavilion, which add a sense of mystery and profundity to Yellow Dragon Cave.

The Golden Palace 金殿

The Golden Palace, the symbol of the Wudang Mountains, is the sign of Wudang Taoism reaching a high peak under the support of the imperial power.

Standing in front of the Golden Palace, you can have a panoramic view of the beautiful scene of Wudang Mountains, as far as 400 kilometers. All the peaks are stopping at the static moment, just like raged waves, which wonderfully advertises major prestige and lofty imperial power.

The Golden Palace, with a height of 5.45 meters and flying eaves decorated by dragon, phoenix, sea horse, and immortals, is the highest one in the ancient Chinese construction grade. Bronze constructed, the Golden Palace was gilded by gold outside. All the parts were so perfect matched that there is without any crevice. Enduring about 600 years' wind and rain, thunder and lightening, cold winter and hot summer, the Golden Palace is still shining as if it was newly built up. Hence, the Golden Palace, national treasure, not only presents the wonderful Chinese ancient architecture skills, but also reveals the wisdom of Chinese people and ancient scientific achievements.

The Golden Palace is the integration of intelligence and creativity, and also the display of art and beauty. The inside walls of the Golden Palace were lightly carved with soft floating clouds lines. Purple mantel, clean and smooth, reflects a gentle and harmonious color. The statues of Emperor Zhenwu, Golden Boy and Jade Girl, and the Generals of Water and Fire are being worshiped inside of the Golden Palace, with delicate portray and distinct personality.

Golden Clock Pavilion and Jade Drum Pavilion are in front of the Golden Palace. On the two sides of the Palace, there are Lot House and Stamp House for pilgrims to draw lots and stamp the holy mark. Behind those houses is Parents' Palace, which is the holy place for pilgrims showing respect to Emperor Zhenwu's parents.

The Hall of Official Wang 灵官殿

Getting into the South Sky Entrance to Purple Gold Palace and then ascending the steps, you will reach the dim and gloomy corridor of the Hall of Official Wang, who in Taoism, is the guard and supervisor to rule mountain gates, overlook the altars, protect the laws, and settle the disputes of immortals. The Hall, in front of the Golden Palace, is the right place to carry on the last spiritual baptism to the pilgrims, so has special importance.

With the limitation of mountain shape, the Hall of Official Wang is a little stone hall closely attached to the rock. Inside of the stone hall lays a tiny tin hall, which is the evidence of the application of using tin as the building materials. The construction skill and the artistic shape of the tiny hall are also worth praising. As the first tin-made historic relic, it is very precious.

In the Taoist system of god, Official Wang takes the responsibility to punish the disloyal ones. There is a horizontal board inscribed, "Holy Kindness Covering All the Earth", which has double meanings: one is to praise the Emperor for his kindness to his people; the other one is to praise Emperor Zhenwu for his favor to nourish the whole earth like sunshine, rain and dew.

The South Sky Entrance 南天门

In accordance with Chinese legend, the South Sky Entrance is the most important gate to get into Heaven and the imperial palaces of Jade Emperor. There are three gate holes in the South Sky Entrance, Holy Gate, Ghost Gate, and Human Gate. Ghost Gate is the symbolic gate, which is always closed since it was built up because there is no permission for the evil ghosts to appear at the worshiping palaces. Holy Gate is closed except when the imperial families visit this place, but human gate is always open for all the pilgrims to pay homage to Emperor Zhenwu.

The walls joining the South Sky Entrance is called Purple Gold Wall, with 2.4 meters of basic foundation and 1.26 meters of top. The solid wall is the perfect display of Emperors Yongle, Zhu Di's order "As Solid and Everlasting as the Sun and the Moon."

In the period of Emperor Yongle, people constructed the famous Golden Palace on the top of Heavenly Pillar Peak in Wudang Mountains. But there were no walls around the Palace at that time, until 1419, Emperors Yongle of the Ming Dynasty, Zhu Di commanded to build Purple Gold Wall on the top of Heavenly Pillar Peak. Eventually, the whole project cost about 5 years, using gigantic and solid stones to make such a wonderful wall, which imbues everyone with a surprise.

In the period of Emperor Yongle, it was very restrictive to enter into Purple Gold Wall, just as the popular saying goes "the Forbidden City in the North, Purple Gold Wall in the South." Therefore, we can see that the Golden Palace of Wudang Mountains played the same role as the Forbidden City in history.

Miao Hua Cliff 妙华岩

Miao Hua Cliff is located in the waist of Peripatetic Peak of Wudang Mountains. Although few people visit this place, it plays a very important role in the development of Wudang Taoism. Miao Hua Cliff, where the surroundings are very quiet and beautiful, the forest is dense, the birds are singing and the flowers are blooming, is also called Miraculous Flowers Cliff.

About the 8th century, some hermits had practiced austerities here. In the Yuan Dynasty, Taoist temples had formed a rather considerable scale here. In the tenth year of Emperor Yongle of the Ming Dynasty, temples were renovated. Miao Hua Cliff became the center of China Taoism with a high reputation in the Yuan Dynasty; many outstanding hermits cultivated themselves, composed and published books on Taoism here.

The outside part of the buildings in Miao Hua Cliff was damaged in early years. Now there remain three stone-caved training beds, which are delicately carved. It is said that they were the places for Taoists to practice the Static Qigong.

Behind the middle training bed, there is a small cave, through which we can find an artificial square pond. It was said that this small pond provided the oil for 30,000 persons without stopping in years in the Ming Dynasty when the people built Wudang Mountains.

7. Miraculous Wonders in Wudang Mountains 武当奇观

Seahorse Spitting Fog 海马吐雾

On the eaves of the Golden Palace of Wudang Mountains have many decorations of beautiful birds and beasts: sky horse, lion, dragon, god, ox, seahorse and so on. Now and then the seahorse will spit fog from the mouth, and several days after the spitting, there will be a heavy thunder-rain, so Seahorse Spitting Fog has become a famous wonder in the Golden Palace.

Thunder and Lightning Tempering the Golden Palace 雷火炼殿

Every summer in Wudang Mountains will appear the wonder of Thunder and Lightning Tempering the Golden Palace. That time, a fit of thunder makes people faint and deaf; lighting penetrates right to the Golden Palace like a sword; so there will be full of colorful lights that make viewers amazing and surprised. The Golden Palace is as bright as new after 600 years' tempering of thunder and lightning.

A Thunderbolt on the Land 平地惊雷

Heavenly Pillar Peak is 1612 meters high. During the days of thunder-rain, there often are black clouds gathering at the foot of the peak, thicker and thicker, more and more onrushing, then suddenly a lightning splitting the sky and a thunderbolt shouting in the airs. But there are still blue sky and white clouds over the Golden Palace.

God-made Xuanwu 天造玄武

Xuanwu, whose shape is like the play between a tortoise and a snake, is the god in the north in ancient Chinese legend. Seen from the sky, the shape of Heavenly Pillar Peak is just like a large tortoise, and the walls and buildings are just like a divine snake winding around the tortoise; which form a miraculous picture of tortoise and snake. The miraculous view makes the viewers can't help thinking whether there is a coincidence between human's wisdom and the nature.

Tides Going-up in the Inland Lake 陆海奔潮

After every rain and snow, there will be boundless white clouds among Wudang Mountains, just like the waves and tides in the sea, going up and rolling down. That time, all the mountains, full of changes, are beautiful and charming beyond description.

A Large Stele on the Back of a Tortoise 龟驮巨碑

In Yuxu Palace there are four stele pavilions, in each of which has a large stele on the back of a tortoise, as heavy as 90 tons. The stele is full of arts and crafts, with flying dragons on the head. The large tortoise sits there steadily, vivid as living.

Xuanyue Gate 玄岳门

Xuanyue Gate was a wooden-like building made of large green stones. The ancient craftsmen made best use of all kinds of techniques to carve many designs, such as swans, clouds, and flying dragons. The building, demonstrating the highest level in stone carving at that time, was listed in the collector's item of Chinese stone carving arts.

The Copper Statue of God Official Wang 铜灵官像

The biggest statue of God Official Wang in Wudang Mountains is 2.22 meters high, made of copper. God Official Wang, with loricae on body and a gold whip in hand, red faced and three-eyed, has the vigor to punish all the bandits who are against god's will to do bad things. According to the legend, there had the evil frightened to kneel before the statue.

The Statues of Six God Generals 六甲神像

The six God Generals were the generals of Emperor Zhenwu. The statues, ordered to make with copper by one of the emperor in the Ming Dynasty, different in shape, are with a height of around 2 meters each. The statues are artworks of Chinese copper melting arts in the Ming Dynasty.

Dragon-Head Incense 龙头大香

The building of Dragon-Head Incense, also called Dragon-Head Stone, 2.9 meters long and 0.3 meters wide, below which is a steep valley, is one of breathtaking wonders in Wudang Mountains. Before, many visitors, in order to show their respect and piety for god, moved on the back of dragon to offer incenses, lot of which slide off the back and died. The Emperor of the Qing Dynasty had sent orders not to move on the back of dragon to offer incenses.

Crows Picking up Foods 乌鸦接食

Crows are looked on as God Birds by Wudang Taoism and its folk followers. If visitors cast peanuts, rice and other foods into the sky on the top of Crow Hill or Golden Peak, crows will gather to pick up these foods from all directions.

Thousand-year-Old Stone Hall 千年石殿

Thousand-Year-Old Stone Hall, a wonder in ancient Chinese buildings, wooden-like, was made out of large green stone, even the small parts and decorations. That the building was precisely designed and carefully carved and that the building was established on the cliff are beyond humans' imagination.

72 Hills Surrounding Heavenly Pillar Peak 72 峰朝大顶

Heavenly Pillar Peak, with a height of 1612 meters, is pointing upward into Heaven. There are 72 hills surrounding him like lotus, which makes the grandeur of 72 Hills Surrounding Heavenly Pillar Peak.

The Hanging Pine on South Cliff 南岩悬松

On South Cliff, there hangs a thousand-year-old pine, just like a huge snake flying in the air, sometimes visible and sometimes not when there is cloud or fog, which makes the viewers happy and full of imaginations.

Nine-Turning Yellow River Walls 九曲黄河墙

Nine-Turning Yellow River Walls are the corridor walls built in accordance with the rise and fall of the mountain. The levelly thick walls, fluent and pleasant curves, green-tiled roofs, are like two huge dragons flying and the Yellow River turning again and again. The huge walls do not only make people feel the long history of the corridor, but also demonstrate royal buildings' grandeur and luxury. It is said that Emperor Zhenwu had studied here when young, so the walls have another implication that his process of studying was devious and difficult.

One Pillar with Twelve Beams on 一柱十二梁

In Crown Prince Slope scenic spot, there is a building called Five-Cloud Tower, in which has a huge pillar with 12 beams crossed on, which is the perfect combination of mechanics and aesthetics and demonstrates the ancient's outstanding creativity, so has been praised as one wonder of ancient Chinese buildings. It is said that Emperor Zhenwu had studied and cultivated here for 42 years, then succeeded in becoming the rock of society.

Four Mountain Gates in One Li 一里四道门

In the temples of Crown Prince Slope scenic spot, there are four huge Mountain Gates in less than one li (500 meters), which makes four different temple yards. It is said that Emperor Zhenwu had studied and cultivated here, so the four gates means that life is like traveling through the Mountain Gates and that only step by step can we succeed.

Ten-li Fragrance of Osmanthus 十里桂花香

In front of the Imperial Scriptures Hall of Crown Prince Slope scenic spot stands a 300-year old osmanthus. Every Mid-autumn, when the osmanthus is blooming, people can smell the fragrance from ten lies away. Sweet fragrance, cool wind, everlasting spring, blue sky and white cloud, purple fog and green smoke form one famous scenic spot in Crown Prince Slope. It is said that Emperor Zhenwu had studied and cultivated here for 42 years, then succeeded in understanding Taoism, so the osmanthus has an implication that we can enjoy the success and become famous after having experienced lots of difficulties.

The Clay Statue of Green Dragon and White Tiger 青龙与白虎泥塑

The clay statue of Green Dragon and White Tiger is the biggest one in Wudang Mountains, with a height of five meters. The dragon and the tiger, with loricae on body and spears in hand, serious and solemn, is vivid as living, demonstrating justice gods' special features of Wudang Mountains. According to the record, the statue was sculptured by Liu Chuxuan, one famous student of the famous sculpture master of the Yuan Dynasty. That all clay statues ordered to build by the emperors were designed and sculptured by Liu shows the preciousness of the clay statue of Green Dragon and White Tiger.

The Copper Statue of Zhenwu 真武铜像

The copper statue of Emperor Zhenwu in a sitting position is the biggest one in Wudang Mountains, with a height of 1.9 meters. The statue, demonstrating Chinese highest level in smelting arts during the 15th century, has been made the first-rate culture relic under the state protection.

Five-Dragon Well 五龙井

There are five wells in two lines in the temple yard of Five-Dragon Palace, where ancient emperors paid religion service there, having a very high status. It is amazing that when someone bails water from one well, the other four wells will wave too.

The Divine Tortoise Spitting Water 神龟吐水

There is a sweet everlasting spring behind the Grand Hall of Purple Cloud Palace. The ancient people had carved a stone tortoise without a head at the mouth of the spring, so there flows sweet spring, also called Divine Water, from the neck of the tortoise.

Double Hills of Purple Cloud 紫霄双峰

In front of Purple Cloud Palace, there are two hills standing among Lotus Hills, like two stone shoots pointing upwards into heaven. The two hills, just like two brushes, are writing articles with the sky as paper.

The God Temple on the Cliff 悬崖神庙

On the top of South Cliff grow pines and vines, waving with the wind, like a curtain; below the Cliff is a deep valley, the voice of the stream sounds like a thunder. At the middle of the Cliff built a God Temple, Mountain Gate, Fasting Room, Taoist Rooms, and the Grand Hall, all of which show that the ancient people were clever in wisdom and brave in heart.

Golden Monkeys Jumping over the Stream 金猴跳涧

In the deep forests there are many monkeys playing, some are grasping the long vines to jump over the stream like swinging a swing; some are moving on an old tree and then jumping over the stream, ...all of them make people happy and laugh.

8. Wudang Traveling Routes (one-day travel) 武当山旅游线路（一日游）

Route A

To meet the tour team in Wudang Mountains: Laoying (by car)— Qiongtai (by tram rail)—

Golden Top (by tram rail)— Qiongtai (by car)— South Cliff Palace (by car)— Purple Cloud Palace (by car)— Crown Prince's Slope (by car)— Laoying (returning trip).

The tourist features of this route:

- On the way from Laoying to Qiongtai by car, we can enjoy the beautiful scenery of Wudang Mountains.
- On the way to Golden Top by tram rail, we are now traveling among the peaks, and then we are floating in the clouds, just like gods…
- On Golden Top, we can visit Golden Palace and Palace of Harmony, and talk about Taoism with Taoists…
- In South Cliff Palace, we can visit the palaces on the cliff, offer incenses on the Dragon-Head Stone, drink the spring water and worship the Gods in Taoism…
- In Purple Cloud Palace, we can have the chance to watch Taoist religion service…
- On Crown Prince's Slope, we can appreciate the appearance of God Zhenwu; enjoy the turning of Nine-Turning Yellow River Walls and the wonder of one pillar with twelve beams…

Accommodation:

- To have lunch in South Cliff Palace.
- To have supper in Laoying.

Some relative explanations:

- Zhongguan Temple, an important view-site in this route, is the beginning point of Wudang tram rail. But for lack of time, we will not stay there.
- When we go and return to Golden Top, we all take a tram rail for the sake of time.

Relative promises:

- To meet the tour team outside of Wudang Mountains for the sake of clients.
- To provide qualified travel guides with you through the routes.
- To provide best service to you, so as to help you visit all the scenic spots.

Notes:

If there is some certain Force Majeure (natural disaster, changes and error of air and rail, bad weather, political situation, or some rules and regulations made by the government) that leads to extra expenses, the travel agency is not responsible.

Route B

To meet the tour team in Wudang Mountains: Laoying (by car)— South Cliff Palace (on foot)— Betelnut Temple (on foot)— Yellow Dragon Cave (on foot)— Ancient Divine Road (on foot)— Sky Entrance (on foot)— Golden Top (by car)— Qiongtai (by car)— Laoying.

The tourist features of this route:

- On the way from Laoying to South Cliff Palace by car, we can enjoy the beautiful scenery of Wudang Mountains; in South Cliff Palace, we can visit the temples on the cliff, offer incenses on the Dragon-Head Stone, drink the spring water, and worship the gods in Taoism…
- In Betelnut Temple, we can look for the track of Betelnut Immortal; worship Zhang Sanfeng, the founder of Wudang Boxing…

- In Yellow Dragon Cave, we can visit the relics of LiShizhen, the famous doctor of the Ming Dynasty; drink the spring water from the Cliff…
- In Sky Entrance Palace, the boundary of the mortal and the immortal, we can walk into Heaven with all immortals…
- On the Ancient Divine Road, there are dense forests, pleasant flowers, singing birds, and a flight of stone steps…
- On Golden Top, we can visit Golden Palace and Palace of Harmony, and talk about Taoism with Taoists…
- On the way to Zhongguan Temple by tram rail, we are now traveling among the peaks, and then we are floating in the clouds, just like gods…

Accommodation:

- To have lunch on Golden Top (may be on the way).
- To have supper in Laoying.

Relative explanations:

- Zhongguan Temple, an important view-site in this route, is the beginning point of Wudang tram rail. But for the lack of time, we will not stay there.
- When we go for and return to Golden Top, we all take a tram rail for the sake of time.

Relative promises:

- To meet the tour team outside of Wudang Mountains for the sake of clients.
- To provide qualified travel guides with you through the routes.
- To provide best service to you, so as to help you visit all the scenic spots.

Notes:

If there is some certain Force Majeure (natural disaster, changes and error of air and rail, bad weather, political situation, or some rules and regulations made by the government) that leads to extra expenses, the travel agency is not responsible.

9. Wudang Traveling Routes (two-day travel) 武当山旅游线路（二日游）

Route A:

To meet the tour team in Wudang Mountains:

The first day: Laoying (by car)— Crow Hill (on foot)— Betelnut Temple (on foot)— Yellow Dragon Cave (on foot)— Sky Entrance Palace (on foot)— The Ancient Divine Road (on foot)— Sky Entrance (on foot)— Golden Top (by tram rail)— Zhongguan Temple (by car)— South Cliff Palace.

The second day: South Cliff Palace (by car)— Purple Cloud Palace (by car)— Peripatetic Valley (by car)— Crown Prince's Slope (by car)— Rubbing-Needle Well (by car)— Laoying.

The tourist features of the route:

- On the way from Laoying to Crow Hill, we can enjoy the beautiful scenery of Wudang Mountains.

- In Betelnut Temple, we can look for the track of Betelnut Immortal, worship Zhang Sanfeng, the founder of Wudang Boxing.
- In Yellow Dragon Cave, we can visit the relics of Li Shizhen, the famous doctor of the Ming Dynasty; and drink the spring water from the cliff.
- In Sky Entrance Palace, the boundary of the mortal and the immortal, we can walk into heaven with all gods.
- On the Ancient Divine Road, there are full of dense forests, pleasant flowers, singing birds, and a flight of stone steps.
- On Golden Top, we can visit Golden Palace and the Palace of Harmony, talk about Taoism with Wudang Taoists.
- On the way to Zhongguan Temple by tram rail, we are now traveling among peaks and then floating in the clouds, just like gods.
- In South Cliff Palace, we can visit temples on the cliff, offer incenses on the Dragon-Head Stone, drink the spring water and worship gods in Taoism.
- In Purple Cloud Palace, we can have the chance to watch Taoist religion service;
- In Peripatetic Valley, we can play with the monkeys, walk on the hanging bridge and climb the cliff.
- In Crown Prince's Slope, we can appreciate the appearance of God Zhenwu; enjoy the turning of Nine-Turning Yellow River Walls and the wonder of one pillar with twelve beams.
- In Rubbing-Needle Well, we can visit the place where Emperor Zhenwu cultivated and understood the gist of rubbing a pontil into a needle.

Accommodation:

- To have lunch on Golden Top or on the way and in South Cliff Palace.
- To have supper in South Cliff and Laoying.
- To have a sleep on Crow Hill.

Some relative explanations:

- Zhongguan Temple, an important view-site in this route, is the beginning point of Wudang tram rail. But for the lack of time, we will not stay there.
- When we go for and return to Golden Top, we all take a tram rail on the first day for the sake of time.

Relative promises:

- To meet the tour team outside of Wudang Mountains for the sake of clients.
- To provide qualified travel guides with you through the routes.
- To provide best service to you, so as to help you visit all the scenic spots.

Notes:

If there is some certain Force Majeure (natural disaster, changes and error of air and rail, bad weather, political situation, or some rules and regulations made by the government) that leads to extra expenses, the travel agency is not responsible.

Route B:

To meet the tour team in Wudang Mountains:

The first day: Laoying (by car)— Qiongtai (by tram rail)— Golden Top (on foot)— Sky Entrance (on foot)— the Ancient Divine Road (on foot)— Sky Entrance Palace (on foot)— Yellow Dragon Cave (on foot)— Betelnut Temple (on foot)— South Cliff Palace.

The second day: South Cliff Palace (by car)— Purple Cloud Palace (by car)— Peripatetic Valley (by car)— Crown Prince's Slope (by car)— Rubbing-Needle Well (by car)—Laoying.

The tourist features of this route:

- On the way from Laoying to Qiongtai, we can enjoy the beautiful scenery of Wudang Mountains.
- On the way to Golden Top by tram rail, we are now traveling among the peaks and then floating in the clouds, just like gods.
- On Golden Top, we can visit Golden Palace and the Palace of Harmony, talk about Taoism with Wudang Taoists.
- On the Ancient Divine Road, there are full of dense forests, pleasant flowers, singing birds and a flight of stone steps.
- In Sky Entrance Palace, the boundary of the mortal and the immortal, we can go to Heaven with the gods in Taoism.
- In Yellow Dragon Cave, we can visit the relics of Li Shizhen, the famous doctor of the Ming Dynasty; drink the spring water from the cliff.
- In Betelnut Temple, we can look for the track of Betelnut Immortal, and worship Zhang Sanfeng, the founder of Wudang Boxing.
- In South Cliff Palace, we can visit temples on the cliff, offer incenses on the Dragon-Head Stone, drink the spring water and worship gods in Taoism.
- In Purple Cloud Palace, we can have the chance to watch Taoist religion service.
- In Peripatetic Valley, we can play with the monkeys, walk on the hanging bridge and climb the cliff.
- In Crown Prince's Slope, we can appreciate the appearance of God Zhenwu; enjoy the turning of Nine-Turning Yellow River Walls and the wonder of one pillar with twelve beams.
- In Rubbing-Needle Well, we can visit the place where Emperor Zhenwu cultivated and understood the gist of rubbing a pontil into a needle.

Accommodation:

- To have lunch in Golden Top and South Cliff Palace.
- To have supper in South Cliff Palace and Laoying.
- To have a sleep on Crow Hill.

Some relative explanations:

- Zhongguan Temple, an important view-site in this route, is the beginning point of Wudang tram rail. But for the lack of time, we will not stay there.
- When we go for and return to Golden Top, we all take a tram rail on the first day for the sake of time.

Relative promises:

- To meet the tour team outside of Wudang Mountains for the sake of clients.
- To provide qualified travel guides with you through the routes.
- To provide best service to you, so as to help you visit all the scenic spots.

Notes:

If there is some certain Force Majeure (natural disaster, changes and errors of air and rail, bad weather, political situation, or some rules and regulations made by the government) that leads to extra expenses, the travel agency is not responsible.

10. Wudang Traveling Routes (three-day travel) 武当旅游线路（三日游）

Route A:

To meet the tour team in Wudang Mountains:

The first day: Laoying (by car)— Zhongguan Temple (by tram rail)— Golden Top (on foot)— Sky Entrance (on foot)—the Ancient Divine Road (on foot) — Sky Entrance Palace (on foot)— Yellow Dragon Cave (on foot)— Betelnut Temple (on foot)— South Cliff Palace.

The second day: South Cliff Palace (by car)— Purple Cloud Palace (by car)— Peripatetic Valley (by car)— Crown Prince's Slope (by car)— Rubbing-Needle Well (by car)—Laoying.

The third day: Laoying (on foot)— Yuxu Palace (by car)— Yuanhe Temple (by car)— Xuanyue Gate (by car)— Chongxu Temple (on foot)— Laoying.

The tourist features of this route:

- On the way from Laoying to Qiongtai by car, we can enjoy the beautiful scenery of Wudang Mountains.
- On the way to Golden Top by tram rail, we are now traveling among the peaks, and then we are floating in the clouds, just like gods…
- On Golden Top, we can visit Golden Palace and Palace of Harmony, and talk about Taoism with Taoists…
- On the Ancient Divine Road, there are full of dense forests, pleasant flowers, singing birds and a flight of stone steps.
- In Sky Entrance Palace, the boundary of the mortal and the immortal, we can go to Heaven with the gods in Taoism.
- In Yellow Dragon Cave, we can visit the relics of Li Shizhen, the famous doctor of the Ming Dynasty; drink the spring water from the cliff.
- In Betelnut Temple, we can look for the track of Betelnut Immortal, and worship Zhang Sanfeng, the founder of Wudang Boxing.
- In South Cliff Palace, we can visit temples on the cliff, offer incenses on the Dragon-Head Stone, drink the spring water and worship gods in Taoism.
- In Purple Cloud Palace, we can have the chance to watch Taoist religion service.
- In Peripatetic Valley, we can play with the monkeys, walk on the hanging bridge and climb the cliff.

- In Crown Prince's Slope, we can appreciate the appearance of God Zhenwu; enjoy the turning of Nine-Turning Yellow River Walls and the wonder of one pillar with twelve beams; in Rubbing-Needle Well, we can visit the place where Emperor Zhenwu cultivated and understood the gist of rubbing a pontil into a needle.
- In Laoying view-site, we can visit the biggest temple relic of Yuxu Palace, Wudang Taoist prison, Yuanhe Temple, and the beautiful stone torii Xuanyue Gate.

Accommodation:

- To have lunch on Golden Top, in South Cliff Palace, and in Laoying.
- To have supper in South Cliff Palace, and in Laoying.
- To have a sleep on Crow Hill the first day, in Laoying the second day.

Some relative explanations:

- Zhongguan Temple, an important view-site in this route, is the beginning point of Wudang tram rail. But for the lack of time, we will not stay there.
- When we go for and return to Golden Peak, we all take a tram rail on the first day for the sake of time.

Relative promises:

- To meet the tour team outside of Wudang Mountains for the sake of clients.
- To provide qualified travel guides with you through the routes.
- To provide best service to you, so as to help you visit all the scenic spots.

Notes:

If there is some certain Force Majeure (natural disaster, changes and errors of air and rail, bad weather, political situation, or some rules and regulations made by the government) that leads to extra expenses, the travel agency is not responsible.

Route B:

To meet the tour team in Wudang Mountains:

The first day: Laoying (by car)— Zhongguan Temple (by tram rail)— Golden Top (on foot)— Sky Entrance (on foot)— the Ancient Divine Road (on foot)— Sky Entrance Palace (on foot)— Yellow Dragon Cave (on foot)— Betelnut Temple (on foot)— South Cliff Palace.

The second day: South Cliff Palace (by car)— Purple Cloud Palace (by car)— Peripatetic Valley (by car)— Crown Prince's Slope (by car)— Rubbing-Needle Well (by car)— Laoying.

The third day: Laoying (by car)— Danjiangkou City (by car)— Laoying.

The tourist features of this route:

- On the way from Laoying to Qiongtai by car, we can enjoy the beautiful scenery of Wudang Mountains.
- On the way to Golden Peak by tram rail, we are now traveling among the peaks, and then we are floating in the clouds, just like gods…
- On Golden Top, we can visit Golden Palace and Palace of Harmony, and talk about Taoism with Taoists…
- On the Ancient Divine Road, there are full of dense forests, pleasant flowers, singing birds and

a flight of stone steps.

- In Sky Entrance Palace, the boundary of the mortal and the immortal, we can go to Heaven with the gods in Taoism.
- In Yellow Dragon Cave, we can visit the relics of Li Shizhen, the famous doctor of the Ming Dynasty; drink the spring water from the cliff.
- In Betelnut Temple, we can look for the track of Betelnut Immortal, worship Zhang Sanfeng, the founder of Wudang Boxing.
- In South Cliff Palace, we can visit temples on the cliff, offer incenses on the Dragon-Head Stone, drink the spring water and worship gods in Taoism.
- In Purple Cloud Palace, we can have the chance to watch Taoist religion service.
- In Peripatetic Valley, we can play with the monkeys, walk on the hanging bridge and climb the cliff.
- In Crown Prince's Slope, we can appreciate the appearance of God Zhenwu; enjoy the turning of Nine-Turning Yellow River Walls and the wonder of one pillar with twelve beams; in Rubbing-Needle Well, we can visit the place where Emperor Zhenwu cultivated and understood the gist of rubbing a pontil into a needle.
- In Danjiangkou City, we can visit Danjiangkou Reservoir, the biggest man-made lake in Asia, also the beginning point of the mid-line project of China Water South-to-North Transmission.

Accommodation:

- To have lunch on Golden Top, in South Cliff Palace, and in Danjiangkou City.
- To have supper in South Cliff Palace and in Laoying.
- To have a sleep on Crow Hill the first day, then in Laoying the second day.

Some relative explanations:

- Zhongguan Temple, an important view-site in this route, is the beginning point of Wudang tram rail. But for the lack of time, we will not stay there.
- When we go for and return to Golden Peak, we all take a tram rail on the first day for the sake of time.

Relative promises:

- To meet the tour team outside of Wudang Mountains for the sake of clients.
- To provide qualified travel guides with you through the routes.
- To provide best service to you, so as to help you visit all the scenic spots.

Notes:

If there is some certain Force Majeure (natural disaster, changes and errors of air and rail, bad weather, political situation, or some rules and regulations made by the government) that leads to extra expenses, the travel agency is not responsible.

11. Wudang Traveling Routes (four-day travel) 武当山旅游线路（四日游）

Route A:

To meet the tour team in Wudang Mountains (the team number should be less than 15, and the numbers should all be healthy and able to walk a long way).

The first day: Laoying (by car)— Crown Prince's Slope (by car)— Peripatetic Valley (by car)— Purple Cloud Palace (by car)— South Cliff Palace.

The second day: South Cliff Palace (by car)— Zhongguan Temple (by tram rail)— Golden Top (on foot)— Sky Entrance (on foot)— the Ancient Divine Road (on foot)— Sky Entrance Palace (on foot)— Yellow Dragon Cave (on foot)— Betelnut Temple (on foot)— South Cliff Palace.

The third day: South Cliff Palace (on foot)— Shang Yuan (on foot)— Zhong Yuan (on foot)— Xia Yuan (on foot)— Five-Dragon Palace (on foot)— Pure Sunshine Cliff, Lingxu Cliff, Pray-Realizing Cliff, Five-Dragon Peak (at the choice of health and time).

The fourth day: Five-Dragon Palace (on foot)— Hermit Cliff (on foot)— Divine Mother's Temple (on foot)— Benevolence and Reverence Temple (on foot)— Haokou Village (by car)— Laoying.

<u>The tourist features of this route</u>:

- The first day: on Crow Prince's Slope, we can appreciate the appearance of God Zhenwu; enjoy the turning of Nine-Turning Yellow River Walls and the wonder of one pillar with twelve beams; in Peripatetic Valley, we can play with the monkeys, walk on the hanging bridge and climb the cliff; in Purple Cloud Palace, we can have the chance to watch Taoist religion service; in South Cliff Palace, we can visit the palaces on the cliff, offer incenses on the Dragon-Head Stone, drink the spring water and worship the Gods in Taoism...
- The second day: on the way from Laoying to Qiongtai by car, we can enjoy the beautiful scenery of Wudang Mountains; on the way to Golden Top by tram rail, we are now traveling among the peaks, and then we are floating in the clouds, just like gods; on Golden Top, we can visit Golden Palace and Palace of Harmony, and talk about Taoism with Taoists; on the Ancient Divine Road, there are full of dense forests, pleasant flowers, singing birds and a flight of stone steps; in Betelnut Temple, we can look for the track of Betelnut Immortal, and worship Zhang Sanfeng, the founder of Wudang Boxing;
- The third day: we can explore the secret of hermits in the caves, visit the relics of ancient hermits; and appreciate the grandeur of Five-Dragon Palace;
- The fourth day: we can visit many temples and caves where immortals and Taoists cultivated; travel in the national level Forest Park.

<u>Accommodation</u>:

- To have lunch in a farmer's home, then on Golden Top, and the other two on the way.
- To have supper in South Cliff Palace, and Laoying.
- To have two night on Crow Hill, the third night in Five-Dragon Palace.

<u>Some relative explanations</u>:

- Zhongguan Temple, an important view-site in this route, is the beginning point of Wudang tram rail. But for the lack of time, we will not stay there.

- When we go for and return to Golden Top, we all take a tram rail on the first day for the sake of time.
- This route is very long, so the traveler should be healthy and follow the guide.

Relative promises:

- To meet the tour team outside of Wudang Mountains for the sake of clients.
- To provide qualified travel guides with you through the routes.
- To provide best service to you, so as to help you visit all the scenic spots.

Notes:

If there is some certain Force Majeure (natural disaster, changes and errors of air and rail, bad weather, political situation, or some rules and regulations made by the government) that leads to extra expenses, the travel agency is not responsible.

Route B

The first day: Laoying (by car)— Zhongguan Temple (by tram rail)— Golden Top (on foot)— Sky Entrance (on foot)— the Ancient Divine Road (on foot)— Sky Entrance Palace (on foot)— Yellow Dragon Cave (on foot)— Betlenut Temple (on foot)— South Cliff Palace.

The second day: South Cliff Palace (by car)— Purple Cloud Palace (by car)— Peripatetic Valley (by car)— Crown Prince's Slope (by car)— Rubbing-Needle Well — Laoying.

The third day: Laoying (on foot)— Yuxu Palace (by car)— Yuanhe Temple (by car)— Xuanyue Gate (on foot)— Chongxu Temple (by car)— Laoying.

The fourth day: Laoying (by car)— Danjiangkou City (by car)— Laoying.

The tourist features of this route:

- The first day: on the way from Laoying to Qiongtai by car, we can enjoy the beautiful scenery of Wudang Mountains; on the way to Golden Top by tram rail, we are now traveling among the peaks, and then we are floating in the clouds, just like gods; on Golden Top, we can visit Golden Palace and Palace of Harmony, and talk about Taoism with Taoists; on the Ancient Divine Road, there are full of dense forests, pleasant flowers, singing birds and a flight of stone steps; in Yellow Dragon Cave, we can visit the relics of Li Shizhen, the famous doctor of the Ming Dynasty; and drink the spring water from the cliff; in Betelnut Temple, we can look for the track of Betelnut Immortal, and worship Zhang Sanfeng, the founder of Wudang Boxing.
- The second day: in South Cliff Palace, we can visit the palaces on the cliff, offer incenses on the Dragon-Head Stone, drink the spring water and worship the Gods in Taoism; in Purple Cloud Palace, we can have the chance to watch Taoist religion service; in Peripatetic Valley, we can play with the monkeys, walk on the hanging bridge and climb the cliff; on Crown Prince's Slope, we can appreciate the appearance of God Zhenwu; enjoy the turning of Nine-Turning Yellow River Walls and the wonder of one pillar with twelve beams; in Rubbing-Needle Well, we can visit the place where Emperor Zhenwu cultivated and understood the gist of rubbing a pontil into a needle.
- The third day: in Laoying view-site, we can visit the biggest palace relics, Yuxu Palace, Wudang Taoist prison Yuanhe Temple, the best stone torii, Xuanyue Gate.

- The fourth day: in Danjiangkou City, we can visit Danjiangkou Reservoir, the biggest man-made lake in Asia, also the beginning point of the mid-line project of China Water South-to-North Transmission.

Accommodation:

- To have lunch in Golden Top, a farmer's home, Laoying and Danjiangkou City.
- To have one supper in South Cliff Palace, and the other three in Laoying.
- To have a night on Crow Hill, and the other two in Laoying.

Some relative explanations:

- Zhongguan Temple, an important view-site in this route, is the beginning point of Wudang tram rail. But for the lack of time, we will not stay there.
- When we go for and return to Golden Top, we all take a tram rail on the first day for the sake of time.

Relative promises:

- To meet the tour team outside of Wudang Mountains for the sake of clients.
- To provide qualified travel guides with you through the routes.
- To provide best service to you, so as to help you visit all the scenic spots.

Notes:

If there is some certain Force Majeure (natural disaster, changes and errors of air and rail, bad weather, political situation, or some rules and regulations made by the government) that leads to extra expenses, the travel agency is not responsible.

12. Exploring Travel in Wudang Mountains (four days) 武当山探险游（四日）

To meet the tour team in Wudang Mountains (the team number should be less than 10, and the members should be healthy and able to walk a long time).

The first day: Laoying (by car)— Haokou Village (on foot)— Five-Dragon Palace.

The tourist features of the route: along the Ancient Divine Road, we can visit the national level Forest Park, Benevolence and Reverence Temple, Hermit Cliff, Divine Mother's Temple; after visiting Five-Dragon Palace, we can chose to visit Five-Dragon Palace, Taoist Grave, Lingxu Cliff, Pure Sunshine Cliff, Pray-realizing Cliff, Five-Dragon Peak in accordance with the strength of the team members.

The second day: Five-Dragon Palace (on foot)— South Cliff Palace.

The tourist features of this route: on the way to South Cliff Palace, we can visit Xia Yuan, Zhong Yuan, Shang Yuan, Black Tiger Temple and other ancient buildings, and South Cliff.

The third day: South Cliff Palace (on foot)— Golden Top.

The tourist features of the route: along the Ancient Divine Road, we can visit Yellow Dragon Cave, Sky Entrance Palace, Meeting Immortals Bridge, Sky Entrance, Worshiping Gate, then get to Golden Top and the Palace of Harmony.

The fourth day: Golden Top (on foot)— Lüjiahe Village (by car)— Laoying.

The tourist features of this route: on the way to Lüjiahe Village, the first Folk Song Village of

China's Han Nationality, we can visit Miaohua Cliff, Qingwei Palace, and Wudang Gorge.

Accommodation:

- To have lunch on the way to Five-Dragon Palace, in South Cliff Palace, and on the way to Laoying.
- To have supper in some certain temple or a farmer's home, in South Cliff Palace, on Golden Peak, in Lüjiahe Village or Laoying.
- To have the first night in Five-Dragon Palace, the second in South Cliff Palace, and the third on Golden Top.

Some explanations:

- The team number should be less than 10, and the members should be healthy and able to walk a long time.
- All the members should follow the guide, please not leave the team halfway by oneself.

Relative promises:

- To meet the tour team outside of Wudang Mountains for the sake of clients.
- To provide qualified travel guides with you through the routes.
- To provide best service to you, so as to help you visit all the scenic spots.

Notes:

If there is some certain Force Majeure (natural disaster, changes and errors of air and rail, bad weather, political situation, or some rules and regulations made by the government) that leads to extra expenses, the travel agency is not responsible.

13. Relevant Tourist Lines Recommended 旅游线路推荐

Wudang Mountains — Xi'an City, Shaanxi Province

Wudang Ancient Buildings Complex, China Terracotta Warriors and Horses, one is the holy mountain in the world, the other is underground kingdom. Both of them have profound Chinese culture connotations, attracting the attentions of all the people in the world.

Wudang Mountains — Beijing City

"Build Wudang Mountains in the south, the Imperial Palace in the north." The same Emperor of the Ming Dynasty built the two large royal building complexes at the same time, which demonstrated the highest level of China's architecture art of all dynasties.

Wudang Mountains — Mount Emei, Sichuan Province

One is the holy land of Taoism; the other is immortal kingdom of Buddhism. To visit the two famous religious mountains at the same time, appreciated their miraculous charms of Taoism and Buddhism…

Wudang Mountains — Shaolin Temple, Henan Province

Shaolin Boxing is to charge the opponent by the tough acts and defeat him with bravery; Wudang Boxing is to charge the opponent by the gentle acts and control him with stillness. Wudang Mountains and Shaolin Temple are the cradles of Chinese martial art…

Wudang Mountains — Shennongjia Forest — The Three Gorges

The biggest ancient buildings group of China Taoism, the mystery green treasury in the country, and the most attractive landscape gallery in the great Changjiang River are the best places to visit.

14. Some Notices in Wudang Mountains 武当山的一些注意事项

Notes When Consuming in Wudang Mountains 景区消费注意事项

- Please not buy anything in the shops without a business license.
- Please not buy any "antique" or "curio" unless you are a connoisseur.
- Please not believe the legend of "man-shaped Reshow" "one-thousand-year lingzhi", which are once in a blue moon.
- Please buy something after you have set the bargain and remember to ask the invoice.
- Please ask for help from the Bureau of Business Management when your interests are damaged.
- When your interests are damaged, please dial 110, and remember to do the following:

  1) remember the name and number of the shop.

  2) remember the place, time and process of the case.

  3) tell your guide your location, and your telephone.

  4)wait for the executive officials to deal with the case.

Notes When Choosing a Travel Agency 挑选旅行社注意事项

- Please make sure whether the travel agency provides many kinds of choices and the travel plan is detailed or not. The travel plan, or the travel arrangement, should involve information on accommodation, meal, and view-site and so on; the more detailed, the better. Besides, the more detailed, the less possibility for the travel agency to change the arrangement at a will.
- Please make sure whether the travel plan is reasonable or not.
- Please make sure how many view-sites and meals contained in the travel agency fees, and how many things done by yourself. And also you should know the ticket contains just one or all gates, less that there will be some arguments.
- Please make sure that what the standard of meal is, for meal is the most important thing when outdoors. When you know the standard, you can imagine what kind of meal you will have, and you can have a measure to ask for refund if the travel agency has not arranged the meal for some reasons.
- Please make sure the name, location, and standard of the hotels.
- Please make sure that what kind of transportation vehicles you will have, imported cars, or home-made cars, and the types of cars, which will play a great role in your comfort during the travel.

Notes When Exploring in Wudang Mountains 武当山探险游注意事项

- Please know all things about the travel line, arrange all things well and get all things ready for start.

- Please have some certain knowledge and skills on self-help visiting. For instance, the best seasons to visit Wudang Mountains are spring and autumn; but there will be rainstorms in these seasons, for escaping, you mustn't stay in a deep valley for fear of a flood or a cliff for fear of a landslide.
- Please visit Wudang Mountains with others, not a single, for visiting alone consists of many inconvenient and unsafe factors.
- Please be careful in choosing the travel lines; do not get far away from the main road.
- Please arrange your time reasonably so that you can come back before the evening.
- Please make good preparations against the stings or spites of mosquito, snake and other things like.
- Please pay more attention to your wearing: the shoes should be skidding-proof and the clothes and trousers should be covered all your body, for fear of sliding and being wounded.
- Please take enough food and water, not eat any mushrooms or unknown fruits.
- Please take your communication means or other things to call for help (such as flashlight, whistle, horn), and medicines for first aids.
- Please not hunt, make a fire in the field, collect specimen, or leave wastes in the mountain.

Notes When Climbing the Mountain on Foot 徒步登山注意事项

- Please wear sports shoes, traveling shoes, or rubber-soled cloth shoes, but not leather shoes, new shoes, or sandals.
- Please climb at a reasonable speed, not be so anxious that run or jump, which will make you tired and hurt.
- Please climb on the stone steps, not on the mountain slope, for the sake of safety and easiness; you can have several times' rest, but the rest time should be less than 10 minutes each time.
- Please concentrate on climbing, not look here and there, for fear of sliding. A saying goes in Wudang Mountains like this: "when walking, not enjoy the scenery; when enjoying the scenery, not walk."
- Please remember to take with you some heavy clothes and umbrella, or raincoat because that the weather here is full of changes and the wind here is also strong. And remember not open the umbrella in the place with a draught lest taking you away.
- Please buy a crutch if you are middle-aged or old-aged, which will help a lot when climbing.
- Please remember to ask the way if you don't know how to go, not have a try by yourself.
- Please keep the pace, often have a rest, and drink something containing salt if you are not so strong.

The Rights You Have When You Travel 享有的权利

In accordance with the 24th Article in the 4th Section of Traveling Management Regulations of Hubei Province, the travelers have the following rights:

- To know the real conditions of traveling service, and have the right to ask the travel agency to provide the information on service contents, standard, and fees.
- To have the right to choose the travel agency, service ways, and service contents.

- To enjoy relative service in accordance with the agreement.
- To have the protections of your personal property and safety.
- To have the respect in your personality, folk customs, and religious belief.
- To enjoy other reasonable rights during the traveling.

The Duties You Have When You Travel 应履行的义务

In accordance with the 26th Article in the 4th Section of Traveling Management Regulations of Hubei Province, the travelers should fulfil the following duties:

- To observe social morality.
- To protect tourist resources, infrastructures, and environment.
- To respect the native folk customs, and religion belief.
- To observe the rules and regulations on traveling sequence, safety, and sanitation.
- To fulfill the agreement between you and the travel agency.
- To fulfill the other duties you should according to the relative laws.

Notes When You Visit Halls and Temples 游览道教宫观注意事项

Wudang Mountains is a famous Taoist mountain where the Taoist organizations have their own beliefs and custom taboos, so the travelers should pay more attention to respecting these, which can't be overlooked, or the incorrect behaviors will hurt Taoists and arouse unhappiness. The travelers must remember the following notes:

- To greet these Taoists "Sir", or "Master", but not "Taoist", or other insulting terms; as to the old nuns, you should greet them "Sir", "Master", but not "Antie", or "grandma".
- To show your respect by ways of crossing your hands to the stomach and then lowering the head, but not shaking hands, hugging, touching Taoist heads or other unsuitable actions.
- Not to talk about age, birthday, or marriage with Taoists, or they will be unhappy.
- Not to interrupt them when the Taoists are having meal, reading scriptures, and cultivating.
- Not to talk loudly, discuss or comment the offerings and deities in the halls and temples, especially, not to tough or point these deities. You should leave quietly when there is a religious service.

Notes When Visiting Wudang Mountains 游览武当山注意事项

- The travelers should protect cultural relics and trees and flowers in the scenic spots; not to write or inscribe on the relics, damage trees and flowers and ancient buildings, or hurt wild animals.
- Please not to take photos in the halls and temples in accordance with the cultural relics laws.
- Please not to smoke in non-smoking zone.
- Please keep the sanitation of view-site, not leave any wastes.
- Please observe social morality and do everything in a gentle way.

Shopping Guarantee 购物保障

- If you meet some troubles in shopping, please connect with Customer Service Department by service hotline or by E-mail, which will deal with the trouble that you meet in shopping.
- If the goods you have ordered are not received on time, please connect with Customer Service Department by service hotline or by E-mail, which will inquire it about at once and give you a

prompt answer.

- If the goods you have received are too damaged to use, please post them back to us, we will exchange them for you free of charges, and also we will compensate your post fees.
- If you have some troubles in using the goods, please connect with us in time, we will be ready to help you.

Tel: 0719—8658637 Fax: 0719—8658637 E-mail: chinawudang@china.com

Notes to Shopping 购物提示

- If you are going to buy some works of modern calligraphy, painting, and sealing cutting, please acquaint yourself with the information of the author at first, then connect with him and bargain the price.
- If you want some pictures of Wudang Mountains for commercial use, please make sure the names of the pictures, then remit money to us in accordance with the tag prices. When we receive your remittance, we will post your pictures by E-mail.
- If you want some books, picture collections, souvenirs of Wudang Mountains, please make sure the names of the pictures, then remit money to us in accordance with the tag prices. When we receive your remittance, we will post these you want through post office.
- Most of the video products provided by our net are teaching materials for Wudang Martial Art, Wudang Regimen, accompanied with performances and skills explanations, which are manufactured, owned, traded only by China Wudang Net. If you want some teaching material please make sure the names of the pictures, then remit money to us in accordance with the tag prices. When we receive your remittance, we will post these you want through post office.

Chapter 6 Ancient Buildings in Wudang Mountains 武当山古建筑

The ancient buildings in Wudang Mountains have been famous in the world for their beauty, size, and grandeur, so that Wudang Mountains was listed World Cultural Legacy by UNESCO on December 17, 1994.

Most of the ancient buildings, devised and planed in accordance with the legend of Emperor Zhenwu's self-cultivation, assembled all the traditional building skills, and revealed that feudal emperors' rightful power and great and solemn Heaven. They also have shown that Taoism worships Nature, to the extent of contributing great and beautiful royal palaces, mysterious and wonderful Taoism, quiet and classic gardens, and other features. The ancient buildings, the reflection of ancient scheme, plan and architecture, are also a wonder in the history of world buildings, especially the highly harmonious unity of artificial buildings and natural landscapes, gives reason to surprise all the people in the world.

The Golden Top, the soul and symbol of Wudang Mountains, is also the symbol of Wudang Taoism's growing to the peak under the support of the royal families. Here you can enjoy Chinese traditional buildings, smelting and foundry, and also the fantastic natural wonders and enchanting legends.

The South Cliff, the main scenic spot in Wudang Mountains where are full of changing views, is the best combined building between artificial and natural views among the 36 cliffs in Wudang Mountains. Especially, when evening coming, the lights here become a new interesting view.

The Purple Cloud scenic spot, full of green pine trees and cypresses, and with a comfortable climate, has been called the home of gods. The buildings here, solemnly arranged, spaciously set out, are imbued with the royal atmosphere of Taoist rites. Statues of gods worshiped in the halls and temples, tables, offerings, and sacrificial service ceremony are forming the mysterious world of god.

The Five-Dragon scenic spot, full of deep and tense forests, is mysterious and primordial so that it has been called the place of pray-realizing. That many famous Taoists came here to cultivate and succeeded in cultivation and the royal families of the Tang Dynasty ordered to build Taoist halls and temples is a testimony to the development of Wudang Taoism.

Ancient building masters made full use of the mountain shapes and topography, so that all the buildings here are cleverly and harmoniously displayed, each with a sense of mystery. Here are everlasting springs, quiet and restful, which makes all visitors reluctant to leave.

Laoying, the base from which the Ming Dynasty built upon Wudang Mountains, is full of scenic spots and places of interest. Now, as the center of politics, economy, and culture of Wudang Mountains Special Economic Zone of Tourism, Laoying is the starting point of a visit to Wudang Mountains and the center for visitors to stay. It has beautiful scenery, is simple and honest in folk style, convenient in transportation, and complete in its range of community buildings.

Taoist Palaces and Temples 道教宫观

During the Ming Dynasty, the emperors ordered to build Wudang Mountains in a large scale, so there built the Palace of Harmony, Qingwei Palace, Purple Cloud palace, Sky Entrance Palace, South Cliff Palace, Five-Dragon Palace, Yuxu Palace, Jingle Palace, Meeting God Palace, and Benevolence and Reverence Temple, Head-Turning Temple, Spring Temple, Fuzhen Temple, Yuanhe Temple, which, with the other nunneries, pavilions, and bridges, formed a large Taoist ancient building complex in the famous Wudang Mountains.

"Palaces", the place for the emperors and gods to live in, are most of the religious buildings ordered to build by the emperors. "Temples", also called towers, formerly referred to the ancient places to climb up and have a wider view and the places to meet gods. Later, people name all Taoist buildings palaces and temples.

Taoist palaces and temples, the places for Taoists to worship gods and practice their self-cultivation, developed from Chinese traditional palaces and halls, god temples, and altars. So Taoist palaces and temples did not only inherit Chinese traditional building theories, arrangements and methods, but also added Taoist aesthetic and value theories in their arrangements, body style and structure, which formed their own style.

The halls to worship Taoist Gods, the founder of Taoism were set on the central axes in all Taoist palaces and temples; the side halls to worship other gods were on the both sides. This kind of symmetrical arrangement demonstrated Chinese ranking theory that the most respective sits in the middle. Symmetrical buildings also demonstrated the kind of aesthetic taste to pursue peace and safety, and keep steady-going and solemn.

Most of Taoist palaces and temples were built in proportion with one and another yards, forming row upon row of development trend. For, Taoism thought that this kind arrangement can collect vitality and meet all gods from all directions, and also easy to distinguish the ranks of gods.

Wudang Taoist palaces and temples were built in accordance with the mountain shapes, with a single building yard as a unit, and with the set axes to connect all these changing building groups, which made these palaces and temples have many changes among the symmetrical arrangements, but the former don't harm the latter's whole building style. This kind of building group, proceeding forward step by step, stood out the artistic result of building space, making the building grander.

All the Grand Halls of Wudang Taoist palaces and temples were built under a very high building rule, such as the eaves protruding a lot and winding upward, swan's kiss and decorations on the backs making charming curves, which made the heavy roofs charming and elegant. Especially the platforms under the heavy walls and in front of the solemn halls, made the whole building solemn and steady, forming a kind of harmonious beauty between the straight and the curve, the dynamic and the static, the tough and the tender.

Most of Taoist palaces and temples in Wudang Mountains were built among the forests, surrounded by deep valley, ancient trees and weeping vines, which provided good places for Taoists to approach the nature so as to return to the simplicity and practice their self-cultivation, also the best places for the followers of Taoism and visitors to have a visit.

Golden Hall (Golden Top) 金殿

Golden Hall is located on the top of Heavenly Pillar Peak, the highest mountain in Wudang Mountains. That the hall was made of copper and decorated by gold with multi-eaves in the form of a hall, was the highest rank of building theory that only the emperors had the right to use during that time.

Golden Hall is 4.4 meters wide, 3.15 meters deep, and 5.54 meters high. There are twelve big beams on which laid other small building structures, two dragons facing each other on the two sides of the ridge, weeping and round eaves on which decorated with immortals, dragons, phoenixes, sky-horses and other lively looking birds and animals.

Golden Hall was made of copper, but all the pillars, beams, tiles, eaves, windows and doors were carved with beautiful pictures. In accordance with the history, the ancient people first founded small parts, then installed them into a whole, Golden Hall. All the parts connected each other perfectly, without any signs of artificial carving, just like made by gods.

Experienced nearly 600 years' corroding of cold winters, hot summers, wind, rain, thunder and lightening, Golden Hall is still as bright as before. So it is worth considering as the treasure of Chinese traditional copper foundry.

Copper Hall (of the Yuan Dynasty) 铜殿

The Copper Hall on the top of Small Lotus Peak, the earliest copper hall of the Yuan Dynasty preserved in China, was founded in the early years of the 14th century, which is the valuable object to research copper foundry of the Yuan Dynasty.

The Copper Hall was formerly put on the top of Heavenly Pillar peak, naming Golden Hall. Later, when Emperor Yongle of the Ming Dynasty ordered to build Wudang Mountains in a large scale, he thought it small in size, so founded another big one, and moved the Copper Hall of the Yuan Dynasty to Small Lotus Peak.

The Copper Hall was finished founding in the 11th year of Emperor Dade in Wuhan City, the capital of Hubei Province. The hall is 2.44 meters high, 2.165 meters deep and wide. There are posies on the walls to narrate the names of Taoists who had collected money for the hall and names and addresses of Taoist believers who had offered money to the hall.

The Copper Hall, transferred from Heavenly Pillar peak, so was also named Zhuanyun Hall. In Chinese, Zhuanyun means that the luck is turning for better, so there added one more view in Golden Top. It is said that if people walk around the hall, their luck would turn for better, so all the visitors would like to walk around the hall when they visit Golden Top.

Tin Hall 锡殿

The Hall of Official Wang on the top of Golden Top, is a tin hall made in the Ming Dynasty.

This wood-like building in the form of a hall was like a model, small but exquisite, made of tin. It is the only one building made of tin found in Wudang Mountains, so it is very precious. Its matured foundry and beautiful shape are the testimony of Chinese application of tin in the 15th century.

Official Wang, in the system of Taoist gods, is the god to guard the Mountain Entrance, observe the altar and supervise the rules, who settles the disputes both in heaven and on the earth. The Hall of Official Wang in front of Golden Hall plays a special role in baptizing the visitors for the last time.

Stone Hall 石殿

Stone Hall, one of the famous buildings in Wudang Mountains, is also named Taiyi Zhenqing Palace. It is said that when Emperor Zhenwu succeeded in cultivation and flied into heaven, he lived in a place called Taiyi Zhenqing Palace. So we can say that Stone Hall was built for him by his followers in the mortal world.

The Stone Hall is a miracle among Chinese ancient buildings. Its wood-like structure, and all the building parts were carved from large blue stones and then installed into a whole building. On the wall, there inscribed four Chinese characters which means “A Miracle in the World”.

The Stone Hall, accurately devised and subtly inscribed, was built on the steep cliff, whose large project and difficulties are beyond humans' imagination. So it is considered as one artistic curiosity of Chinese ancient large stone building.

The hall was built in the Yuan Dynasty, whose construction lasted for 27 years. The builder of the hall was Zhang Shouqing, a famous Wudang Taoist, who came in Wudang Mountains at the age of thirty, led the Taoists to plant trees and carve cliffs, and left the later generations the Stone Hall, a miracle in the world.

Wooden Hall 木殿

The Grand Hall of Purple Cloud Palace, built in the Song Dynasty, is located at the foot of Flag-Stretching Peak in Wudang Mountains. The wood-made Taoist ancient building of supporting beam structure, making use of the fall of mountain shape, was built on a three-layer platform, which made it grander and more magnificent.

The Grand Hall, the only one hall of multi-eaves and mountain-like structure that preserved in Wudang Mountains, is very wide and deep and with green tiles and red walls. All the beams in the hall were carved with pictures; the hall was decorated in a simple and unsophisticated way; the arrangements in the hall were solemn and rarefied; the ridge was decorated with all kinds of birds and animals; the eaves were decorated with four flying dragons and four phoenixes; which all made the hall solemn and miraculous.

That Purple Cloud Palace was the place for the royal families to pray for good fortune made its arrangement solemn and furnishings rarefied. The gods and immortals worshiped in the hall, and divine tables, offerings, tools for religious service formed the miraculous world of gods. The emperors of the Song, Yuan, Ming, Qing dynasties often set orders to pray for a good harvest and a peaceful and steady reign in the hall.

Brick Hall 砖殿

The halls and temples made of bricks in Wudang Mountains are most distributing in the area of Five-Dragon Palace. Most built in the caves, so they are not big. Brick halls, most of wood-like structure, were accurately devised and symmetrically built. This kind of building feature fully demonstrated Taoist aesthetic theory to pursue for steadiness, self-control and quietness.

Some experts, judging from the shape and building feature of the hall, thought that the hall was built in the Song or Yuan Dynasty and that it is the important object to study Wudang Taoist buildings.

During the Song and Yuan dynasties, many profound Taoists came into Wudang Mountains to practice their self-cultivation, for they wanted to be away from the mortal world. Later, their students or followers set up temples to worship them where they cultivated.

The Wall 城墙

Golden Hall was built on the top of Heavenly Pillar Peak in 1416. Three years later, Emperor Cheng set an order to build a wall named Purple Gold Wall around Golden Top and demanded that the construction of the wall around Golden Top should follow the fall of mountain shapes, without any changes of the mountain and that the wall be strong and steady.

The construction lasted five years. The 344 meters long wall, made of one-thousand-Jin heavy stones, is standing on the steep cliffs, but strong and steady; winding around Golden Top, just like an aura encircling Golden Top, making the visitors surprise at its magnificence and grandeur.

In the wall there are four stone-carved entrances in the four directions, which represent Sky Entrances in Heaven. The four entrances, standing on steep cliff and facing forward, demonstrate the solemnity of the world of gods.

There once had a saying like that "The Imperial Palace is in the north, Purple Gold Wall in the south". The Imperial Palace was the place for the royal families to live in. Purple Gold Wall here referred to Golden Top in Wudang Mountains. So we can understand that at that time Wudang Mountains had an important status same to the Imperial Palace in Beijing.

Sky Entrance （神道）天门

There built three great Sky Entrances in the ancient divine road to Golden Top of Wudang Mountains. The three Sky Entrances, made of bricks and stones, with green tiles and red walls, are standing in order among thousands of stone steps and guardrails. Surrounded by floating fogs and color clouds, they are grand in vigor.

That the ancient builders built three Sky Entrances in the ancient divine road is full of miracles. The Sky Entrances, the main gate to enter into Heaven, whose grandeur and steadiness foiled the solemnity of the world of gods, made the visitors have deeper and deeper respect for gods. At the same time, when the visitors suddenly find the great Sky Entrances standing in front of them after a period of hard traveling, they will be excited and full of energy, which is the sublimation of aesthetic taste. In accordance with the records, when the visitors came to the Sky Entrances, they used to feel excited and shout joyfully, whose echoes lasting for a very long time.

Ba-Shaped Mountain Gate 八字门

All the high-ranking gates of the palaces and temples in Wudang Mountains were built in the Ba-shape structure. (here Ba is one of Chinese character, 八, eight.)

Ba-shape mountain gate, the masterpiece of the Ming Dynasty, was composed of the three parts: base, wall, and tile roof. There are elliptical embossing of double phoenixes or roses in the middle and in the four corners of the wall, as lively as living, showing the high artistic level of earth foundry.

Ba-shape mountain gate, the important symbol of royal buildings in Wudang Mountains, is great and imposing so as to be seen five kilometers away, which does not only demonstrate the solemnity and seriousness of royal power, but also has the miracle and mystery of god's power, making visitors be imbued with piety.

Five-Cloud Building 五云楼

Five-Cloud building, usually is the place for Taoists to live in, have an important status in Taoist palaces and temples in Wudang Mountains. For instance, there once built Swan Building, Cloud Building, Sky Lake Building in Palace of Harmony.

Five-Cloud Building on Crown Prince's Slope is the highest wooden building preserved in Wudang Mountains, with five stories. Ancient people conformed to the cliff and built the building, without a digging here, achieving the double effects both in whole arrangement and practicability.

When you enter into the building, you will find there are full of changes: all the halls and rooms, devised in accordance with the mountain shape, are vagarious in structure and changing. There is one big pillar on which laying twelve beams standing up to the top floor, which is a miracle in Wudang Mountains. Architect home and abroad and visitors all speak highly of consummate craftsmanship involved in the building.

The Bridge　桥（剑河桥）

The ancient buildings in Wudang Mountains were built among the mountains and the valleys, so it was necessary to build bridges to connect with them. It is said that there are sixteen famous stone bridges and lots of bridges of less importance in Wudang Mountains.

The stone bridge best preserved in Wudang Mountains is Tianjin Bridge, or Sword River Bridge, a main drag on the ancient divine road, which was built in the Yuan Dynasty and rebuilt in the Ming Dynasty.

The three-holed bridge is very flat, with 19 pairs of decorated stone rails on which carved dragons, phoenixes and other rare birds and animals, all as lively as living. The water under the bridge is clear and clean; the forests around the bridge are green and dense, which make you happy and fresh when you walk on the bridge.

The Pavilion　亭（黄龙洞亭）

The pavilion, as the important symbol of Chinese garden buildings, has been much demonstrated and applied in Wudang Taoist buildings. In accordance with the statistics, there are fifteen famous pavilions in Wudang Mountains, among which Yellow Dragon Cave Pavilion is the representative one.

Yellow Dragon Cave Pavilion, one of the representative small buildings in Wudang ancient building complex, is located on the ancient divine road to Golden Top. The pavilion is quite proper and even in building devise, color, size, shape and its location, so the visitors all like to have a rest here when they pass the pavilion to Gold Top.

Yellow Dragon Cave Pavilion has some certain connection with Wudang medicines; eye medicines and other kinds of medicines produced here were famous in the country in history. There are four steles on the upper part of the pavilion, on two of which inscribed four Chinese characters that mean “Famous all over the world”, on the other two of which wrote some notes on applications and prices of these medicines produced here. Some experts thought that the pavilion has the only one billboard of the Ming Dynasty found in Wudang Mountains, for there is information on prices.

The Altar　坛（太子坡祭坛）

An altar is the hathpace special for sacrificing gods and ancestors.

There is an altar on Crown Prince’s Slope, which was built in the early years of the Ming Dynasty. Composed of three parts, base, wall, and rails, all made of stones, the altar is the only one preserved in Wudang Mountains, as good as before. There is one big clock in the pavilion;

when hitting, all the mountains around will echo the ding.

The Cliff Temple 岩庙（玉虚岩）

It is said that there are 36 cliff temples in Wudang ancient buildings. The cliff temples, built at the waist of the mountains or on the steep cliffs, demonstrated ancient builders' strong spirits to build rooms on the cliff and their lofty skills.

Yuxu Cliff is the biggest one in size and steepest one in location among the 36 cliff temples, for there are mountain gate, fasting room, chambers, grand hall, and other Taoist buildings in the cave on the steep cliff. When you enter into the cave, you will find the relics of the buildings and some color josses here and there.

The Stele Pavilion 碑亭（龟驮碑）

There are twelve large stele pavilions preserved in Wudang Mountains, which is the only phenomenon in China Taoist buildings, also the symbol of highest rank building. In every pavilion there is a big tortoise backing an imperial stele, which is one form of ancient posy, to show that in ancient Chinese traditional culture, only the big tortoise was qualified to deliver important orders to the people.

The stele pavilion often has a mountain-like roof, four doors at the four directions, red walls and green tiles. The stone carving of the tortoise with imperial stele on its back is very large, usually as high as ten meters, and as heavy as over 100 tons. On the large stele inscribed imperial orders. The tortoise is just going to move with the large imperial order stele on its back, as vividly as living, which is the rare artistic work of stone carving in the world, very precious.

Chapter 7 Wudang Martial Arts 武当武术

1. The Gist of Wudang Gongfu 武当功夫精髓

Wudang Gongfu, one important school of China Martial Arts, has a very long history. Wudang Gongfu, ingesting the ways to keep healthy and prolong the lifespan, collecting the skills to fight, is not only a special school of Martial Arts, but also a whole system of Martial Arts in theory.

Wudang Gongfu, as a culture, taking root in the fertile soil of thousand-year long Chinese civilization, containing profound Chinese philosophical theories, has combined traditional theories of Taiji, Yin-Yang, Five-Element, Eight-Diagram into boxing theories, boxing skills, boxing-exercising rules and attacking policies, same to studying the laws of life activities. So we can say that Wudang Gongfu is the crystal of Wudang Taoism in the process of studying the life.

It is said that when Zhang Sanfeng, the founder of Wudang Boxing, was cultivating in Wudang Mountains, he met a fight between a magpie and a snake. That the magpie was flying up and down to attack and the snake was therefore shaking the body and raising the head to fight back gave him some inspiration and understood Taiji Theory so that created Wudang

Boxing.

The origin legend of Wudang Gongfu and the pose of the snake in the fighting have visually demonstrated the gist of Wudang Gongfu: to overcome the tough in a tender way and to win the enemy by striking only after he/ she had struck; and to ascertain the position and then defeat the enemy.

After many boxing masters' enriching and developing, Wudang Gongfu has derived many schools and kinds, such as, Taiji Boxing, Form-and-Will Boxing, and Eight-Diagram Palm, Taiji Spear and Taiji Sword; Qigong, Hard Gongfu, stunts and some kinds of Qigong. From then on, Wudang Gongfu has walked out of the deep mountains and become one important school of China Martial Arts.

The Nature of Fist Position 拳法自然本体说

Every progress of Wudang Gongfu is the result of imitation of biology's and non-biology's framework, shape, character, and ability. Even in the ancient years of Wars, the leading art to activate bones and muscles and to regulate breath to the effect of keeping fit, was just imitating birds' and animals' actions to keep one healthy and prolong one's life span. During the late years of the Eastern Han Dynasty, the famous doctor Hua Tuo, learned from the actions of tiger, deer, bear, monkey and bird, invented a kind of gymnastics, *Five Animal-mimic Frolics*. In the following dynasties, regulatory Qigong had great development. Some men of letters and Taoists invented Eight Trigrams Boxing, Twelve Trigrams Boxing, on the base of the ancestors' work. Judging from regulatory Qigong to Taiji Boxing, the imitation of activity characters of all creatures in the natural world is the secret to keep body healthy and regenerate physical strength.

During the formation and development of Wudang Gongfu, those inventors have learned from all creatures, imitated the shapes and learned their intentions, grasped their strong points to make human beings stronger and stronger. This kind of imitation of biology and non-biology, from actions, tools, names, ways, to characters, is a harmonious returning to Nature, is the exertion of Taoism "Nature and Humans are connected". Here "Nature" refers to the natural world, "Nature and Humans are connected" refers to that human beings and Nature are communicated in the reality and that all the activities of human beings is just conforming to Nature. Only by conforming to Nature can we live and develop. Exercising all the reasonable actions of biology and non-biology to prolong their off-springs, and achieving a balance between Nature and humans, can make human beings live forever among the universe.

In Taiji Boxing, Taiji, namely extremity, really means that working in the unlimited universe and combining Yin and Yang in the Nature. China's *Book of Changes* has named the former original unity Taiji, root of the universe, germ of all creatures in the heaven and world. Naming a boxing Taiji was to show the unification between humans and Nature by means of boxing. The progress of exercising boxing is the progress to achieve a unification between humans and Nature.

Wudang Gongfu succeeded in achieving the whole effect of cultivating body and mind, which is the material performance of Universe Unity Theory in boxing.

Wudang Gongfu pays more attention to purifying learners' mind, proposes that the progress should begin from mind to body, then from body to mind. The learners should first purify their minds, remove all other thoughts, just concentrate on boxing, which is the concentration of mind, or going into quietness of mind. Only by concentrating on one's mind and going into quietness of mind, can he concentrate his mind and sense on activating body, changing temperament, and making himself stronger and healthier in the exercising of boxing.

But other boxing pays more attention to body exercise, proposes that human body is the carrier of Gongfu. The body, strong or weak, decides Gongfu, strong or weak. But the carrier has two parts, body and mind, and mind is more important than body, so we should cultivate our minds to make the strength strong, then the body, and then the whole.

In the body exercises of Wudang Gongfu, the changing ways of stretching out and drawing in, standing up and stooping down, crossing and turning, bowing downward and facing upward, are the exercising methods with the axis of waist, which is the general hinge of upper body and lower body. In exercising or fighting, the body moves about, in accordance with the changes of fighting, using waist to carry strength, then performing the changes by waist, chest, head, hands and feet. No matter what change is, this is the basic rule of Wudang Gongfu.

Wudang Gongfu does not emphasize only the formality of body exercise, but also the harmony of cadence; cadence, not same to, but is held in rhythm of Wushu acts, with differences and connections. In Wudang Gongfu acts, there appears both shape and content, cadence of contents and rules and forms of shape, which are both tangible and intangible. Cadence in reality refers to inner feelings, shaping the law of body exercise. Without cadence, the boxing acts will become rigid, without law, disorderly.

In one word, the axis of waist and the harmony of cadence further perform Wudang Gongfu's character of nature and unity between body and mind, upper part and lower part, attack and defence, part and whole.

The Theory of Yin-Yang of Fist Position “拳法阴阳”技击论

Deeply influenced by Taoist theory that Yin and Yang (the positive and the negative) are opposite and unified, Wudang Gongfu has developed a theory of Yin-Yang of fist position with its own characteristics.

Taoism regards the world as a unity that is both opposite and unified, which was named Yin-Yang in *Book of Changes*. The combination of the two opposite aspects of Yin-Yang has produced unlimited changes.

Wudang Gongfu canonizes the theory of Yin-Yang both in theory and skills of boxing. In view of skills, every act and change take Yin-Yang as the base, or root. The Formulas of Eight-Diagram Palm said that Eight-Diagram Palm has relied on Yin-Yang, and has held five elements (mental, wood, water, fire, and earth). A Book on Taiji Boxing has said that Taiji, or extremity, is coming from the unlimited universe, the chance to move or wait still, the mother of Yin and Yang. *The Digests of Taiji Boxing*, proposed that every act of Wudang Boxing, no matter it is open or close, active or still, tough or tender, visible or invisible, real or false, slow or quick, all change in accordance with the basic law of Yin-Yang. So boxing learning should begin with understanding the unlimited universe and the basic law of Yin-Yang. He can't learn boxing well who does not understand the law of Yin-Yang.

As how to make full use of the tactics of opposite Yin and Yang in real fighting, Wudang Gongfu proposes that we should consider the rival and us as a unity that Yin and Yang are opposite, judging from these transforming law between Yin and Yang, attack and defence, advance and retreat, right and left, up and down, active and still, tough and tender, for and against, open and close, take adequate counter measures in view of rival's character of acts, so that we can defeat the rival without any wound. A Book on Taiji Boxing has proposed many skills, such as, depart when the rival is moving towards, meet when the rival is still; not do excessively or wantingly; take direct skill after a curving one; evade away when the rival is stronger than us; attack when the rival is in a worse position than ours. Only by understanding these transforming law between Yin and Yang, can we make best use of these tactics of attacking or evading away. Only this can help us make a prompt decision in accordance with the situation and the rival, then make easy and quick changes so that defeat the rival.

To sum up, if we understand the transforming changes between Yin and Yang, we can make full use of all positions, directions, angles, potentials that benefit us, then we can escape from death but put the rival into a trap and to death, by means of leaping and evading, or beating back the rival with his own attack, or keeping the rival's powerful attack at bay by a powerless act. All tactics that propose the transforming law of Yin and Yang, waiting still for holding the rival in play, seizing direction and way of the rival's attack, then beating back belong to Wudang Boxing.

The Tactics of Winning by Striking Only After the Enemy Having Struck "后发制人"战术论

Wudang Gongfu takes winning by striking only after the enemy had struck as its tactics, which is same to Taoism's theory of "inaction", "nothing desired", and "being not the first one in the world."

Lao zi, the famous philosopher had proposed that man should think less for oneself and have little desire. He thought that the best way to rule a country was to make the civilians' stomachs full while heads muddled, to make their body and bone strong while their spirit and willing weak. He also proposed the proposition of ruling a country by inaction, in other words, the king does nothing while the civilians will be self-cultivated; the king keeps quiet while the civilians will do their proper business; the king does nothing while the civilians will make themselves rich; the king has little desire while the civilians will have a good rest. On the base of the above propositions, he further proposed the ideology, not to be the first one in the world. He said, "I have three treasures that I keep and protect forever, which are kindness, frugality, and being not the first one." Here "kindness" referred to that the king should love his civilians just like parents to their children; "frugality" was same to that the king should live a simple life and have a simple mind, and not think much for extravagance and luxury; "being not the first one" meant that the king should be modest and folksy.

Influenced by the above ideology, in tactics, Wudang Gongfu emphasizes the importance of winning by striking only after the enemy had struck. That is to say, if some certain enemy attacks us, we should take it easy and wait still to look for and grasp the chance to beat back even when the enemy has a sign of movement. *A Detailed Explanation of Taiji Boxing* has said that we keep still when the opposite makes no actions, we make quick actions when the opposite has a sign to move, which is the tactics that strikes after the opposite's act but heat him earlier before he does me. Some other books, such as *A Book on Taiji Boxing*, *Forty-eight Formulas of Eight-diagram Palm*, have the same statements; all emphasize the policy of striking later but heating earlier. Striking later but heating the opposite earlier can happen only on the condition of evading away the attack to make the attack go by the board. The strategical theory of striking later but heating earlier has two points: one is that we should not over-emphasize the power of subjective thinking, but respect the objective situation, remembering that all one's acts are to adapt and beat the opposite; the other is that we should try to get initiative chance, especially when in a passive predicament, whose policy is to evade away the attack and then to beat the opposite out of his expectation.

The Origin Legend of Keeping Healthy “养生健身”起源说

Wudang Gongfu emerges as the demand of health in Taoism.

Adopting realistic attitudes towards life, extremely devoting much attention to this life, and pursuing happiness, wealth, longevity and living forever, which are held in esteem in Taoism. Besides, it is thought in Taoism that the ordinary persons are likely to become celestial being in the contemporary age rather than in the posthumous time. The aim of becoming celestial being can be achieved through the cultivation of the spirit and flesh.

In Taoism, cultivating to be supernatural being demands the practice of vital energy that needs breathing exercises. Then, practicing shadowboxing is in need. The motions of Wushu are led into the practice of breathing that is also permeated in the process of shadowboxing, thus forming the Gongfu mechanism: Gongfu excising inside and shadowboxing outside, combing inside and outside but taking inside as the dominant factor. Gradually the complete system of Wudang Gongfu comes into being.

The thinking-way of Taoism is to attach importance to intuition and comprehension. Grasp the features of objects by mental perception in order to understand the essence profoundly, which is the basic characteristic of the thinking of Wudang Gongfu. Movements, offence and defence of Wudang Gongfu can be imparted, viewed and learned. However, the different mood, charm, internal temperament and vigor are comprehended deeply in the repeatedly practice and ponderousness after perceived by intuition. This thorough process is penetrated with hardworking, studying with concentration and proficiency. Only after accumulative experience can the charm be captured. Meanwhile, and the entry to a certain mood is the key to true essence of the occult. The way through intuition and practice reflects the profound influence that Wudang Gongfu exerts on the flesh, spirit, thought and ethics, and represents the social purpose of effect and cultivation.

Wudang Boxing, a unity of internal and outside Gongfu, contains the social function of self-defence. The offence and defence at all times and all countries advocate the force, tempo, intensity, bigness winning smallness, quickness winning slowness, and strength winning weakness. But only in Wudang Boxing are bigness, smallness, quickness, slowness, strength and weakness looked at dialectically. The saying of "Four taels lifting a thousand jin" and the moving mode: conquering toughness by gentleness, defeating strength by weakness, subduing quickness by slowness—have enriched the theory and practice in the East and West and have contributed to the world culture. The strategic characteristics and their social efficacy coincide with the purpose of preserving health, which is the fundamental differentiation between Wudang Boxing and other boxing schools, and is the essential dynamic factor in expanding function of improving health.

In the theory of Wudang Gongfu, the cultivation of essence, energy, spirit and their relationship between each other are held significantly. It is thought that essence is the root, providing the basic substance for the body growth, that energy is the carrier to essence, which is circulating through the whole body by the form of energy and supplies the energy to physiology continuously, and that spirit is the manifestation and result of the endless energy, which can maintain the thought and other activities. A system of requirements result in this principle. On the one hand, the potentiality of self-defence is tapped; on the other hand, making use of motions of offence and defence to harmonize the vital energy and blood, to mitigate the collateral channels, and to incorporate Wushu and health, by means of which the vitality is reinforced to accomplish the aim of longevity. The theory of preserving health, developed and perfected, is the result of combining the strong desire for living and pleasure-seeking.

The Orbit Theory of Arc Movement **"圆弧运动"轨迹说**

The arc movement is taken as the motion requirement and moving orbit in Wudang Gongfu, which is the expansion of philosophical thought of Taoism.

Lao zi said, "All the things come from something, something from nothing" (The Classic of *The Tao and Teh* by Lao zi, the seventieth chapter). Thus, a transformable circle is formed. As for *Diagram of the Taiji*, it is a circle of transformation between Yin and Yang. Since the relation between the creation in the universe and Taoism is manifested in a mutually transformable circle, moving orbit is the best diagram of the infinitude. Naturally, Wudang Gongfu chooses this optimizing pattern having great vitality to preserve the health, which is also the root cause for attaching importance to the circle.

In view of the aim, effect and pursuit of the shadowboxing, Wudang Boxing devotes much attention to the circle and arc in the permutations and combinations of motions and moving orbit, such as Eight-Diagram Palm laying on circle. The moving orbit is that a big circle contains a small one and then there is no circle in form; however, the circle still exists in the mind. Circle or arc is permeated in each motion: directing palm, rising legs, walking, posing feet, even practising strength by thought, and so on. In this case, the Eight-Diagram Palm is called circle-interlocking palm.

The Diagram of Taiji, applied to the boxing by the founder of Chinese boxing, has become the badge of Taiji Boxing. Accordingly, the mode and route are the arc, curve and circle. There are three-circle rhymes in the Form-and-Will Boxing: the chest should be round and sinking, the back round like a monkey, and fist round like a triangle, which are three normative requirements and show the significance of the circle.

Taiji Boxing, Form-and-Will Boxing, and Eight-Diagram Palm are based on arc, which is not only manifested in the route and pose, but also in the feature of body movement. So, the movement going around about the waist taken as an axis is penetrated with circle and arc. With the change of motions, all kinds of arc movements, in other words, a big arc containing a small one, a big circle containing a small one, the flat circle, the standing circle, and the orbit are formed. It is reasonable to say that the rule of those is a circle.

The explosive force of Wudang Boxing is related to the arc. Taiji Boxing shows spiral force, Form-and-Will Boxing drilling force, and the Eight-Diagram Palm twinning force. All that makes the strength bold and vigorous, which is the special requirement of conquering toughness by gentleness.

Concerning the attack and defence in the shadowboxing, the force is steadier going in the spinning approach and it is not easy to be caught by the opponent. In the defence, the application of the circle and arc can augment the enduring area of the strength and prolong the functionary time nicely up to the status of "four teals lifting a thousand Jin".

In one word, the orbit of arc movement is the foundation of the boxing, weapon, pattern and standard.

Tips

Zhang Sanfeng, the famous Wudang Taoist, with high moral probity, had visited all the famous mountains in China. He had created Wudang Inside Gongfu, the gist to overcome the enemies and the best ways to keep healthy and prolong the lifespan. The Emperor ordered halls to be built for him, and lots of people learned and still are learning from him.

Qualified coaches of Wudang Boxing give you a face-to-face teaching of Wudang Gongfu, to ensure that you can learn the real Gongfu and make friends here.

Wudang International Tourism & Martial Art Festival is held every year in Wudang Mountains, Hubei Province, where masters of Martial Arts from all over the world will come to take part in the competition.

Wudang Gongfu Performance Team, whose main duty is to carry forward Wudang Gongfu and whose team members are skillful in boxing, has accepted invitations both at home and abroad to demonstrate the mysterious Wudang Gongfu.

2. Wudang International Tourism & Martial Art Festival 武当国际旅游武术节

Every autumn in recent years, there holds Wudang International Tourism & Martial Art Festival in Wudang Mountains, which is an international culture fair, sponsored by Hubei

People's Government, undertook by Hubei Tourism Bureau, Hubei Committee of Ethical and Religious Affairs, Shiyan People's Government, and Wudang Mountains Special Zone of Tourism and Economy.

There are full of colorful and interesting activities in Wudang International Tourism & Martial Art Festival. We will invite first-rate arts group and famous artists to give performances; hold such culture exchange activities as Wudang photograph, arts, calligraphy, specialties, for the purpose of showing up Shiyan City and Wudang Mountains, especially miraculous landscapes and profound artificial views in Wudang Mountains, the World Culture Legacy, Five-A Degree tourist zone and other tourist resources.

During the festival, there will hold International Exchange of Wudang Boxing, Wudang Taoist religion service, Wudang exploration travel, and the competitions and performances of Wudang Taiji Boxing, Wudang Traditional Boxings, Taiji Hand-Pushing, Free-hand Operations, and weapons.

Masters and researchers of Wudang Martial Art will come together to research, exchange their studying results on Wudang Martial Art, so as to widely spread Wudang Gongfu.

Wudang International Tourism & Martial Art Festival will also invite important officials in from governments, social influential persons, and the foreigners who have business cooperation with Shiyan City and/or Wudang Mountains Special Zone of Tourism and Economy. So we can say it is a real and true fair of Wudang tourism and martial art, which is worth your visiting.

3. Wudang Gongfu Performance Team 武当功夫团

Wudang Mountains is famous for Taoism and Martial Art. Wudang Martial Art, on the base of Chinese Taoist philosophy, with regimen and keeping healthy as its principle and Taoist philosophy as its boxing theory, has developed into Wudang Gongfu with profound philosophy and miraculous skills. But for thousands of years, Wudang Inside Gongfu had just been transferred secretly in a small circle, so that the outsider can't have a chance to appreciate their charm.

During the past ten years, Wudang Mountains Special Zone of Tourism and Economy has employed many masters of Wudang Martial Art and formed Wudang Gongfu Performance Team to research and collected a series of Wudang Gongfu and give performances of Wudang Gongfu, so Wudang Gongfu has unveiled her mysterious veil and shown her real appearance.

Wudang Gongfu Performance Team, since her forming, has been invited to give exchanging performances in Russia, America, England, France and so on, which have achieved great successes. In the performance, the viewers have the chance to appreciate Wudang Eight-Diagram Tactics of Nine Directions, Wudang Tactics of Seven Stars, Wudang Sword, Wudang Taiyi Flowing Palm, Wudang Taiji Boxing, Xuantian Sword, Eight-Diagram Flowing Palm, Taiji Knife, Xuanwu Cudgel and so on.

The performance of Wudang Gongfu Performance Team has become an important part in Wudang tourism. The team will give two performances every day on the Crown Prince's Slope, so that visitors can visit Wudang Mountains and enjoy Wudang Gongfu at the same time, which has been spoken highly by the visitors home and abroad.

Wudang Gongfu, Chinese excellent culture legacy, has been loved by more and more people in the world. Now there are more than eight billions people exercising Wudang Taiji Boxing. Wudang Gongfu Performance Team has played an important role in spreading Wudang Taoism and Wudang Gongfu, Wudang Tourism.

4. Sayings and Proverbs on Martial Arts 武术类谚语

Southern-style Boxing and Northern-style Leg; Eastern-style Spear and Western-style Cudgel 南拳北腿，东枪西棍

Wushu in the Changjiang River reaches and the south of the Changjiang River is characterized by many acts, steady stake, violent boxing, and a small place to exercise, so that there has a saying, a place as small as a sleeping ox is enough to exercise Southern-style Boxing. Wushu in the Yellow River reaches and the north of the Yellow River is characterized by big shape, fast speed, powerful legs, running and jumping, and a big place to exercise, so that there is a saying, the boxing fights four directions. The southern-style boxing and the northern-style boxing have their own priorities and striking features. The Hui People lived in the northwest China are good at playing stick, called Ali Stick. While the famous spears in the early periods were mainly popular in the eastern China, especially in Shandong Province and Henan Province. The saying of East Spear and West Stick was first spread in the Hui People in the northwest China.

The Spear is the king of all weapons. 枪为百兵之王

This saying shows the power of the spear, for it has a strong force, high speed in attacking and defense, many changes in real fight, which make the rival difficult to protect.

The Knife is the general of all weapons. 刀为百兵之帅

The knife, one of the earliest weapons in China, is the weapon most often used. The acts of knife emphasize split, cut, point, slice, which is easier than the acts of spear, so most of the generals and soldiers choose to use a knife.

The Sword is the scholar of all weapons. 剑为百兵之秀

The sword, as one of the earliest weapons in China, has been substituted by other weapons in many wars. Later, the swordplay has developed into two kinds: one has a long fringe; when exercising, the sword is like a swimming dragon, full of charm. The other has a short fringe; when exercising, it has many changes in acts and paces, violent movements, which are very useful in fighting. Both the two have a charm of a scholar, so it has been named the scholar of all weapons, compared with musical instruments, chess, and book.

The cudgel is the head of all weapons. 棍为百兵之首

The cudgel is the most original weapon. He who doesn't know Wushu can freely use a cudgel to protect himself. It is very common to use a cudgel as a weapon, so has been named the head of all weapons.

The spear is like a swimming dragon, and the cudgel a whirlwind. 枪如游龙，棍如旋风

We say that the spear just hits one point like a swimming dragon, but the cudgel hits a big direction like a crazy devil. The spear, in order to puzzle the rival, can't hit the point directly, but in a curving way, just like a zigzagging dragon. The cudgel, for the purpose of hitting the rival, should be as quick and violent as a whirlwind; only this can have the power to defeat the rival.

The exercise of single knife depends on the movement of the bare hand, double knives the movements of the legs, big knife the mouth of the knife. 单刀看手，双刀看走，大刀看口

This saying explains the basic requirements when exercising the three kinds of knife plays. When we exercise a single knife, one hand holds the knife; the other one is bare, which is to balance the former one. The standard, balance, use, usefulness, beauty depend on the bare hand's cooperation, so the exercise of a single knife depends on the movement of the bare hand. The acts and changes of double knives are realized through the proper cooperation of the hands and the legs, otherwise, the double knives will meet each other, even do harm to oneself. So when the masters of Wushu appreciate the double knife play, they first look at the paces of the two feet, so we say that the exercise of double knives depends on the movement of the two legs. The big knife is a long and heavy weapon. Only the proper use of the cutter point can we display the power of big knife well. So there has the above saying.

Wushu has eight basic acts, which should practice more and often. 武术讲八法，拳脚要踢打

The Eight Acts refer to eight basic acts, namely, hand play, eye play, pace play, mentality, breath, strength, and Gongfu, which are the basic acts for all kinds of Wushu. Without the eight acts, you can't succeed in exercising Wushu; but the eight acts can only shown in the practice and can be achieved in the practice. This saying means that only through continuing practice can we grasp the Eight Acts.

Exercise vital energy inside, the bone and muscle outside. 内练一口气，外练筋骨皮

The advantage of Wushu exercise is that it can exercise vital energy inside and the bone and muscles outside. Through the exercising of Wushu, we can strengthen the vigor of the body, improve the function of the innards, speed the metabolism, so we can be full of energy and prolong our life spans. And through the exercising of Wushu, we also can make our body strong, muscles developed, bones hard, ligaments soft, skins healthy, giving a healthy and charming performance.

When we practice the stand everyday, our Gongfu improves everyday accordingly. 架子天天盘，功夫天天增

To exercise the stand is to exercise the sets of Wushu. The development history of Wushu shows that all the Wushu develops from free combat to a set of acts, which is the highest stage in Wushu development, no matter it is boxing or weapons. Wushu acts are a series of movements formed by combating skills, which is to help the learners practice them skillfully. Only practice more and often can we improve our strength and resistance. So if we want to have a full display of Gongfu, we must practice them everyday.

Exercise body essence, vital energy and mentality inside, hands, eyes and body outside. 内练精气神，外练手眼身

According to Chinese traditional medicine, body essence, vital energy and mentality are the three most important things. The transformation of the three can speed up metabolism so as to keep healthy and prolong the lifespan. The acts of Wushu are fulfilled through hands, eyes and body. The exercising of hands, eyes and body is the performance of the exercising of body essence, vital energy and mentality. The two parts depend and help each other, can't exist without the other one.

Boxing emphasizes three things: skill, medicine, and art. 拳讲三术：技、医、艺

Skill, medicine, and art are the three performances of Wushu. To exercise Wushu is to combat, so all kinds of Wushu are centered in skills; all emphasize the methods of skills, which is the attacking character. At the same time, the exercising of Wushu can strengthen our body, regulate the functions of all organs, and heal some diseases, so as to keep healthy and prolong the lifespan. Healing bones, hitting points, massage, guiding of Qigong, are indispensable parts of Wushu, which is the medicine character. Wushu is an art of his own, is a unity of these beauties, strength, speed, rhythm, skill, and shape, which is the artistic character of Wushu.

Exercise Wushu without exercising the waist, Gongfu can't be high. 练武不练腰，终究艺不高

The waist is the king of all the body; when the waist is flexible, all the body is flexible; when the waist is rockbound, all the body rockbound. The waist play is the key to display all the body's movement. The movements of shoulders, elbows, wrists, legs and kneels all depend on the management and cooperation of the waist. So we say that the waist is the axis of the body. If we can exercise the waist as soft as a snake, we can freely perform all kinds of acts. On the other hand, the waist play is the base for attacking acts. So if we can't exercise the waist play well, we can not succeed in learning Wushu.

Exercising Boxing without a stake, just as building a room without a pillar. 练拳无桩步，房屋无立柱

Stake work, one of private Gongfu, is the work that all schools of Wushu emphasize. Stake work is one method to regulate the breath so as to strengthen our strength by standing still. To name it stake is because that the exerciser should stand there as still as a pole; after a long time exercising, the exerciser can stand on foot as steady as the stake of a pole. Stake work has two kinds: regimen stake work and attack stake work. If a boxing learner lacks of stake work, his acts will be powerless; so the opponent will easily hit him down.

Exercise boxing without real effect, he gets no result in the end. 打拳不练功，到老一场空

To exercise boxing is not same to exercising Gongfu. Boxing refers to the way of exercising, the Gongfu the real effect of exercising. He, who just pays attention to the ways of exercising but not the real effect, will learn Gongfu in a skin-deep way, without any value of use. Exercising

Gongfu has many purposes, such as increasing strength, improving softness, enhancing alertness, exercising endurance, expanding lung capability, and boosting reaction speed. Only exercising both the way and the Gongfu, can we learn real Gongfu, so that we can overcome the others.

As steady as Mount Tai, as quiet as a virgin. 稳如泰山，静如处子

This saying emphasizes that when fighting, we should be in a calm mood; only this can make us calm and easy enough to grasp his intention, without being cheated by the opponent, so that we can make correct reactions to defeat him. When fighting, we can't be excited, for in an excited mood, we will make us in disorder so as to let out our shortcomings, even be defeated by the opponent.

Poking away one-thousand-kilogram attacked by a four-tael force 四两拨千斤

This saying emphasizes that we should use wisdom to defeat the opponent when fighting. Wisdom refers to being good at changes, so as to well deal with surprise attack. Only these masters who are good at Wushu and has many experiences can deal with surprise attacks in a wise manner. When getting to the wisdom stage, we can defeat the attack in a wise manner, or with the opponent's strength. The bigger the attack of the opponent is, the more violent the attack hit back, and the worse the opponent will be. We deal with the violent attacks in a small strength, as the saying "Poking away one-thousand-kilogram attacked by a four-tael force" goes.

Pay 70% attention to the feet, 30% to the hands. 七分看脚，三分看手

70 percent and 30 percent refers to the relationship between the major and the minor. When one fights with the other, he should pay more attention to the opponent's feet and minor attention to his hands, because that the direction and speed of the opponent are related to his pace. If his proper pace is held by the opponent, he is doomed to be defeated by the opponent before the opponent begins to attack. The direction of the opponent's feet and kneels forecasts his direction to attack, so attention to the opponent's feet is very necessary. This saying offers a good method to take the initiative and overcome the rival in a very easy way.

Attacking where, look where; looking where, attack where; attacking and looking the same way, we can make a powerful act. 拳到眼到，眼到拳到，拳眼齐到，招招见效

This saying explains the three methods to cooperate one's hands, feet and eyes in fighting. When Wushu masters can deal with the opponent's attack in a wise way after many practices, they also can make subconscious reactions to surprise attack. The movements of hands and feet often go before that of eyes, so the eyes should follow hands and feet quickly, which is that attacking where, look where. In fighting, the clever masters can sense the opponent's intention by a look, and make relative reaction, which is that looking where, attack where. When one's Gongfu comes to a very high level, the speeds of hands, feet and eyes are nearly the same, with high veracity and agility.

Wait still for the opponent's act, strike only after the enemy has struck 以静待动，后发制人

Here the still refers to that we should give a relative still performance so as to regulate our strength and wait for the attack in a casual way, compared with the opponent. The still also refers to that we should have a calm mood to watch carefully all the movements of the opponent. Here the act refers to such unimportant and false movements made by the opponent so as to cheat us, and the attacks of the opponent earlier than ours. In fighting, we should first wait still for the attack of the opponent, then look for his mistakes, so that we can find a chance to defeat him, which is the meaning of the saying.

Wait still when the opponent is still; hit him earlier when he makes a small movement; make reactions later than the opponent, but hit him earlier than he does. 彼不动，我不动；彼微动，我先到；后人发，先人拳

It is very right that he takes the initiative by an earlier attack in fighting, but there often has many miraculous effect when strike only after the opponent has struck. Many schools of Wushu and masters propose to strike only after the opponent has struck. Striking only after the opponent has struck doesn't refer to that the speed should be lower than that of the opponent, but that making reaction later and hitting the opponent earlier. This means that when strike after the opponent, our speed must be quicker than that of the opponent. Wait still when the opponent is still, which means that we should not make movements earlier than the opponent. Hit him earlier when he makes a small movement, which means that when the opponent shows his intention, direction and attacking skills, we should make proper reactions at once so as to defeat him before his attack. Make reactions later than the opponent, but hit him earlier than he does, in other words, make reactions later, but reach the target and defeat the opponent than he does us.

Make reactions later, but hit the target earlier; make three attacks after the opponent's movement; make reactions later and hit the target later. 后发先至，后发三至，后发后至

The three sentences tell us the three methods to fight against the opponent. The first emphasizes that we must make quick reactions to fight against when the opponent has struck, but has not hit us. The second emphasizes that we should make reactions to fight against the opponent by continuing tactics, letting him to have the chance to rest a little. The third means that if the opponent's attacks are very quick and violent, we should evade away until his power is decreased, and then make quick and violent reactions to defeat him. All the three sentences have one common point, being good at grasping the right time so as to make attack and defence automatically.

Make an attack earlier than the opponent, but hit him later. 先人发，后人至

To make an attack and hit the target earlier is to emphasize the importance of taking the initiative. To make an attack later than the opponent but hit him earlier is to emphasize that we should strike only after the opponent has struck and attack while defense. To make an attack earlier than the opponent but reaching him later is to mean that when in fighting, we should make an attack before the opponent but defeat him only after he has made a reaction, not defeat him by a blow, whose purpose is to charge the opponent in a smart way. This is the method to make the opponent take the failure in heart with our lofty Gongfu.

The will should not be performed by the form, or we can't succeed in fighting. 有意莫带形，带形必不赢

Here the will refers to the intention of making an attack or an evasion; the form, the movements of all the body parts. In fighting, our intention of making an attack or an evasion can't be discovered by the opponent, or, the opponent understands our intention and makes corresponding preparations, so that our intention will be a failure. How does the opponent understand our intentions? By the form of body, for the form can explain the will. For example, some light movements of hands and feet, a slight incline of the body, and a slight shake of the muscle can tell the opponent that we are going to attack. Clever masters even can sense the opponent's intention by his feeling, breath and eyesight. On the other hand, clever masters are also good at hiding their intentions, or make no preparing positions, or a false position to cheat the opponent to make a false decision, so that defeat him out of his expectations. In order to achieve the above purpose, the attack should be as quick as possible.

Walk as plough the earth; stand there steady as has root in the earth. 迈步如行犁，落脚如生根

When exercising Boxing, we propose that the upper part of the body should be as easy as possible; the lower part should be steady as possible. Being easy means that being in a relaxed mood, so that the upper part can be in the mood to attack or defense all the time. Being steady emphasizes the importance of a steady stake. When we have a steady stake, we can stand there without a little shake, no matter how the opponent pushes, or hits us. If we can have steady feet, we can walk out the right position in a pace, so as to squeeze down the opponent's attacking center and make an counter-attack or an evasion easily according to our intentions. If we have a steady stake and walk on steadily, we display all the power hidden in the body, so that defeat the opponent successfully.

Fight the opponent is like walking on; treating the opponent as the grass. 打人如走路，看人如蒿草

This is one psychological hint made by oneself when in fighting. This hint may help us remove our worries about the opponent's higher height, stronger body, loftier skills, and even greater fame, make us in an easy and calm mood to believe that we will succeed in the fight, so that we can display our real Gongfu without any interference outside.

The boxing has no acts; the will has no thought, which is the real purpose to exercise boxing. 拳无拳，意无意，无拳无意是真意

When exercising Wushu to a certain stage, a casual act can have the effect of attacking, so that we needn't make any preparations for attacking and thinking, for the head has managed all parts of the body to an automatic degree, can automatically make a proper decision and some reactions to any surprise attack. It seems that the will and the movement has lost their connections at that time, all reactions are automatic, which is that the boxing has no acts, the will has no thought, the real purpose to exercise boxing. That the will has no thought doesn't mean that the head really has no thought, but a quick thinking. The order from the head to the acts is so quick that the thought and the acts seem to happen at the same time, without the thinking of the head. That the boxing has no acts doesn't mean that the boxing really follows no acts, but not obeys the acts to the letter, should change our acts in accordance with the changing situation, to the purpose of defeating the opponent.

Charge the opponent by a blow, or fight with him by long time competition. 不招不架，只是一下；犯了招架，十下八下

The character of Wushu is continuing attacking; the principle is defeating the opponent as soon as possible. Even if we strike after the opponent has struck, we should also hit the opponent earlier than he does on us, for several rounds can determine the result of the fighting between the two. When fighting against others, we should end the fighting as soon as possible, for the result can be determined by several minutes or several seconds; the long time fighting we see in the movies does not demonstrate the principle of Wushu. So Wushu demands the learner to be clever and alert, brave and violent, so that he can charge the opponent in several minutes. If we can charge the opponent in several minutes, we should understand that our Gongfu is not able to achieve a quick success, so we have to fight against the opponent for a long time, which demands Gongfu and strength.

The soft acts with tough movements in can't be defeated; the tough acts with soft movements in have unlimited power. 柔中有刚攻不破，刚中有柔力无边

The tough is hard and strong; the soft is tender and flexible. The tough acts refer to that the acts have a quick, large, explosive power; the soft acts refer to that the acts are everlasting and can turn the opponent's attack into nothing. The tough also means that the spirit and mentality are very strong, will break rather than bend; the soft also means being strong-minded, never giving up. The soft acts with tough movements in means that we should use explosive power among the soft acts at the proper time. The tough acts with soft movements in means that we should use several clever acts to follow and hold in playing the opponent's acts. When the tough acts without soft movements in meet with the opponent's tough acts, both will be damaged; when the tough acts without soft movements in meet with the opponent's soft acts, they will be held in play by the opponent. When the soft acts without tough movements in meet with the opponent's soft acts, they have no chance to succeed; when meet with the opponent's tough acts, they are hard to succeed. Only fight with both tough acts and soft ones can we be easy and free to deal with the opponent's attacks, so that defeat him in the end.

5. Masters of Wudang Martial Art and the Boxing 武当武术大师和功法

Master Zhao Shouli, male, born in 1944, is an advanced middle school teacher, excellent teacher of P.E. in Hubei Province. He, as the 18th inheritor of Long-Style Heart School, was enlisted into Hundred Masters of Wudang Martial Art. He learned Form-and-will Boxing from his father when he was very young, then he met by chance the 17th inheritor of Long-Style Heart School, profound Taoist Song Chenyi, who accepted him as a student and taught him Yoga and Long-Style Boxing. In 1957, he learned Taiji Boxing from Taiji master Li Yunlong. During his study in Beijing University of Physical Education, he learned Yang-Style Taiji Boxing and Hand-Pushing from Guo Zhongyuan, the famous master of Hebei Province. In the 1960s, he learned Six Harmony Boxing and Swordplay from Cao Peishan, the master of Six Harmony School, in Shandong Province. In the 1970s, he learned the Eight Diagrams from Sun Baohe. In the 1980s, he learned Wudang Swordplay from Guo Gaoyi, the profound Taoist of Long-Style School.

He has been researching Wudang Martial Art theory and skills, collected and compiled many kinds of boxing and swordplay and published lots of papers.

He has been given many prizes in martial art competitions sponsored by Hubei Province and other provinces.

Here are the names of martial art:

Wudang 37-Pattern Chunyang Swordplay 武当三十七式纯阳剑

Wudang 37-Pattern Chunyang Swordplay, the apple of inner exercise skills, was created by Sun Lutang, the master of Form-and-Will School, on the base of Form-and-Will theory, so also named Form-and-will Swordplay. This swordplay, having absorbed all the strongpoints of all boxing schools, can balance the breath of Yin and Yang inside to cultivate healthy energy, so as to get rid of diseases and keep healthy. When exercising swordplay, the mind is very important, and the movements of eyes, hands, body, and feet should follow the mind, the word, according to form-and-will theory.

Wudang 37-Pattern Chunyang Swordplay is mainly made up of 13 sword movements, cooperated by the mind and feet, so steady and powerful when moving on or retreating.

Here are the names of 37 Patterns:

(1) Starting position

(2) The hiding dragon jumping out of the sea

(3) The Immortal directing the way

(4) Giving three swords when retreating

(5) Flapping the sword

(6) Waving the sword upward

(7) Walking on and slanting the sword

(8) Hugging the moon in the arms

(9) Waving the sword around

(10) Flapping the sword

(11) Pushing the boat with the current

(12) Fair lady working at the shuttle

(13) The white monkey offering peaches

(14) The cat attacking at the rat

(15) Waving the sword in one side

(16) Pushing the window to see the moon

(17) Whipping the willing horse

(18) Blowing the sword straightly

(19) Cutting the back

(20) The dragonfly touching the water

(21) Waving the sword as touching the sea

(22) Hugging the moon in the arms

(23) Waving the sword overhead

(24) Turning around and holding the sword in both hands

(25) Waving the sword under the feet

(26) Retreating and waving the sword to the opponent

(27) The black Tiger running out the den

(28) Turning back and flapping the sword

(29) Waving the sword around violently

(30) Clipping the monkey downside up

(31) The dragon putting out its paws

(32) The black Tiger running out the den

(33) Giving three flowing sword

(34) The dragon turning back

(35) The hiding dragon jumping out of the sea

(36) The dragon returning to the sea

(37) Closing position

Long-Style Xiantian Eight Diagrams Palm 龙门先天八卦掌

Long-Style Xiantian Eight Diagrams Palm, just taught by mouth among the Taoists of Long School, is not familiar to the public. Cao Zhenyang, the 25th inheritor of Long School, has been spreading Long-Style Xiantian Eight Diagrams Palm, with its own outstanding features.

The Palm observes the Eight Diagrams theory and has a set of patterns in each small part, which are ever flowing and full of changes, with the effect of cultivating regimen and attacking and defending. The Palm organizes its patterns in accordance with the characters of easy changing and harming each other of the Eight Diagrams, and precise in structure. In exercising, the mind is guarding the breath, which make the man comfortable and relaxed. The following are the acts:

(1) Turning palm

The white swan displaying the wings

The moon and the sun working the shuttle

Turning in Taiji position

The tiger guarding the mountain

(2) Qi Mountain mooing-phoenix palm

The moon and the sun walking together

The phoenix worshiping the sun

The swallow touching the water

The phoenix landing in Qi Mountain
Turning over and displaying the wings
The swallow touching the water
The phoenix landing in Qi Mountain
The phoenix putting up the neck to moo
The phoenix worshiping the sun
The tiger guarding the mountain

(3) Raging fire golden hook palm
The moon and the sun working the shuttle
The iron scratching the silver hook
Raging fire blazing out
The iron scratching the silver hook
Raging fire becoming more violent with the wind
The iron scratching the silver hook
Raging fire tempering the gold
The iron scratching the silver hook
Raging fire burning the mountain
The iron scratching the silver hook
Raging fire running upward
The iron scratching the silver hook
Raging fire returning to the stove
The tiger guarding the mountain

(4) Violent tiger crossing the forest palm
The moon and the sun working the shuttle
The dragon meeting the tiger
The dragon waving its tail
The dragon meeting the tiger
The dragon waving its tail
The dragon meeting the tiger
The tiger guarding the mountain

(5) Returning wind peripatetic palm
The moon and the sun working the shuttle
The arrow moving fast as the falling star
Taking away the goat conveniently
Two dragons fighting for one pearl
Waving the cloud and cover the rain
The arrow moving fast as the falling star
The wind returning to the deep valley
Putting out the palms violently

The tiger guarding the mountain

(6) White horse crossing the river palm

The moon and the sun working the shuttle

The arrow moving fast as the falling star

Jumping down the horse near the river

Putting the palm upward

Jumping down the horse near the river

Putting the palm upward

Stopping the horse near the cliff

The white horse crossing the river

Facing flowers

Turning right in a Taiji position

The tiger guarding the mountain

(7) Black bear guarding the mountain palm

The white swan displaying the wings

Crossing the mountain on a horse

Separating the mane

Attacking the two ears of the opponent with the two hands

The black bear bumping the mountain

The violent tiger waving the tail

The moon meeting and passing the sun

The black bear turning back the head

The black bear turning over the back

(8) Divine mother ever-flowing palm

The moon and the sun working the shuttle

Thundering in the clear sky

The white snake sleeping on the grass

Turning around and kicking the clock

The white snake putting out its tongue

Putting the palm upward

Hammering the ear

Facing the flowers

Falling flowers landing on the earth

Opening the bow

The dragon waving the tail

Turning left in a Taiji position

The white swan displaying the wings

Changing Yin and Yang

Closing position

Wudang Eighteen Elbows of Nine Direction 武当九宫行宫十八肘

Wudang Eighteen Elbows of Nine Direction, created from Wudang Long School, is also named Taiyi Softening Exercise.

Wudang Eighteen Elbows of Nine Direction takes as its theory Taoist principle "the map of a river, the book of Luoyang, four images, eight diagrams, and nine directions", and consults the theories of Yin and Yang and Five Elements, supplied with relative movements of feet, body, hands, and elbows, so that the exercising can improve the learner's agility in walking, turning, escaping, approaching and retreating, so as to make a progress in martial art. If exercise it often, it can help balance Yin and Yang, regulate the muscles and blood, and make the learner agile and smart.

Here are the names of the acts:

(1) Starting position
(2) Pushing the boat with the current
(3) Stooping down to draw water
(4) The dissipater turning back the head
(5) Waving the sleeves to play with flowers
(6) The immortal waving the sleeves
(7) The falling star dropping quickly
(8) The dragon diving into the water
(9) The golden rooster shaking the wings
(10) The wind waving the willow
(11) The ancient tree twisting its roots
(12) The black dragon waving the tail
(13) Three rings covering the moon
(14) Clapping the hands and putting forward
(15) Poking away the clouds to see the sun
(16) The dragon turning back the head
(17) Flowing the water and moving the cloud
(18) Waving the sleeves to play with the flowers
(19) The monk offering the cudgel
(20) The surprised horse withdrawing the front feet
(21) The dragon diving into the water
(22) Seeing the flowers in the mirror
(23) The iron immortal worshiping the Buddha
(24) Waving the sleeves to play with the flowers
(25) The immortal waving the sleeves
(26) The falling star dropping quickly
(27) The dragon diving into the water
(28) The golden rooster shaking the wings

(29) The wind waving the willow
(30) The ancient tree twisting the roots
(31) The black dragon waving the tail
(32) Three rings covering the moon
(33) Clapping the hands and putting forward
(34) Poking away the cloud to see the sun
(35) The dragon turning back the head
(36) Flowing the water and moving the cloud
(37) Waving the sleeves to play with the flowers
(38) The monk offering the cudgel
(39) The surprised horse withdrawing the front feet
(40) The dragon diving into the water
(41) Seeing the flowers in the mirror
(42) The iron immortal worshiping the Buddha
Closing position

13-Pattern Taiji Static Qigong 太极静功十三式

This set of patterns is coming from Master Chen Jisheng of Qigong regimen.

This exercise is coming from Taoism, collecting all the theories of Taoism, Confucianism and Buddhism, laying importance to static movements, or inactiveness. Exercising 13-Pattern Taiji Static Qigong can activate the bones and joints of waist, hip and legs, cultivate the mood and the character, and regulate the breath and blood, so as to get rid of disease, keep healthy and prolong the lifespan.

Here are the names of the acts:
(1) Wuji position
(2) Taiji position
(3) Big feet
(4) Collecting the tail of the swallow
(5) Holding the knees and walking on
(6) Touching the big legs
(7) A single whip
(8) Chopping the hand
(9) Separating the mane
(10) Big feet
(11) Collecting the tail of the swallow
(12) Half closing and half opening
(13) Taiji closing position

Wudang Eight Diagrams Flowing Palm 武当八卦连环掌

Eight Diagrams Palm is the famous internal boxing of China, with profound theories and agile acts. The Palm, bearing in mind the theory of Eight Diagrams, is to realize the mind through all the parts of the body, quick and flexible.

Here are the names of the acts:

(1) Single changing palm

Hiding the flowers under the leaves

The dragon turning over the body

The grazing boy directing the way

Giving three flowing palms

(2) Double changing palm

The dragon turning over the body

Closing the door and pushing the moon

The white snake twisting the body of the man

The swallow touching the water

The bird putting out its tongue

(3) Turning body palm

The dragon touching the sea

The Golden needle touching the flower

Hugging the moon in the arms

Sweeping the arm of thousand soldiers

The dragon turning around

(4) Following palm

The bird flying into the sky

Poking away the grass to look for the snake

Making the lion to catch the ball

The dragon turning around

(5) Turning back palm

The dragon turning around

The dragon diving into the sea

Pushing the mountain into the sea

The swallow touching the water

The boy offering the fruits

The immortal holding the tray

(6) Penetrating body palm

The dragon turning around

The immortal directing the way

Opening the door and giving an iron fan

The swallow penetrating the shade

Taking off the clothes to give away the place

The dragon turning back the body

(7) Shaking body palm

Hiding the flowers under the leaves

Holding up Mount Tai

Turning over the body

The black bear putting out the palms

Chopping the mountain to save his mother

The dragon turning around

(8) Escaping body palm

The dragon turning around

Poking away the clouds to see the sun

The swallow touching the water

A single whip

Opening the window to see the moon

The dragon turning back the body

Wudang Songxi White Rainbow Swordplay 武当松溪白虹剑

White Rainbow Swordplay has a long history, with lots of followers and students. During the late years of the Qing Dynasty, the trigger men of Tianjin City had spread this swordplay to Sichuan Province and Qinghai Province where there have been many changes and progress in spreading.

This swordplay, simple in theory but profound in morality, is to perform the bravery and generosity of swordsmen and knights-errant, explain the principles of being wise and brave. The learner should observe the six principles: "civility, piety, hermit, self-restraint, kindness, frugality", melt the mood and character into the sword. There are many changes, but all steady and simple, without any changes of coldness and power, only by which can display the main thought of this swordplay.

The sword has no fringe or sword-finger, for the purpose of real fighting, not for the performance, which is mainly relying on jumping pace, walking pace, attacking pace, and arrow pace, free to attack or retreat.

Here are the names of the acts:

(1) Climbing the high mountain to see the moon

(2) Bringing out the knife to cut the water

(3) Throwing a dart in a horse

(4) Poking away the clouds to see the sun

(5) Giving a sword to run after the wind

(6) Holding the pearl in both hands

(7) Lifting the clothes to hide the sword

(8) Closing the door not to receive the visitors

(9) Nie Zheng killing the prime minister

(10) The blood dying the rainbow

(11) Kicking the vertebra against the waves
(12) Waving the sword upward
(13) Sun Bin fighting wisdom with Pang Juan
(14) The white ox turning the hoofs
(15) Sun Bin reducing the stoves
(16) Hiding the sword in a fish
(17) Zhuan Zhu killing his colleagues
(18) Surrounding the city to carve up the territory
(19) Stealing the beam and changing the pillar
(20) Yao Li cutting his arm
(21) Killing Qing Ji in a clever manner
(22) Retreating to hold the helm
(23) Holding back nine oxen
(24) Moving the boat against the current
(25) Picking up the pearl in the deep sea
(26) Bian He offering the jade
(27) Backing the thorns to ask for mercy
(28) Hou Yin guarding the city
(29) Zhong Er returning to Jin Country
(30) Surrounding Wei Country to save Zhao Country
(31) Autumn wind and Yi River
(32) Jing Ke killing Emperor Qin
(33) Waving the sword as a rainbow
(34) The ancient strange triggermen
(35) The white rainbow crossing the sky
(36) Healthy energy penetrating the sun

Yang Qunli, male, born in 1953, was graduated from Martial Art Department of Wuhan University of Physical Education, China. Now he is a national judge of martial art, advanced martial art coach, at the seventh degree in Chinese martial art.

He has been working in Wushu teaching for many years, and has taken the team to take part in the competitions presided by Hubei Province and the nation, where his students has obtained more than 400 prizes.

Besides Wushu teaching, he also works hard at scientific research, having published many papers and books, among which *A Research on Boxing System and Content of Wudang Boxing* has been awarded the Third Prize by the State Ministry of Education, *Simplified Wudang Boxing* the Scientific Prize by Hubei Province.

He has been the Chief Referee in Wudang Mountains International Festival of Martial Art for several sessions. He has also been the Chief Referee in national competition of martial art for many years. Now he is a committee member of China Association of Martial Art, of Hubei

Association of Martial Art, and Standing director of Wudang Boxing Seminar.

He has taken Wudang Gongfu Performance Team to give exchange performances overseas, achieving several great successes. Here are the names of Gongfu:

Wudang Taiyi Five-element Boxing 武当太乙五行拳

Wudang Taiyi Five-Element Boxing, one important school of Wudang Wushu, was invented in the year of Emperor Hongzhi of the Ming Dynasty by Wudang Taoist Zhang Shouxing, the leader of Long School of Wudang Taoism. On the base of Taiji Thirteen Acts invented by Wudang Taoist Zhang Sanfeng, and the Play of Five Animals invented by Hua Tuo, the famous doctor of the Han Dynasty, after absorbed Taoist theory of breathing and guiding, Zhang Shouxing invented Wudang Taiyi Five-Element Boxing.

Chinese ancient philosophers selected the five different elements from the material world, water, fire, wood, gold, and earth, and considered them the basic elements to form all things in the world, naming them "the Five Elements". By use of the relationship between the five elements that help and harm each other, they expressed the law that all things are helping and harming each other at the same time. The ancient masters of martial art, on the base of Chinese traditional culture, used Five-Element Boxing and human body as the carrier to explain boxing theory and exercising rules.

1. On the base of the form, capability, and orientation of the Five Elements, the ancient masters made the basic boxing acts a system of five elements: walking on, walking back, turning to the left, turning to the right, and standing in the middle. Taiyi Five-Element Boxing, from movement program to movement route, is following the theory of the Five Elements to the letter.

2. Through combining the Five Elements with human body and observing the theory that all the elements are helping and harming each other at the same time, the ancient masters expressed Taoist theory that human and nature are unified, with a purpose to go for naturalness and return to simplicity. Using the still as the base and the soft as the form, organically combination of regimen and attack, are the guiding line for Taiyi Five-Element Boxing.

3. The ancient masters used the theory that all the elements are helping and harming each other at the same time to standardize boxing. So there are Yin and Yang penetrating into the acts that the boxing has an everlasting violent power.

Here are the names of the acts:

(1) Preparing position

(2) Starting position: having a long breath

(3) White monkey running out of the den, double peaks respecting the sun

(4) Stopping the horse on a cliff, clouds arising from the deep sea

(5) The dragon waving the water; thunder shouting and flood overflowing

(6) The rhinoceros looking up for the moon, then turning back and support the sky

(7) The blue lion hugging the ball in his legs, lightning appearing over the hall

(8) The leopard biting a beauty, when facing upward, surprising the wood

(9) The giant eagle displaying his wings, surprising all the animals

(10) The deer picking up Lingzhi, bowing to drink the spring

(11) The snake spitting the spit, playing with other stronger animals

(12) The carp jumping from his feet, making the waves wave violently

(13) The male eagle looking over the mountain, catching two from the group of chickens

(14) The swan jumping into the sky, waving the wind and the cloud

(15) The monkey stealing the medicine, making the fire in the stove extinguish

(16) The crocodile worshiping the moon, making the sea quiet and safe

(17) The black bear pulling out his palms, surprising the forest

(18) The hoptoad jumping out of the shell, sleeping drunken in the lake

(19) The pie standing on the plum tree in the cold winter

(20) The dragon returning to the sea, quieting his mind.

(21) The wild horse waving his manes, running at a high speed;

(22) The monkey returning to his den, drawing back his character

(23) The phoenix flying into the sky, all the other birds singing to pay respect

(24) The tiger sleeping on the platform, protecting his den forever

(25) Drawing back the hands and having a long breath

(26) Closing position: combining the still with the active

Wudang Twelve-Act of Nine-Direction Turning 武当九宫旋转十二法

Wudang Taoist Regimen comes from Taoism. As to regimen, Taoism observes the principle that "The laws are natural and follow the Nature"; in other words, under the guiding line of Nature, we cultivate our natural bodies, so as to activate our lives.

Twelve-Act of Nine-Direction Turning is a simplified Gongfu exercised by Taoists in their daily life, which has simple acts, easy to study and exercise. All the acts can be exercised one by one, or from the first to the last, without any limitation of place or time.

Twelve-Act of Nine-Direction Turning has the following characters: activating the whole body, including the upper and the lower parts; exercising both the still and the active; combining the form and the spirit into one, including the inside and the outside; and circulating the vitality and the breath.

Exercising Twelve-Act of Nine-Direction Turning has these effects to keep healthy and prolong the lifespan: to build up the heart, cultivate the liver, grow the lung, firm the kidney, conduce the cerebrum, regulate the breath, exercise the character, and cultivate the mood. Therefore a long time exercising of Twelve-Act of Nine-Direction Turning can help get rid of disease so as to keep healthy and prolong the lifespan.

Here are the names of the acts:

(1) Being easy and quiet to let circulate the breath

(2) Looking up to the sky and then down to the earth to activate the neck and the waist

(3) Looking forward and turning back to look backward to activate the neck and the waist

(4) Shaking the head to activate the neck

(5) Combing the hair to help activate the head

(6) Floating over the water to regulate the breath

(7) Washing the face and massaging the private part to cultivate the nerve and the vitality

(8) Standing and pressing the private part to cultivate the vitality

(9) Going around and patting the kidney to firm the kidney

(10) Massaging the belly to regulate the breath

(11) Shaking the body to return to the easy

Simplified Wudang Boxing 简化武当拳

Simplified Wudang Boxing is one kind of Gongfu combined Static Qigong with Dynamic Qigong, which takes Zhang Sanfeng, the founder of Wudang Inside Exercise's Taoist laws as the base, Taoist theory as the core, and keeping healthy, self-cultivation, and protecting oneself as the purpose.

The acts of Simplified Wudang Boxing are created on the base of these excellent boxing: Wudang Taiyi Five-Element Boxing, Wudang Peripatetic Boxing, Wudang Stretching Palm, Wudang Taiji, Wudang Hammer, Wudang Pure Positive Boxing, Zhaobu Taiji, and Wudang Five-Element Regimen.

The skill characters of Simplified Wudang Boxing: cleanness and quietness as the base, roundness and softness as the form, cultivating the breath as the principle, inside and outside exercises, natural acts, Yin-yang skills, proper balance between the still and the active, the tough and the soft helping each other, combination of boxing and Qigong, and a unity between humans and the Nature.

Simplified Wudang Boxing has been approved by Hubei Science and Technology Commission, which said that Simplified Wudang Boxing had made Wudang Martial Art have its own simplified acts for the first time, better satisfy the need of keeping healthy, prolonging the lifespan and self-protection, also achieve a great success in developing Wudang Martial Art in a scientific and standard way, which had filled the blank history of this skill.

Here are the names of the acts:

(1) Circumvolving the world

(2) The dragon jumping out of the sea

(3) The cold hen looking for food

(4) The tortoise playing with the water

(5) The god directing the way

(6) The white snake shooting the shuttle

(7) The five dragon swimming secretly

(8) The gold snake winding the beam

(9) The blue dragon turning back the head;

(10) The cat attacking the rat

(11) The giant eagle displaying the wings

(12) The monkey sitting in the den

(13) The little boy teaching the sea

(14) The Taoist opening the door

(15) The dragon sleeping in the lake

(16) Golden Hall turning for better fortune

(17) Wasps returning to the nest

(18) The black bear turning over the back

(19) Closing position

The First Movement of Chen-style Taiji Boxing 陈式太极拳老架一路

Chen-style Taiji Boxing is one of the oldest schools of Taiji Boxing, which originated in Wudang Inner Exercise, flourished in Chen Village, Wen County of Henan Province during the later period of the Qing Dynasty and the beginning of the Republic of China. Passed on from generation to generation by the family of Chen, improved on the basis of the original acts, it has developed into the First Movement and the Second Movement today, which are different from each other in act, speed, strength, form, moving capacity, and difficulty.

There are 75 acts in the First Movement of Chen-style Taiji Boxing, relying mainly on the applications of covering, stroking, pressing forward and pushing, supplemented by the applications of picking, lining up, elbowing and leaning to one side. The ways to use one's strength rely on the strength of twining supplemented by using one's power. The actions are required to be gentle on the basis of using one's power, meeting and overcoming hardness by softness. It is characterized by slowness, gentleness and steadiness in the appearance. Because of its slow acts, this Boxing can be divided into the high, the middle and the low grades. The amount of physical exercises can be regulated, so this Boxing is not only suitable for healthy people to strengthen body building but also suitable for the weak and chronic to cure diseases and keep fit. It takes eight to ten minutes to practice this Boxing.

Here are the names of the acts:

(1) Starting position

(2) Diamond hammer

(3) Fastening one's clothes lazily

(4) Six sealing and four closing

(5) Single whip

(6) Diamond hammer

(7) The white goose displaying the two wings

(8) Diagonal slanting

(9) Brushing knees

(10) Stepping forward three steps

(11) Diagonal slanting

(12) Brushing knees

(13) Stepping forward three steps

(14) Covering the hands and punching with the fists

(15) Diamond hammer

(16) Turning around and throwing a fist
(17) The blue dragon emerging from the water
(18) Pushing with two hands
(19) Throwing a fist under the elbow
(20) Stepping back and whirling arms on both sides
(21) The white goose displaying the two wings
(22) Diagonal slanting
(23) Flashing the back
(24) Covering the hands and punching with the fists
(25) Six sealing and four closing
(26) Single whip
(27) Moving hands like clouds
(28) Reaching high to tough the horse
(29) Rubbing with the right foot
(30) Rubbing with the left foot
(31) Kicking with the left foot
(32) Stepping forward three steps
(33) The god taking everything in one hand
(34) Turning over and kicking the two feet
(35) Throwing a fist to protect the heart
(36) Whirling legs
(37) Kicking with the right foot
(38) Covering the hands and punching with the fists
(39) Small catching
(40) Holding head to push the mountain
(41) Six sealing and four closings
(42) Single whip
(43) Front moving
(44) Back moving
(45) Parting the wild horse's mane
(46) Six sealing and four closings
(47) Single whip
(48) Fair lady working at the shuffle the fairy weaving at the shuttle
(49) Fastening one's clothes lazily
(50) Six sealing and four closings
(51) Single whip
(52) Waving hands like clouds
(53) Sweeping the lotus twice
(54) Fall-split

(55) The golden cockerel standing on one leg

(56) Stepping back and whirl arms on both sides

(57) The white goose displaying the two wings

(58) Diagonal slanting

(59) Flashing the back

(60) Covering the hands and punching with the fists

(61) Six sealing and four closings

(62) Single whip

(63) Waving hands like clouds

(64) Reaching high to touch the horse

(65) Crossing legs

(66) Hammering under the hip

(67) The ape stretching forward to get the fruit

(68) Single whip

(69) The dragon jumping up from the ground

(70) Stepping up in the position of seven stars

(71) Retreating and mounting the tiger

(72) Sweeping the lotus twice

(73) Throwing a fist to the head of the opponent

(74) Diamond hammer

Closing position

The Second Movement of Chen-style Taiji Boxing 陈式太极拳老架二路

There are 42 acts in the Second Movement of Chen-style Taiji Boxing, which are complex, fast, violent and springing, and among which there are running, hopping, jumping, escaping, attacking and other movements. It is characterized by quickness, hardness and jumping. Judging from the outside, it is not different from other boxing in its quickness, hardness and jumping, but in essence it has the characteristics of its own: to constantly spin the waist, turn back, twist forearm, rotate the shoulder, twist the ankle and kneels so as to form the integrated spiral actions in which one movement leads to all the movements, which can get the general effect of opening and freeing, closing and gathering, opening with closing and freeing with gathering.

Because this Boxing is quick in speed and strong in explosive force, it's suitable for the youth, the adults, and healthy people to practice. It takes two minutes to practice this Boxing.

Here are the names of the acts:

(1) Starting position

(2) Diamond hammer

(3) Fastening one's clothes lazily

(4) Six sealing and four closing

(5) Single whip

(6) Throwing a fist to protect the heart
(7) Diagonal slanting
(8) Turning back with diamond hammer
(9) Turning around and throwing a fist
(10) Throwing a fist under the hip
(11) Chopping with the hands
(12) Turning over the flowers by brandishing the sleeves
(13) Covering the hands and punching with the fists
(14) Giving a elbow to the waist of the opponent
(15) Punching with big and small fists
(16) Fair lady working at the shuffle the fairy weaving at the shuttle
(17) Riding backward on a dragon
(18) Covering the hands and punching with the fists
(19) Changing position inside
(20) Forming as a beast's head
(21) Palm cutting
(22) Turning over the flower by brandishing the sleeves
(23) Covering the hands and punching with the fists
(24) Subduing the tiger
(25) Cleaning off the eyebrows of the opponent
(26) The yellow dragon stirring water for three times
(27) Thrusting the left fist forward
(28) Thrusting the right fist forward
(29) Covering the hands and punching with the fists
(30) Sweeping the foot circularly
(31) Covering the hands and punching with the fists
(32) Hammer blowing
(33) Covering the hands and punching with the fists
(34) Pounding and turning around
(35) Punching twice on the left and punching twice on the right
(36) Turning back to attack directly
(37) Attacking the haunt
(38) Giving a fist to the waist of the opponent
(39) Parrying the elbow
(40) Attacking the haunt directly
(41) Turning back and moving in directly
(42) Diamond hammer
Closing position

Wudang Sanfeng Taiji Swordplay 武当三丰太极剑

Wudang Taiji Swordplay has been playing an important role in Wudang Boxing and weapons, which was taught by the former famous martial art master Sha Guozheng. Wudang Taiji Swordplay is characterized by distinct acts, broad position, smoothness and naturalness, proper proportion of the slow and the quick, softness and twisting, and elegance and steadiness, helpful to keep healthy and prolong the lifespan.

Here are the names of the acts:

(1) Stepping forward and covering the sword

(2) The immortal directing the way

(3) Three rings covering the moon

(4) Moving in the position of the big star

(5) The swallow touching the water

(6) Waving the sword on both sides

(7) The boy lifting the stove

(8) Yellow bees returning back home

(9) The cat attacking at the rat

(10) The dragonfly touching the water

(11) The snake twisting the willow

(12) The swallow returning back the nest

(13) The big bird displaying the wings

(14) Whirling rightward

(15) Moving in the position of the small star

(16) Whirling leftward

(17) The fisherman fishing fish

(18) Poking away the grass to look for the snake

(19) Hugging the moon in the arms

(20) The sleeping bird flying into the forest

(21) The dragon waving the tail

(22) The dragon jumping out of the water

(23) The wind folding the leaves of lotus

(24) The lion shaking the head

(25) The tiger hugging the head

(26) The wild horse jumping over the valley

(27) Turning over to stop the horse

(28) The gold needle pointing southward

(29) Flipping the dirt against the wind

(30) Pushing the boat with the current

(31) The falling star chasing the moon

(32) The sky-horse running in the sky

(33) Stepping on the snow to look for the plum
(34) Gold flowers falling down the earth
(35) Picking up the curtain
(36) Waving the sword like a wheel on both sides
(37) The swallow picking up the soil
(38) The wild horse separating the mane
(39) The birds flying in all directions
(40) The swimming dragon playing with the water
(41) Fishing the moon in the deep sea
(42) Standing up to subdue the tiger
(43) Poking the sea
(44) The rhinoceros putting up the head to look the moon
(45) Shooting the wild goose
(46) The dragon putting out the paws
(47) Painting Taiji
(48) The phoenix displaying the wings
(49) Flying obliquely
(50) The swan displaying the wings
(51) Striding over the rail on both sides
(52) The immortal painting the picture
(53) The monkey offering the fruit
(54) The flowers falling on both sides
(55) Fair lady working at the shuttle
(56) The tiger waving the tail
(57) The fish jumping over the dragon gate
(58) The dragon twisting the post
(59) Fair lady touching the flowers
(60) The leaves falling with the current
(61) The wind sweeping the plums
(62) Breaking the gold stone
(63) The clever girl sewing the clothes
(64) The black clouds covering over the head

Wudang Horsetail Whisk 武当拂尘

The horsetail whisk, one of Taoist religion service materials, also the thing that Taoists will take with when they practice cultivation and travel around, has been developed into one kind of soft weapon with its own special characters.

The acts of Wudang Horsetail Whisk are mainly made up of blowing upward, sweeping downward, throwing, twisting and picking, whose features are relaxed, nimble, elegant, overcoming the tough with gentle acts, and the tough and the gentle helping each other.

Here are the names of the acts:

Starting position

(1) Turning around the body

(2) The yellow dragon covering the head

(3) The old tortoise trying the way

(4) Stepping in the position of the five elements

(5) The black tiger beating a way

(6) Sweeping thousands of soldiers

(7) Turning over the rivers and the seas

(8) Putting up the whip behind the horse

(9) The monkey shrinking the body

(10) Twisting the bamboo

(11) Breaking Wu Mountain at the waist

(12) Poking away the clouds to see the sun

(13) Looking around on both sides

(14) The Monkey offering the fruits

(15) Touching the sea

(16) The dragon waving the tail

(17) The horse kicking the leg

(18) The falling star chasing the moon

(19) Subduing the dragon and the tiger

(20) Turning back to see the moon

(21) Attacking directly at the yellow dragon

(22) Whipping the horse to run faster

(23) Balancing Yin and Yang

(24) Sitting on the mountain

Closing position

Wudang Swordplay 武当剑

Wudang Swordplay is the most representative swordplay among all the weapons of Wudang School. Wudang Swordplay pays more attention to Taiji waist, eight-diagram pace, form-and-will strength, and Wudang mentality. There has a saying about Wudang Swordplay going like "Wudang Swordplay has no set theory of patterns", for it will change according to the movements of the opponent, and change acts between the real and the false, hard to predict.

Wudang Swordplay is mainly made up of these acts: whipping, taking, lifting, fending away, attacking, pointing, penetrating, straight blow, stirring, pressing, blocking and chopping.

Here are the names of the acts:

(1) Lifting the hands to begin the position

(2) Looking forward and backward

(3) The immortal directing the way

(4) Spreading flatly the carpet
(5) The snake moving out of the den
(6) Directing the single whip
(7) The phoenix displaying the wings
(8) The snake twisting the body
(9) The yellow dragon turn over the body
(10) The cat attacking at the rat
(11) The weaver working at the needle
(12) Spreading flatly the carpet
(13) The snake moving out of the den
(14) Directing the single whip
(15) The gold roster shaking the hairs
(16) Pushing open the window to see the moon
(17) The phoenix whirling around the nest
(18) Offering an incense upward
(19) Ridding on a mule back forward
(20) The yellow dragon turning over the body
(21) The cat attacking at the rat
(22) The weaver working at the needle
(23) Poking away the grass to look for the snake
(24) The swallow returning back to the nest
(25) Directing the single whip
(26) The gold roster shaking the hairs
(27) Pushing open the window to see the moon
(28) Hugging the moon in the arms
(29) Sending the bird into the forest
(30) Hugging the scepter to meet the emperor
(31) The phoenix displaying the wings
(32) Fishing the fish
(33) The rhinoceros putting up the tail
(34) The yellow bees flying out of the nest
(35) Hugging the tiger to return to the mountain
(36) The bittern stepping on the lotus
(37) The dragon swallowing the water
(38) The dragon diving into the sea
(39) The male eagle displaying the wings
(40) Hugging the tiger to return to the mountain
(41) Directing the single whip
(42) The gold roster picking up the grain

(43) The snake moving backward
(44) Pushing the boat to leave the sea
(45) The yellow dragon stirring the sea
(46) The black dragon waving the tail
(47) Picking a peach under the leaves
(48) Poking away the grass to look for the snake
(49) The cat attacking at the rat
(50) Poking away the grass to look for the snake
(51) The cat attacking at the rat
(52) Turning back to stop the horse
(53) Hiding the needle under the sleeve
(54) Putting upright the sword
(55) The dragonfly touching the water
(56) Waving the sword like a wheel on both sides
(57) The swallow picking the soil
(58) The fish jumping over the dragon gate
(59) Cutting Mount Hua downside up
(60) Withdrawing the sword

Wudang Taiji Swordplay　武当太极剑

Wudang Taiji swordplay is mainly made up of these acts: chopping, penetrating, pointing, straight blowing, picking, taking, fending away, whipping, lifting and so on, which is characterized by clear sword acts, gentle movements, mild rhythm, a unity of body, sword and mentality, full of vigor.

Here are the names of the acts:

Preparing position
(1) The immortal directing the way
(2) The cloud rings covering the moon
(3) Turning back to see the moon
(4) Moving in the position of the big star
(5) The swallow touching the water
(6) Sweeping on both sides
(7) Moving in the position of the small star
(8) The swallow returning to the nest
(9) The cat attacking at the rat
(10) The dragonfly touching the water
(11) The yellow bees returning to the den
(12) The bird displaying the right wing
(13) Whirling the sword leftward
(14) Whirling the sword rightward

(15) Poking away the grass to look for the snake

(16) Hugging the moon in the arms

(17) The sleeping birds flying into the forest

(18) The black dragon waving the tail

(19) The wind folding the lotus

(20) The lion shaking the head

(21) The tiger hugging the head

(22) The wild horse jumping over the valley

(23) Turning back to stop the horse

(24) Pointing the sword southward

(25) Flipping the dirt against the wind

(26) Pushing the boat with the current

(27) The falling star chasing the moon

(28) The sky-horse running in the sky

(29) Picking up the curtain

(30) Whirling the sword like a wheel on both sides

(31) The phoenix displaying one wing

(32) Fishing the moon in the deep sea

(33) Hugging the moon in the arms

(34) Touching the sea

(35) The rhinoceros facing upward for the moon

(36) Shooting at the wild goose

(37) The monkey offering the fruits

(38) The phoenix displaying the wings

(39) Pouring the wind on both sides

(40) Shooting at the wild goose

(41) The monkey offering the fruits

(42) The flowers falling on both sides

(43) Fair lady working at the shuttle

(44) The tiger stirring the tail

(45) The fish jumping over the dragon gate

(46) The dragon twisting the post

(47) The immortal directing the way

(48) Pointing the sword southward

(49) Withdrawing the sword and returning to the original position

Closing position

Taoist Yuan Limin, born in Jingzhou City, is a martial art coach, vice-chairmen of Wudang Martial Art Performance Team of Wudang Mountains.

Influenced by the customs of studying martial art in his hometown, he began to study folk traditional martial art when he was very young. For he was working very hard, the teacher loved him so much that taught him as much as possible.

At the age of eleven, enlightened by his teacher, he came to Wudang Mountains to study Wudang Martial Art. There are many strict rules and regulations in Taoism, and Wudang Martial Art is just spread among Taoists only; but he was persevere and modest to ask for advice, after many years' testing and with his own good base, he finally learned genuine Wudang Martial Art.

Living in Wudang Mountains and influenced by Taoist Culture, he got great interested in Wudang traditional culture. Knowing that there is a tight relationship between Wudang Martial Art and traditional culture, he made up his mind to work hard at culture, asked for advice from these profound Taoists, so as to make a big progress both in moral cultivation and skills application.

He loves Wudang Culture and Wudang Martial Art very much, taking as his own duty spreading Wudang Martial Art.

The following are these competitions that he have taken part in:

In 2001, he was awarded Swordplay Champion in Wudang Boxing International Friendship Competition.

In 2001, he composed a play of martial art to take part in Wudang Mountains International Tourism Festival, having made great success.

In 2002, he composed and performed the main programs to celebrate the Third Anniversary of Macao Returning, giving Macao people the chance of enjoying Wudang Martial Art in their own eyes.

In 2002, he took part in Wudang, Shaolin, and Emei Masters competition held in Mount Emei, on behalf of Wudang Mountains.

In the spring festival of 2002, he led a team to take part in Wudang, Shaolin, and Emei Masters Competition held in ShenZhen City, on behalf of Wudang Mountains.

In April of 2003, he was invited to give a performance of Wudang Martial Art in Taiwan Province, which became the hot topic of the province.

He has also, as a Wudang inheritor, given many performances of Wudang Martial Art to leaders of the Central Government, leaders of foreign countries and friends home and abroad.

Here are the names of Gongfu:

Wudang Taoist-Exclusive Taiji Boxing 武当秘传太极拳

Zhang Sanfeng, the founder of Wudang Inner Exercise, on the basis of understanding the gist of Taiji and watching the fight between a swallow and a snake, created Taiji Boxing.

It has been hundreds of years since the founder created Wudang School, which has developed into many schools of Taiji Boxing with their own outstanding features. However, Wudang Taiji Boxing was not seen by others, just like a mystery, so that there was a saying to the effect that Wudang Taiji Boxing was lost in spreading. In the fact, Wudang Taiji Boxing was not lost in spreading, but exclusive in spreading. Because that Wudang Taiji Boxing was Taoist exclusive in temples with strict rules and regulations, it is not easily seen by the common people.

In the 1980s, Wudang Taiji Boxing appeared in a Martial Art Competition. When saw this, all the masters present cried in joy, "This is the real Wudang Taiji Boxing! Wudang Taiji Boxing has not been lost in spreading."

This Boxing is special in manner, detailed in explaining the theory of Taiji Boxing created by Zhang Sanfeng, which has been regarded as the masterwork of profound Taoists of all generations.

Here are the names of the acts:

(1) Having a breath and standing there still

(2) Moving in the direction of Taiji

(3) Poking away the clouds to see the sun

(4) Hugging the moon in the arms

(5) Poking away the clouds to see the sun

(6) Hugging the moon in the arms

(7) Seahorse Spitting fog in both right and left directions

(8) Turning around the body in both right and left directions

(9) Crossing the hands

(10) The lion turning back the head

(11) Collecting the tail of the swallow

(12) Pushing open the window to see the moon

(13) The phoenix worshiping the sun

(14) Turning backing the head to see the moon

(15) Fishing the moon in the deep sea

(16) Tucking the clothes

(17) Fishing a needle in the deep sea

(18) The immortal jumping over the valley in both right and left directions

(19) Subduing the dragon and tiger

(20) Picking a peach under the leaves

(21) The general Hanging the stamp

(22) Official Wang putting up the whip

(23) Waving the single whip downward

(24) GuanYu combing the beards

(25) Picking a peach under the leaves

(26) Jumping forward and waving the hands

(27) Putting out the hand to touch the horse

(28) Fighting right and left in the direction of the Seven Stars

(29) Stepping back whirling arms on both sides.

(30) Circling the knees and moving forward

(31) The dragon jumping out of the sea

(32) Crossing the hands

(33) Separating the feet on both sides

(34) Giving a hammer under the elbow

(35) Pushing back the sleeves on the small elbows on both sides

(36) Standing on one foot on both sides

(37) Hugging the moon in the arms

(38) Fair lady working at the shuttle on both sides

(39) Pushing back the sleeves on the big elbows on the both sides

(40) Lying drunkard in the lake

(41) Obliquely brushing knees and twisting steps

(42) Fighting right and left in the direction of the Seven Stars

(43) Carrying the mountains on the shoulder

(44) Putting out the hand to touch the horse

(45) Turning back to place the lotus

(46) Bending a bow to shoot at the tiger

(47) Tucking the clothes on both sides

(48) Closing position

Wudang Taoist-Exclusive Five-Form Regimen 武当秘传五形养生功

Wudang Mountains, the cradle of Wudang Inner Exercise, through hundreds of years' succeeding and development, has formed a set of internal regimen system which combines keeping fit, regimen, attacking and defending into one.

Wudang Taoist-Exclusive Five-Form Regimen, one of the excellent exercises succeeded by Wudang Taoists, is the required course that every Wudang Taoist must study. This regimen is made up of five big forms of tortoise, snake, dragon, tiger, and swan, which, derived from the powerful and holy creatures in Chinese traditional culture, will cooperate with five elements, so as to harmonize human body functions, make the man vigorous in blood and breath, clear in mind and sharp in eyes, and smart in thinking.

Here are the names of the acts:

The form of tortoise

The tortoise, in Chinese traditional culture, was one kind of creature who could predict the future, enjoy a long life and clever, do everything steady and quiet. In the five elements, the tortoise belongs to water; so practicing this regimen can increase energy, strengthen the kidney, and make the body soft and flexible.

(1) Starting position

(2) Guarding the breath into the pubic region

(3) Having a deep and long breath

(4) Xian-Yu Putting up the ancient cooking vessel

(5) Creeping on the earth to look for the root

(6) The tortoise grasping the moon

(7) The tortoise playing with the water

(8) The tortoise spitting out the medicine

Closing position

The form of swan

The swan, in Chinese traditional culture, had the following characters: transcendence and escaping from the common world, elegance and purity. In the five elements, the swan belongs to fire; the heart in the body. Practicing this regimen often can make the man vigorous in energy, salubrious in mind and mood.

(1) Starting position

(2) Guarding the breath into the pubic region

(3) Flying leftward and right ward

(4) The swan displaying the wings

(5) The swan playing with the water

(6) The swan standing on the peak

(7) The swan is going to fly

(8) The swan cleaning the eyes.

Closing position

The form of snake

In Chinese traditional culture, the snake and the tortoise were a unity, called Xuanwu. In the five elements, the snake belongs to metal, the lung in the human body. Practicing the regimen often can cultivate the lung and make the body soft.

(1) Starting position

(2) Guarding the breath into the pubic region

(3) Turning around the body

(4) The snake twisting the willow

(5) The snake moving out of the den

(6) The snake moving into the den

(7) The snake creeping on the earth

(8) The snake turning over the body

Closing position

The form of tiger

In Chinese traditional culture, the tiger was the symbol of power and unruliness. In the five elements, the tiger belongs to soil. Practicing the regimen often can cultivate the spleen and stomach, strengthen the bones and muscles.

(1) Starting position

(2) Guarding the breath into the pubic region

(3) The tiger washing the hands and face

(4) The tiger crouching down to listen to the wind

(5) The tiger attacking at the prey

(6) The tiger standing there still to look around

(7) The tiger swallowing the prey

(8) The tiger turning back the head

Closing position

The form of dragon

In Chinese traditional culture, the dragon was a creature of wisdom and cloud, with the characters of predicting the future and ordering the clouds to rain. In the five elements, the dragon belongs to wood. Practicing the regimen often can cultivate the liver and gallbladder and make vigorous in blood and breath.

(1) Starting position

(2) Guarding the breath into the pubic region

(3) The dragon putting out the paws

(4) The two dragons playing with the pearl

(5) The dragon waving the tail

(6) The dragon twisting to control the pearl

(7) The swimming dragon and the flying phoenix

(8) The dragon diving into the sea

Closing position

Wudang Dan Swordplay 武当丹剑

Wudang Dan Swordplay, or Wudang Dan School Swordplay, is said to have been created by Zhang Sanfeng, the founder of Wudang Martial Art. Zhang Songxi, Wudang Taoist of the Ming Dynasty, had spread this swordplay in Siming Mountain, Zhejiang Province, so it is also named Siming Swordplay.

Wudang Dan Swordplay contains two kinds of swordplay: single man exercising and double men exercising. The single men exercising includes the sky, the earth, and the man three levels swordplay, which mainly consists of thirteen patterns of changes, such as taking out, taking away, lifting, feeding away, attacking, thrusting, pointing, straight blow, stirring, chopping and so on. When exercising, the man should act in a Taiji waist, Eight-Diagram paces, turn around like rolling pearls in a plate and walk like rolling wheels. The swordplay is everlasting, light, elegant, as soft as floating cloud and flowing water, as light as a swallow flying through the forest.

Wudang Dan Swordplay, alternating with the real and feint acts, changing between Yin and Yang, displays the stage of Taoist elegance and quietness.

Wudang Taiyi Floss Palm 武当太乙绵掌

Taoists use water to explain Taoism, thinking that water does not complain about when staying below, just adjusts to the surrounding, softly and quietly; however, water also can build up energy and power so as to break stones and cut mountains.

Wudang Floss Palm, derived from the “Water” philosophical theory of Wudang Inner Boxing, is delicate and exquisite, for floss is soft. Wudang Taiyi Floss Palm, alternating with the tough and the tender, changing between Yin and Yang, neither hard-shelled nor stagnant, is soft in appearance, but powerful in force. That the tough is easily to be broken and that the soft can succeed forever demonstrate Taoist gist of overcoming the tough by the tender acts. Taiyi, in Taoism, is the extremity. Wudang Taiyi Floss Palm is one extreme boxing that takes the softness as the gist.

Wudang Taiyi Peripatetic Palm 武当太乙逍遥掌

Wudang Taiyi Peripatetic Palm is one Taoist-Exclusive Gongfu of Wudang Inner Boxing, which takes deep respiration and guarding as the core and emphasizes the cultivation of inner exercise.

In skills, Wudang Taiyi Peripatetic Palm emphasizes the following skills, separating muscles and breaking bones, catching the muscles and veins, attacking the points and so on. When exercising or walking, the man has an elegant and natural manner of Taoist characteristics.

Here are the names of the acts:

(1) The purple gas coming from the east

(2) The black tiger sitting in the den

(3) Two dragons playing with a pearl

(4) The river vehicle carrying loads, left-style

(5) The river vehicle carrying loads, right-style

(6) Poking away the grass to look for the snake

(7) Two immortals teaching Taoism

(8) The ancient tree twisting roots

(9) The wild goose displaying the wings

(10) The swallow touching the water

(11) The white snake spitting the tongue

(12) Three plates falling down the ground

(13) The hungry tiger attacking at the prey

(14) The pie sitting on the branch

(15) Transferring the flowers and engrafting the tree

(16) Holding the pagoda in the hand

(17) The logger asking the way

(18) The green dragon jumping out of the water

(19) Poking away the cloud to see the sun

(20) Transferring the flowers and engrafting the tree

(21) The wind shaking the lotus

(22) The white monkey guarding the cave

(23) Pushing the boat with the current

(24) The snake and the pie fighting for the food

(25) Running the thread through the eye of the needle

(26) The yellow dragon twisting on the post

(27) The founder reflecting the light

(28) The morning sun in Wudang Mountain

(29) The moon knocking the mountain gate
(30) Sweeping the devils
(31) The black tiger walking into the den
(32) The storming sea running after the waves
(33) Containing the secret and hiding the mentality
(34) The Eight Immortals traveling in the sea
(35) Hiding flowers under the leaves
(36) The thunder fire tempering the hall
Closing position

Wudang Xuanwu Cudgelplay　武当玄武棍

Wudang Xuanwu Cudgelplay, one Taoist-Exclusive Gongfu of Wudang Inner Boxing, is the cudgelplay for Taoists to protect the mountain and guard the temples.

Wudang Xuanwu Cudgelplay, simple and clear, seems to be soft and powerless, but as powerful and violent as running flood and storming sea. When exercising, the cudgel has the softness of a snake and the composure of the tortoise. The cudgel, on the basis of blowing, pointing, hanging, teasing, sweeping and fending, emphasizes the unity of the body and the cudgel, looking for the straight acts among the cursive movements and changing between Yin and Yang.

Here are the names of the acts:
Starting position: the purple gas coming from the east
(1) Offering an incense to the sky
(2) The immortal cutting the mountain
(3) The dragonfly touching the water
(4) Walking on and tucking up the clothes
(5) The green dragon jumping out the water
(6) The yellow bees flying out of the den
(7) Falling star chasing the moon
(8) The wild goose falling down the ground
(9) The white snake spitting out the tongue
(10) The lion turning back the head
(11) Sweeping thousands of soldiers
(12) Walking on and tucking up the clothes
(13) The seven stars worshiping the North Pole
(14) Subduing the dragon and the tiger
(15) The dragon jumping out of the sea
(16) Subduing the dragon and the tiger
(17) The black tiger sitting in the den
(18) The wind sweeping the clouds
(19) The wind shaking the lotus

(20) The black dragon waving the tail
(21) The yellow bees flying out of the den
(22) The pie sitting on the branch
(23) The wind sweeping the clouds
(24) The wind shaking the lotus
(25) The white monkey offering the fruits
(26) The tortoise looking up for the moon
(27) Carrying the mountain on the shoulders
(28) The tortoise playing with the water
(29) The wind sweeping the clouds
(30) Hiding the flowers under the leaves
(31) The black tiger sitting in the den
(32) The ancient tree twisting the root
(33) The white snake spitting out the tongue
(34) The yellow bees flying out of the den
(35) Stopping the horse on the cliff
(36) Two dragons playing with the pearl
(37) The phoenix displaying the wings
(38) The big star nodding the head
(39) The white monkey offering the fruits
(40) Poking away the grass and looking for the snake
(41) The white swan flying up
(42) The black dragon waving the tail
(43) Sweeping all the devils
(44) Turning back to look at the moon
(45) Lifting the ancient cooking utensil with two hands
(46) The rabbit kicking the eagle
(47) The gold roster opening the wings
(48) The swan standing among the hens
(49) The black tiger inspecting the mountain
(50) The five dragons worshiping the Emperor Jade
(51) Handing the incense and worshiping the ancestors
Closing position

Tan Dajiang, or Kong De, male, born in 1947, now is the vice-editor-general of Wudang Magazine, Secretary-General of China Wudang Mountains Wudang Boxing Academy. Having been working hard at Wudang Martial Art, Wudang Culture, and Taoist Regimen, he is a famous expert in Inner Medicine Regimen, Taoist, researcher of Taoism Culture, enjoying a very great fame home and abroad.

The books that he has published are the following: *Wudang Qigong*, *The Ancient Mystery of*

Wudang Mountains, *A Research on Wudang Boxing* (co-author), *A General Introduction of Wudang Martial Art, The Notes to The Collection of Muscle-Changing and Marrow-Cultivating, Wudang Inner School, The Notes to Leyu Hall Quotations, The Collection of Taoist Couplets, A General Introduction of Wudang Zhao Pu-Style Taiji Boxing* and so on. Besides these books, he has also published one-million-word articles in the relative publications all over the country.

The prizes he has attained are the following: the Second Prize in Qu Yuan Cup Hubei Highest Literature Prize, the Excellent Paper and Achievement Prize in Vitality Cup International Traditional Medicine Papers Competition, the Third Prize for Science Progress sponsored by the State Department of Physical Education. His stories have been compiled into *The Collection of China Couplet Artists, Experts Section of China Cyclopedia*, and so like books.

The main concurrent posts of social science he has had: a member of News Commission of China Martial Art Association, member of China Couplet Academy, committee of Hubei Martial Art Association, member of Hubei Folk Artist Association, Secretary-general of China Wudang Mountains Wudang Boxing Academy, advisor of Chang'an International Taiji Boxing Academy, advisor of Harbin Eight Diagrams Palm Academy, guest professor of Zhejiang Province Xinchang Taiji Academy, advisor of Henan Zhao Pu-style Taiji Boxing Association, honorary chairman of Wuhan China Wudang Boxing Academy and so on.

Here are the names of Gongfu:

Muscle-Changing Exercise 易筋功

This Muscle-Changing Exercise, selected from *The Illustration to Muscle-changing and Marrow-cultivating Internal Exercise* by Zhou Xuguan of the Qing Dynasty, consists of the ten big patterns: Righting the body, Folding the body, Moving the body, Siding the body, Twisting the body, Sitting the body, Halving the body, Head standing the body, Bending the body, and Turning over the body.

The ten big patterns, all having a priority to exercise under the general principle of "Changing Muscles and Cultivating Marrow", are the effective ways for the weak and the ill to suit the remedy to the case. A comprehensive cultivation of the ten big patterns can dredge all the veins in the body, activate the blood and breath, strengthen the muscles and bones, cure disease and prevent disease, keep healthy and prolong the lifespan, even make the man more powerful in fighting. If the exerciser can cultivate Static Qigong, at the same time when cultivate Dynamic Qigong, which will be more helpful in cultivating the character and mood.

To speak in simple words, "Changing Muscles" is to cultivate the life; "Cultivating Marrow" is to cultivate the character, which is one way for Taoist and Buddhist to teach the super Tao.

The ten big patterns are the lower-hand acts of Changing Muscles and Cultivating Marrow. When you understand the truth of cultivating Taoism, you will understand that all the laws are flexible and changing. So we hope that the learners can understand the truth from the exercise, and then understand the ways to cultivate from the truth, which is a genuine shortcut.

Here are the names of Muscle-Changing Exercise

Righting the body

(1) Standing in a ring-arch

(2) Offering the pestle to start the exercise

(3) Putting the paws and displaying the wings

(4) Two phoenixes worshiping the sun

(5) The flying eagle displaying the wings

(6) Holing a pagoda in both hands

(7) Three peaks facing each other

(8) The dragon putting out the left paw

(9) The dragon putting out the right paw

(10) Side legs standing

(11) Crossing the ten fingers

(12) Touching the belly

(13) Putting out the palms flatly

(14) Opening the two palms

(15) Overlapping the two palms and supporting backward

(16) Overlapping the two palms and pushing forward

(17) Turning over the palms and supporting forward

(18) Opening the two palms

(19) Pointing the palms up into the sky

(20) Overlapping the palms and supporting the sky

(21) Overlapping the two palms and pushing forward

(22) Turning over the palms and supporting forward

(23) Opening the two palms

(24) Overlapping the two palms and supporting backward

(25) Offering the pestle and returning to the original position

(26) Facing upward

Closing Position

Folding the body

(1) Offering the pestle on a horse

(2) Bowing down to hug the post

(3) Nodding the head

(4) Driving the river carriage backward

(5) Raising the head and hanging the tail

(6) Closing the palms to calm one's breath

(7) Putting out the hands to relax the veins

(8) Standing up

(9) Stepping on the cloud and poking away the fog

(10) Supporting the sky and controlling the earth

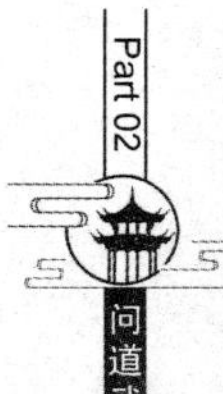

(11) Relaxing the arms and legs

(12) Hanging a clock

(13) Standing right like a pine

(14) Offering the pestle and returning to the original position

(15) Facing up

Closing position

Moving the body

(1) Putting out the left foot

(2) Putting out the right foot

(3) Whirling the right foot and then standing

(4) Whirling the left foot and then standing

(5) Putting down the palms and stamping the feet

(6) Relaxing the eyebrows

(7) Holding the fists to activate the strength

(8) Side legs standing on a horse

(9) Supporting the palms on a horse

(10) Moving round the left hand (I)

(11) Moving round the left hand (II)

(12) Moving round the left hand (III)

(13) Moving round the left hand (IV)

(14) Hanging the fists and unwinding the body

(15) Moving round the right hand (I)

(16) Moving round the right hand (II)

(17) Moving round the right hand (III)

(18) Moving round the right hand (IV)

(19) Hanging the fists and unwinding the body

(20) Crossing the left foot

(21) Crossing the right foot

(22) Round light over the head

(23) Round light in the heart

(24) The swimming fish opening the wings

(25) The swimming fish separating the wings

(26) Hammering backward

(27) Hammering forward

(28) Putting out the palms and relaxing the body

(29) Withdrawing the palms and relaxing the body

(30) Waving the palms and relaxing the body

(31) Holding the palms and relaxing the body

(32) Massaging the belly to dredge the breath

(33) Crossing the hands and returning to the original position

Closing position

Siding the body

(1) Putting up the left hand to support the sky

(2) Turning over the right hand to bring out the knife

(3) Opening the bow and shooting leftward

(4) Relaxing the shoulders flatly

(5) The swan shaking the wings

(6) Offering the pestle and making a knot

(7) Facing up

(8) Closing position

Twisting the body

(1) Offering the pestle on a horse

(2) Turning leftward and hugging backward

(3) Turning leftward and lifting the hands

(4) Turning leftward and bending over to the ground

(5) Hugging backward and turning leftward

(6) Turning rightward and hugging backward

(7) Turning rightward and lifting the hands

(8) Turning rightward and bending over to the ground

(9) Hugging backward and turning rightward

(10) Pulling the ox's tail leftward

(11) Pulling the ox's tail rightward

(12) Offering the pestle and turning leftward

(13) Offering the pestle and turning rightward

(14) Offering the pestle and turning to the middle

(15) Crossing the feet and jumping up

(16) Facing up

(17) Offering the pestle and returning to the original position

(18) Closing position

Halving the body

(1) Offering the pestle on a horse

(2) Throwing the rein on a horse

(3) Withdrawing the rein on a horse

(4) Tidying up the clothes on a horse

(5) Tidying up the helmet on a horse

(6) Driving a horse with the wind

(7) Stopping the horse leftward

(8) Stopping the horse rightward

(9) Side legs standing on a horse

(10) Exchanging something with others on a horse

(11) Tidying up the saddles forward

(12) Throwing the rein forward

(13) Throwing the rein on both sides

(14) Tidying up the saddles backward

(15) Lifting the rein forward

(16) Throwing the rein forward

(17) Throwing the rein on both sides

(18) Climbing a pine on a horse

(19) Lifting the ancient cooking vessel on a horse

(20) Lifting the rein forward

(21) Throwing the rein forward

(22) Throwing the rein on both sides

(23) Tidying up the saddles backward

(24) Offering the pestle on a horse

(25) Facing up

(26) Offering the pestle and returning to the original position

Closing position

Head standing the body

(1) Offering the pestle on a horse

(2) Closing the palms and flattening the wind

(3) Letting the four parts on the ground

(4) Putting out the left foot and relaxing the body

(5) Putting out the right foot and relaxing the body

(6) Standing on the ground and returning to the original position

Closing position

Bending the body

(1) Offering the pestle on a horse

(2) Crossing the hands upward on a horse

(3) Crossing the hands downward on a horse

(4) Waving the hands on both sides

(5) Standing on the ground with two feet and the pestle

(6) Offering the pestle and returning to the original position

(7) Facing up

(8) Closing position

Ten Trigrams Boxing 十段锦

Ten Trigrams Boxing, one of Chinese traditional regimen exercise is an easy-to-learn set of exercise to practice regimen and hairdressing, cure disease and keep healthy, with a long history, which was very popular in the Qin Dynasty, then applied by Confucians, Taoism, and Buddhism. This exercise has no limitation of time, suitable for the old and the young, the male and the female. This exercise also has pertinence, that is, if you want to practice hairdressing, you should practice more face exercise; if you want to cure and prevent eyes disease, you should practice more eye exercise, and so on.

Tan Dajiang, having been researching Taoist Medicine and Ten Trigrams Exercise for thirty years, understands deeply the curative effect to cure disease and keep healthy and maintain beautiful, so tidies them up and performs them by himself, with the purpose to enlighten the learners.

Face Exercise

This exercise is to activate the blood and moisten the face, so as to get rid of spots in the face, make the face smooth, soft, and healthy.

Eye Exercise

This exercise is to cultivate the eyesight and cure the eyes disease, as well as some troubles in wind and kidney.

Nose Exercise

This exercise is to cure the nose diseases and cultivate the lung.

Tooth Exercise

This exercise is to make the teeth strong and tight, concentrate the mind and cure the toothaches.

Mouth Exercise

This exercise is to cultivate all the internal parts of the body, activate the blood and supply the breath.

Head Exercise

This exercise is to cure some troubles in the head, clear head and beautify the hair.

Ear Exercise

This exercise is to cure drumming in the ears, make the ear more alert and improve the listening capability.

Waist Exercise

This exercise is to strengthen the kidney, cure the troubles in the waist and make the vertebra flexible.

Knee Exercise

The health condition of a man has something to do with his knees and legs. This exercise is to cure the troubles in the knees, increase the strength and flexibility of the knees, so as to keep healthy and prolong the lifespan.

Belly Exercise

This exercise is to improve the functions of the spleen and the stomach, so as to help digesting the food, and cultivate the public region and the healthy energy.

Eight Trigrams Boxing　八段锦

This exercise is a set of Dynamic Qigong which is easy to learn, time-compassing, helpful to cure disease and keep healthy, and suitable for all sorts of people, compiled by Tan Dajiang, China famous expert in Inner Medicine Regimen, Taiji Medicine inheritor of Wudang Mountains Sanfeng Hermit School, who, on the basis of the gist of breath-guiding and boxing of all generations of Wudang Taoists, combined the living characters of modern people with the manners of physical education sports. This exercise is clear and quick in rhythm, elegant in movement, and proper in activating all the parts, bones and joints of the body. This exercise is easy to learn and to remember by heart, which can be practiced singly or wholly, in a long time or in a short time, with a wide applicability and popularity.

Seeing the moon and picking the stars

This exercise is to move the neck, shoulder joints, arms and the back, so as to cultivate the spleen and the stomach and improve the eyesight.

Looking around on both sides

This exercise is to improve the flexibility and harmony of the waist, knees and neck by way of turning the waist, exchanging the knees, and turning around the neck, so as to prevent some diseases in the bones and joints. Turning around the neck on both sides, holding the fists, and staring backward can cure and prevent fatigue, strengthen the vital energy and strength, and improve the eyesight.

The Ancient tree standing against the wind

This exercise is to activate the bones in the bosom by way of putting up and waving the arms, so as to cultivate the inner parts of the bosom.

The Swan beginning to dance

This exercise is to strengthen the function of the inner parts of the bosom by way of opening the bosom on one hand; to improve the flexibility of the six main joints on the other hand.

One pillar supporting the sky

This exercise is to cultivate the balance capability of the body, strengthen the toughness and flexibility of knee and hip joints, and to improve the strength.

Hating the earth for no door

This exercise is to strengthen the functions of waist and kidney and the toughness of the legs so as to get rid of fatigue by way of bending over the waist and nodding the head.

The swallow displaying the tail

This exercise is, on the basis of the former exercise, to further strengthen the flexibility of waist and knee joints, cultivate the vertebra, so as to prevent and cure some troubles in the neck and the back vertebras.

Hugging the ball and returning to the field

This exercise is to open and relax the bosom on one hand, and to absorb the vital energy into the public region to nurse the life by way of hugging the ball in both arms on the other hand.

Taiji Thirteen-Sword 太极十三剑

Chen Qing, the master of Dart in the Qing Dynasty, invented Taiji Thirteen-Sword, formerly named Thirteen-Act of Darts. Taiji Thirteen-Sword was developed from the base of thirteen acts of sword. All the acts intensely connected, require right cooperation of hands, eyes, body, acts, and feet, especially some skillful actions.

Here are the names of these acts:

(1) Preparing act

(2) Displaying the two arms like a swan

(3) Directing a way like a god

(4) Hiding a needle under a leaf

(5) Touching the sea

(6) Cleaving Mount Tai

(7) Clutching the rein to stop the horse

(8) Attacking a rabbit like a hungry eagle

(9) Standing on one foot like a roster

(10) Jumping downward like an eagle

(11) Hugging the moon in the arms

(12) Running after the moon like a falling star

(13) Hanging the clock upside down

(14) Wrapping the flag with the current

(15) Chopping the thorns to beat a way out

(16) Hugging a lute in the arms

(17) Waving the tail like a tiger

(18) Hugging the moon in the arms

(19) Cleaving Mount Tai

(20) Clutching the rein to stop the horse

(21) Pointing to the South

(22) Playing with the hoptoad

(23) Pointing to the South

(24) Returning home like a swallow

(25) Hanging the clock upside down

(26) Turning back like a tiger

(27) Climbing the mountain to run after the moon

(28) Jumping upward

(29) Touching the sea

(30) Looking for a pearl in the sea

(31) Jumping out of the sea like a dragon

(32) Wrapping the lotus leaves

(33) Turning over like a snake

(34) Jumping out of the sea like a dragon
(35) Pulling the boat with the current
(36) Going down like a snake
(37) Facing upward
(38) Crossing through the rainbow
(39) Kicking the branch to get the peach
(40) Clutching the rein to stop the horse
(41) Offering the book like the Golden Boy
(42) Attacking the sky like an eagle
(43) Flying upward like a dragon
(44) Offering the lute like the Jade Girl
(45) Mooing like a roster to pronounce the dawn
(46) Respecting the phoenix

Wudang Songxi Sword 武当松溪剑

Wudang Songxi Sword, the special sword of inner exercise, is famous for clear acts, beautiful actions, high speed, and violent force. The exercising of Wudang Songxi Sword will make the man's actions smart, the body light and the waist flexible.

Here are the names of these acts:

(1) Casting the net to catch fishes
(2) Sweeping the leaves with the current
(3) Spitting out the tongue like a snake
(4) Twisting the pole like a dragon
(5) Waving the tail like a fish
(6) Crossing the shuttle like a Vega
(7) Separating the mane
(8) Nodding like a stone
(9) Turning over like a pigeon
(10) Producing clouds under the feet
(11) Upholding the fire to burn the sky
(12) Waving the flag with the current
(13) Hitting the horse to run faster
(14) Standing on one foot like a roster
(15) Strolling on the sand beach
(16) Touching water like a swallow
(17) Fishing the moon in the sea
(18) Overlapping the head with snow
(19) Neatening the clothes with the pace
(20) Dragging a knife like a monkey
(21) Jing-Ke Killing Emperor Qin

(22) Turning around while riding a horse
(23) Running after the moon like a falling star
(24) Surprising a snake
(25) Touching the water like a swallow
(26) Waving the fan against the wind
(27) Waving the tail like a tiger
(28) Dancing violently like a snake
(29) Touching the sky with the left hand
(30) Jumping over a stream
(31) Floating a boat in a quiet lake
(32) Leaving out of the wild goose group
(33) Separating the grass to look for the snake
(34) Cleaving Mount Tai
(35) Penetrating the heart with a sharp sword
(36) Waving the fan against the wind
(37) Neatening the clothes with the current
(38) Waving the fan against the wind
(39) Waving the tail like a tiger
(40) Killing the cetacean by crossing the sea
(41) Hiding in the deep sea
(42) Penetrating the sun like a white snake
(43) Touching the water by the clothes
(44) Chopping the thorns to beat a way out
(45) Carving the clouds and cutting the moon
(46) Attacking the rat like a clever cat
(47) Casting the sand against the wind
(48) Pulling into the willow downside up
(49) Pointing the way like a god
(50) Returning to the root like the falling leaves

Wudang Taiji Sword 武当太极剑

Wudang Taiji Sword is famous for its characteristics, such as light and tender, everlasting and changing, form following the will, and charming performance. When exercising Wudang Taiji Sword, the man is now like a swimming dragon, and then like a steady mountain, with the proper combination of the active and the still, the tough and the tender.

There is full of connotations in Wudang Taiji Sword, whose body, pace, and acts are flexible, with a very high value in skill and art.

Here are the names of the acts:

(1) Starting position
(2) Walking one foot out and pointing the sword

(3) Turning back and pointing the sword
(4) Going down and sweeping the sword
(5) Touching both sides of the right and the left
(6) Separating the feet and drawing back the sword
(7) Crossing the feet and pointing the sword backward
(8) Going down while the legs are like ridding a horse
(9) Walking one foot out and pointing the sword
(10) Turning over and cleaving the sword
(11) Walking one foot out and penetrating the sword downward
(12) Standing on one foot and pointing the sword downward
(13) Going down and sweeping the sword
(14) Kicking the feet back and pointing out the sword
(15) Jumping and pointing out the sword
(16) Turning over and pointing out the sword
(17) Walking on and penetrating the sword
(18) Walking on and cleaving the sword
(19) Walking one feet out and penetrating the sword downward
(20) Jumping and penetrating the sword downward
(21) Walking one foot out and drawing back the sword
(22) Turning back and pointing out the sword backward
(23) Lifting one foot and cleaving the sword
(24) Standing on one foot and penetrating upward
(25) Drawing back the foot and sweeping the sword
(26) Facing upward and bridging the sword
(27) Turning back and drawing back the sword
(28) Standing on two feet together and pointing the sword downward
(29) Walking on and waving the sword
(30) Facing upward and waving the sword
(31) Standing still and taking hold of the sword
(32) Jumping and penetrating downward
(33) Resting the feet and pressing the sword
(34) Lifting one foot and pointing the sword
(35) Standing on one foot and bridging the sword
(36) Walking one foot out and cleaving the sword
(37) Resting the feet and pointing the sword backward
(38) Crossing the feet and sweeping the sword
(39) Resting the feet and hugging the sword
(40) Crossing the feet and sweeping the sword
(41) Walking one foot out and waving the sword

(42) Standing up and pointing out the sword

(43) Crossing the feet and penetrating back the sword

(44) Walking one foot out and pointing out the sword

(45) Walking one foot out and penetrating the sword

(46) Walking on and penetrating the sword

(47) Drawing back and then sweeping the sword

(48) Standing on the two feet and pointing out the sword

(49) Drawing back the sword and returning to the starting position

Wudang Original Taiji Boxing 武当原式太极拳

Wudang Taoist Zhang Sanfeng created Wudang Original Taiji Boxing, formerly named Zhang Sanfeng Original Taiji Boxing that is famous for its ancient boxing position and easy to learn, natural movements and flexible to change. When exercising this Boxing, we should going down and standing steadily on the two feet, so we can easily get a steady position and move downward the inner Qigong inside; therefore there is much value in keeping healthy and attacking.

Here are the names of the acts:

(1) Taiji starting position

(2) Lifting the hands

(3) Pulling out the hands to the left

(4) Pulling out the hands to the right

(5) Grasping the tail of the swallow

(6) Waving the lute

(7) Lifting the hands

(8) Walking on while keeping the kneels together

(9) Grasping the tail of the swallow

(10) Walking on while keeping the kneels together

(11) Grasping the tail of the swallow

(12) Walking on while keeping the kneels together

(13) Grasping the tail of the swallow

(14) Walking on and lifting the sinker

(15) Closing the hands by half

(16) Lifting the hands

(17) Walking on while keeping the kneels together

(18) Hugging the tiger in the arms and then putting it in the mountain

(19) Tamping the sinker under the arm

(20) Scattering the monkeys

(21) Flying in a declining way

(22) Waving the lute

(23) Lifting the hands

(24) Fishing a needle in the sea
(25) Drawing back the feet
(26) Flying in a declining way
(27) Displaying the arms
(28) Waving the hands
(29) Pointing out the arm to touch the high horse
(30) Turning back and separating the feet
(31) Walking on while keeping the kneels together
(32) Tamping the sinker while keeping the kneels together
(33) Turning back and tamping the sinker
(34) Kicking one foot out
(35) Turning over and kicking two feet out
(36) Turning back and kicking backward
(37) Shooting the tiger with a bow
(38) Walking on and pulling out the hands
(39) Walking on while keeping the kneels together
(40) Grasping the tail of the swallow
(41) Drawing back the feet and lifting the sinker
(42) Closing the hands by half
(43) Hitting the two ears with the two hands
(44) Separating the mane
(45) Shooting the shuttle
(46) Waving the whip downward
(47) Displaying the two arms
(48) Waving the hands
(49) Standing on one foot
(50) Scattering the monkeys
(51) Flying in a declining way
(52) Waving the lute
(53) Lifting the hands
(54) Fishing a needle in the sea
(55) Drawing back the feet
(56) Flying in a declining way
(57) Displaying the two arms
(58) Waving the hands
(59) Walking out the right foot and pressing the arms
(60) Walking out the left foot and pressing the arms
(61) Pulling out the palms under the arms
(62) Crossing the feet and pulling out the palms

(63) Shooting the tiger with a bow

(64) Walking on and pulling out the hands

(65) Walking on with a position of the seven stars

(66) Walking on like riding on the tiger

(67) Turning back and pulling out the hands

(68) Shooting the tiger with a bow

(69) Walking on and pulling out the hands

(70) Waving the lute

(71) Closing the hands

(72) Taiji concluding position

Liu Deyi, the only inheritor of Wudang Taoist-Exclusive Five-Element Regimen, has enjoyed a long life of 82 years by 2004, who, having been practicing this exercise from very young, has succeeded in this excellent regimen and benefited a lot from it. Though he is over eighties, he is still alert in ears and eyes, soft in muscles and strong in bones, as energetic as the young, which is the sound proof of the wonderful effect of Wudang Taoist-Exclusive Five-Element Regimen.

He learned this exercise from his father, Liu Yurong, a man of Dengzhou, Henan Province, who came to be a Taoist in Wudang Mountains when he was young. Later, Liu Yurong secularized from Wudang Taoism and settled in Yunxi County, Hubei Province. When he made a fortune in business, he established Yunxi Charity Association, to build bridges and repair roads, help the weak, protect the wild animals, with a high reputation; so he was regarded as the active pioneer to carry out "Practicing humanism before practicing Taoism" proposed by Wudang Taoism. This exercise is coming from Wudang Taoism and original in every acts and every theory, so it is very valuable.

Thanking for LiuDeyi's belief, he has offered the whole set of exercise and performed it by himself. We believe that the spreading of Wudang Taoist-exclusive Five-element Regimen will do a lot to Chinese traditional culture and human's health.

Here are the names of Gongfu:

Wudang Taoist-Exclusive Five-Element Regimen 武当道门五行养生秘功

"The Five Elements" was Chinese ancient important philosophical theory on world forming, which thought that Taiji, the unity of Yin and Yang, produced Yin and Yang, and then Yin and Yang produced all the things in the world. The ancient philosophers thought that the five elements of things, wood, fire, earth, gold, and water have their own characters of moving and changing. The characters of the five elements lie in that they have opposite aspects to each other, so can cooperate with each other, so as to bring in many changes of the things in the universe.

The theory of the five elements was also introduced into ancient medicine, which corresponded "wood, fire, earth, gold, and water" to "liver, heart, spleen, lung, and kidney" of the body, the five senses organs of "eye, tongue, mouth, nose, and ear" "muscle, vein, flesh, skin, and bone" of the body, and pointed out that when practice regimen and keep healthy, the man should obey the laws of the five elements. So we can say that Wudang Taoist-exclusive Five-element Regimen is one kind regimen for Wudang Taoists to cultivate the body and the character, with a profound foundation of Chinese traditional culture.

This exercise is made up of the five big patterns, massaging, standing, sitting with the legs crossed, sleeping cursively and sleeping flatly, abiding by human body health theory, with some effects to strengthen the vitality, cure diseases and prolong the lifespan.

Here are the names of the exercises:

Massaging

(1) Sitting with the legs crossed in a Wuji manner

(2) Turning around the body in a Taiji manner

(3) Facing up and putting the two palms upward to support the sky

(4) Massaging the face

(5) Massaging the hair

(6) Massaging the forehead

(7) Massaging the eyes

(8) Massaging the temples

(9) Massaging the nose

(10) Massaging the ears

(11) Beating the body to dredge the veins

(12) Stamping the feet to relax the body

Standing

(1) The gold pillar standing steadily to protect the medicine

(2) The phoenix nodding the head and turning the eyes and the neck

(3) Beginning to practice when the roster cries

(4) Standing upright and poking the general vein

(5) Shaking the body like a goose and softening the shoulders and the arms

(6) Pushing and pulling four times and then putting the palms upward

(7) The swan displaying the wings to fly around

(8) The hungry tiger jumping at the prey

(9) The monkey offering the fruits to the seniors

(10) Sweeping the floor with the wind and blowing on both sides

(11) The immortal directing the way and looking the sword-finger

(12) The rhinoceros looking up at the moon

(13) The dragon twisting the post

(14) Getting the moon in the deep sea and standing in horse-riding position

(15) The boy touching the sea and reaching for the heels

(16) Closing Yin and Yang and then turning the body

(17) Watching the fight on a horse and increasing the power of palms

(18) The flying wild goose displaying the wings slightly

(19) Getting the sea and looking up, then closing and opening the arms

(20) Shaking the two oars to pushing the waves

(21) Hugging oneself and turning around

(22) Putting the hands on the waist and then turning around with four kicking

(23) The swan massaging the knees and pressing slow private parts

(24) Strolling on the road

(25) Pressing palms to calm the breath and shaking the whole body

(26) Making the vital essence into the public region

Sitting with the two legs crossed

(1) Sitting with the two legs crossed and breathing normally

(2) Looking oneself and moving the eyes quietly

(3) Turning the eyes and the neck to look far away

(4) Massaging the public region and moving the breath through the body

(5) Massaging the two breasts

(6) Rubbing the palms, poking the fingers and touching the shoulders

(7) Pushing forward, grasping backward and displaying the arms

(8) Whirling the hands in a Taiji manner

(9) The wild goose flying into the shy

(10) Turning the palms in the manner of Yin and Yang

(11) Pushing and pulling slightly four times

(12) Turning the body with fingers to fingers

(13) Hugging the knees with the two hands in the manner of lotus

(14) Kicking one foot upward

(15) Massaging and beating the body to end the exercise

Sleeping with the two legs crossed

(1) Sitting with the two legs crossed and breathing normally

(2) Sleeping flatly

(3) Sleeping leftward

(4) Sleeping rightward

(5) The tiger sleeping in the wood waiting for the chance

(6) Two immortals transferring to make Yin and Yang close together

(7) The sleeping swan displaying the wings and waving slightly

(8) The tortoise moving into the den and then through the mountain

(9) The bear standing on the cliff and moving on two knees

(10) The little boy playing and climbing the two feet

(11) Beating the lower part to shaking all the body

(12) Standing to make the vital essence into the public region

Sleeping Flatly

(1) Sleeping flatly on the back and waving the inner parts of the body

(2) Sleeping on one side and shaking to cultivate the liver and the spleen

(3) Sleeping on the stomach and shaking to strengthen the waist and the kidney

(4) Relaxing the muscles and poking the bones to dredge the veins

(5) Massaging the hands and feet and poking the tips of them

(6) Hitting and catching the body to activate the muscles and bones

(7) Massaging the arms and legs

(8) Kicking the feet on both sides

(9) Sleeping with the two feet kicking forward repeatedly

(10) Bending the knees and kicking two times to change muscles and veins

(11) Opening and then whirling the legs

(12) Closing the legs and pressing slow private parts

(13) Hugging the knees and massaging the belly

(14) Opening and closing the arms and the legs as a frog swimming in the water

(15) Bowing the leg to touch the belly to the Achilles' heel

(16) Turning the body and moving the vital essence into the public region

Wudang Martial Art Education 武当武术教学

Wudang Mountains is famous all over the world for its Taoism and Martial Art. Wudang Martial Art, coming from China Taoist culture, having the efficacy of cultivating the body and character, protecting oneself and defending the enemies, is the elite of China martial art, and the treasure of oriental culture.

Wudang Martial Art is deeply connected with Taoism. Taoism emphasizes cultivating and regimen, whose real purpose is to research the laws of life activities so as to enjoy a longer life. Wudang Martial Art is the crystal produced during Wudang Taoism studied life, the result of changing the Static Qigong for cultivating the body and the character into boxing skills for protecting oneself and defending the enemies. To keep on exercising Wudang Martial Art and respect Wushu morals, can develop one's potential and wisdom, make one healthy and strong-minded, and dispel the diseases and prolong the lifespan.

Here the followings are provided: Wudang Taiji Boxing, Form-and-Will Boxing, Eight-Diagram Palm, Wudang Taiyi Five-Element Boxing, Simplified Wudang Boxing, Wudang Taiyi Peripatetic Palm, Wudang Sword, Wudang Taiyi Whisk, Wudang Xuanwu Cudgel, Wudang Sword of Drunken Eight Immortals, Eighteen-Elbow of Nine Directions and other excellent martial art formulas.

Wudang Martial Art education, one tutor for one student, is provided by the successors of Wudang Martial Art and advanced Wushu coaches, who have profound accomplishments in Wudang Martial Art moral cultivation and martial art skills, and lots of experiences in martial art education and training.

Wudang Martial Art education takes the mode of club teaching and pays more attention to individual different needs. From the fundamental theories of Wudang Martial Art to the material acts, teachers and coaches will be with you, and give you a systemic and earnest instruct, performing exercising and material education. We also provide relative VCDs performed by these coaches, enabling you to watch and exercise Wudang martial art as much and correctly as possible.

Warmly welcome those enthusiasts who cherish health and love Wudang Martial Art to study Wudang Martial Art here. We will be offering best service for you all the time, making all of you succeed in learning.

Chapter 8 Wudang Regimen Culture 武当养生文化

Wudang Taoist Culture of Regimen, started from the period of prehistory, famous in the Qin Dynasty, gone through several dynasties for thousands of years, formed its own system in the Ming Dynasty and became famous all over the world, has been a miniature of China Taoist Culture of Regimen.

During the process, Wudang Taoist Culture of Regimen has observed Taoist theory of "Nature and humans being a unity" "The fate of humans being decided by humans but not Nature" and the optimistic philosophy to decide one's own fate by oneself, and has absorbed all things and methods related to regimen from Confucius, medicines, martial arts, and witchery, so has formed its own regimen culture system with its own characteristics, which is rich in content and profound in meaning.

Here are the cultural meanings of Wudang Taoist culture of regimen:

1. To cultivate character and life. The character refers to man's one part in spirit, and the other part in material. To cultivate the character is to enlighten one's wisdom and understand theories of nature and man on one hand; to set right philosophy and cultivate one's moral culture so as to have active sense of social responsibility on the other hand. To cultivate the life is to exercise the body so as not only to prolong the lifespan, but also to make one become an immortal god, which has been taken as the general principle and ideal for regimen.

2. To cultivate both in static and dynamic ways. Wudang Taoism, learned from the shortcomings and lessons of the former Taoism and Confucius, has summed up its own experience from practice. Especially, Zhang Sanfeng had improved Taiji Boxing and made it one of the best ways to cultivate for Taoists. And on the basis of regimen theory and moral principles, he had brought into play the miraculous attacking power of cultivation.

3. To cultivate with the help of medicines. Wudang Taoist Culture of Regimen advocates the self-sense that one's life is determined by oneself and emphasizes the importance of self-cultivation on one hand, advises to make full use of natural offerings to help and accelerate one's self-cultivation on the other hand, for Nature and humans are a unity.

4. To cultivate step by step. On methods, Wudang Taoist Regimen advocates cultivating

from the most fundamental things, such as walking, standing, sitting, sleeping, and guiding breath, then to the higher-level regimen, for only this can we succeed in cultivation, or we will fail.

5. To make full use of all things and methods useful for regimen. This means that we should combine and absorb all kinds of theories and methods that are useful for regimen, no matter which school and what forms they are. We should not only exercise insider power and outside power, but also make use of herbs, acupuncture, massage and so on. In addition, we can take other forms that are good to prolonging lifespan and cultivating character, such as food, drink, reading, music, and traveling.

6. To take active and inactive measures. Taoist Culture of Regimen, something related to self-cultivation, is observing general Taoist theory. We should take the inactive measures as the main body, the active measures as the methods and the steps. The inactive measures, or the inactive actions, mean that all we do should follow Nature. The active measures, or the active work, mean that we should work hard to fully conform to Nature.

Taoism and Regimen 道教与养生

Extending the lifespan to living forever has been human beings' ideal and pursuit from the time when man had the self-consciousness. This fine ideal and desire is revealed and reflected in religious conceptions, literatures and arts of every nationality all over the world.

China, the cradle of Taoism, is a nation with brilliant civilization and long history. Chinese nation, known for its emphasis on life, has longed for the long lifespan and living forever. Many people began sedulously to probe the secret for eternal life from the time of ancient Qin Dynasty. For thousands of years, the ancestors of Chinese people have created and invented various ways with different efficacy to extend the lifespan. The colorful regimen culture reveals the advanced sciences and outstanding intelligence of Chinese nation. The precious heritage of history and culture is worth our exploring and utilizing.

Taoism is the native traditional religion of China, whose main feature is pursuing a long lifespan and practicing austerities. Taoism is also a kind of religion that loves life and abhors death. Taoism concerns most about the protecting and prolonging the life as well as longing for the eternal life.

During the founding period of Taoism, *A Book on Peace and Tranquility* and other ancient books showed a tendency to pursue eternal life. The first volume of *Taoist Deposits* also reveals this kind of meaning. Taoism considers that human being is the noblest creature of all the creatures, and human being regards the life as the most precious. So owing to this concept, Taoism advocates human being should spare no efforts to cherish the life and promise longevity. Taoism does not only carry forward the good tradition of this culture but also puts it into its own creed and practice.

Taoism, consisting of two big parts, never-die belief and regimen ways, assuring "My life is up to me instead of God", has always been pursuing the ways leading to an eternal life. Just with the support of this positive attitude, numerous Taoists have probed the means earnestly for two thousand years. There are many regimens means in Taoism, such as, holding the breath, inhalation and exhalation, directing the obstructed place, massage and so on, most of which do effect if they are done in proper way. Professionals and scholars in the fields of medicine and regime home and abroad have acknowledged all of these regimens. So, if there was not a firm belief of "My life is up to me instead of God", nor Taoist persevering practice, the heredity of Chinese culture could not have left such a special regimen idea and means.

So Taoist Regimen is not only occupying an important position in Chinese regimen, but also a treasure house to be tapped.

Preserving Heath by Mentality 精神养生

Preserving health by mentality is to promote the psychological health by means of soothing spirit and enlivening life with a view to improving physical and mental health under the guiding of the concept that heaven and men are corresponding. Modern medical research has discovered that the worst among all the unfavorable factors that lead to person's death is unhealthy mood.

1. Soothing the spirit to improve health

(1) Attaining mental tranquility in quietude

Quietude refers to the state of keeping calm without worldly desires in spirit. The ease can be attained by banishing distracting thoughts. The methods for attaining mental tranquility in quietude are the following:

1) Diminish selfish motives and lower the sensual desires for fame and wealth. Proceeding from actual situations, and the abstinence in sensual desires can relieve unnecessary loads on mind, and make one easy to be sound in body and mind.

2) Take good care of the mind, keep with whole-hearted devotion, banish distracting thoughts and expel the vexation. Only by tranquility, calmness, and mildness, can harmonization and happiness and sanity be accomplished, which is beneficial to the study and work, to the regular life and to the longevity.

(2) Determination and moral cultivation

1) The proper spiritual nourishment demands the right outlook on life. Those who are imbued with confidence and have correct aims in life can obtain moral cultivation and modulation of the spirit to promote health.

2) Keep a firm conviction and be hopeful for life.

3) The lofty morality and psychological tranquility and straight-forward character are favorable to the physiological function proceeding harmoniously and regularly. Thus, one can be full of vigor and healthy.

(3) Being optimistic

Cultivate the character by moral behaviors from the angle of specific details. It is said in *The Analects by Confucius*, "Work so hard as to forget to eat, and be so happy as to forget grief, without being aware of senility." Optimism is the best nutrition that can adjust sentiments, ease the morale and resist senility.

(4) Keeping balance in mind

High-tempo competition environment easily results in worries, exhaustion and nervousness.

If they can't be handled well in time, the psychological health will be harmed. Therefore, it is important to develop the psychological quality and competitive awareness that is initiative and great sense of responsibility. Those who possess responsibility will seek for the knowledge, technique and interest, so they broaden the vision and substantiate the life.

2. Adjustment of mood

(1) Abstinence

Abstinence is to soothe feeling and forestall the excess of the seven human emotions, namely, joy, anger, sorrow, fear, love, hate, and desire, for the balance in the mind. Whatever one meets, try to restrain the anger that is regarded as the worst taboo in the cultivation and that is the most harmful to health. Anger not only harms the liver, but also the heart, stomach, and brain and leads to many diseases. Morals can control the anger, and so can the way of reminding. Besides, when the fury is over, one should self-examine his anger and draw a lesson to form a habit of not being angry little by little.

(2) Unbosoming

Give vent to the pent-up feelings through the appropriate means to recover the balance in the mind as soon as possible.

(3) Transferring

1) Sublimation is a way, showing the reason over misfortunes and holding devotion to the career with the power of sense and sensibility, by which the anguish can be weakened. Furthermore, be detached. Detachment means that treating with indifference in life and behaviors should break away the disadvantageous environments.

2) Divert affections and banish distracting thoughts and gloominess to change unhealthy mood and habit.

3) Sports also can enhance the vigor of life and ameliorate harmful feelings.

(4) Controlling through viscera

Fury harms liver but sadness surpasses fury; happiness harms heart but fright surpasses happiness; contemplation harms spleen but fury surpasses contemplation; melancholy harms lung but happiness surpasses melancholy; fright harms kidney but contemplation surpasses fright, which generalize the dialectical relation between the spirit and viscera, and interaction between physiology and pathology. Therefore, the particular method has been created, sensibility corrected by sensibility, for instance, amusing can generate laugh, stimulus can do fury, guiding can do fright. Adroitly guide action according to circumstances and blaze the accumulated gloominess to achieve coziness.

On Dynamic Qigong 动功论

Chinese Qigong can be divided into two main parts, the Dynamic Qigong and the Static Qigong. The former one is the basis of the second one as well as the correct gateway to Qigong. So, concerning to practicing Qigong, Taoists have made a general principle of tempering the static with the dynamic and have created a set of dedicated ways to practice Qigong, such as, "from the dynamic to the static" "to control the dynamic by the static" "to help the tough by use of the tender ways" and "to relieve the blood vessels by breathing", whose purpose is to cure sickness and to strengthen the body.

The patterns of the Dynamic Qigong vary from one school to another; however, they have the interlinked ways and identical points.

The most important rhyme is "softness", whose implication is the following items:

Firstly, the whole body should be as soft as a baby, which means that the four limps, muscles and joints should be as soft as a baby's. In other words, you should soften the bones, muscles, skins, flesh and so on, so as to be without a little toughness and strength.

Secondly, the breath should be soft and be controlled by the diaphragm, which means that when you practice Dynamic Qigong, you should keep your breath in the diaphragm. As a result, only softness can contain toughness, change into toughness and even control toughness, having a large degree of tenacity. So softness can be equal with toughness; however, toughness cannot be equal with softness. When we understand the sense of softness and toughness, we also know the difference between "inner exercise" and "outer exercise". Although the two denominations both practice breath, they still have the differences.

The usages of "controlling the breath into diaphragm" and "being soft", can be described in the four rhymes, "ascending" "descending" "opening" and "closing". The key point of the rhymes depends wholly on the sub-diaphragm. In other words, exhalation and inhalation starts and ends with sub-diaphragm. Ascending and descending; opening and closing all converse to the sub-diaphragm. That's to say, whenever a movement is made, the sub-diaphragm is the starting point. Whenever a movement is finished, the sub-diaphragm is the ending place. All these relationships demonstrate that "the breath should be soft" and "the breath sinks to the diaphragm" is active and free, not rigid and harsh. Free and active use of the breath is the gist of being soft in the inner exercise; rigid and harsh use of the breath is the performance of being strengthened in the outer exercise.

Thirdly, the breath should be gentle and continuous, which means that the exhalation of the old and the inhalation of the new should be "continuous", and "neither existent nor dead". In other words, you should adjust your aspiration into long and slim one, just as the silkworm spins continuously and endlessly. Its theory is like a spider knitting its web. The spider must knit the vertical threads first, then the horizontal threads. After finishing this task, the spider returns to the web core and waits patiently in order to deal with the other worms but let them plunge into the cobweb. At the same time, it catches and eats them quickly. So is the procedure of using the virtuous breath to resist the evil breath and defeat the disease.

Fourthly, the movement should be as soft as snake, which refers to every action and every gesture should be "as soft as without bones". The large joints, such as, elbow, arm, hip, and leg move as a snake with the performance of heading the head high and winding the hip. Small joints, such as, wrist, finger, ridge and neck should move as a silkworm, with the performance of wriggling and outflanking.

Fifthly, the sense of touch should be as gentle as stream, which refers to two factors: the external factor, such as, the surrounding persons and weather; the internal factor, especially the internal viscera. It means that the external movement of fists and feet, the performance of various body frame movements should unite harmoniously with the internal aspiration and cycling breath. No matter what kind of unexpected things happen, such as, the assaulting of adventitious people, the invading of cold, or the stop of the breath, you should apply the principle and method of "being soft". To deal with these diseases, you should use the virtuous breath and give a blow as the flowing water, just like the murmuring stream and sluggish trickle of water. Using this principle and aiming at the impended places, you will attain the effect of "using softness to control toughness". As a result, the whole breath is unobstructed and your lifespan is prolonged.

The above is the content of "being soft" in Dynamic Qigong.

In addition to the above things, we should pay more attention to the change between Yin and Yang, as well as the moving of the strength among the bowels.

Under the direction of "being soft", every movement of framework and every gesture will produce a certain change of breathing, which can be embodied in the speed of the movement, the quantity of flowing, the change between Yin and Yang, the connection of the main and the collateral channels. The beginners of Qigong experience the movement of virtual breath by the following phenomenon, ache, numbness, swell, heat, cold, and frigidity. When their Qigong learning rises to a higher level, they will have different experiences. The former ache and numbness change into comfort and relaxation. They feel suddenly refreshed as if have drunk some sweet dew. Even if you get tired after the work, you can practice Dynamic Qigong attentively; the fatigue will vanish and resume your spirits.

On Static Qigong 静功论

Static Qigong is one kind of Qigong, a system of deep breathing exercises, opposite to Dynamic Qigong. With regard to the external form, Static Qigong needs to sit cross-legged quietly with hands clasped, mouth and eyes closed, compared with the boxing and dancing with joy.

As to the theory and method of Static Qigong, there are many schools, each of which has their own strong and weak points. The works by God of the Third Cave of Taoist Canon, belonging to Taoist scripture, involves 21 volumes, where 32 methods of the aspiration and exhalation are recorded. Those methods are the reference value to Qigong.

In a word, cooperating with Dynamic Qigong, Static Qigong can improve the effect in therapy and hygiene. Meanwhile, the proportion of Dynamic and Static Qigong is just appropriate. According to the regular process of practising Wushu, one should begin with Dynamic Qigong, and then, the period of Static Qigong comes. Gradually, Dynamic Qigong is diminished; correspondingly, Static Qigong is increased. As time goes on, Static Qigong is mastered in highly skills with an eye to accomplishing the quiet state only by internal exercise. Thus, the promotion of health and the efficacy of the cure are obtained naturally.

The following are the ten essentials in practising:

(1) Confidence. Believe firmly that Qigong can cure the disease and preserve the health.

(2) Perseverance. Adhere to practice and don't stop halfway just because the efficacy is

inconspicuous.

(3) Bearing aches in the waist and legs, and keep on with wholehearted devotion.

(4) Seizing the opportunity to practice and integrate it with life and work at all time and all places.

(5) Seeing whether methods are suitable. Some methods are beneficial to you, and persevere in it. Otherwise, it should be abandoned.

(6) Analyzing dialectically, during the practice, various phenomena that the energy extends all over the body producing coolness, pins, aches, and shocks. They symbolize the moving of vital energy and pulse. Treat them normally without considering whether they are good or bad. Don't pursue it intentionally and don't be frightened.

(7) Being relaxed and adjusting the posture at the beginning.

(8) Harmonizing the aspiration and exhalation.

(9) Concentrating attention and combining the vital energy and spirit.

(10) Massaging the whole body, namely, face, head, ears, eyes, palms, shoulder, waist, legs, and feet after practicing.

The mnemonic rhymes, various meticulous procedures, can be applied separately. To sum up, curing viscera separately is the most exquisite.

Static Qigong has a relation with the environment. The existence of all can determine one's consciousness; the contact with nature can affect the vital energy. Therefore, in ancient times, rule, wealth, companion, and place had been emphasized. That is to say, the peaceful and secluded spot is important to practice Static Qigong.

So according to the previous two points, you can reach a very high level, no matter which school that you are practicing. Externally, you practice bone, skin, and muscle until these parts are as tough as iron, as soft as still water. If you attain a high degree of perfection, you will know better the thorough breathing channel as you know your own figures. Then you will have a strong basis of your tranquil movement. It's the right way to move from Dynamic Qigong to Static Qigong, which will make you achieve a satisfying result in Qigong.

Chapter 9 Wudang Culture 武当文化

1. Selected Books on Wudang Culture 武当文化书籍

Bamboo Slip Book of the Chu Kingdom and Silk Book on Lao zi 楚简与帛书老子

The Tao and Teh by Lao zi, the Chinese famous ancient philosopher, has enjoyed a long history of more than 2,000 years. The rulers of the feudal dynasties took it as a magic weapon to make the country rich and the people strong; the oracles took it as the model of their behaviors, and the common civilians took it as the standard of their social life, which made it become more and more popular not only in China, but also in the whole world and published over and over again. With the passing of the time, more and more people came to find that in the Book there are many points of view are ambiguous, not easy to understand correct, especially, the explanations and misleading of the translators of generations made some sentences of the Book more difficult to understand. Some researchers even had hooked in them and could not have found a way out.

The Tao and Teh written on bamboo slips unearthed in one grave of the Chu Kingdom, Guodian Village, Jingmen City, Hubei Province, like a bolt, told us that *The Tao and Teh* written on bamboo slips is the origin book made by Lao zi, those difficult words and sentences are the addition by the men of the later generations.

This Book, taking *The Tao and Teh* written on the bamboo slips as the original version, consists of fifteen pieces on the basis of the paragraphs in the bamboo slips, among some of which there are small chapters with a few explanations in a piece; all of them are translated into modern free poetry. There are many topics in the book, such as the formation of the universe, the progress and change of the world, the developing theory of the society and human beings, the behaviors of oracles and the ruling methods of the former feudal rulers and so on. The book, peculiar in design, clear and elegant in the poems, concise and comprehensive, is worth the relevant experts and researchers' researching and the common readers' reading and collecting.

Edited by Zou Anhua,

Press: National Press

A Collection of Wujiagou Village Folk Stories 伍家沟村民间故事集

Wujiagou Village, lying at the foot of Wudang Mountains, the holy land of China Taoism, was the suburb of the former Junzhou City. Judging from the micro-environment, the village is very small and out-of-the-way; from the macro-environment, the village was not far from the profound soil of Chinese historical culture. On the contrary, the special situation had made it possible that the small village could have stored many ancient cultural agents in and could have brought in many interesting verbal stories.

These verbal narrative stories, with a strong myth sense of Taoist culture, have been an important part of Wudang Mountains Taoist culture. These fancy stories about ghosts and apparitions, though sound ridiculous today, reflected the simple and beautiful inner world of Chinese ancient working people, and contained many deep social theories worthy of thinking. These stories, gone down from generation to generation by means of verbal communication, are more simple and original than those in other places. Among them, there are some certain ancient cultural relics full of research value that can be compared with those relics unearthed from the ground... These stories have preserved the major characteristics of Chinese folk literature, including the simplicity of the oral language. In a word, they are worth researching from many aspects of view.

Wujiagou Village is like a twinkling star of folk culture in the northwest of Hubei Province. May the flowers of stories to manifest the beautiful mind and artistic wisdom of the Wujiagou Village people live forever and blossom happily!

Edited by Li Zhengkang

Press: Shandong Literature Press

Wudang Legend Stories 武当传说故事

A mountain is not famous for its height, but for the immortal living in. Emperor Zhenwu worshiped in Wudang Mountains, the China holy land of Taoism, had succeeded in becoming celestial being here. Sword River, Needle-rubbing Well, Crown Prince Slope, Pavilion to Dress and other scenic points are all connected with Emperor Zhenwu. The famous Taoist Zhang Sanfeng, just like the Monk Jigong in Buddhism, half-human-half-god, had lived here and created the world-famous Wudang Boxing. When we follow the races of these famous ancient gods, visit the profound Taoists here, we will find that all the way is full of mysteries and fancies, just like in a dream, or in the world of God. Great mountains and rivers, mysterious religion, centuries-old history, magnificent buildings work together to make an attractive rainbow. Since it is rare to see rainbows, so the rainbow is bound to make people full of interest, imagination and enthusiasm, therefore a lot of legend stories come into being.

Legend stories, the sublimation of social life and the crystal of human feeling, can endow all the materials in the world with life and make them have the feeling of happiness and sorrow vice verse. At the same time, these stories can infect the listeners with their strong emotion, to move them into the stories and enjoy the same feelings of the heroes and heroines of the stories.

When you visit Wudang Mountains, you can just only enjoy the superficial charm of them, but if you read Wudang Legend Stories at the same time, you can appreciate the inner charm too.

Press: Wuhan Press

Fighting Stunts with Short Weapons for Wudang Taoists Exclusively 武当秘传短兵绝技

Wudang Internal Boxing, a kind of very ancient boxing schools, is not only effective in keeping healthy and prolonging the lifespan, but also famous in the Martial Art filed for its special fighting character of overcoming the active by means of keeping still. Because most of the boxing skills are falling to attack, closing one's points, changing one's muscles and so on, Wudang Internal Boxing have been just spread exclusively among the Martial Art field.

The skills and tricks of four short weapons edited in the Book are these exclusive for Wudang Internal School, many of which are the first time to open to the world, having very high value for exercising and researching, especially suitable for the martial art fans and professionals. Wudang Short Cudgel-play introduced in the Book is a series of skills and tricks for short weapons with the emphasis on overcoming the active by means of keeping still and fighting back later but attacking the opponent earlier, whose acts are ancient and simple, effective in attacking, having a special effect to defeat the opponent by one act. They who are fond of fighting skills can learn a lot from it. Wudang Snake-shape Swordplay, when exercising, walking in the shape of the Eight Diagrams, moving the waist according the theory of Taiji Boxing, waving the sword as quick as a bolt, can make you appreciate the mysterious charm of Wudang swordplay. Wudang Horsetail Whisk, one of Taoist exclusive skills and tricks, whose acts are elegant, flexible and have very high value in keeping healthy and safeguarding oneself, is suitable for middle-aged and elderly people. Night Walking Knife, a kind of hieroglyph skills made up of many styles of the Eight Diagrams, Form and Will, Taiji Boxing, is very popular in martial arts competitions home and abroad and especially suitable for teenagers to learn and practice.

Editors: You Mingsheng, Zhao Rong

Press: Beijing University of Physical Education Press

Fighting Stunts in a Near Distance for Wudang Taoists Exclusively 武当秘传短打绝技

Fighting Stunts in a Near Distance for Wudang Taoists Exclusive, has set forth in details Wudang Internal Boxing's theory of Yin and Yang and pointed out the gist of the theory, main points of fighting skills in a near distance, achieving the effect of making the finishing point for people to get to know and understand the origin, development, style and gist of Wudang Internal Boxing.

This Book mainly introduces some of the fighting stunts in a near distance of Southern-style Wudang Internal Boxing, from easy to difficult, easy to understand and exercise by oneself. You will learn something from this reference book for Wudang Boxing, no matter you have leaned a little of martial arts or not.

Editors: You Mingsheng, Zhao Rong

Press: Beijing University of Physical Education Press

The Secrecy of Wudang Internal School 武当内家派述秘

Wudang Martial Arts has come of Wudang Mountains, the Holy land of China Taoism. However, it is not the product of religion, but the crystal of Chinese nation's excellent traditional culture with Taoist school as its representation. It, from theory to practice, always demonstrates Chinese nation's traditional social, moral, and universe conception, good hopes to keep healthy and prolong the lifespan, and their elegant and civilized aesthetic sense, which is the reason for Wudang Martial Arts has the strong vitality.

With the spreading and development of Wudang Martial Arts both in home and abroad, more and more Wudang Martial arts fans, disciplines of all schools of Wudang Martial Arts, experts and researchers who are interested in martial arts history, are eager to know more about the essence and process of Wudang Martial Arts. Here are the purpose for the author to write this book: to make it a reference book for Wudang Martial Arts, easy for people to consult; to make it a book of Wudang Martial Arts for these fans to research and exercise; to make it a series of articles on martial arts and Qigong, for experts in martial arts exercising and martial arts history to continue their further researches.

Editor: Tan Dajiang

Press: People's Physical Education Press

A Note to Wudang Mountains Couplets 武当山对联辑注

A Note to Wudang Mountains Couplets, made up of more than seven hundred couplets chosen from nearly twenty thousand couplets written on Wudang Mountains, covering view points, immortals, Taoism, and martial arts, is the most complete collection of couplets written on Wudang Mountains that has ever found.

These materials for the Book are coming from Wudang Taoists hand-written books, all kinds of literature and the writer's interview and visit on the spot. In the book, the writer has given some brief introduction to the view points and immortals connected with the couplets.

Editor: Tan Dajiang, Guo Xuyang

Press: Shiyan City Society of Poetry, Calligraphy and Painting.

Notes Collection of Wudang Mountains Histories 武当山历代志书集注

Wudang Mountains, also called Supreme Harmony Mountains, was respected by the emperors of the Ming Dynasty as the Greatest Mountain and the Mountain to run the Country. As a world-famous holy land of China Taoism and a mountain of colorful literature, Wudang Mountains has the tradition to compose the history records for it. According to the literature, there have been ten pieces of *Wudang Mountains Histories* from the Song Dynasty to the rule of Republic of China, eight of which have been collected. They are complete and systematic reference books about Wudang Mountains, the comprehensive literature to manage the country and the society.

The eight kinds of mountain histories in the book are largely identical in style and content but with some minor differences, each of which has their own priority. Judging from these eight separate parts, each demonstrates the universality and particularity of different things at different stage; judging from the comprehensive view, these eight parts work together to demonstrate the continuity and completeness of different things.

Recording the history of Wudang Mountains and the changes of feudal governments, you can understand the history of Wudang Mountains more than 2,000 years;

Recording the enchanting mountains and rivers, magnificent halls and temples in words and pictures, you are moved to go and have a good time there;

Recording the history of Emperor Zhenwu, the first god of Wudang Mountains, you can understand its origin, development and the rule to progress;

Recording feudal runners' decrees of generations to Wudang Mountains, you can sense out the close relationship between Wudang Mountains and the feudal governments of different dynasties and its important role in the feudal society;

Recording precious birds, beasts, plants, and miraculous things, you can know the beauty, miracle and richness of Wudang Mountains;

Recording the relics of those immortals and hermits, important words on Taoism of those profound Taoists, you can have reference to consult;

Recording the poems and calligraphy of men of letters of generations, you can improve your comprehensive knowledge when you appreciate the poems and calligraphy;

In a word, *Wudang Mountains Histories*, though impenetrable Taoist outlook to protect one's life by keeping inactive and cultivating regimen and character, Confucian's ethic theory of the three cardinal guides specified in feudal ethical code and the five cardinal common senses, and lots of feudal and superstitious narrations to pay a tribute to the feudal kings and to spread the power of gods and ghosts, contain a great many of historical events, which is very useful to research Wudang Mountains' history, politics, military affairs, economy, culture, Taoism, architecture and literature.

Editor: China Wudang Literature Series Composing Committee

Press: Hubei Press of Science and Technology

Wudang Mountains History 武当山志

The New Edition of Wudang Mountains History is one of the key items among the State's Social Science Developing Project.

The composers of the book, from a perspective of a historian, on the basis of collecting many materials and choosing the picks of the old histories and absorbing the new research achievements, have finished the book with some strong regional features after eight years' hard working and seven times' changing and improvements.

This book is not only properly narrating in details the grand vigor and charming scenery of Wudang Mountains and excellent Taoist cultural relics, but also demonstrating in full passion the great achievements in carrying forward the cultural relics, civilizing the people and building the viewpoints, which shows the temporal spirit of the new edition. This book is not only important to boost the tapping of Wudang Mountains and the development of culture and tourism, but also contributing to China's regional history treasure and socialist spiritual civilization.

The New Edition of Wudang Mountains History comprehensively records Wudang Mountains regional natural viewpoints and human histories, from the emerging of Wudang Mountains to the year of 1990.

The book has made full use of materials coming from former county histories, mountains histories, Taoist books, records and other relevant scriptures, the researches of the writers on the spot and the research achievements of temporal experts.

Editor: Wudang Mountains History Composing Committee

Press: Xinhua Press

A Collection of Immortals on Wudang Mountains 武当神仙大观

Wudang Mountains was regarded as the birthplace of Emperor Zhenwu. Wudang Taoist basic belief is worshiping Emperor Zhenwu as well as other gods. During its prosperous period, there were more than ten thousand gods worshiped in Wudang Mountains, which was looked upon as divine mountains for all gods to come.

This book, on the basis of relevant ancient literature and Taoist books, referring to modern related monographs, having combined gods former worshiped and now worshiped in Wudang Mountains, objectively introduces all gods' names, images, status, positions, and their origins respectively. This book contains Emperor Zhenwu, Taoist gods, stars gods, Taoist founders, celestial immortals, protectors of family life, protectors of all kinds of productions, protectors of marriage and birth, gods in the hell and so on, which divided into twelve chapters.

This book, on the basis of the composers' comprehensively looking for materials and elaborately selecting and composing, is credible in materials, polished in diction, brilliant in both words and pictures, and suited for both refined and popular tastes.

Editor: China Wudang Culture Series Composing Committee

Press: Wuhan Press

A Collection of Wudang Martial Arts 武当武术精粹

Wudang Martial Arts, also called Wudang Internal Boxing, come from Wudang Taoist School and taken Lao zi's inactive philosophy as its theoretical basis, are characterized by paying more attention to internal cultivation, demonstrating Taoism by way of martial arts and overcoming the tough by the soft.

The main body of Wudang Martial Arts is Taiji Boxing, one of the biggest schools of Chinese traditional martial arts, one representative of internal boxing schools, which has contributed a lot in helping people cultivate regimen, keeping healthy and promoting cultural exchanges.

The Eight Diagrams Palm, Form and Will Boxing, Dacheng Boxing and other boxing changed from and influenced by Taiji Boxing, are becoming more and more popular in China and even all over the world. At the same time, there has produced more than one hundred minor schools of fighting skills and tricks from Wudang Internal School. *A Collection of Wudang Martial Arts* is the gist collecting of Wudang Martial Arts, after the composers' many years' hardworking and elaborate selecting.

Editor: China Wudang Culture Series Composing Committee

Press: Hubei Press of Science and Technology

Wudang Internal Pulse Cultivation 武当真宗丹脉

Taiyi Hunyuan Fundamental Theory, also called Wudang Internal Pulse Cultivation, or Taiyi Miraculous Power, is one part among a series of Wudang traditional cultivation. The practicing methods and theoretical basis, in accordance with the guiding lines of cultivating internal pulse and demonstrating external power proposed by Zhang Sanfeng, the founder of Wudang Boxing, have demonstrated the cultivating features of Wudang Gongfu, such as coming into Taoism through martial arts, demonstrating Taoism by way of martial arts, and at last combining martial arts and Taoism into one.

In the beginning period of Taiyi Hunyuan Fundamental Theory cultivation, the Book has mentioned the theories of one element, two politeness, three abilities and four quadrants, and given some advice on cultivation practice, as well as validated the guiding effect of cultivation theories and traditional culture left by ancient oracles in Taoist cultivation.

Editor: Liu Tiecheng

Press: Wudang Magazine Editorial Board

Research Reference for China Taoist Culture and Wudang Culture 中国道教文化、武当文化研究索引

Taoism is the native-born religion in China, whose ideological origin is connected with many doctrines of the Qin Dynasty, which has been much mentioned in the researches on Taoist history.

Taoism and Taoist culture are the important components of Chinese culture. There have been many experts in China who has researched in Taoism. Taoism researchers of generations have made a lot of contributions to the development of Taoist theory and culture; they have not only enriched the theoretical basis of Taoism, but also researched and developed religious regulations and etiquette of Taoism.

This book has embodied all the relevant monographs, pictures and thesis on Taoist culture published in China mainland (including some of them published in Hong Kong, Macao and Taiwan) during the years between 1950 and 2000.

The book contains nearly five thousand entries arranged in the big parts of research reference for China Taoist Culture and research reference for Wudang Taoist Culture.

Editor: Yang Shiquan

Press: China Press of Science and Culture

China Wudang Medicine Prescriptions 中国武当医药秘方

The author, Shang Rubiao, born in Xiangyang City, Hubei Province, was graduated from Hubei University of Chinese Medicine. He has attended in advanced studies in Affiliated Orthopedics Hospital of Wuhan University of Physical Education, Affiliated Orthopedics Hospital of Chengdu University of Physical Education, Liaoning University of Chinese Medicine, Shenyang Intestinal Tract Hospital. In March, 1996, he was employed vice-chief physician of the No. One Hospital of Danjiangkou City, Hubei Province, one of the first leaders in their chosen field of learning of Danjiangkou City.

This book introduces the common senses for the using of Chinese herbs. This Book has given a systematic and comprehensive introduction of each herb with picture appended, from living environment, characters, harvest season, processing methods, medicine effect, taste, to prescriptions. This book has embodied nearly 3,000 pieces of prescriptions that are high in curative effect but low in prices and safe in application.

This book can be a reference for the clinic doctors, also for fans of Chinese medicine to read and learn.

Editor: Shang Rubiao

The Collection of Taoist Couplets 道教对联大观

Couplets, the excellent culture art of Chinese characteristics, are the gems among Chinese culture art treasure. They are excellent works of Chinese characters, with concise words but profound meanings, precise rhyme and charming image, which can add salt to human's life, and make people hope for the better future and appreciate the special art.

China Taoist couplet is the culture crystal that has combined literature, art, philosophy, and ethic into one, which has a close relationship with Taoism culture. Taoist ancestors and their followers have created many couplets with profound meaning and charming images to air gods in Taoism. *The Collection of Taoist Couplets* compiled by Mr. Kong De, is the promising research item, which will play an important role in spreading Taoism culture.

Author: Tan Dajiang

Press: Religion Culture Press

The Notes to Leyu Hall Quotations 乐育堂语录注解

The Notes to Leyu Hall Quotations is a book on Taoist medicine. During the years of Emperor Daoxian of the Qing Dynasty (1841—1860), master Huang Yuanji taught the ways to make medicine to his students in Leyu Hall, and then his students collected and compiled his ten years' words into a book of four volumes, named *Leyu Hall Quotations*.

Among all the Taoist books on medicine, *Leyu Hall Quotations* is the special one written in simple words. Its real value lies in explaining the theory of Taoism, and having combined medicine cultivation into social life practice, without avoiding facing the social life or talking big words, so that it has been recommended by all the Taoists. *Leyu Hall Quotations*, with the detailed notes by Kong De, is very useful for those who want to study Taoist medicine by themselves.

According to records, Huang Yuanji, lived in the Yuan Dynasty, had studied Taoism and medicine from Zhang Sanfeng, which was recorded in *The Collection of* Zhang Sanfeng. It was said that he had been a hermit for many years, and then began to gather students and teach Taoism during the years of Emperor Daoxian of the Qing Dynasty, enjoyed a long life of 500 or 600 years.

Author: Tan Dajiang

Press: Shiyan City Qigong Science Academy

Wudang Zhao Pu-style Taiji Boxing 武当赵堡太极拳大全

Wudang Zhao Pu-style Taiji Boxing, one of the ancient China Taiji Boxing, was formed and widely spread in Zhao Pu Town, Wen County, Henan Province.

Through many generations' neatening, practice, Wudang Zhao Pu-style Taiji Boxing has become one kind of Taiji Gongfu popular among the folk. Wudang Zhao Pu-style Taiji Boxing has its own attacking features and outstanding characteristics in patterns and boxing system, with 75 patterns, gentle and flexible, which can exercise to keep regimen or protect one. For the exercise of Wudang Zhao Pu-style Taiji Boxing can make the bones strong, improve the inner strength, and better the health condition so as to prolong the lifespan outside; cultivate the mood and character inside.

Wudang Zhao Pu-style Taiji Boxing, with the theory and skills, compiled from the easy to the hard, is good to well understand the characters and requirements, so as to learn and grasp the gist of Wudang Zhao Pu-style Taiji Boxing.

Press: World Books Press Company

A Research on The Tao and Teh 《道德经》探玄

There have been many experts researching and adding notes to 5,000-word *The Tao and Teh* in the past 2,000 years. In the history, militarist, legist, orator, expert of martial art, fortune-teller, all looked for their root and cause in *The Tao and Teh* and found their theoretical base and behavior rules.

A Research on *The Tao and Teh* is the first time for the author to explain systemically *The*

Tao and Teh from the perspective of regimen, after many years' cultivation and studying all editions of *Tao and Teh*. In the book, the author has pointed out the limitations of applying the relative understanding method in people's thinking, and should consult the reference directly in the research on universe, only by which can we understand the real relationship between human life and the universe of nature.

The book has given many easy-understanding explanations on what rules should observe when cultivating Taoism, how to start, how to avoid going astray, and how to make some progresses, which is not only helpful in instructing keeping healthy and prolonging the lifespan, but also in studying and applying other sciences.

Press: Beijing University of Physical Education Press

Notes to The Collection of Muscle-Changing and Marrow-Cultivating 易筋洗髓大全注解

Changing Muscles and *Cultivating Marrow* are the two books on the ways to cultivate Taoism, for changing muscles can be strong in muscles and strength and cultivating marrow can help you cultivate the mood and the character. The two books are very mysterious, so it is not easy to understand the gist of them.

Notes to The Collection of Muscle-Changing and Marrow-Cultivating is the book compiled by Mr. Kong De after his intensive reading of *Changing Muscles* and *Cultivating Marrow*, which is very helpful for those who want to study Taoism and practice cultivation.

Author: Kong De

Press: Wudang Journal Company

The Holy Land, Wudang Mountains 仙山武当

Wudang Mountains, a famous fairy mountains of long history, profound culture and China Taoism, is one of the splendid pages in the oriental cultural codes and records with unique style and enchanting grace. It has not only range upon range of mountains which are magnificent and majestic but also the unique beauty appearing in all her glory and pretty & bright charm, which can be described beyond words.

This Album of paintings, excellent both in pictures and language, fully shows the feeling and setting, the imagery, the hidden and the visible in Wudang Culture, which truthfully displays the most beautiful aspect of Wudang Mountains to us.

Editor: Wang Guangde

Press: Religious Culture Press

Paintings of Wudang Mountains 仙山武当画册

As the famous Taoist mountain in China, Wudang Mountains merges into an organic whole the splendid natural scenery, the grand wonderful ancient architecture and the extensive and profound Taoist culture. In 1994 UNESCO listed it in the roster of World Cultural Legacy.

In order to let more people know it better and come nearer it, the Chinese photographer, Yin Daolu, with his love to Wudang Mountains and pursuit of art, finished this album of painting after two years of hard work. This album vividly shows and reflects the real ethos and romantic charm of Wudang Mountains.

Yin Daolu, a member of China Association of Photographers, has published five volumes of photographic works, some of which have won prizes in the 17th Chinese Photographic Exhibition and the Photographic Competition of Asiatic and Pacific Area.

Author: Yin Daolu

Press: China Photographic Press

2. Rare Paintings in Wudang Mountains 武当绘画

The Pictures of Emperor Xuan's Auspicious Signs 玄帝吉兆图

The Pictures of Emperor Xuan's Auspicious Signs, Taoist pictures of the Ming Dynasty, mainly narrated the auspicious signs showed by Emperor Zhenwu, the leader god of Wudang Mountains in the mortal world, with two parts: in the sky and on the earth; one picture and one narration.

The pictures of Emperor Xuan's auspicious signs are the earliest interlinking pictures found in China, which played an important role in the history of Chinese Arts.

The Pictures of Wudang Mountains Auspicious Signs 武当山吉兆图

The Pictures of Wudang Mountains Auspicious Signs, drawn in the Ming Dynasty, mainly portrayed the auspicious signs showed over Wudang Mountains when all the palaces and temples were finished in the Ming Dynasty, which were full of miraculous color. The pictures were precisely devised and fresh colored; with a very high value in art.

Fresco (I) 湿壁画一

This is located in the Grand Hall of Needle-Rubbing Well in Wudang Mountains, with eight small parts, which narrated the following stories: the young Emperor Zhenwu was determined to study and spread Taoism, so that he moved the gods in Heaven and enlightened him to cultivate in Wudang Mountains, then he left home for Wudang Mountains.

Fresco (II) 湿壁画二

After cultivated in Wudang Mountains for several years and met many hardships, Emperor Zhenwu felt depressed and returned home; met a old rubbing a large pontil into a small needle in the form of an old grandma, which made him understand the theory "Perseverance makes success/ Persistence is success" and then returned to Wudang Mountains and continued his cultivation.

Fresco (III) 湿壁画三

Emperor Zhenwu succeeded in becoming a profound immortal after forty-two years' hard cultivation and flied into sky with the escort of five dragons.

Fresco (IV) 湿壁画四

Emperor Zhenwu killed all evils and monsters after he flied into sky so that Jade Emperor commanded him and ordered him to guard Wudang Mountains.

The Pictures of the Eight Immortals 八仙图

The Eight Immortals were the eight famous Taoist gods in Chinese folk tale, who often traveled between heaven and earth to help people from the trouble, worshiped by the people and their stories are widely-spread in China.

The Pictures of the Eight Immortals portrayed the vivid visions of the eight immortals with heavy and fresh colors, having a very high value of art appreciation.

3. Rare Sculptures in Wudang Mountains 武当雕塑

The Wood Sculpture of God Zhenwu 木雕真武像

The Wood Sculpture of God Zhenwu is one of the top-quality products among wood sculptures of the Ming Dynasty, which is large in scale, true to life, appearing calm and composed, pleats of the clothes being seen clearly, fine and smooth in graceful lines, and is the biggest one of first grade among the wood sculptures preserved in Wudang Mountains. After 600 vicissitudes of life, it's still in good shape without being worm-eaten or rotten. It assembles the pith and marrow of the skills of sculpture, colored drawing and antiseptic in the ancient China.

The Wood Sculpture of Golden Boy 木雕金童

The wood sculpture of Golden Boy is beautiful in shape with exquisite skill. It stands on the left of the sculpture of God Zhenwu, with volumes in hands, gazing at the front calmly, elegant and dignified in bearing with a respectful, cautious and serene expression. It belongs to the same model of the wood sculpture of God Zhenwu, harmoniously in entirety and has a considerably high value in arts and research.

The Wood Sculpture of Jade Girl 木雕玉女

The wood sculpture of Jade Girl wears the phoenix coronet with various jewelry. With brush, ink, inkstand in hands, she gazes forward, looking respectfully and submissively with a dignified and steady manner. The clothes of the patterns are perfectly engraved with graceful, mellow and full lines. It belongs to the same model of that of God Zhenwu, harmoniously in entirety and has a striking artistic effect.

The Clay Sculpture of Blue Dragon 泥塑青龙

Blue Dragon is the patron saint of Wudang Mountains, aiming to play up the impressive and dignified manner of God Zhenwu.

The clay sculpture of Blue Dragon, five meters high, is the biggest clay sculpture of Blue Dragon preserved in Wudang Mountains. Because of its large scale, and also in case that the arms holding the weapons would not be too heavy to get broken, the designer, with great wisdom, arranged a small blue dragon to play on the body of the huge dragon so as to hold up the arms and make them solider.

Fine and smooth in graceful lines, the clay sculpture, wearing a suit of armor and holding weapons, is of high stature, sturdy and intrepid, making people awed by the sight, which reflects the dignity and prestige of benefactors in Wudang Mountains.

The Clay Sculpture of White Tiger 泥塑白虎

The white tiger is the patron saint of Wudang Mountains, aiming to play up the impressive and dignified manner of God Zhenwu. The clay sculpture, five meters high, is the biggest clay sculpture of white tiger preserved in Wudang Mountains.

Because of its large scale, and also in case that the arms holding the weapons would not be too heavy to get broken, the designer, with great wisdom, arranged a small white tiger to play on the body of the huge tiger so as to hold up the arms to make them solider, which revealed the ancient people's superb skills. Wearing a suit of armor, with weapons in hand, the white tiger has a genial expression on its face, looking vivid and lively.

Wood Sculptures of Four Imperial Gods—Jade Emperor 玉皇大帝

The word "Imperial" is used to describe emperors who, in Taoist Books, are said to be the creators of all the creatures in universe, commanding all the gods. Jade Emperor, the head of the four imperial gods, is the highest god worshiped by Taoism.

This wood sculpture is a statue of Jade Emperor in a seating posture, 0.62 meter high, elegant and poised, just like the emperor on earth. Wearing a royal crown, delicately dressed, he looks imposing, which makes people feel that he is paramount and the most distinguished.

Wood Sculptures of Four Imperial Gods—Emperor of the North Pole 北极大帝

Emperor of the North Pole, assisting Jade Emperor to control cosmic inventory, the heavenly bodies, the four seasons, the three world (Hades, Earth and Heaven) and the mountains, the suzerain of all phenomena, can summon wind and rain, and order the gods of thunder and lightening and ghosts.

This wood sculpture is a statue of Emperor of the North Pole in a seating posture, 0.62 meter high. Wearing a royal crown, looking plump and smooth-skinned, he looks elegant and stately. This statue is carved to a nicety and looks vivid and lively.

Wood Sculptures of Four Imperial Gods—Emperor Heaven 天皇大帝

Emperor Heaven, assisting Jade Emperor to control the South and North Poles, heaven, the earth and human beings, is also the god in charge of the wars on earth.

The seating sculpture of Emperor Heaven, 0.60 meter high, is delicate in shape, with a full face, appearing calm and composed. Pleats of clothes are seen clearly with fine and smooth lines. This statue is carved to a nicety and looks vivid and lively.

Wood Sculptures of Four Imperial Gods—Goddess of Mother Land 后土皇地祇

Goddess of Mother Land is in charge of Yin and Yang, the births of all creatures and the beauties of the land, the mountains and the rivers.

The seating sculpture is 0.60 meter high, elegantly dressed with well-rounded figure. With fluent lines, the sculpture wears a benign expression, kind and calm, which reveals the beauty of mother's intimation and gentleness and has a high value in religion, history and art.

The Stone Sculpture of God Zhenwu 石雕真武

It's a jade stone sculpture. God Zhenwu, with long hair handing down over his neck, bear-footed, is plump in figure, powerfully built with heroic bearing and kind expression.

The sculpture is fluent in scale and vivid in shape. Although it shows only a moment in the dynamic process, by imagination we can feel the incisive philosophy of living in seclusion and doing nothing beyond the limitation of time and space.

The Wood Sculpture of Lao zi 木雕老子

Lao zi, father of the Taoism of the Qin Dynasty in China, wrote *The Tao and Teh* with supreme wisdom, regarded as the holy classic of Taoism.

The wood sculpture of Lao zi, 1.96 meters high, is covered with god foil and painted colorfully. Kind-faced, with silver hair waving, this sculpture looks very vivid and lively. He does not only seems to be sermonizing but also to be absorbed in thought, which shows vividly the internal world of the man of great wisdom and also ignites people's boundless imagination and unlimited thought.

The Dragon-Head Incense 龙头香

This stone carving, hanging in the air over the steep cliff, is one of the famous perilous interests of Wudang Mountains.

The Dragon-Head Incense is made up of two dragons' heads, 3 meters long, 0.55 meter wide. The ancient artisans used the sculpture-in-the-round, engraving, screen sculpture, etc, which made it look like soaring up in the air.

Stone Sculpture of Xuanyue Gate 玄岳门石雕

The stone sculpture on which says "Running the Country by Xuanyue" is 20 meters high, 12.8 meters wide, joggled together by component parts made of huge blue stones. Using these skills, such as high relief, engraving, sculpture-in-the-round, shadow carving and so on, the ancient artisans carved the red-crown crane, auspicious clouds, hovering dragons, ruyi, the Eight Immortals, etc. decorated with the pictures of flowers and birds, which are of excellent workmanship with a sense of mystery and wonder.

This huge stone sculpture is compactly lying out, giving the viewers a sense of extravagant impression with the power of stability and majesty. Therefore, it's honored as art treasure of Chinese stone sculpture, for its superb skills.

The Stone Sculpture of Tortoise Carrying a Stele 龟碑石雕

There are twelve imperial stele pavilions, in which there are stone sculptures of tortoises carrying steles. Holding high its head and coiling its tail, the holy tortoise, with the power of legs, bearing on its back thousands of tons, still stands extremely steady. These sculptures are steady and heroic in shape, hailed as the acme of perfection.

The Wood Carvings of Imperial Scripture Temple 皇经堂木雕

On the railing and partition windows of Imperial Scripture Temple, there carved some rare birds and unusual animals and many things and people in Taoism, such as the red-crown crane, auspicious clouds, the eight celestials welcoming guests etc, among which the Eight Immortals take up the majority, which is the common phenomenon of Taoist palaces.

The wood carving of Imperial Scripture Temple, decorated with colored patterns, makes the whole building splendid and elegant with delicate design, which also reflects the social life, religious belief and aesthetic and tastes, regarded as an excellent masterpiece with high value of art and religion research.

The Holy Board of Emperor Xuan　玄天上帝圣牌

The holy board of Emperor Xuan, imperially made in the Ming Dynasty, by the best quality porcelain in the court porcelain kiln, is 1.01 meters high, and 0.5 meters wide. It's joggled together by seven component parts such as the pedestal, border board, the center of the board and so on.

On the pedestal auspicious clouds and the red-crown crane are carved; high above are two border boards with the vivid and lively pictures of the hovering dragon playing with a pearl on the auspicious clouds; on the top of the board is the vivid pattern of ruyi with auspicious dragon in the floating clouds.

This holy board, delicate in shape, is the only one preserved in Wudang Mountains with very important historical relic value.

4. Rare Calligraphy in Wudang Mountains　武当书法作品

In The White Jade Hall　白玉京中

This horizontal inscribed board hangs above the architrave of Imperial Scripture Temple, on the top of Golden Peak, which makes clear the building idea and usage of this Temple. This board is flat with frames on which are carved the pictures such as three dragons playing with a phoenix, two couples of dragons and phoenixes, and the red phoenix worshiping a deity and so on.

In accordance with Taoism, in heaven there is the golden imperial palace in the center of which is the White Jade Hall where the god of heaven lives. This board shows that Imperial Sculpture Temple is of high position just like the centering hall in the Imperial Palace, and is the residence of Emperor Heaven for all the gods to have an audience with him.

Thanking Gods for Their Great Favor　酬谢神恩

This board, made of wood, is an inscribed horizontal board with red background and gold characters. This board is flat with frames painted gold on which there are six dragons with two dragons playing with a pearl on the top, two dragons playing in the water in the bottom, and each dragon on the left and the right.

This is a board to redeem the vow of the devotee, that is, to thanks gods for their great favor, reflecting the customs and morals of the people in Wudang Mountains, making a vow and redeeming a vow is handed down from generation to generation.

The Kind Bodhisattva Helps All the Folk　慈航普渡

This is a flat scraper with black background and gold characters, dedicated by the devotee in Gucheng County, Hubei Province, in the 28th year of Emperor Daoguang of the Qing Dynasty.

The journey of salvation, originally a Buddhism term, means that the process of the great merciful Bodhisattva's liberating all living beings from the human world of woes. It's said that Bodhisattva is infinitely resourceful, especially to save the suffering women. People believe in "delivering all living creatures from worldly sufferings" in the hope of finding a god who will help anyone regardless of their richness or poverty. Then Bodhisattva is worshiped to satisfy many people's wishes. This board intends to praise and show Bodhisattva's ability and virtue.

Incarnation from the Imperial Palace 金阙化身

This board, hung in the hall of Purple Clouds Palace, is an inscribed horizontal board with running script. It's a flat scraper made of wood, which is still well preserved after renovation.

These four characters originate out of the one hundred titles of God Zhenwu, the main god in Wudang Mountains, symbolizing that he is the incarnation from the Imperial Palace.

So High to Touch the Sky 峻极于天

This was made in the Qing Dynasty. There is a pun in the meaning: it praises not only the magnificence of Pure Sunshine Palace which is almost connected to heaven but also praises the boundless beneficence and power of God Zhenwu.

The Palace of Heaven and Earth 两仪殿

This board, hung over the lintel of the stone door of South Cliff Palace, is a vertical wood board with black background and gold characters written in the official script.

"Liangyi" just means the heaven and the earth. According to *Book of Changes,* there is Taiji, supreme ultimate in changes that produces the heaven and the earth. So "Liangyi" also means Yin and Yang, opposite principles or forces existing in nature and human affairs.

The Great Kindness of God Zhenwu is Just Like Sunshine 神光普照

This board, hung over the lintel of the door of Crown Prince's bedroom in South Cliff Palace, is an inscribed horizontal board with running script. High above the frame is carved the picture of two dragons playing with a pearl; below the frame is carved the picture of two phoenixes facing the rising sun; on each side is carved the bat with auspicious clouds. These pictures are all high relief decorated with gold. The meaning of this board is that the great kindness of God Zhenwu is just like the sunshine.

Standing on the Earth but Holding up the Sky 生天立地

This board, hung over the central shrine of Imperial Scripture Temple on Golden Top, is an inscribed horizontal board with running script. It's a flat board with gold background and black characters that was written by Emperor Daoguang in the Qing Dynasty. The calligraphy looks stately, solid, forceful and vigorous with free and easy strokes.

The Bravery God Zhenwu to Subdue the Devils 始判六天

This board, hung over the lintel of Purple Clouds Palace, was made by the local official in the later period of the Qing Dynasty. There are many explanations about this board, praising and commenting Wudang Mountains, God Zhenwu and cultivation ambit.

In accordance with the legend of Wudang Mountain, after God Zhenwu ascended to heaven, devils appeared and fought with each other in heaven. When Supreme God of Originality was delivering the sermon in heaven, the dirty and evil things such as black poison and blood burst into the South Heavenly Door. Supreme God of Originality was so angry that he ordered God Zhenwu to subdue the devils. With bravery God Zhenwu led 300,000 soldiers and generals from heaven to subdue the devils overnight. These four characters are the comment of that expedition of God Zhenwu.

Super God is powerful and kind 太上能仁

"Taishang" means Lao zi, worshiped by Taoism as a god and patriarch who is supreme and regarded as existing every time at every place but seen only by wise people. "Neng" means ability; "Ren" means kindness, sympathy, affection and protection. The meaning of the four characters is that Lao zi has a kind heart to every one, stays with the kind-hearted people and will come to help you overcome the difficulty when you meet a disaster.

The Wisdom, Thought and Spirit God Zhenwu can last forever like the spring 体慧长春

The general idea of these four characters is that God Zhenwu's boundless wisdom, thought and spirit can last forever. His spirit, just like spring, encourages every devotee to work persistently to draw lessons so as to get wisdom and ability. Only in this way human beings can be young and happy forever.

Wudang Mountain is Prosperous like the Sun 协赞中天

This huge board with these four characters, hung over the architrave of Purple Clouds Palace, intends to praise not only the prosperity of the royal temples and palaces of Wudang Mountains in the most prosperous period of the Ming Dynasty but also praises the fabulous geographical location of Wudang Mountains which can react to heaven because God Zhenwu can protect Wudang Mountains, subdue devils and pray for gods to get rid of disasters.

Miraculous Gate 玄妙之门

This board is an inscribed horizontal board with seal characters. It's a wood flat board with gold background and black characters decorated with gold powders.

According to Lao zi, Taoism is the most mysteriously wonderful way. In accordance with the scriptures, Yuan is Yang, the masculine principle in nature, which means force and dynamic state; "Mu" means Yin, the feminine principle in nature, which means gentleness and peace. The door of "Mu" is the door of Yin and Yang when they are united together. Taoism thinks that Tao is just like the great mother body that can bear everything on earth. The four characters just mean that the senses are mysteriously abstract and wonderful.

Effective to All Praying 有求必应

It is an inscribed horizontal board with seal characters. It's an intaglio with black background and gold characters. It's a board dedicated by the devotee who redeemed their vows to praise and thank God Zhenwu's efficacious power.

The Sky World beyond the Clouds 云外清都

"The Sky World", heaven in Taoism, is the highest fairyland of gods. The meaning of these four characters is to praise the high grade of Purple Cloud Palace of Wudang Mountains, which is just like the Three Qings fairyland of the three spaces. At the same time, it also praises that the beautiful scenery in Purple Cloud Palace is just like the paradise on earth.

The First Pace to Wudang Mountains 云严初步

There is a pun in the meaning of this board, its metaphoric meaning is that God Zhenwu began to cultivate himself here when he was young; at the same time, it shows the dedicator's all sorts of feeling well up in his mind when he came to Wudang Mountains, which shows the dedicator's wish to visit Wudang Mountains again.

5. VCDs of Wudang Mountains 武当光盘作品

The Mysteries of Wudang Mountains 武当探秘

Wudang Mountains is world renowned for its enchanting natural scenery, splendid buildings of palaces and temples, melodious Taoist music, mysterious Wudang Martial Art, long-history Taoist culture, exquisite rare treasures, and so on. *The Mysteries of Wudang Mountains* will show all these to you and let you explore and feel the mysteries of Chinese Taoism holy land.

The Mysteries of Wudang Mountains, true, audio-visual and refined, will be the best choice of your reference material and treasured souvenir, either you have been to Wudang Mountains or you are going to visit Wudang Mountains.

Press: Hubei Jiutong Press

Manufacturer: Shiyan Television Station, Hubei province; China Wudang Net

Muscles-Changing Exercise to Direct the Body 易筋运身功

Muscles-Changing Exercise, Chinese traditional excellent regimen cultivation exercise, has been handed down from generation to generation for its miraculous effect, such as relaxing all the pulses of the body, improving blood circulation, developing one's muscles and strengthening one's body, curing and guarding against diseases, prolonging lifespan and showing one's robustness and bravery in attacking and defending.

This Exercise has ten patterns all together, which is discovered, neatened and performed by Mr. Kong De, the secretary-general of China Wudang Mountains Research Association of Wudang Boxing, a famous master of Inner Medicine Regimen, and scholar of Taoist Culture.

It contains the demonstrative edition and the teaching edition. This exercise is the excellent set of patterns collected by http://www.wudangwang.com.cn/.

Demonstrated by: Kong De

Press: China WudangNet

Wudang Taiyi Five-Element Boxing 武当太乙五行拳

Wudang Taiyi Five-Element Boxing is the principal kind of boxing in Wudang Martial Art. This Boxing is superb in skills and complicated in theory, whose stepping position and body position are simple and unsophisticated, and emphasizing slow and gentle acts with strength. In the view of attacking and defending, it pays more attention to grappling, whose palms are heavy and explosive, with relaxing and gentle acts as the basis, and strength starts from inside, so as to fully show the distinctive feature of Wudang Inner Exercise. To practice it more can regulate and improve physiological function, keep a good health and sound mind, postpone the coming of decrepitude, and has an active effect in health preservation and the practice of attacking and defending.

This Boxing is demonstrated by Mr. Yang Qunli, a senior coach, national referee of martial art, and seventh class master of martial art. He has been teaching and training martial art for decades, abundant in teaching experiences.

It contains the demonstrative edition and the teaching edition. This exercise is the excellent set of patterns collected by China Wudang Net.

Demonstrated by: Yang Qunli

Press: China Wudang Net

Wudang Taoist-Exclusive Five-Element Boxing 武当秘传五行拳

Wudang Mountains is the cradle of Wudang Inner Exercise, which, passed down from generation to generation for thousands of years, has formed a system of inner cultivation integrated by body-building, regimen, attacking and defending.

Wudang Taoist-Exclusive Five-Element Boxing is an excellent set of inner exercise exclusive to Wudang Mountains Taoists, which is the compulsory work of each Taoists of generations. This Exercise is formed by five patterns: the shapes of tortoise, snake, tiger, dragon and crane which are inspirited from holy and powerful creatures in Chinese traditional culture, to regulate the biological function of the human body so that it can make people be in the best state in which they are full of vital energy and blood, with free mind and bright eyes, vigorous and quick-witted.

The inheritor of this Exercise is Taoist Yuan Limin, 34 years old now. At the age of 11, he came to be Taoist in Wudang Mountains where he has been learning the art of martial with famous masters. With a deep love of Wudang Culture and Martial Art, he has been a distinguished Taoist with profound learning in martial art virtue and skills. He has been invited many times to take part in the games and martial activities all over the world and won many prizes.

It contains the demonstrative edition and the teaching edition. This exercise is the excellent set of patterns collected by China Wudang Net.

Demonstrated by: Yuan Limin

Press: China Wudang Net

Wudang Taoist-Exclusive Taiji Boxing 武当秘传太极拳

Wudang Taoist-Exclusive Taiji Boxing, simple, unsophisticated and elegant with long flavor, tone and hidden profound secret, is the most exclusive the inheritors of Wudang School. In the process of long history, because its very strict disciplines and the special cultural background of Wudang Mountains and Taoist quiet and inactive theories, it was not widely spread.

Wudang Taoist-Exclusive Taiji Boxing is taught in the temples of Wudang Mountains, which requires to practice forms, acts, posture externally and practice mentality, physical strength internally so as to cultivate the inner body essence, vital energy and mentality as inner exercise, concentrate one's spirit, ease one's mind, lead vital energy, urge one's body with vital energy and cultivate both internally and externally. This Exercise can make up the learners' positive breath, remove the obstacles from the main and collateral channels, harmonize the viscera, maintain the normal biological function of the human body and improve immunity so as to cure diseases, keep fit, prolong one's lifespan and protect oneself.

Mr. Yuan Limin, a distinguished Taoist with profound learning in martial art virtue and skills, has presented this exercise out to realize Zhang Sanfeng's wish, that is, to prolong the lifespan of the heroes all over the world.

It contains the demonstrative edition and the teaching edition. This Exercise is the excellent set of patterns collected by China Wudang Net.

Demonstrated by: Yuan Limin

Press: China Wudang Net

Wudang Taoist Five-Element Regimen 武当道门五行养生秘功

Wudang Taoism has achieved many successes in the active exploration of life science, among which Wudang Taoist Five-Element Regimen is one of the achievements of the excellent regimen culture.

"Five elements" is an important philosophical perspective in the ancient Chinese theory of the development of the world. From this perspective, nature is made up by the five elements: metal, wood, water, fire and earth. The wax and wane of the five elements makes nature change accordingly, which does not only affect man's fate but also makes the universe and all creatures circulate unlimited. The ancient medicine had invoked the five-element theory, too.

Wudang Taoist Five-Element Regimen, Wudang Taoist regimen exercise to cultivate the body and the character, has a solid foundation of Chinese traditional culture. It observes human's health principles in every aspect, so as to have a distinctive efficiency to cure the diseases and prolong one's lifespan.

Mr. Liu Deyi is the only inheritor of the Exercise, from which he has benefited a great deal. Now he is at his eighties, but he, hale and hearty, can still hear and see quite well with lithe muscles and strong bones.

It contains the demonstrative edition and the teaching edition. This Exercise is the excellent set of patterns collected by China Wudang Net.

Demonstrated by: Liu Deyi

Press: China Wudang Net

Wudang Twelve-Act of Nine-Direction Turning 武当九宫旋转十二法

Wudang Taoist Regimen stems from Taoism, which lays emphasis on the idea of cultivating the natural body in the natural way, that is, through the process of training vital essence to build up man's vital energy and training vital energy to build up man's mentality, to make man's body essence, vital energy and mentality gather together, and the body and mind can be balanced so as to restore the body essence to grow the brain and strengthen life energy.

Wudang Twelve-Act of Nine-Direction Turning is a simple skill in the Taoist cultivation, which has a few routines and is easy to learn. One can practice any single routine or the whole set of patterns anywhere without a time limitation. If practice it for a long time, it can coordinate vital energy and blood circulation, concentrate one's attention and make one energetic so as to cure diseases, keep fit and prolong one's lifespan.

It contains the demonstrative edition and the teaching edition. This Exercise is the excellent set of patterns collected by China Wudang Net.

Demonstrated by: Yang Qunli

Press: China Wudang Net

Simplified Wudang Boxing 简化武当拳

Simplified Wudang Boxing has eighteen routines all together. Theoretically based on Wudang Inner Thought of Wudang Boxing, The technical acts are based on the creams of ten kinds of inner boxing, such as Peripatetic Boxing, Chunyang Boxing, Taiyi Five-Element Boxing, Natural Boxing, Taoist-Exclusive Taiji, Hammer, Eight-Step Longxin Palm, Taihe Boxing, Zhao Pu Style Taiji Boxing and so on.

This Exercise pays emphasis on the unity of heart, mind-intention, vital energy and the human body so as to keep fit, cure diseases and prolong the lifespan.

The chief compiler of this Exercise, Mr. Yang Qunli, is a national referee for martial art, the Seventh class master of martial art. He has been teaching and training martial art for decades and has made many achievements in the scientific research and teaching of traditional martial art.

It contains the demonstrative edition and the teaching edition. This Exercise is the excellent set of patterns collected by China Wudang Net.

Demonstrated by: Yang Qunli

Press: Hubei Jiutong Electronic Press

6. Famous Painters in Wudang Mountains 武当画家

Mr. Zhao Jiafu 赵家富先生

Zhao Jiafu, born in 1962, graduated from Hubei Institute of Fine Arts and gained Bachelor of Art in 1986, and then graduated from the sixth session of Canvas Studying Class of Central Academy of Fine Arts in 1993. Now he is an assistant professor of Shiyan Institute of Education, member of Hubei Artists Association, chairman of Shiyan Canvas Arts Commission.

His canvas works have been displayed in all kinds of big exhibitions sponsored by the nation, and the province, many of which have gained prizes and been published in some important arts magazines. Such as:

2003, *The Mountain is also Civil in a Static View* was enlisted in Walking together into the New Century—the Third Session of Chinese Canvas Exhibition.

2003, *The Cloud is also Auspicious in a Static View* was enlisted in the Second Session of Hubei Paintings Exhibition, Hubei Canvas Arts Exhibition.

2003, *Spring Wind and Clear Sound* was awarded Excellent Prize in Hubei Arts Exhibition of Universities and Colleges.

2002, *Tibet Scenery III* was awarded the seventh session of Hubei Masters Prize.

2002, *Tibet Scenery III* was enlisted in Words of Materials—Hubei Exhibition of Small 2000, *The Autumn in a Static View* was awarded Silver Prize in Hubei Teachers' Art Works Exhibition.

2000, *The Old Friends* was enlisted in the Ninth Session of Hubei Arts Works Exhibition.

2000, *The Charm of Hubei Province when the Moon Rises* was enlisted in China Arts Today.

1999, *Gold Stele* was awarded the third session of Hubei Masters Prize.

1995, *The Greenland Afar* was enlisted in the First Session of China Scenery Canvas Exhibition, and was compiled in China Scenery Canvas.

Canvas and Sculptures.

Mr. Yao Qiang 姚强先生

Yao Qiang, male, born in 1961, graduated from Hubei Institute of Fine Arts and gained Bachelor of Art in 1986, graduated from Canvas Material and Skills Studying Class of Lu-Xun Arts College in 1991, and graduated from Sketch and Canvas Skills Studying Class of St.Petersburg Insititute for Painting, Sculpting and Architecture, Russia. He was invited to visit the United States, Canada, France, Italy, Germany, Holland, and some other countries in the South-east Asia, and the world-famous art museums. Now he is the dean of Art Department, Hubei Industrial Polytechnic, assistant professor, director of Hubei Arts Association, committee member of Hubei Art Instructing Commission of Universities and Colleges, President of Shiyan Artists Association, and outstanding experts of Hubei Province.

His canvas works have been displayed in all kinds of big exhibitions sponsored by the nation, and the province, many of which have gained prizes and been published in some important arts magazines. Such as:

In September of 1994, his canvas work *Static Object* took part in China Teachers' Arts Work Exhibition and was awarded Excellent Prize, the First Prize in Hubei Teachers' Arts Works Exhibition, and was also compiled in Journal of Pictures.

In November of 1994, his canvas work *The New Life* was awarded Gold Prize in the First Session of China Canvas of Static Objects Exhibition, was bought by Just Auction Company of England, the first-rate art gallery of the world, and then was sought at the highest price in Hong Kong 1995 Spring Auction Fair, having an important influence in the world.

In September of 1995, his canvas work *The Island in April* was selected as Best Works in China Canvas of Scenery Exhibition, displayed in many countries and then compiled in Journal of Pictures.

In September of 1997, his canvas work *A Woman in the Snow Land* was awarded Excellent Prize in Hubei Art Works Exhibition, and then was awarded Silver Prize in 2001 Hubei Teachers' Works Exhibition.

In October of 1999, his canvas work *The Life* was enlisted in Hubei Exhibition of the Ninth Session of China Arts Exhibition.

In May of 2002, his canvas work *The man in the Himalayas* was awarded the Highest Learning Prize in Hubei Exhibition of Small Canvas and Sculptures.

In July of 2003, his canvas work *Shepherding in the Grassland* was awarded Gold Prize in Hubei Arts Works Exhibition of Universities and Colleges, Canvas Art Prize in the Second Session of Hubei Canvas Exhibition, and was enlisted in Best Works Exhibition of the Third Session of China Canvas Exhibition.

Mr. Hu Shengqi　胡盛骑先生

Hu Shengqi, male, born in 1970, graduated from Hubei Institute of Fine Arts in 1994, and then completed the First Session of Advanced Canvas Studying Class, Russia in 2002. Now he is a teacher in Art Department of Shiyan Institute of Education, a member of Hubei Art Department Association, member of Hubei Water Color Academy, the vice-secretary-general of Shiyan Artists Association, and chairman of Shiyan Water Color Art Commission.

His painting works have been displayed in all kinds of big exhibitions sponsored by the nation, and the province, many of which have gained prizes and been published in some important arts magazines. Such as:

In 1994, his watercolor work *A Static Object* was awarded Excellent Prize in the Second Session of Biyearly Exhibition of Hubei Water Color Academy, and compiled in Journal of Pictures.

In 1995, his watercolor work *The Chair that My Grandfather Sat on* was enlisted in 1995 Hangzhou, China Water Color Exhibition.

In 1996, his watercolor work *A Static Object* with Tulips was enlisted in the Third Session of China Exhibition of Water Color and Powder Paintings, and compiled in Exhibition Works Collection of the Third Session of China Exhibition of Water Color and Powder Paintings.

In 1997, his watercolor work *A Static Object with Carnations* was enlisted in 1997 Hubei Art Works Exhibition.

In 1997, his watercolor work *A Static Object on the Table* was enlisted in 1997 China Youth Water Color Exhibition, and compiled in Works Collection of China Youth Water Color and Powder Paintings.

In 1998, his watercolor works *In Front of the Window* and *Stories in the Summer* were enlisted in the Fourth Session of Biyearly Exhibition of Hubei Water Color Academy, and compiled in Hubei Water Color Collection.

In 1999, his watercolor work *For the Forgetting Memories* was awarded Silver Prize in the Ninth Session of China Art Works Exhibition, and compiled in Best Works Collection of the Ninth Session of China Art Works Exhibition and Water Color Collection of the Ninth Session of China Art Works Exhibition.

In 2000, his watercolor work *The Wind in July* was enlisted in the Fifth Session of China Water Color and Powder Paintings Exhibition, and compiled in Works Collection of the Fifth Session of China Water Color and Powder Paintings Exhibition.

In 2000, his watercolor works *Uncompleted Words* and other four were compiled in Journal of China Art Today.

In 2001, his watercolor work *Declining Shadow* was awarded Gold Prize in the First Session of Hubei Teachers' Art and Shooting Works Exhibition, and compiled in Hubei Teachers' Art Works Collection.

In 2001, his canvas work *A Lotus* was enlisted in Studying and Overcoming— China Small Canvas Exhibition, and compiled in Picture Collection of Studying and Overcoming— China

Small Canvas Exhibition.

In 2002, his canvas works *A Horse* and *Frost* were awarded Learning Prize in Words of Materials— Small Canvas Exhibition.

In 2002, his watercolor work *Ode* was awarded Excellent Prize in the Ninth Session of Hubei Masters' Works Exhibition.

In 2002, his watercolor work *Fresh Flowers and Green Fruits* was enlisted in Best Works Exhibition of China Water Color.

In 2002, his canvas works *A Water Jug and Homeland* were enlisted in To Commemorate 60 anniversary of Yan'an Art Meeting — Hubei Art Works Exhibition.

In 2003, his watercolor Air-dried *Lotus* was enlisted in Best Works Exhibition of China Small Water Color.

In 2003, his canvas work *Spring Planting* was awarded Silver Prize in teachers group of Hubei Art Competition of Universities and Colleges.

In 2003, his canvas *Just Like One* was awarded Excellent Prize in the Second Session of Hubei Canvas Exhibition.

Chapter 10 Taoist Music of Wudang Mountains 武当音乐

Taoist music is performed during the Taoist rituals where activities are carried out to celebrate the immortal's birthday, beg for god's blessing, expel and conquer devils or deliver the soul of the deceased. It is an essential part of Taoist rituals that aims to create the religious atmosphere and thus strengthen believers' aspiration for the fairyland and their adoration of immortals.

The early ritual activities claimed lineage going back to the ancient sacrifice ceremony by the wizards. Sutra used to be chanted directly and there was no record of musical chanting. Taoist music was initiated round in the Northern and Southern dynasties and the Tang Dynasty witnessed its heyday. Emperor Gao of the Tang Dynasty once ordered music performers in imperial temple to compose Taoist tones. Emperor Xuan of the Tang Dynasty asked priests and chancellors to present Taoist songs and he produced and taught Taoist music in person. Xue Tao, a poetess in the Tang Dynasty, wrote such lines in her poem: dressed in long robes as those worn by the Celestial Worthy of Primordial Beginning, holding lotus flowers to follow the example of numerous immortals, music performers get together whenever there is a singing and dancing festival, to chant the songs of Bu Xu (Pacing the Void) in chorus with their heads bending. This poem is a manifestation of the prosperity of Taoist music of that time. At the end of the Tang Dynasty and the early beginning of the Five Dynasties, a famous Taoist priest named Du Guangting compiled *A Complete Collection of Taoist Rituals*, which epitomized Taoist ritual activities of the previous dynasties and further standardized Taoist ceremonies. Up till then, Taoist music had been greatly diversified: besides the original simple percussion instruments, blowpipe and plucked string instruments were added.

The Song Dynasty proved another significant period in the development of Taoist music. Emperors Tai, Zhen and Hui of the Song Dynasty engaged themselves in the music composition successively and totally produced dozens of pieces. Emperor Hui, with an overwhelming enthusiasm for Taoism, promoted a Taoist priest named Lin Lingsu to an important position for the amending of the rituals through supplementing or abridging work. Priests were selected out of the temples to study Taoist music on a nationwide basis. It is in this period that string instruments were included.

During the Yuan Dynasty, Taoism was divided into the Zhengyi (Orthodox) and Quanzhen (Complete Reality) sects, each influencing and characterizing the styles of Taoist music in their own ways: the former values quiet self-cultivation and its music is endowed with seclusion, quietness and detachment, while the latter attaches importance to rituals and magic figures, hence its music firm, vigorous, classic and elegant.

In the early period of the Ming Dynasty, Emperor Zhu Yuanzhang established the Institute of Metaphysical Sect (later changed into the Taolu Department) to manage national Taoism. He endeavored to rectify Taoism and ordered Taoist priests to draw up ceremonious standards, which contributed to the normalization of Taoist music. In Emperor Yongle period of the Ming Dynasty, Emperor Cheng, Zhu Di, wrote *The Great Ming Metaphysical Sect Musical Chapters*, which included three parts, that is Altar Eulogy, Xuanwu (God) and Hongen Lingji zhenjun (Perfected Lords of Vast Mercy and Numinous Salvation). This book subsequently included The Zhengtong Daocang (*Taoist Canon of the Zhengtong Reign*) and proved of great referential value in the study on the ancient music of the Ming Dynasty.

As an ancient form of religious music, Taoist music had established its unique style with invariable abundance in Taoist beliefs and aesthetic thoughts underlying the connotation of its musical forms and emotional appeal. It mainly served for eulogizing immortals, begging for blessing and averting calamity, releasing the purgatory of the departed and maintaining internal cultivation. There are two kinds of Taoist musical forms, the Yang Tune and the Yin Tune: the former is mainly used in the morning altar class and ritual praying exercise, while the latter in evening altar class and ceremonious sparing practice. The underlying aestheticism is a manifestation of the pursuit of longevity and the In-activeness (without action or effortless doing) in Taoism. The tones are solemn, serene, quiet as well as appealing. It can be grand and magnificent in serving for summoning and dispatching immortals. While fulfilling the function of conquering and exorcising devils, it is powerful and resolute. In blessing and celebrating activities, it appears brisk and merry. To sing the praises of immortals, it becomes tranquil and graceful. Lastly, the music performed in praying and self-cultivation becomes melodious and celestial. It is under the musical background that Taoist ritual activities are further infused with solemnity, seriousness, respectfulness and mysteriousness. Vividly and harmoniously, the musical instruments seem to have brought the fascinated listeners back to every fairyland which used to be visualized in their minds.

Taoism has a close relation with the custom and convention of the Han People and advocates both receptiveness and detachment. Accordingly, Taoist music is closely related to the traditional music of the Han People with resort to considerable absorption and blending of the tones and performances in imperial and folk musics. With its popularity, Taoist music is widely accepted and thus strengthens its homiletic and recreational functions.

Taoist music consists of vocal music and instrumental music, which has formed various musical patterns, such as solo, chanting, unison, ensemble and accompaniment, and so on. Vocal music takes the majority of ritual music performances, including eulogy, praise, gatha, song of Bu Xu (Pacing the Void), and chanting. Among them, eulogy, praise, song of Bu Xu and gatha are independent tunes, consisting of either two sentences, four-sentenced sub-paragraphs or longer paragraphs. The rhyme in the music serves as the melody to create the atmosphere and intensify the emotions. Different from the normal cases, melodies (i.e. sutra) express the ritual performers' wishes and petition through their praying to the deities or eulogizing of immortals.

Melodies preserve harmony with sutra and mix miscellaneous tunes naturally and consistently, whereby an integral ritual activity comes up. The instruments in Taoist music comprise all those used in the Han People's music, among which three patterns are used most, i.e. percussion music (consisting of bell, drum, chime stone, cymbals, wooden fish, etc), blowpipe music (including Sheng, pipe, flute, Xiao, etc) and plucked strings music(comprising Guqin, Erhu, Banhu, Ruan, etc).

Many Taoist priests were renowned musicians in the Chinese history, among whom the most famous one is Hua Yanjun (also addressed as A Bing). His masterpiece *Erquan Yingyue/ Two Springs Reflecting the Moon* still remained unique and incomparable in Chinese national music.

In the years of Emperor Yongle of the Ming Dynasty, 400 Taoists were drafted into Wudang Mountains from the temples throughout the whole country to conduct ritual activities. Being erudite and well-informed about Taoist ritual music, these senior priests from different regions and various Taoist schools merged their respective Taoist music into one, which established Wudang Taoist music as a quintessential gathering of different styles of Taoist music over the country; hence a gradual formation of Taoist musical system with both individuality and commonness.

Taoist music of Wudang Mountains is rich in tracts as well as in the variety of names. At present, about over 100 pieces of Taoist music are preserved and collected in *China*'s *Taoist Music of Wudang Mountains*.

Chapter 11 Wudang Taoist Teas 武当道茶

1. Fragrant teas coming from famous mountains

Wudang Mountains, the famous holy land of China Taoism, is the first of the four Taoist

Mountains. Wudang Mountains Taoism has had a long history since the Spring and Autumn Period when some visiting Taoists made temples by grasses in Wudang Mountains and practiced self-cultivation and Taoist activities. Wudang Taoism had a fast development during the Wei, Jin, Southern and Northern dynasties. In the years of Zhenguan Ruling of the Tang Dynasty, Yao Jian, the magistrate of Wudang prefecture prayed for rain under the imperial order and succeeded, so Emperor Li Shimin ordered to build Five-dragon Palace. In the late years of the Tang Dynasty, Wudang Mountains was listed one of the seventy-two fortune lands of Taoism.

In the years of Song, Yuan, Ming and Qing dynasties, Taoist activities were more and more. The Emperors of the Song and Yuan dynasties conferred Wudang Zhenwu God and respected as Home God of the Whole Country, and took Wudang Mountains as one of the important places to pray God and celebrate longevity. When Emperor Yongle of the Ming Dynasty came into power, he ordered to build the Imperial Palace in the north and Wudang Mountains in the south, where 300,000 artisans worked for thirteen years to finish building thirty-three building complexes, with a total construction area of 1,600,000m^2. Wudang Mountains was respected as the Supreme Mountains, the Mountains to rule the country and the highest Imperial Temple and the center of China Taoism activities. The biggest number of the Taoists in Wudang is over 13,000, so that it was the biggest Taoism place and the First Mountain of China Taoism.

Wudang ancient buildings are on the top of the mountains, in the steep cliffs, and among great pines and cypresses, extending from Junzhou Town to Tianzhu/ Heavenly Pillar Peak for about 70,000 meters. During the late years of the Yuan Dynasty and the early years of the Ming Dynasty, Wudang Taoist Zhang Sanfeng created Taiji Boxing here and was regarded as the founder of Wudang Boxing. After the inheritance and spreading of many generations' Taoists, Wudang Boxing has been one of the key schools of Chinese martial arts, named as Shaolin Boxing in the north and Wudang Boxing in the south.

Wudang Mountains was included in the first list of Key State Scenic Spots by the State Council in 1982, and the Ancient Building Complex in Wudang Mountains was listed in World Cultural Heritage in 1994, and 64 ancient building complexes were under the state protection in 2006, Wudang Boxing and Wudang Temples and Palaces were listed in the State Intangible Cultural Heritage, and Wudang Mountains Taoist medicine and temple fair were listed in the Provincial Intangible Cultural Heritage.

Wudang Mountains is covering 312 km^2, where are strange peaks, steep cliffs, valleys and ravines, covered by clouds and fogs all year round, full of change. The main one, Tianzhu/ Heavenly Pillar Peak, 1,612 meters-high, is rising up into the sky like a pillar. Seventy-two peaks are around Tianzhu Peak just like paying respect for it. Xu Xiake, the famous geologist, traveler of the Ming Dynasty, Wang Shizhen, the litterateur of the Ming Dynasty, Mi Fu, one of the famous calligraphers and other poets thought highly of its scenery.

Wudang Mountains has had suitable natural conditions for tea, which belongs to subtropical monsoon climate, with a clear vertical temperature and the temperature decreases with the height of the altitude which has three climate zones, high, middle and low, 1,200-1,600 meters and an average climate 12℃, 750-1,200 meters and an average climate 10.0℃-12.0℃, below 750 meters and an average climate 15.9℃ respectively. The annual average humidity of Wudang Mountains is about 10.0℃-12.0℃, annual rainfall 900-1,200mm, and frost-free season 163-254 days. Since the Yuan Dynasty, Wudang Mountains has been not cold in winter and not hot in summer, an ideal place for summer resort.

Wudang Mountains is rich in medicinal plants and Compendium of Materia Medica recorded over 1,800 Chinese traditional medicines, while Wudang Mountains has had over 400 kinds. According to the medicinal plants survey of 1985, here are 617 kinds in Wudang Mountains. Therefore, Wudang Mountains has been called Natural Medicine Warehouse. Here is of mild climate, warm in winter and cool in summer, a suitable place for tea tree to grow.

2. Fragrant teas coming from magical 30°N

Northern latitude 30° is the most magical zone in the Earth where Bermuda Triangle, Egypt Pyramid and Sphinx, the Hanging Garden of Babylon, ancient Mayan civilization, Chinese Sanxingdui Ruin Site, Himalaya, the highest peak in the world and the deepest submarine trench are located.

In China, northern latitude 30° is the production zone for best teas, such as West Lake Dragon Well, Junshan Silver Needle, Mengding Ganlu Tea and other seven famous traditional teas. Wudang Mountains is in the Zone, which is the reason for producing fragrant teas.

Special geographical landscape is the basis for teas' fine quality. The diversity of the landscape has created the conditions for different kinds of teas, including some phosphor, zinc, selenium and some organic matter, which are very helpful for the forming of tea characters. Some researches have proved that the height of latitude is closely connected with the tea's fragrance, just as the saying goes, high mountains covered by clouds and fogs produce best tea.

Suitable climate is the key point for the forming of teas' fine quality. Northern latitude 30°N is the boundary zone between subtropic zone and temperate zone, of a moderate climate and relatively plenty rainfall, suitable for most of the animals and plants including tea trees to grow.

Good ecological environment is the guarantee for teas' fine quality. Suitable climate and diverse geographical changes has led to biological diversity. In the tea gardens of Wudang Mountains, there are well-protected forest, robust plantations, fertile soil, therefore the tea tree here is strong in fighting against illness and insects, and there are mony natural enemies of tea tree insects, including birds and spiders, which has made the tea gardens here have complete self-regulation system and the main production zone of green and organic teas.

Generally speaking, with the southern movement of the latitude, the tea leaves are bigger and bigger, the content in the tea leaves are more and more, including EGCG, polyphenols and amino acid, the taste is stronger and bitter. Vice versa, with the decrease of the latitude, the temperature is lower and lower, the tea leaves are smaller, polyphenols and other contents are fewer, and the taste is weaker. While, northern latitude 30°N is of comfortable temperature, which makes the tea have balanced form and content, polyphenols and amino acid accounting for 10%, regarded as the best condition for making fine green tea.

3. Types of ancient Wudang Taoist tea

Qianlin Tea

Qianlin is the forest in the moon according to Taoist literature, which has been recorded in many books and literature. Qianlin tea was one of the famous tribute teas. Wudang Mountains prefecture would sacrifice two Jin of Qianlin Tea. The rare Qianlin Tea, Wudang Tribute Tea, has been a special and magical part of Wudang Culture as a unique Taoist tea culture.

Qianlin Tea was the oldest Taoist tea in China, which was recorded in the books written in the Northern Song Dynasty and Pilgrimage to the West by Wu Cheng'en of the Ming Dynasty. Many records proved that Qianlin Tree was the symbol of rare tree in Taoist wonderland.

A Summary of Hubei Teas, Junzhou Annals, Annals of the Qing Dynasty and other important books all recorded Qianlin tree, Qianlin tea, which were cherished by the Taoists, not drunken by the common people. And Chinese ancient classics have recorded that the magical Wudang regiment tea had many beneficial effects, including getting off heat and curing diseases.

As to the taste of Qianlin Tea, there are many versions as early as in the Yuan and Ming dynasties, such as bitter first and then fragrant, can have three or four infusions. Many people cherished it as a tea treasure.

The tea leaves grown in the ancient Qianlin tree of Wudang Mountains, different from the common tea leaves, can be smell a special fragrance before drinking it, which is everlasting so that it can be infused more times than other ordinary tea leaves. Therefore, the unique and lasting fragrance has been the key point to separate it from other tea.

Orange Tea

In *Travel in Taihe Mountains* by Yuan Zhongdao, one of the famous litterateurs, Orange Tea, a kind of regiment health tea created by Wudang Taoists was recorded. During the Ming Dynasty, many pious followers came to Wudang Mountains and paid sacrifice to the Hall of Emperor Zhenwu through lots of seasonal fruits. The Taoists here shared the sacrificed fruits with the followers and put some teas into the slightly dried oranges with some herbs as to make Taoist tea after many times of steaming and sunning, which can be stored for five, ten or even fifty years, and the longer the storage year, the better effect in curing cough, reducing phlegm, and relieving fever. What's more, the tea flavor is mild, fresh and lingering.

Yuan Zhongdao drank the Orang Tea when he visited Qizhen Cave, which had a long impression on him so that later he asked others to send him the Orang Tea from one-thousand li away Wudang Mountains. When Zheng Chenggong succeeded in resuming the sovereignty over Taiwan, the process of making Orange Tea was spread there and loved by the residents there. Taiwan people like to drink Orange Tea by putting tea and orange peel into the boiling water with some rocky candy. So the tea is sour, sweet, bitter, fragrant and astringent, a very special flavor with some light tea and dried orange peel.

Liver-curing Tea

Liver-curing Tea was already created in the years of Emperor Qianlong of the Qing Dynasty, respected as the Imperial Tea. Wudang Liver-curing Tea is prepared by natural wild flos puerariae of high connotation of isoflavone and saponin, which has very good effect of relieving liquor and protecting liver in accordance with *Shen Nong*'s *Herbal Classic, Master Index of Medicine Specialty, and Compendium of Materia Medica,* and other medicine books. There is a saying going like that drinking wild flos puerariae can make you have one thousand cups of wine without being drunk, in other words, if you drink wild flos puerariae fifteen minutes earlier before you drinking wine, your wine potential will be quickly enlarged because flos puerariae can dissolve wine quickly and reduce the pressure of liver. Wudang Liver-curing Tea is made of wild flos puerariae come from the deep mountains, whose power of dissolving wine is 8 or 10 times of that of man-planted ones.

Medicinal Tea

Medicinal Tea has had over two thousand years' history since the Han Dynasty, which has been recorded in the medical books of many dynasties, such as *Treatise on Cold Pathogenic and Miscellaneous Diseases* by Zhang Zhongjing of the Eastern Han Dynasty. In the Southern Dynasty, the famous doctor Tao Hongjing recorded that the medicinal tea can make the drinker to sleep easily. In the Tang and Song dynasties, tea therapy theory was formed, recorded in *Revised Compendium of Materia Medica.* Especially, the imperial doctor Hu Sihui recorded many kinds' medicinal tea making process and effects, whose book is the relatively complete one recording medicinal tea. The famous doctor Li Shizhen had a much deeper study of medicinal teas, he recorded medicinal teas' functions, major functions and sixteen prescriptions for headache, toxic heat, diarrhea, and dissolving other poisons in *Compendium of Materia Medica*. In the Qing Dynasty, the tea therapy was very popular and tea medicine were part of the royal families' medicines.

In the wide and high Wudang Mountains, there have been many profound Taoists cultivating hermit and studying Taoist teas so that they created many medicinal teas with different functions, such as, increasing positive energy and dissolving poisons, producing saliva and slaking thirst, moistening negative energy and dryness syndrome, warming cold and curing stomach. Wudang Taoists are fond of drinking teas and good at putting some herbs into the tea as to wake up and get rid of fatigue, stimulate appetite and digestion, clear heat and dissolve poisons, and cure diuresis and diarrhea, and so on.

4. Types of modern Wudang Taoist teas

(1) Shengshui Tribute Tea

Shengshui Tribute Tea is produced from the deep Shengmu Mountains, Zhushan County, Hubei Province, where the special climate, soil and ecology has made the tea of best character, clear tea soup, long and strong fragrance, fresh taste, recognized as one of the rare ecological tea of strong fragrance.

According to the legend, in the Emperor Wuzhou of the Tang Dynasty, Prince Luling was exiled to Fangling (now Fangxian County), when he went through Zhushan County and had the tea by chance, finding that the character is special and of best quality, offered it to his mother Wu Zetian, the Queen. After drinking the tea for three years, the Queen became healthy and younger in appearance, so that she named the tea Shengshui Tribute Tea and ordered to build Imperial Tea Garden and Shengshui Temple for a purpose of spreading the making process of Shengshui Tribute tea. For its long history, best quality, and fine workmanship, the tea was awarded Gold Medal in China International Agriculture Exposition for three consecutive sessions.

(2) Shengshui Wudang Taoist Tea

Shengshui Wudang Taoist Tea is produced from Wudang Mountains, the world famous holy land of China Taoism, one of the major tea origin places and the core water source area of the mid-line project of South-to-North Water Diversion. The tea gardens are in the deep mountains of about 500-1,000 meter above the sea level, with a fine ecological environment, rich natural resources, as the premium tea garden determined by the Ministry of Agriculture and Hubei strong-fragrance green tea base and organic tea production zone. Shengshui Wudang Taoist Tea is of special character, unique and lasting flower fragrance, thin and straight in form, green and clear in soup, and fresh and happy flavor. Shengshui Wudang Taoist Tea is famous for its green, strong fragrance, pure and mild taste and the unique Taoist culture flavor, very popular among the customers in many big cities, including southeast Asia and European Union.

(3) Shengshui Cuifeng/ Green Peak Tea

Shengshui Cuifeng Tea is made from the local specialty, the quality single-bud of Zhushan Dark Big Leave in a combined process of traditional skills and modern theory. The tea is tight, thin, round and straight in the form, green in color, special and long flower fragrance, fresh green and clear tea soup, pure and mild taste, and rich in Se and Zn and other elements.

(4) Shengshui Maojian/ Needle Tea

Shengshui Maojian Tea is made of fine tea leaves in strict production standard through low temperature, oxygen absorbing and other modern skills to keep fresh, hence the fine quality, unique natural flower fragrance, tight, thin, round and straight appearance, fresh and lingering taste.

(5) Wudang Yinjian/ Silver Sword Tea

Wudang Yinjian Tea is famous for Wudang Sword as a high-level gift tea. The dried tea leaves are flat, smooth and straight like swords, and the tea soup is tender green, clear, long orchid fragrance and linger taste. Wudang Yinjian Tea is taking the creative idea from Wudang Sword for its outer form is same as a silver sword, with a very high appreciation value. The tea has been awarded Golden Medal in 1995 China Agriculture Exposition, and Chinese International Tea in 1998 by the Ministry of Agriculture of the PRC.

(6) Wudang Zhenjing/ Needle Well Tea

Wudang Zhenjing Tea is famous for the legend of grinding a iron stick into a needle, created through Taoist traditional process. The dried tea leaves are tight and thin as needles, green in color, and the tea soup is tender green and clear, and lingering taste. Since the creation in 1987, the tea has been awarded ten times province-level prizes, and listed in Hubei Top Tea in 1992, one of the Top Fifteen Organic Teas, and Hubei Top Brand since 2002.

(7) Wudang Qifeng/ Strange Peak Tea

Wudang Qifeng Tea is named from the seventy-two peaks respecting the Golden Summit of Wudang Mountains. The dried tea leaves are thin, twisted, free and moistening, and the tea soup is tender green and clear, fresh and lingering in taste. The tea was awarded the Best Tea of Northwest Hubei in 1990.

(8) Wudang Taoist Tea King

Wudang Taoist Tea King, also called Wudang Taiji Regiment Gongfu Tea, is the gist of Wudang Taoist regiment tea practice. The dried tea leaves are twisted, moistening, yellow-gold in soup, clear, pure and mild, and lasting fragrance and taste, which is good for digestion, bacteriostasis, and regiment.

(9) Wudang Taihe/ Supreme Harmony Tea

Wudang Taihe Tea was the tribute tea of Wudang Taoists for the imperial families of the Ming and Qing dynasties, named from Wudang Mountains, also called Taihe Mountains. The dried tea leaves are tight, smart, like dragon's teeth, and the tea soup is tender green, of lasting fragrance and taste, and the boiled tea leaves are standing upright in the cup, with very high value in appreciation and aesthetic. The tea was awarded the Best Tea of Hubei Province in 1992, and the Second Prize of China in 1994.

(10) Wudang Daohong Tea

Wudang Daohong Tea is one of the Taoist regiment teas, made by Taoist traditional process. The dried tea leaves are tight and smart, black moistening in color and the tea soup is red and charming, fragrant and sweet, and of lasting taste.

5. Making process of modern Wudang Taoist Teas

Making process of modern Wudang Taoist green teas

The making process includes fresh leave picking, spreading, fixing, rolling and forming, whose technical points are the following:

(1) Fresh leave picking

The fresh leaves of Wudang Taoist Tea is characterized by smallness and tenderness, of which the spring leaves are the best and the summer leaves the worst. The best Wudang Taoist Tea is famous for its early green tea and its smallness and tenderness, whose requirements are very strict. The key points for picking the fresh leaves are carrying out by stage and in turn and making in level. Not qualified fresh leaves, insect-hurt leaves, and the leaves with rainwater, dew, dirt and pollution are not picked. When picking the fresh leavers, the worker should use a correct method and should not do damage to the fresh leaves.

(2) Spreading

Spreading is the managing of picked fresh leaves between collecting into the tea house and fixing process.

Wudang Taoist green tea emphasizes the spreading in the making process of fresh leaves, especially for the best quality green teas, or, the insufficient spreading will affect the making effect and product quality.

The spreading of fresh leaves will evaporate some water and reduce the cell strength as to make the leaves flexible, good for fixing to a more balanced and complete extent. During the spreading, some grass smell gives off and tea fragrance forms. The spreading also promotes the hydrolyzing of protein, polysaccharose and other polymeric compounds, which is good to increase the content of free amino acid, soluble sugar and other low molecular objects as to strengthen the tea's flavor and fragrance.

The spreading of fresh leaves is better to be carried out in strip mat and soft plaque, which requires the place to be clean, free and cool, far away from sunning and raining. Nowadays, spreading machine for fresh leaves has come into being, saving place and time. The correct thickness of spreading is no more than 10cm, while the high-quality leaves should be thinly spread and the low-quality ones should be thickly spread. During the spreading, the leaves should be turn over every two or three hours as to make the leaves lose water in a balanced way. The turning-over should be soft and not hurt the leaves. The spreading should be not longer than ten hours, more or less is not good to the forming of characters. Usually speaking, when the water content of the spread leaves is about 70%, the leave color is changing from bright green to dark green, the leave surface gloss is basically disappeared, the leaves will be soft and fragrance will be smelled, when the leaves are suitable for fixing.

(3) Fixing

Fixing is one of the key process of Wudang Taoist green tea's character forming, which requires high temperature to inactivate enzyme's activity in a short time as to prevent polyphenols' oxidation and acquire the three-green character of green tea. The fixing can give off green smell, develop tea flavor, evaporate some water as to make the tea soft, flexible, easy for rolling into some certain form.

Fixing can be carried out by hand and by machine. Hand fixing is finished by using of sloping wok or pan whose bottom temperature is about 200℃. The volume of tea leaves of each fixing should be no more than one kg, and the time should be 5-7 minutes. When the fixing is OK, put the leaves out of the wok or pan quickly and spread thinly so as to lower down the temperature in a fast way. Machine fixing is usually carried out by microwave fixing machine, while the tea fragrance is not good, which is suitable to perform the second fixing of best quality green tea as to make up for the lack of fixing in the first stage. Steaming fixing is carried out by steaming fixing machine by way of inactivating enzyme's activity quickly through hot steam.

In fixing process, both hand fixing and machine fixing should abide by the following three principles of fixing in high temperature and changing from high temperature to low one, combining spreading and steaming while more spreading and less steaming, and longer fixing for tender leaves and shorter fixing for older leaves. When the weight of fixing leaves decrease by 40%, the leave color is changing from bright green to dark green, the leave surface gloss is basically disappeared, no red color, the leaves will be soft and fragrance will be smelled, when the leaves are flexible and easy to form a group, meaning the fixing is correct.

(4) Rolling

Rolling is making the tea leaves roll up into slim stripes, which is beneficial for form outer appearance and relatively damage some leave cells as to let out the in-contained contents and improve the tea water's concentration and consistency. Mass green tea leaves are in need of rolling, while best green tea leaves don't need this, for the leaves are already qualified for forming. The tea leaves without rolling are very slow in letting out in-contained contents so that the tea water is light and the dried leaves are bigger.

Rolling can be carried out by hand and machine. Hand rolling is for small volume of best green tea, while machine rolling is for the mass production of big volume green tea. Hand rolling is usually on bamboo mat or plaque, making tea leaves into slim stripes by way of hand, arm and upper body strength, lasting 10-25 minutes. Machine rolling is putting tea leaves into the machine and rolling them, different machine type meaning different rolling bucket diameter. Slim and tender leaves should be rolled in smaller rolling machine for better effect, while many bigger leaves are suitable to be rolled in bigger rolling machine. Both hand rolling and machine rolling should obey the pressing principle, light, heavy and light. When 80% of the tea leaves are rolled into slim stripes, the leave cells are damaged to 45%-55%, and the rolled leaves are wet and sticky, the rolling process is finished.

(5) Forming

Mass green tea has no special requirements on the form, but best Wudang Taoist tea emphasizes the forming. There are many kinds of best Wudang Taoist teas, which are different in forming methods, such as flat shape, roller, needle and so on. Different form has different forming methods, here are the methods of flat shape, roller, and needle.

a) Forming method of flat shape tea. The forming methods are grasping, shaking, lifting, extending, pulling, pushing, buckling, throwing, grinding, and pressing.

Grasping: making the tea leaves in one's hands exchange inside out and classify them and make them straight and tight. The actions is separating the thumb from the other four fingers, the palms downward with a arc shape. When the tea leaves are in the other side of the wok or pan, grasp them back and repeat the actions, which is suitable for medium and low quality tea leaves.

Shaking: making the water and grass smell in the tea leaves give off completely and all the tea leaves touch the wok and realize a balanced frying. The palm is upward, five fingers separated, with a light and slow move so as to make the tea leaves fall into the wok evenly.

Lifting: making the tea leaves flat. The thumb is separated from the other four fingers, palm opened and fingers upward, lifting 70% of the leaves in the hand to the middle of wok.

Extending: making the tea leaves in the wok move as to be easy for shaking. Taking the leaves to the edge of the wok and then make the palm upward and use the four fingers catch the leaves.

Pulling: making the tea leaves flat, smooth and clean by using four fingers and palm to press the leaves as to make them flat into stripes.

Pushing: making the tea leaves smooth, stripe, flat by using five compacted and unbent fingers to tightly press the leaves and pushing the leaves towards wok bottom and front wok wall as to make the leaves flat and smooth.

Buckling: making the tea stripes tight, straight and balanced, especially for medium and low quality teas. The hand movements are like that of grasping.

Throwing: making the tea leaves in the hand exchange from inside out and classify tea stripes as to make the tea leaves arranged in order. When the leaves are near the wok edge, catching them with four compacted finger and upward palm, then throwing the leaves into the wok for a purpose of classifying leaves and giving off water.

Grinding: making the tea leaves flatter, smoother. The hand movements are same to that of pushing, but one should grind from front to back or right to left in a fast speed as to make hand, tea and wok wall grind each other continuously and increase tea leaves' smoothness.

Pressing: making the tea leaves flatter and smoother. The hand movements are same to that of grinding, but more powerful, repeatedly, making the tea leaves flatter, evener and smoother.

b) Forming method of roller shape tea. The forming of roller shape tea is characterized by rubbing ball, when the wok temperature is down to 60℃-65℃, both hands' fingers closing and bending as to hold the warm tea leaves into the palms and rub it quickly for 4-6 rounds into a ball and then put into the wok and let it scatter by itself. Each wok tea leaves can be rubbed into 3-4 balls, when all balls are done, scatter them all together. The wok temperature is changing from low to high, then to low. When the leaves' water connotation is about 20%, scramble and roll the tea leaves lights so as to make them scramble each other. Roll each ball three to five turns and then scatter it till they are rolled and the water content is less than about 13%. Rolling the balls for 12-15 minutes and then turn them over lightly to make them dry completely. Nowadays, the rolled tea has the machines to make forms, same to heating machine, rolling and heating at the same time.

c) Forming method of needle shape tea. Needle shape tea is thin and straight like needles, whose forming method is same as polishing containing rubbing and tight polishing. Rubbing is performed when the wok temperature is about 60℃-80℃, with two palms classifying and rubbing, from light to heavy, till the tea leaves are 60%-70% dry. Tight polishing contains classifying, rubbing, piling and cutting, when all the tea leaves are thin, tight, round, smooth, with a 90% dryness, which last for 30-40 minutes, they can be gotten out of the wok for spreading and sunning.

(6) Drying

Wudang Taoist green teas want long-time storage so that the water content must be kept at a very low level. Drying can evaporate water and make the water content decrease to 4%-6%, suitable for long-term storage and quality and further forming of tea leaves' color, fragrance and flavor. The drying of best Wudang Taoist tea is carried out at the same time of forming, drying in forming and forming in drying.

The drying of Wudang Taoist green tea leaves has three stages. Firstly, decreasing the water content from 60% to 40%, mainly for evaporating water and preventing the further action of the former process and stopping the activity of the remained enzyme, where there is short-time high temperature and small volume of tea leaves. Secondly, decreasing the water content from 40% to 20% where the tea leaves are easy to form as the key period called forming stage. The forms of Wudang Taoist green tea are different, so the requirements are different too, but almost all forming of Wudang Taoist tea is finished in this stage, which requires low temperature, long time and suitable volume each time. Thirdly, decreasing the water content from 2% to about 4% is the main stage of Wudang Taoist green tea forming fragrance. The temperature is of very important influence upon the fragrance, which is the key period for fire process and which requires low temperature, long time and suitable tea volume. At the latter part of the third stage, there is some special process in the practice for improving its fragrance and appearance as to achieve a better quality.

The drying methods of Wudang Taoist green tea contain stoving, frying, stoving and frying, and sunning. Stoving is performed by way of stove or stoving machine; frying is performed by way of wok or machine; stoving and frying is performed through stoving and then frying or frying and then stoving or stoving, frying and then stoving again; and sunning is performed in the sunlight.

The measuring method of drying for Wudang Taoist green tea is by hand rubbing, rubbing the tea leaves into powers easily means the water content is qualified. All the requirements of green tea leaves' drying can be performed in this way.

Making process of modern Wudang Taoist black teas

The making process includes fresh leave picking, deteriorating, rolling, fermenting, and drying, whose technical points are the following:

(1) Fresh leave picking

The picking of fresh tea leaves of Wudang Taoist black tea is same to that of green tea, requiring that they are thin, tender, even and fresh. Fresh tea leaves can be classified into bud-tea, one bud and one leave, one bud and two leaves, one bud and three leaves, generally speaking, mainly picking one bud and two or three leaves.

(2) Deteriorating

The loss of water content and the change of internal material, the deterioration of tea leaves, leaves' texture changing from tough into tender, leave color changing from fresh green into dark green, and fragrance changing with the quality, are called deteriorating. The deteriorating of Wudang Taoist black tea is same to the spreading of green tea making, while the former is longer and heavier. The deteriorating has water loss in physical aspect and internal material change in chemical aspect, which is the basic process of forming the character of Wudang Taoist black tea. After spreading, water evaporation is the mainbody in the early period, then with the extending of the time, fresh leaves' water loss comes to a certain point and internal resolution becomes more and more.

The deterioration of fresh leaves has two kinds, sun deteriorating and indoor deteriorating, the latter has natural deteriorating and heating one. Sun deteriorating is usually carried out before 10 o'clock and after 15 o'clock, sunning for 30 minutes and then spreading for 1-2 hours in a cool and open place. After sun deteriorating, fresh leaves become soft and rolled, and has a special flower fragrance, while the short points are fast process and difficult to control, easy to damage the quality and character.

Indoor deteriorating is spreading tea leaves on the special shelves, which has 8 or 12 layers with a space of 20 cm on which a bamboo mat or plaque. In a fine day, open the door and windows, speed the deteriorating; in a rainy day, close the door and windows to keep the inside temperature. The deteriorating time is different in accordance with the change of season, weather and tea leaves, which is hard to control.

Indoor heating deteriorating is making use of deteriorating slot which is made up of stove, blowing machine and slot, 10 meters long, 1-1.5 meters wide and 0.80 meter high. Under the deteriorating slot are even heating slope and heating blowing machine, on the slot are iron or bamboo mat or plaque, spreading tea leaves 2-2.5 kg in one square meter with a thickness of about 20 cm, blowing cool or warm wind. Spreading fresh leaves in the slot and blowing hot wind, the deterioration will be sped up and the time be shortened. When the wind is 35℃, the time is about 3-4 hours.

Generally speaking, deteriorating should follow a principle, tender leaves deteriorating longer while older leaves deteriorating shorter, preventing lack or excess in deteriorating. The standard for suitable deterioration is, the leave losing its color, changing from bright green to dark green, no flag, focal edge or red leave; the water content is about 60%-64%; leave texture is soft and no sound when rubbing, making balls by hand and then they will not scatter easily and quickly; most of the grass smell is lost and fragrance or flower flavor is smelled.

(3) Rolling

The purpose of rolling deteriorated leaves is same to that of green tea, while the major role of rolling of Wudang Taoist black tea is to break leave cells and mix ecologic enzyme with substrate as to promote the fermenting. The strength in rolling of Wudang Taoist black tea is heavier that that of green tea, and more times of complete pressing and longer period. Rolling has light, heavy and light stages. Heavy deteriorated leaves should be pressed heavy and rolled short, light deteriorated leaves should be pressed light and rolled long, tender leaves should be light pressed and rolled short, old leaves should be pressed heavy and rolled long, when the temperature is high rolling should be short, when the temperature is low rolling should be long. Keeping on rolling until all the bud and leave are rolled into tight stripes without loose overlapping, the stripe percentage is over 95%, holding the tea billet in hand tightly there will be some tea juice flowing out, opening the hand there is no loose tea balls, there is a strong grass smell and the tea cells are broken 78%-85%, which means that the rolling is correct.

(4) Fermenting

The fermenting of Wudang Taoist black tea is also called wormwood red, meaning putting the rolled tea leaves into a special fermenting plat in a certain thickness and in a certain humidity and temperature, the chemistry objects in the tea billet is having oxidation and changing color. Therefore, the fermenting of black tea needs suitable environment and condition to enhance the activity of enzyme and promote the oxidation of polyphenol composition and have a complete ferment, forming the special color, flavor and fragrance of black tea.

The fermenting of Wudang Taoist black tea is usually carried out by piling and natural fermenting, some affordable tea houses have had special fermenting room and realized temperature-and-humidity controlled fermenting. And some tea houses use fermenting car to achieve automatic control of temperature and humidity and automatic turning. During the fermenting process, the fragrance and color of fermenting leaves will change as the following: fragrance is changing from grass-smell, fragrance, orchid fragrance, fragrans fragrance, fruit fragrance, light fragrance, to no fragrance; the color is changing from green, yellow, yellow-red, red, to dark red. If the leaves are yellow-red, having fruit fragrance, the tea leaves are correctly fermented. The fermenting should not be less or more, while in the practice, we should abide by the rule, rather be lack than be excessive.

(5) Drying

The drying of Wudang Taoist black tea is mainly making use of high temperature to inactivate the activity of ecological enzyme in the fermented leaves as to stop their fermenting and keep the character formed by fermenting, and then evaporating the water in the leaves to decrease the water content to about 6% as to tighten the tea stripe and fix the outer form for storing and transporting. At the same time, drying will give out most of the grass smell of low boiling point and stimulate and keep the fragrance materials of high boiling point, acquiring the special sweet fragrance of Wudang Taoist black tea.

The drying of Wudang Taoist black tea usually abides by the principle, drying by different time, high temperature first and low temperature then, meaning at the beginning high temperature in a fast speed and then low temperature in a slow speed. The first temperature is 100℃-120℃, the complete fire is 90℃-95℃, and then spread and cool the leaves quickly. Nowadays, many products of Wudang Taoist black tea emphasize heating temperature, same as that of oolong tea, while high-quality Wudang Taoist black tea should keep the natural fruit fragrance formed in the fermenting as much as possible.

Currently, high-quality Wudang Taoist black tea is learning from best Wudang Taoist green tea in making forms, including roller, needle, plat and other shapes.

Making process of modern Wudang Taoist oolong teas

The making process of modern Wudang Taoist oolong teas has combined the making processes of green tea and black tea, the deteriorating, rolling of oolong tea is same as deteriorating, rolling and fermenting of black tea, whose material change is almost same. Making green is the key process of Wudang Taoist oolong tea to form its special character. The whole processes are, picking of fresh leaves, sunning, making green, frying green, rolling and drying and heating by fire, whose making requirements are the following:

(1) Picking of fresh leaves

The spring leaves are the best for oolong tea, the autumn leaves second, and the summer ones the worst, for spring oolong tea has the best flavor and the autumn oolong has the best fragrance. Oolong tea requires the leaves have some certain maturity, usually when all the peak buds are fully spread, not like green tea or black tea, emphasizing on the tenderness. When the tea tree has three-five leaves on the new treetop and six or seven top leaves and forms standing buds, pick one bud with two or four leaves. Spring tea leaves are usually picked around grain rain, summer tea leavers around summer solstice, great heat tea leaves around autumn beginning, and autumn tea leaves around the autumn equinox, different picking season is separated by 40-50 days. The best time for picking oolong tea leaves is between 10 o'clock and 14 o'clock in a fine day, when the quality is the best.

(2) Sunning

Sunning includes cooling, sunning and cooling. The first cooling is spreading tea leaves on indoor floor or bamboo mat to low their temperature and recover the activity. Sunning is to promote the evaporation and physical change by spreading tea leaves on bamboo mat in the sun. The correct sun is weak or medium, usually before 10 o'clock in the morning and after 16 o'clock in the afternoon, lasting 10-30 minutes and tuning them over two or three times. After sunning, cool the leaves to give out water content and decrease temperature as to recover leaves' activity and slow the speed of water evaporation for making green.

(3) Making green

Making green is the special process of oolong tea production, including many times of shaking green and cooling green. Shaking green is to make tea leaves jump, turn and scramble, break the leave edge to promote the oxidation of enzyme and form a special character. Cooling green in making green also called waiting green, is spreading the shaken leaves and wait for a while for a purpose of coordinating the forced change in shaking and adjusting the speed of enzyme oxidation. Shaking green and cooling green is performed in turn. The breaking of leave edge cell and slight oxidation will make the leave edge to show red and the leave center to show yellow green, forming the special character of oolong tea.

Making green of oolong tea is usually making use of bamboo mat and shaking by man or machine, then spreading the leaves on the bamboo mat evenly for cooling. The whole process has former and latter stages.

a) The former stage of making green. The main purpose is to promote the water evaporation and recovery of green leaves' activity, as well as speeding up the water content giving off and appropriately damaging leave texture cells, making preparations for the latter internal material changes.

The first shaking green: making the leaves to have slight green smell and some tight status.

The second shaking green: making the leaves to smell green and some red points in the edge.

Sunning is making the leaves to change from tight status to softness and sleep closely on the bamboo mat.

b) The latter stage of making green: the main purpose is to promote the deep change of internal materials, shaking for a long time and in a heavier style, as to make the leave edges have enough breaking face and promote the oxidation of polyphenols and the water evaporation.

The third shaking green: making the leaves to have strong green smell and red edges.

The fourth shaking green: making the leaves to have some slight green smell and clear red points.

The principle of making green of oolong tea is making green on seeing green and making green on seeing the sky, which means that making green is changed and adjusted with the change of leaves' physical and chemical characters, season, weather and other factors. During making green, the process is determined by leave color, fragrance and water content as to promote the forming and development of fragrance and flavor.

(4) Frying green

The frying of oolong tea is different from that of green tea, the former is mainly preventing leaves' ecological enzyme's activity, stopping enzyme's oxidation and giving off grass smell of low boiling point. The requirements for frying oolong tea are high temperature, speed, more stewing and less spreading, of the temperature 250℃-350℃, lasting 3-4 minutes.

(5) Rolling and drying

Oolong tea is specially emphasizing rolling as to make form in the rolling process. Oolong tea materials are of some certain maturity and less form-ability so that form can be finished by more steps. Rolling process must be accompanied by drying which is involved many processes. The rolling should be performed in high temperature, suitable volume, fast speed and short period, and the pressing should be light, heavy and light again, and the turning speed should be slow, fast and slow again.

(6) Heating by fire

The dried oolong tea leaves need special heating by fire, usually by using of charcoal fire, low temperature and long time, which is good to enhance the tea soup color, flavor and fragrance. The high-quality oolong tea leaves need lower temperature, shorter time, while medium and low quality tea leaves need higher temperature and longer time.

Making process of modern Wudang Taoist dark tea

The making process of wet dark tea is picking of fresh leaves, wrapping, rolling, piling and drying.

The making process of dried dark tea is picking of fresh leaves, wrapping, rolling, sunning, watering, and air-drying.

The former part of Wudang Taoist dark tea is same to that of green tea, here are the different processes and the technique points:

(1) Wrapping of fresh leaves

Dark tea leaves are older in the whole, we should add some water before wrapping as to increase its water content. Adding 10kg water into 100kg fresh leaves, turning the leaves when adding water to make them evenly watered. Dew leaves, rainwater leaves and tender leaves should not be added water, spring leaves should be added less water, summer and autumn leaves more water, tender leaves less water and old leaves more water. The wok temperature should be about 240-250℃, till all the leaves become sticky and fragrant.

(2) Piling

As to the wet leaves of dark tea, pile them directly after wrapping in a dark place and one-meter height and covered by wet cloth to keep wet and warm. When piling, the tea billet' water content should be about 65%, less, add some water. The suitable indoor temperature is above 25℃, when the temperature is higher, the leaves' temperature will be increased quickly so we should turn it over once less it is hurt by the heat. When piling, the leaves' temperature is 30℃, after 24-hours' piling, will be as high as 43℃. The indoor relative humidity should keep at about 85%. The piling period should be different in accordance with the origin place of the tea leaves, one day, one week or even longer. When the piling is OK, the leaves become yellow brown, grass smell disappeared but wine fragrance appear. If you put your hand into the pile, you will feel hot and many water drop among the tea leaves.

As to the dry leaves of dark tea, add water in it to make the water content about 30% and then pile up for fermenting. The piling and fermenting is very long, about one month, during which we should turn it over many times and decrease the pile's height and temperature.

6. The core spirit of Wudang Taoist Tea Culture: Taihe

Wudang Mountains, also called Taihe Mountains, means Supreme Harmony. Wudang Qianlin tea is also called Taihe Tea, so that the spirit core of Wudang Taoist Tea Culture is Taihe, supreme harmony, meaning the the unity of human and nature, emphasizing the harmony between human and nature.

Chinese tea ceremony thinks that tea is the best plant of the south and the rare gift awarded by the Nature. In tea regiment, Taihe means human's desire to return to the nature and include all the world. In planting, picking and making tea, Taihe means human must conform to the rules of the Nature. In drinking tea, Taihe means that all things must be simple and natural, without any artificial actions. In sipping tea, Taihe means that human should love to keep close with the Nature, just like living among grass and trees. Tea ceremony advocates the interactive communication between human and Nature, and melting the boundary between object and man as to achieve a mental comfort.

The process of infusing tea is letting one's heart melt with tea and Nature. Only when the drinker achieve the status of Taihe can he hear the breath of Nature from the boiling water and understand the Nature doctrine from the unity of human and Nature. Chinese tea ceremony takes Quietness as one of Four Truths, meaning that when drinking tea, one should be quiet and not speak or talk, only by this can he appreciate the real taste of tea and experience the happiness of drinking tea. Only by drinking quietly can one realize the perfect integration of human and Nature and approach Taoist status where one forgets himself. The thought of Taihe also reflects in the tea set, especially the bowel with cover. Therefore, Taoists are fond of using bowel with cover to make tea, implying the harmony between heaven, earth and human.

Between heaven and earth are five elements, gold, wood, water, fire and soil. Human has five organs, eyes, ears, mouth, nose and heart. The foods have five tastes, sour, sweet, bitter, hot and salty. Human have five feelings, anger, happiness, thinking, worries and fear. Tea comes from soil and tree, produced from fire and boiling water. Drinking Taoist tea, accompanying five element, nurturing five organs and protecting five feelings are the true essence of Taoist tea.

Chapter 12 Tourguide Words of Wudang Mountains 武当山导游词

Good morning, Ladies and Gentlemen,

Today we'll visit the famous holy land of China Taoism, Wudang Mountains. We will climb up the mountains and visit the scenic spots on way up the mountains, then take the tram rail down the mountains. First, it will take us 45 minutes to visit the Yuxu Palace. Then we will visit the Purple Cloud Palace for about one hour and the South Cliff for 30 minutes. The last two stations are the Golden Summit/ Top and the Golden Palace. They are the most important palaces. We will spend 2 hours on visiting them.

Everyone might be very familiar with the Best Foreign Language Film of the 2001 Oscar, *Crouching Tiger, Hidden Dragon*. At the end of the Film, the actress Yu Jiaolong jumped from the cliff here. I believe that everyone must be fascinated by the Gongfu and the scenery in the movie. Today I will lead you to appreciate its mystery and charm in the reality.

Wudang Mountains, situated in Shiyan City, Hubei Province, China, where there are many high mountains, green forests, and everlasting clean springs, has been called the No. 1 Celestial Mountain in China.

Throughout the history, the federal emperors of every dynasty paid an increasing attention to the creation of buildings in Wudang Mountains, and in the Ming Dynasty, Wudang Mountains was the center of China Taoism.

The ancient buildings in Wudang Mountains, great in size and beautiful in artistic design, built on steep hills or in sharp cliffs to achieve a harmonious unity between the buildings and the Nature, have been praised as the ultimate showcase of China's ancient buildings and has been enlisted in World Cultural Heritage Site.

There are full of attractive places of interest in Wudang Mountains Special Region of

Tourism and Economy, as charming as the rainbow in the sky; especially Wudang Mountains, the famous Taoist Mountain which has combined quietness, wonder, beauty, and elegance into one, has these following famous scenic spots, such as, seventy-two peaks, thirty-six cliffs, twenty-four valleys, eleven caves, three pools, nine springs, ten lakes, nine wells, ten stones, and nine pavilions. There are four distinct seasons with their own features, the mountain is green and full of flowers in the spring; there are wind, thunder, and rainstorm with clouds and fogs twisting the mountain in the summer; the forest are in gold yellow and the laurels send fragrance in the autumn; all the mountain is covered by the white snow in the winter.

Wudang Mountains, the famous scenic spot in China, whose perimeter is over 800 km, about 500 miles, full of beautiful hills and intense forests, was praised as the meeting place of Heaven and Earth. For its enchanting scenery and the legendary home of gods, many Taoists and hermits came to practice cultivation here, so Wudang Mountains has been regarded as the birthplace of China Taoism. Taoism can trace back to the Han Dynasty and after thousands of years' development Taoism has played an important role in politics, economy, culture, and ideology of China. Taoism, with Chinese characteristics and nearly 2,000-year history, is still influencing Chinese life. The main idea of Taoism is harmony. People believe Taoism because they want to reach the perfect combination with the Nature.

It is said that Emperor Zhenwu had been cultivating here for over 40 years and succeeded in becoming god. Zhenwu is named Emperor Zhenwu, the founder or the Grand dad in heaven. This super god is evolved from the image of the ancient northern god, Xuanwu. During the Song Dynasty, Wudang Taoism had developed into some certain size, forming its own organization and system, and also had set up many Taoist buildings. On the days of Emperor Zhenwu's birthday and becoming god, pious people would come here worship Wudang Mountains from all the directions.

Wudang Taoism came to the most prosperous stage in the Ming Dynasty. Emperor Cheng, the third emperor of the Ming Dynasty, Zhu Di ordered to support and develop Wudang Taoism after he became the Emperor. He wrote all the orders by himself, from reconnaissance and devise of Taoist buildings, sending some qualified officials to overlook the project, to the ways and disciplines for Taoists to cultivate and obey. There were all high buildings on the both sides of the 140-km Ancient Divine Road to the Golden Peak/ Top. The series Wudang Taoism palaces and temples, located in Southern China, the Forbidden City, located in Northern China, were the two key constructions under the supervision of Emperor Zhu Di of the Ming Dynasty (1403—1425) during his realm.

After thousands years' development, there produced proud and profound Wudang Culture in Wudang Taoism: nature-upholding Taoist buildings, mysterious Wudang Boxing, Wudang Ways to keep healthy and prolong the lifespan, talking-with god religion service, court-like Taoist music, unrivalled carvings, Chinese traditional medicine and herbs, all are the crystal of Chinese national cleverness.

玉虚宫 Here we are, at the gate of Wudang Mountains, what is standing in front of us is the famous Yuxu Palace! The Yuxu Palace was built in 1413 and was repaired in 1552 because of the destructive fire disaster. It is the biggest palace of Wudang Mountains. The main building of the palace adopted the royal construction style and made full use of plain topography. The symmetric configuration is based on precise axle wire. Undoubtedly, you can feel the magnificence of the palace hall, which is surrounded by palace wall. All of these precious designs add to the Yuxu Palace's dignity and momentum. Here, go straight! This is the Hall Gate. The rare viburnum sumeru stone blocks are subtly sculptured on the gate. Touch the exquisite pattern on the gate and feel the lines. You can not help admiring the artistry of the ancient people. Inside and outside the gate is a pair of pavilions, majestically facing each other. Yeah, so cute! So now follow me, along the wall. Upstairs! You can see the palace wall is just like Halo wandering around Fairy Que. What a fairy-land! People in the Ming Dynasty compared the Yuxu Palace with E-pang Palace. Both of their designs and artistry are really unbelievable! Look afar, tasting the ancients' amorous feelings. Isn't it a marvelous sensation!

Dear friends, now let's get down here and rush toward another paradise!

紫霄宫 Now we are heading to the Purple Cloud Palace. At the foot of Stretching Flag Peak sits the magnificent and boundless Purple Cloud Palace. Here, with the cluster of hills guarding the peaks, the woods of high pine and green cypress deep and remote, and the surroundings elegant and weather comfortable, the place is thought as the Blessed Place in the Purple Cloud Palace View-site.

The Purple Cloud Palace is an apotheosis of construction by employing the particular physiognomy that is cragged in length while wide and plain on breadth. All the buildings are arrayed along the axis. On the axis lie the Green Dragon and White Tiger Palace, Imperial Stele Pavilion, Shifang Hall, the Grand Hall of the Purple Cloud Palace and Parents' Palace from the bottom to the top. The altitude of these buildings gradually rises and the axis symmetries the wing houses of each construction. And through the way of stacking tall sidesteps, the Purple Cloud Palace is divided into three sections of yard, so as to form a kind of group of constructions in which one row is upon row of the other and the primary buildings are more distinctive than the secondary ones. From a far distance, the palace has the atmosphere of imperial worshiping rites.

Historically, the Purple Cloud Palace, because of shouldering the responsibilities of praying for emperors and royal families, had solemn overall arrangement and exquisite furnishings. Inside each various palace, the worshiping deities and celestial beings are ablated. Together with the divine tables, obliging apparatuses and omniscient instruments, all these consist of a mysterious and metaphysical world. The images created by Taoist legends are so vivid by the designs and various on atmosphere. Here, people may differ them from their status, divine responsibilities, specified occupations, dispositions and thoughts.

The feudal emperors of the Song, Yuan, Ming and Qing dynasties often issued their orders to set up altars so as to praise and pray for good fortune, or plead deities to bless the peace of their sovereignty and the plain people or the harvest of crops. In fact, this was a ritual of communicating with the Gods, for Taoism thought that through that way Gods would help the prayers, bless them to be away from the disasters and prolong their lifespan.

At present, the Purple Cloud Palace is not only the best choice to visit, but also the locus of the Taoism Association of Wudang Mountains. Here is the destination of the outstanding Toaist, experts and scholars from all over the world. Furthermore, it is the very source for Taoism researchers to search the origin of Taoism.

南岩 Now we come to the South Cliff. The South Cliff is also known as "Purple Cliff", it faces towards the south, that's how the name comes from. Here you can see that the hills are steep and forbidding, covered by many green trees.

Also I am pretty like to introduce the buildings to you, they are really a great combination of artificial and natural landscapes among all 36 mounts in Wudang Mountains.

The ancient architecture of the South Cliff has broken through the traditional layout to achieve a high degree of harmonious style. So the craftsmen had skillfully made a compact and grand construction in an ups and downs way. The view of the South Cliff is unique and changing, and everywhere is so special. My friends, please enjoy your walking here and taking photos as much as you want.

金顶 Let's get on the bus and go to our next station, the Golden Summit/ Top, which is regarded as the symbol of Wudang Mountains, whose scenic spots include the Huanglong/ Yellow Dragon Hole, Chaotian/ Facing Sky Palace, Golden Palace and the bronze hall of the Yuan Dynasty and some ancient architectures. Here preserved a lot of manufacturers of different dynasties, religious artifacts and other treasures. These are the technologies of casting brilliant pearl in our ancient Chinese architecture, which reveal the wisdom of Chinese people and ancient scientific competence.

Golden Summit/ Top has a strong attraction to visitors and pilgrims. Whenever you stand in front of the Golden Summit, there will be an invisible feeling of shock and respect in your mind. At the same time, you still can enjoy many peculiar natural wonders of the myths and stories.

We are now traveling among the peaks where the Golden Palace is located. The Golden Palace, with a height of 5.45 meters and flying eaves decorated by dragon, phoenix, sea horse and immortals, is the highest one in the ancient Chinese construction grade. Having endured about 600 years' wind and rain, thunder and lighting, cold winter and hot summer, the Golden Palace is still shining as if it was newly built up. In every summer thunderstorms season, it will appear the spectacle of Lightning Golden Summit: when the lighting flashes across the sky, the deafening noise arises, suddenly, the sky is point - blank, what a spectacular sight!

金殿 Now we have reached the Golden Palace, the last palace in Wudang Mountains. Standing in front of the Golden Palace, you can appreciate the magnificent scenery of Wudang Mountains, as far as 400 kilometers. Outside the gilt gold, the entire house, engraved rare birds and peculiar animals, weighs over 80 tons. All the parts were so perfect matched that there is without any crevice. Despite the erosion of wind and rain, thunder and lighting more than 500 years, the Golden Palace, as one of the first-level national treasures, not only represents the wonderful ancient Chinese architecture skills, but also reveals the wisdom of Chinese people and ancient scientific competence.

The Golden Palace is the combination of intelligence and creativity of the ancient Chinese people. It is the development of art and science as well. The inside walls of the Golden Palace were lightly carved with soft floating clouds lines. Purple Mantel, clean and smooth, symbolizes a gentle and harmonious color. It is obvious that the image of Emperor Zhenwu, Golden Boy and Jade Girl, and the Generals of Water and Fire are being worshiped inside of the Gold Palace. We have a panoramic view of beautiful scene as well as its culture. When you close your eyes, do you sense a breath of Taoism?

We will get back to the shuttle bus station by tram rail. You have enjoyed the view of the peaks again. Now let's get on the bus. We have appreciated the scenery as well as its culture. It is not only a mountain but also a heritage full of our ancestors' wisdom. Your current visit to China is drawing to a close. Time has elapsed so quickly and you have visited several scenic spots in this City. The time we stayed together was rather short and really the surface was only scratched, just like what the Chinese people say "looking at the flowers on the horse's back". Every one in the group has been very cooperative, friendly, understanding and punctual. That is what I witnessed and experienced, and as an international guide, it was much appreciated. Thanks a lot for your cooperation!

Parting is such sweet sorrow. Happy to meet, sorry to depart, and hope that we will meet again. Wish you have a nice journey home. Goodbye!

Part 03 探秘神农

Exploring Shennongjia Forest

Chapter 1 Shennongjia Forest Region 神农架林区

神农架东西连巴楚，南北分江汉，是我国南北东西珍稀物种交汇地，有国家重点保护珍稀濒危植物 26 种、动物 73 种，尤以国宝“金丝猴”最为著名，有“华中天然动物园、东方物种基因库”之称。神农架保存有我国南方最完整的上前寒武系神农架群地层剖面，神农顶海拔 3105.4 米，被誉为“华中屋脊”，这里群山巍峨，森林苍茫，石林诡秘多姿，风光四时各异。神农架地处北纬 31°“神秘地带”，野人之谜、白化动物更为其平添了几分奇幻色彩。欢迎您：到中国神农架，看野外金丝猴；登华中第一峰，赏五月杜鹃花；游魅力神农架，探千古野人谜；品神农秋韵，戏南方瑞雪。

Shennongjia Forest Region, lying in the joint zone of Sichuan, Hubei and Shaanxi provinces, as the meeting zone of different natural environments and biological diversities, has been awarded as the Natural Zoo of Central China, and the Species Gene Pool of the Oriental, where have 26 kinds of rare endangering plants and 73 kinds of rare endangering animals, such as, National Treasure, Golden Monkey, complete upper Cambrian stratigraphic section of South China.

With the altitude of 3,105.4m, Shennong Peak is known as “the Ridge of Central China”, where are lofty mountains, virgin forests, peculiar stone forests, and changing scenes in four seasons.

Shennongjia located at north latitude 31°, the famous Mysterious Zone, and is attractive for the wonders of Wild Man and albino species.

Welcome to the mystical Shennongjia to watch Golden Monkey in the wild field, climb the First Highest Peak of Central China, explore the myth of Wildman, and appreciate May rhododendron, autumn aura and southern snow.

Shennongjia Forest Region, located in the northwest of Hubei Province, near Wudang Mountains, occupying 3,253 km^2 is the only well protected one Greenland in Central China land, the only one green treasure in the middle latitude region in the world. Shennongjia Forest Zone, the most characteristic world-level tourist resource, has the only one best-protected sub-torrid forest ecology system in the middle latitude region in the world.

Here are full of charming mountains, dense forests, deep valleys, clean springs, which are isolated from the modern world, well preserving miraculous beauty of the primitive times. The relative topography fall is 2,707.4 meters, so there are the following climates in Shennongjia Forest Zone: hot summer at the foot but spring on the top; color autumn at the waist but ice winter on the top; red, orange, yellow, and green colors are unlimited to enjoy, spring, summer, autumn, and winter are difficult to separate from.

There are beautiful and ancient legends, simple and mysterious folk cultures and folk customs, and primitive ecology culture group in China inner land formed by humans and nature together in Shennongjia Forest Zone. The divine farmer tasting all herbs, the mystery of Wild man, myths and epics of Han nationality, marriage customs of Tujia Nationality, and countryside music all attract the tourists all over the world.

The unlimited sea of forests, well-protected primitive ecology system, abundant biology resources, pleasant climate, simple and special alp culture of inner land, form together charming and changing landscapes. In 1990, Shennongjia Forest Zone was accepted as one member of International Protection Network of Humans and Biology by the UNSCO. In 1995, Shennongjia Forest Zone was again named The Pilot Spot for the Protection of Biology Diversity by World Nature Foundation.

Shennongjia National Nature Reserve is located in the southwest part of Shennongjia Forest Region, Hubei Province, China, covering 70,467 hectares, of which core region is 54.5%, buffer 13.3%, and experimental region 32.2%. The Reserve is composed of two parts, the east part with Laojun Mountain as the core covering 10,467 hectares and the west part with Greater and Lesser Shennongjia as the core covering 60,000 hectares.

Shennongjia Nature Reserve was approved to set up by the People's Government of Hubei Province in 1982, upgraded to national forests and wild animals' nature reserve by the State Council of the P.R.C in 1986, and admitted into World Biosphere Reserve of Human and Biosphere Plan by UNESCO in 1990. Since 1995, China Nature Reserve Management Project of Global Environment Fund has been carried out in Shennongjia National Nature Reserve, and Biodiversity Protection Exemplary Base oriented to Asia has been set up, which is also the permanent exemplary base of global biodiversity protection.

Up to now, Shennongjia National Nature Reserve has been one of the fourteen key regions for international biodiversity study and protection, the key region of China biodiversity by International Biodiversity Study of World Nature Fund, and also the Four-A Scenic Spot of China, one of the fifty-one Forestry Exemplary Reserves, and the first fixed research region of state key research projects.

Shennongjia National Nature Reserve has lots of biological species, the forest coverage up to 96%, such as evergreen broad-leaved forest, evergreen and deciduous broad-leaved mixed forest, deciduous broad leaved forest, needles and broad-leaf mixed forest, and other plants, which is the epitome of the main plantations between subtropical and cool temperate zone in Eurasia. In accordance with incomplete statistics, there are more than 3,400 vascular plants, among them, dove tree and other 25 plants having been listed in State Key Protection Plants List,

116 Shennongjia special plants. There are 493 kinds of wild animals, birds, fishes, and amphibians, and 4,143 kinds of insects, such as Golden Monkey, leopard, and golden eagle. There have been found 43 kinds of new animals and 33 kinds of new plants. Here are 259 kinds of wild animals of important economic and scientific research value.

Here are six peaks over 3,000 meters high, forming the Ridge of Central China, and the watershed of the Changjiang River and Hanjiang River. The highest peak, Shennong Top, of 3,105.4 meters, is the First High Peak in Central China.

Chapter 2 Shennongjia National Geopark 神农架国家地址公园

神农架山高水长，古老神秘，人烟稀少，具有“一山有四季，十里不同天”的立体气候。物种繁多，蕴藏丰富，是驰名中外的“绿色明珠”“天然动物园”“物种基因库”“炎天清凉王国”，其自然风景壮丽、钟灵，可与黄山、华山、峨眉山、泰山、武当山、张家界媲美，且神农架自然保护区与长白山、武夷山，卧龙保护区齐名。自然风景点星罗棋布，有“神农无处不风光”的美誉。由于历史上的原始封闭，人文胜迹甚少，以自然风景见长，她是“华中之屋脊”“金丝猴的故乡”“‘野人’的避难所”“动物的乐园”，又是国际公认中纬度地区植被保存最完整的地方，且具有世界上最完整的上前寒武系地层。神奇的自然景观，丰富的宝藏，动人的传说，可供人们旅游观光，探险猎奇，休憩疗养，科研考察。相传境内炎帝神农氏采尝百草、西汉留侯张子房弃官隐居、薛刚反唐及夔东十三家联明抗清、白莲教军反清起义，这里还建立过苏维埃政权，可供人们追历史之陈迹，发思古之幽情。神农架博大幽深的地理环境、自然资源、传统文化，使不少文人墨客、学者名流发出“大三峡不如小三峡，小三峡不如神农架”“神农天园，国之瑰宝”的赞叹。

神农架自然风景由北至南形成神农架—神农溪—长江三峡、神农架—昭君故里—长江三峡两条旅游线。由南至北形成神农架—武当山旅游线，是湖北省旅游胜地的重中之重，若到湖北观光，不到神农架就不能算领略了荆楚全部胜境。

由于特定的地质背景、地理位置和气候条件，使神农架融众多地质、地貌景观于一体。完整的前寒武系、典型的断穹构造、第四纪冰川遗迹、2000 米以上的剥夷面、高山湿地草甸，以及无处不在的峡谷、河流、瀑布、暗河、泉水、石林、溶洞等等，构成一座得天独厚的地质公园。

湖北神农架国家地质公园自西向东分为六个景区：大九湖景区以发育冰川地貌和高山草甸为特色；板桥景区以侵蚀构造地貌为主；神农顶景区展示了壮丽的山岳地貌和典型的地质剖面；天燕景区峡谷与岩溶地貌发育；香溪源景区以峡谷、河源景观为特色；老君山景区发育断裂构造与水体景观。

Shennongjia Forest Region is world-famous for its abundance of water and steep mountains with height ranging from 480-3,105.4m above the sea level, among them Shennongjia Summit, known as “the Roof of Central China”, is the highest peak in central China. With a complicated geological structure, the deformational structure of Shennongjia Groups is famous for scenic spots. The pre-Cambrian section of Southern China type are the best preserved in the world enjoying exceptional advantage of favorable natural condition resulted in the remoteness and diversity of plant and animal formation. Hence distinguishable and diverse as its climate is, that it is known for "four seasons co-existing simultaneously in a peak, 10 miles could make a distinction". Shennongjia Geopark being the best preserved primitive forest ecosystem among mid-latitude regions up till now, earns it reputation such as Green pearl, Natural Botanical and Zoology Garden, Shelter of Creatures, Gene Pool of Species, Cool Kingdom, etc. It has also the name fame as the home of golden monkey and the mysterious "Wild Man", a Chinese Bigfoot. The Shennongjia Geopark is of beautiful peaks, lake on high mountains and clear air, which provide a charming place for relaxation, vacation and tourism.

From north to south, there are two tourist route: Shennongjia—Shennong Brook—Three Gorges of the Changjiang River; Shennongjia—Zhaojun's Native Place—Three Gorges of the Changjiang River. From south to north, there is the Shennongjia to Wudang Mountains. These are the key tourist line on any Hubei itinerary, hence it is a "must" on the way if the visitor to visit here.

Besides the complete section of the upper pre-Cambrian, there is the typical faulting-dome, Quaternary glacier evidence, the planar erosion surface above 2,000m sea level etc. They constituted a Geopark which abounds in gifts of nature in our country.

From west to east, Shennongjia Geopark is subdivided into six scenic area: Dajiuhu (Big Nine Lake) Area, showing the glacier landform and the marshy grassland of high mountain; Banqiao Area, dominated by the structural landform of erosion; Shennong Top Area, characterized by the mountain range structure and typical geological section; Tianyan Area presenting the valley and karst geomophologica feature; Xiangxiyuan Area, dominated by the valley and the source of the river; Laojunshan Area shows developed of the fault structure and water system.

Chapter 3 Shennong Top Scenic Spot 神农顶景区

神农顶景区的景点均分布在神农架国家级自然保护区内，区内的神农顶、杉木尖、大神农架、大窝坑、金猴岭、小神农架诸山峰，海拔都在 3000 米以上，是大巴山山脉最高处和神农架林区最高一级夷平面，堪称“华中屋脊”。壮丽的亚高山风光，奇异的野生动植物，深藏的矿产资源，动人的故事传说，无不引人入胜。景点有神农顶、风景垭、瞭望塔、阴峪河、金猴岭、太子垭等。九（湖坪）酒（壶坪）公路贯通其间。

The scenic spot of Shennong Top Area distributed over Shennongjia National Natural Reserve Region. The main peak is heaven-kissing mountains, including Shennongjia Summit, China Fir, Big Shennongjia, Dawokeng, Golden Monkey Ridge, Small Shennongjia, etc. Over 3,000 meters above the sea level, it is the highest planar erosion surface in the Daba Mountains, known as "The Roof of Central China". With a richness in mineral resources, a moving legend, the charming scenery is attracting countless visitor from all over the world.

The scenic spots include Shennong Top, Fengjing Cliff, Liaowang Pagoda, Yinyu River, Golden Monkey Ridge, Taizi Cliff, etc. Jiujiu (Jiuhuping - Jiuping) highway passes across there.

积水小潭 There is a small water accumulation pond in the Dalong Deep-pool Vauclusian Valley, circle in form and with the largest diameter 30 meters, and the general depth no more than 2 meters, connecting with its near brook, so that the pool surface is stable no matter the specific water yield of downriver clench lessening and/ or having underground leak halfway. This pond, the formation of Quaternary glacier relic, was a small glacial scour lake originally, which was a depression formed by the dredge of glacier, becomes a lake after long time melting of the water accumulation, fluvial corrosion or underground corrosion.

观音洞 Guanyin Cave is a doline, the height of cave mouth 20 meters and the width 5 meters, dipping to the northwest. Cave body develops along the strata interlayer fissure, the inner of cavity backfilled by the silt, and the underground water draining into Yinyu River through leakage. This cavity is near the watershed area so that the specific water yield is less.

红石沟 Red-Stone Gorge is nominated for its crossing the purple sandshale of Dawo Formation, with sloughing mauve sandshale rubble inside and purple soils around. It is also a U-shape ice gorge, the represent of the first-stage glacial valley in Shennongjia Forest Area, with a length about 6kms, an open wide floor and two little slopes. The both sides of the gorge around Little Longtan Pond are semi-arc ridge, hillock, and big boulder left by the Quaternary glacier activity.

长岩屋 Changyanwu/ Long Cliff House is located at the upper reaches of Hongshigou Glacial U-shape Valley, with a sea level of about 2,600m. Here the floor is open, the valley sides and terrace are scattered with big and small blocks. Tills in the floor are the layers of a set of brown yellow sandstones. The muddy gravel has saffron weathering surface and offwhite fresh inner with poorly sorting and roundness. Most of them are angular, and some have clear polish face. Big boulder in the gorge is the traveled stone left by the Quaternary glacier activity.

金猴岭 The altitude of the Golden Monkey Ridge is 3,019 meters, which is made up of the diabase rock formed by the base magma's inrush about 700 hundred million years ago. Many golden monkey live here. And as a result of the mountain's height and steepness, the rich rain fall, and the stream washing the hard rock, the waterfall generally comes into being. The Golden Monkey Flying Waterfall is about 30 meters high and 5 meters wide, with a quick flow of water. You can have a special sentiment in the exuberant original forest, with the superposed waterfall hanging overhead and flying down.

风景垭 The Fengjing/ Scenery Cliff, formerly named Badong Cliff, which is a mountain pass between the Wangnong Booth and the Dawokeng. The jaws' altitude is 2,785 meters, which is praised as "the first beautiful landscape of Hubei Province". The Cliff is located in the north wing of the Shennongjia Anticline Core, connecting with the Jiucai Cliff fault in the south which tends towards the northeast. After the Mount Yan Movement, along with the continuing ascending of Shennongjia Section, the deep cut-in action continuously happened in the flabby part of the south fault, which brought about the south slope of the jaws cutting in about 1 kilometer, forming the gorge. But the north slope is almost in the same direction as the rock lay, forming an boss-eyed mountain conformation, with a comparatively mild grade.

The Fengjing Cliff is in the bare area of white cloud rock in Shennongjia rock slot river group, and the high angle cranny is full-grown because of the severe squeezing with the plait wrinkle. Rain pouring to filter and etch along the cranny , and the knife-like erosion of wind and frost of millions years, today the strange peaks and beautiful valley and rock forests were carved. And because here is the passage of airflow from north and south, the weather here changes quickly. Stepping onto the top of the mountain, you can see the majestic peaks rising one after another, with gorgeous and varied scenery that enchant visitors with bright flowers and trees covering green slopes, light mist filling the whole valley and throwing out glaring color under the effect of sunshine. So here is also called “Cloud Rain in Rock Forest”.

望夫石 Wangfu/ Waiting-for-Husband Stone lies in the northeast part on the top of Dawokeng Mountain, looks like a woman looking to the distant mountains and valleys in the south, waiting for her husband coming home, hence its name, impressing the visitors with its majestic and precipitous appeal. This stone is made up of white cloud rock in rock slot river, and finally shaped after long-time efflorescence, denudation and water erosion.

瞭望塔 The Observation Tower is located in the top of mountain with the elevation 2,900m, 40m in height, formerly used for fire prevention of the Forest. Ascending onto the scenery platform, the mountains and rivers are viewed completely, such as, mountains in the southwest, the Ridge of Central China, and four water systems of Shennongjia starting from here. The view of the stratum section can help the viewers understand the evolution of Shennongjia, and be lost in limitless thoughts and moods.

Behind the Observation Tower, there are varicolored silicon nature “agate stone” conglomerate. The rock has the basal conglomerate nature, and formed by sea shore aggression movement, whose color is rich and gorgeous. In this rock mass, axiolitic stone is the jade flint, the calcedony the quartz aphanitic aggregate, which is one kind of low-grade jade, hard, smooth and exquisite after polished. The vari-colored silicon stone has had a popular name agate stone.

神农顶 The elevation of Shennongding (Shennong Summit; Shennong Top) is 3,105 meters. It is “the Peak of Central China”, which rises up lofty and steep and looks down upon the other peaks and mountains in the Central China. At the top of the mountain, haphazard stone uncovered, no trees alive, only moss and fern are scattered on the ground, a primitive and desolate sight. The so-called "rock sea", refers to the repeated freezing and melting of weathering causes the base rock to break out and solve into melt rock bits in the severe icing cold area, and finally the rock bits moved to the more smooth mountaintops or slopes.

In the middle of Shennongjia, the dividing range of the Changjiang River and the Hanjiang River is composed by the east extending part of Dabashan Range, or called Shennongjia Range, with an altitude of more than 2,000 meters and a slightly W-S extending, including High-Foot Cliff, Small-Bound Mountain, Big-Bound Mountain, Monkey Rock, Greater Shennongjia, Shennong Top, Raincap Tip, Laojun Mountain, Sun Plateau and so on, and was called “Prince's Boundary” in the history (the subdividing boundary of Prince Luling Manor set by by Emperor Wu Zetian), and also the first-stage watershed of the Changjiang River and the Hanjiang River in

Hubei Province, where there are two water systems of Du River and South River flow in the Hanjiang River in the north of the Mountain, and two water systems of Xiangxi River and Yandu River (Shennong Brook) flow into the Changjiang River.

In the source of valley stream near the peak and the watershed there sometimes exists a funnel-shaped topography. When the climate became cold and the start of glacier happened, the valley source was occupied by ice and snow. When the ice and snow was accumulated to a certain degree, they would flow and then formed glacier. The glacier has great execration to the valley bottom and its margin, so that the funnel was execrated into a trilateral basin under the nearby mountains, just like a sheet of cane chair, which is called cirque in geology. The cirques in Big Dimple and the south slope of Fengjing Cliff developed in a large scale and kept in a good configuration, are the source of U-formed Red Rocky River Glacier Valley.

Dawokeng Cave Formation of Shennongjia Group is a rocky naming unit, whose naming site is near the highway in the north slope, whose stratum thickness is about 353.2 meters. The underpart is mottle siliceous conglomerate, quartz sandstone and shale, of which the conglomerate is marine transgression offshore, the rather steady lithology typical horizon of Shennongjia Group. The top part is light gray siliceous stripe dolomite, mostly in flat wet environment.

Haematite in the ore mountain of Shennongjia Group is the only example of sedimentary rock strata of Proterozoic era in Hubei Province, which was called "Iron Ore Mine of Shennongjia Style", having some rather high value in study and exploitation.

The so-called "Channels & Collateral Rock" is calcite vein in fact, which is mainly found in dolomite in the stratum of Shennongjia Group, Dawokeng Cave and Ore Mine Mountain. Resulted from tectonic force, many freely interlaced fissures are produced and infilled with thin calcite crystal, which grew in a right angle to the surface of fissure. Sometimes the calcite vein is replaced by silicon. As a result, this kind of dolomite cemented by calcite is called as "Channels & Collateral Rock" and taken as a good collection by magic rock fans.

The so-called "Alveolus Rock" is a kind of knot-like dolomite or limestone, formed by being suffered from different weathering. Knot-like dolomite or limestone is a kind of common carbonate rock, different in anti-weathering capability resulting from the difference in components. The knot of the dolomite is easily suffered from weathering and erosion and show network pattern after weathering. Knot-like dolomite or limestone is often found in the top stratum of ore mine mountain and its position is quite stable.

阴峪河 Yinyu River originates in the Baishibiao Mountain at the south of the Bancangxiang Township in the north slope of Shennongjia Mountains, flowing across jungles and cloughs from south to north and then draining into Qiudao River, Fangxian County, whose name comes from the lowing in gloomy valley. The Quaternary glacier engraved U-shape glacial valley in the headwaters and then followed by intensive incising and erosion by rivers and finally the valley came into being. There is "Yixiantian/ One Line Sky" landscape between the mouths of two rivers with the altitude of 800m. There karst landform developed well and has such beautiful landscape as Yangque Cave and Huoshao Cave and so on.

In the fir forest of Bashan Mountain, there is a sharp-ridge and plate-strip rock pillar, whose head is just like a singing rooster, formed by dolomite of Shicao River Formation. There are mainly two groups of columns jointing in a right angle in the rock strata. Because of rock dissolving, ice freezing and collapsing, together with the inhomogeneity of components in rock, various kinds of shapes have come into being.

Some rugged stalagmite groups in the Banbi Rock Area are just like a Rooster Crowing, a Giant Eagle Spreading His Dings, a Rhinoceros Staring at the Moon, a Frightened Snake or Escaped Rabbit, a Jade Prism Sustaining the Sky, a Red Phoenix Facing the Sun, a Jumping Dragon or Advancing Tiger and the like. The lithology of the bedrock, develops with a steep dip angle and jointswell, as the dolomite of Ore Mine Mountain, Shennongjia Group. Because of the location in high mountains and faced with the wind gap, the bedrock has suffered from such erosion as ice freezing, chopping and wind corrosion of physical weathering by rain, snow, wind and frost and karst influence. Due to the different ability of different lithology to endure erosion, the stalagmites display different appearances.

猴子石 Monkey Rock Mountain was named by its similar appearance as monkeys and has an altitude of 2,967m. The lithology of the Peak is sandstone of Liantuo Formation, Nanhua System. To the north, the dolomite of Ore Mine Mountain Formation, Shennongjia Group, forming a stone forest due to karst influence, ice chopping and wind corrosion.

The Neo-proterozoic moraine conglomerate of Nanhua System is located on a watershed between Chaoshui Pond and Monkey Rock Mountain with an altitude of higher than 2,800m, which is very hard and has an almost right dip angle. There remains typical relic of ice margin: frozen rock prism, which comprises mixed moraine conglomerate. The biggest one can be 5m high and the smallest 1.5m high. They linearly arrange along the direction of strata and extend along the ridges and watersheds approximately 2km. Frozen rock prism is a production of physical weathering in a cold and humid climate. Because of repeating freezing and melting, rocks break off and collapse and finally turn into stone stack or stream.

幸福洞 The outcrop stratum in Happy Cave is the Sinian dolomite of Dengying Formation. Happy Cave is a near horizontal karst cave with an altitude of higher than 2,800m, 30m high, 20m long and its mouth opening to the north. It is also an exit of an underground river with a runoff of 300l/s, only 400m far away from the entry. According to the analysis of flow mark from water flow, the cave was ever the entry of the underground river but afterward altered into an exit because of collapse in the faults cross in NS and WS direction.

南天门 Nantian Gate/ South Sky Entrance has an altitude of 2,602.7m and is well-known for its lofty terrain, majestic pass, and beautiful scenery, which is just like the South Heaven in Chinese fables. Lithology of the outcrop in the area is mainly muddy dolomite including sandy slate of Shicao Formation, Shennongjia Group. It has an almost right dip angle, so the rainfall readily leaches along the bedding surface. Over the geological time, it turned into a landform of fairy stones lifting up and thrusting to the sky, which is the so-called "Rock Forest and Sword

Edge".

太子垭 Taizi/ Prince Pass is a pass in the ridge of Taizi/ Prince Slope. Along the road, a bigger and a smaller dolomite are lifting up, just like the form of a mouth of duck. So it is called Duck Rock, too. Duck Rock is consist of moraine conglomerate of Nantuo Formation, which are the bedrock remains of weathering and denuding.

The outstanding characteristic of high mountain relief is the great and smooth terrain, so there is a saying that no plane is found until you clime onto high mountains, for the summits are often the original surfaces formed in different altitude and during different ages. Shennongjia Forest Region can be divided into five grades of original surfaces by the ladder terrain from low to high. Shennong Peak/ Top, the dominant peak of Shennongjia, has an altitude of over 3,000m and is the first-grade surface with the highest altitude. The surface formed by the summits far away is the second-grade surface, just corresponding to that of Taizi Pass.

Chapter 4 Xiangxiyuan/ Honey Stream Source Scenic Spot 香溪源景区

香溪源景区位于神农架林区南部，包括木鱼镇、红花乡、九冲乡及自然保护区一部分。景区内有 209 国道及支岔公路线网络其间。木鱼坪海拔 1200 米，气温凉爽，水源充足，距三峡水利枢纽工程坝址中堡岛仅 100 公里，距林区政府所在地松柏镇 112 公里，离兴山县高阳镇 60 公里，与神农顶景区相邻，是林区开发旅游事业的重点区域。主要景点有神农洞、潮水泉、香溪河等，是旅游观光、科研考察、避暑休息的理想天地。

Xiangxiyuan (Honey Stream Source) Scenic Spot is located in the southern part of Shennongjia Forest Region, including Muyu Town, Honghua Town, Jiuchong Town and a part of Shennongjia National Natural Reserve. Muyu Plateau, the location of Muyu Township, is the key place where the Forest Region develops the tourist industry, which is 1,200m above the sea level, with cool weather and abundant rainwater, 100km away from the Three Gorges Dam and 112km away from Songbai Town where the Capital of Shennongjia Forest Region is located. This area is full of tourist resources, including Shennong Cave, Chaoshui Spring, Honey Stream River and so on, is a nice place for relaxation, vocation, sightseeing and science research.

神农洞 Shennong Cave is a typical limestone solution cave, which has two interconnected mouths with a height difference of 200m, is located to the west and faced to the east, and is characterized by a particular style of balcony because of a wide bottom and narrow top of the cave body. There are several clean and clear water sinks and various appearances of karst landscape due to the dropping rock latex. Moreover, there is an underground river stealthily flowing through the cave, so that the visitors can hear the water sound but can't find its form.

三堆河 The carbonaceous shale, limestone and dolomite of the Cambian Shuijintuo Formation and the Sinian Doushantuo Formation distribute in the area from Sandui/ Three-Stack River to Honghua Plateau where there are silica veins dominated by faults and infilled by thermal fluid in the geological history. The veins have an almost right dip angle and the SiO_2 content can be up to 99.9%, forming a large scale silica ore. Silica rock can be smelt into industry silicon to prepare colored metal alloy, high-grade antichlor, alloy addition agent, high-purity semiconductor, organic silicon, high temperature materials and other materials.

Because silica rock is too hard to be eroded, many bare peaks formed with rare soil and vegetation. For the well-developing joints and fissures, it is easy to collapse to be sharp-ridge peaks, which arrange in order along the strike and are different from round-shape and cascading karst peaks. The silica rock's surface is dyed to red color by leaching iron from pyrite in the surface, joints and fissures of rocks, which has been named Flame Mountain since it seemed as flame in the sun.

Hard and brittle silicon mass have many joints and fracture planes, easy to fall down in the condition of available free face. Several mass was dissected by unloaded fracture planes, becoming unstable, lastly these rock-fall is locating on the gentle slope, in the slope foot or in the Three-Stack River. So it forms three big silicon colluvial stacks, which is the reason that why it is called Three Stacks River.

The Three-Stack River Waterfall is a deferentially-eroded waterfall, whose length is 30 meters and width is 2 meters. The water falls down straightly, like a river collapsing, which is clean and clear just like a white silk. Green mountains around inverts reflection in water, which becomes a green jade flowing away.

潮水泉 Chaoshui/ Tidewater Spring is a karst spring in the dolomitite of Dengying Formation of the upper Sinian system, whose cavity altitude is 1,220 meters, 10 meters higher than riverbed. The Spring comes out under a subsiding cliff, whose mouth is a lentoid fracture, long in 5.5 meters, high 0.05-0.5 meters and deep in 3 meter visibly. Normally Tidewater Spring has three tides everyday, for long time sunshine or before a shower, the period cycle will be longer, but for long time raining the cycle will be shorter. Before a tiding, the sound of skirr comes out first, secondly cool gas spurts out, and tide is well up from the Spring mouth two minutes later. The flux gradually rise up until it is becoming stable(the flux can be 1112l/s). After 15 minute, the flux gradually diminishes down, 24 minute later it stops. Every time the tide lasts about 45 minutes. The formation of Tidewater Spring is closely connected with air pressure and the moving channel of groundwater, a pulse flux caused by a kind of siphon phenomenon.

燕子洞 Yanzi/ Swallow Cave in Chaoshui/ Tidewater River is of 1,260 meters high above the sea level, with the dolomitite of Dengying Formation of Sinian system coming out. It is a outlet of underground river with 6-meter height and 1.2-meter width, controlled by the fractures, whose flux is 175l/s. Seven meters upper to the top, there also develops one dry water-eroded cave with 2-meter height and 1.2-meter width, which is connected with an underground river by karst fractures where the tide spring is below it. With the development of region's raise or valley's cut, the overflow spot of groundwater also adjusts its location downwards, which makes karst channel to obtain the layer character of staircase.

Rocks with dissoluble dolomitite as the mainbody come out in the region of Small Dangyang -

Shennong Sacrifice Garden-Tiansheng Bridge, in steep occurrence and nearly in erection, forming two teams of vertical columnar joints and several fractures. Along with joints, layers and fractures, the karst effect of surface water and groundwater, root cleavage cracking, cold freezing, ice cleavage cracking, rock falling and so on, peak clusters have been made. Mountain peaks are shot high up along the same directional joint, and the peaks, columnar rocks, rock screens often have sharp ridges.

Along the two teams of vertical columnar joints formed by dissoluble dolomitite in Shicaohe Formation, nearly in erecting layers and fractures, the karst effect of surface water and groundwater, root cleavage cracking, cold freezing, ice cleavage cracking, rock falling and so on, makes the formation of rock screen, just like a sword coming out of the sheath.

Along the two teams of vertical columnar joints formed by dissoluble dolomitite in Shicaohe Formation, nearly in erecting layers and fractures, the karst effect of surface water and groundwater, root cleavage cracking, cold freezing, ice cleavage cracking, rock falling and so on, make two side ridges steep, in the ridge peaks there are one team edged columnar rock, same as Shennong carrying herbal medicine, and another one seeming as a patient which lowers his head and back towards the Sacrifice Garden.

Along the two teams of vertical columnar joints formed by dissoluble dolomitite in Shicaohe Formation, nearly in erecting layers and fractures, the karst effect of surface water and groundwater, root cleavage cracking, cold freezing, ice cleavage cracking, rock falling and so on, make two side ridges steep, in the ridge peaks there are one team edged columnar rock, like a Cyprinoid jumping out of water surface, since it is located on a ridge on the one side of Dangyang River, hence the name Cyprinoid Jumping Imperial Door.

鳄鱼石 In the ancient landslide of Shennong Sacrifice Garden, there are some dolomitite floats of Shicaohe Formation fell from the mountains around. The plants is growing in the joints, layers and fractures of the floats, the root cleavage cracking is very distinct, some even bigger like a big bonsai, one of them seems like a crocodile's head, hence the name Crocodile's Head Stone.

For the violent raising in Small Dangyang Region and the deep dropping of the river, Dangyang River and Huangyang River deeply cut the dolomitite bedrock of Shicaohe Formation, which led to edged ridge in the joining part of the two rivers. The dolomitite rock of Shicaohe Formation is very hard, which is good to keep the ridge peak.

Along the joint plane in Shicaohe Formation of Shennongjia Group, Dangyang River cut the rock, which made the columnar peaks stretching out, and the peaks made of dolomitite are just like the edge of knife, forming steep cliff, erecting on the riverside, facing to southeast, so called Dangyang Cliff. Because of varied lithology weathering, there displays yellow, white, gray and other colors in the Cliff, dark or light, forming a natural cliff mural painting, some looking as China Map and running horse. Besides, the two sides of the Cliff often have some stratified karst caves.

神农祭坛 Shennong Altar is a huge ancient landslide, stuffed the river course a long time ago, now the out-bent river is caused by the landslide. The back edge altitude is 1,700 meters and the front edge altitude is 1,300 meters. It is a rocky landslide, whose plane form is like a shoe and the section form like a sidestep. There is a legendary Shennong Statue of cattle head and man body stands in the highest flat (the totem of ancient farming clans). Landslide material is gravel soil with relaxed structure and good penetrability. In the Lower flat there planted a thousand-year-old iron fir, the reason why it is not declined in the thousand years is that the soil is crashed in landslide, good for the roots to develop downwards and draw in enough nutrition and water so as to satisfy the need of photosynthesis of ten-thousand-square-meters' leaves. There also one fragrant fruit tree called "living fossil" grows in the slope of landslide's front edge.

天生桥 The dolomitite of Shicaohe Formation comes out in Tiansheng/ Nature-Made Bridge Scenic Spot, whose altitude is 1,800 meters and covering area is nearly 20 square kilometers. Here peaks are steep and valleys narrow, together with Tiansheng Bridge, Water Curtain Waterfall, and the Huangyan River, forming a majestic, steep and pretty landscape. Here are three tall and straight mountains, Caomao Peak, Yinzi Cliff and Gaodeng Mouth, forming a natural paint screen behind Tiansheng Bridge, Water Curtain Waterfall and the Huangyan River.

The Huangyan River coming from Laojun Mountain and Huangjie Mountain, runs out like a waterfall in a calabash cavity under the Longtou/ Dragon Head Mountain, and the surface of bridge is 40 meters higher than the water surface below, so it is called Tiansheng/ Nature- Made Bridge. A long time ago, the Huangyan River was channeled to the current farmland because of Longtou Mountain, but there is a fracture right at the corner in the Mountain, and upon the long effect of river erosion, the fracture is eroded at last, forming a bilge. So then Huangyan River cut the bending and turned to this way, and formed a steep bank of 3 meters high in the new riverway.

翻水洞 Water-Turning Cave is 250 meters west to Tiansheng Bridge, whose altitude is 1,260 meters and the outlet is in the dolomitite of Shicaohe Formation, which is a karst fracture. The underground river's flux is 844l/s, so much water turns out from the outlet, so it is called Water-Turning Cave, the water's main chemical component is HCO_3-Ca-Mg.

地潭 After flowing out from the underground river in Tiansheng Bridge, the water is flying down to a deep pool about 2 meters deep, forming a water curtain in the Cliff in front of Tiansheng Bridge. The waterfall's height is 30 meters and its width 2 meters. The flying waterfall is flying down from the Cliff and hitting the rock and deep pool, like the Milky Way, and jade pearl splashing, raising drizzly water fog. Under the sunshine, we can seethe bottom through the deepwater in pool, there raises some drizzly water fog over the water surface, and the Cliff forms a painting of "Lianpo and Lin Xiangru", for there displays several varied colors caused by weathering effect .

溶洞 The dolomitite of Shicaohe Formation is scattered in Yijia Slope to the north-east of Tiansheng Bridge. There is a karst cavity in the mountain at the altitude of about 1,500 meters, which is 500 meters deep. In the Cavity, there is odd rocks and strangestalactiteshere and there, and a little stream. The air temperature is exactly negative inside and outside the cavity, warm inside and cold outside, or hot outside and cool inside. It is warm in winter and cool in summer, you may see frost spectacle by chance in the summer, so it is called "Cold-Hot Cavity", which is relative to the big difference in airflow temperature between inside and outside the cavity.

野人峰 Plants often grow in the joint fractures where some soil is kept, when the plants' roots deeply implant in the cliff fractures and grow bigger and bigger, they will split the rock along the fracture, which is the effect of root cleavage, or biology weathering. The dolomitite of Shicaohe Formation, Shennong Group in Zhangba River has many joints, the root cleavage phenomena are seen here and there. The most typical example is Wildman Columnar Peak, which is formed by root cleavage, cold freezing and karst together, now still erecting here.

大千家坪岩溶洼地 The karst depression is 500 meters long and 100 meters wide surrounded by mountains. Beifeng Ground made of diabase is like a big lying dragon north to the depression, whose head looks back on Tongchang Peak (ancient copper mine site), where has much copper mine resources. In the south of the depression, it is Motian Mountain, 50-100 meters lower than the mountains around. Reconstructed by the quaternary era glacier, the depression formed valleys, quaternary accumulational material is more in the bottom with some swamp soil. In the raining seasons there are ringing streams, swamp lakes and mountain grass, wild flower and bees and butterflies. In the autumn, red leaves are everywhere in the mountains.

Around Big Qianjia Ground Karst Depression, along two teams of vertical columnar joints the dissoluble dolomitite of Dawokeng Formation, under the karst effect, root cleavage cracking, cold freezing, ice cleavage cracking, rock falling and so on, forms needle edge peak clusters, karst peaks and columnar rocks, some is a castle, others plane and columnar.

There leave two isolated karst peaks in the center of Big Qianjia Ground Karst Depression, Gates to All Sides, like a castle. There are several sinkholes in the center or edge of the Ground Karst Depression, whose the bottom is inclined to the sinkhole. One of the sinkholes manifests a man-made circle lake in the raining season, called "Heaven Pool".

Gates to All Sides are connected with the underground karst systems along the joints and fractures. When in the raining season, the surface water is drained to Small Qianjia Ground. When the water under the foot of castle in the depression has no time to drain from sinkhole, it will form a temporary moat.

The outlet is located at the end of Small Qianjia Ground Depression in the siliceous strip dolomite of the Dawokeng Formation, whose entrance of cave is 30 meters high, 8 meters wide, and 2,050 meters above the sea level. Around the entrance, there are some piles of collapsed rock. In the cave, the deposit is mainly the coarse sand, well divided. The cave is an export of a hidden river in Big Qianjia Ground originally along the crevasse growth. Presently, the cave does not have a surface current of water, for the underground stream has already dropped or changed its way.

Shicaohe Formation of Shennongjia Group, named by Shicao River, is the biggest stratigraphic unit in Shennongjia Group, whose thickness is 2,301.6m. The lower part is dolomite breccia, gravel; the dolomitic sandstone, dolomitic siltstone and brecciated limestone; the upper part is mainly gray flint strip dolomite, and stromatolite dolomite and the top part is mainly purple-red dolomitic siltstone, siltstone, and argillaceous dolomite, whose halite pseudomorph, splits, and the ripple mark can be seen obviously and the deposit of evaporated lagoon facies is on the rock stratification plane.

The vanadium ore in the Region is mainly in the middle of Zhengjiaya Formation of Shennongjia Group, which is black coal bed containing vanadium and uranium rock with the thickness 32 - 53m, composed of the upper vanadium ore bed and the lower vanadium ore bed, and the coal bed containing vanadium and uranium rock, principally includes charcoal and argillaceous soil, compact and in plate-like structure. It is a big-scale rock series of vanadium, high and rich, whose beneficial component may supply the comprehensive utilization, having some certain industrial prospect.

Under the effect of air, water and biology movements, the surface rock experienced some physics and chemical change, causing rock mass collapsing, shelling off, crashing, and turning into loose materials, which is called weathering. The plants grow in the fractures, with the plants growth, the roots grow bigger and bigger, making the rock fractures become bigger and deeper and collapse at last, which is called biology weathering.

One of the two teams of dissoluble dolomitite vertical columnar joints along Shicaohe Formationt formed karst cavity, there are wind blowed out perennially, so called Wind Tunnel. It is a part of this region's karst cavity system which is connected with each other, and karst cavity system is a ventilating tunnel, the wind tunnel as its outlet.

The two teams of dissoluble dolomitite vertical columnar joints along Shicaohe Formation have had the karst effect, root cleavage cracking, cold freezing, ice cleavage cracking, rock falling and so on, forming edge ridge, and a needle edge columnar rock on the one side of ridge, just like a big dragon perking in the cloud. On the side of Longtou Peak, there is a columnar rock, just like a slim and graceful girl with flower crown on head standing on the side of the big dragon.

The two teams of dissoluble dolomitite vertical columnar joints along Shicaohe Formation have had the karst effect, root cleavage cracking, cold freezing, ice cleavage cracking, rock falling and so on, forming plane rock screen, just like a Token Rock, which is parallel to one of two teams of vertical columnar joints.

香溪河 The Xiangxi/ Honey Stream River, as a tributary of the Changjiang River, is well-known in the world because it has nurtured Qu Yuan, one of the four major persons in world cultural circle and Wang Zhaojun, one of the four major charming women in China. The Honey Stream Source have two, here is the west one, the spring flowing up from the entrance of Qianlong/ Sneaking Dragon Cave, the exit of Zhengjiabao undercurrent. Qianlong Cave was collapsed a long time ago because of the karst, now buried in the breaking huge stones. Roaring water of the spring gathers at one place, so the water yield exceeds 2t/s, and the water quality is pure, Lu Yu, one of famous Chinese scholars once named it the 14th Spring in the world.

The spring of Qianlong Cave falls down into Xianglong/ Taming Dragon Pool, transforming into a waterfall of more than 10 meters wide and two floors high, named Xianglong Waterfall, one of the difference corrosion waterfalls. River water formed different corrosion to several soft and hard rocks which have different ability of anti-eroding in the bottom of the Southern China's tillite. The hard rock layers rise above the incompetent beds which is easy to be corroded and formed steep mountain cliffs. When the water flows in the same direction of the tillite movement, the water is divided into several fluxes by the hard rock layers, flying down swiftly from ten-meters' height. The waterfalls are overlapping, gathering, and dispersing, whose state is changeable.

Zhengjiabao Underground River is located between Shennongjia back slope and Muyu Ground front slope, comes out in the interface of the dolomitite of Shicaohe Formation, Shennongjia Group and the rock layers of Nantuo Formation of Sinian system, whose altitude is 1,400 meters, flux is 2000l/s, main water content is HCO_3-Ca-Mg, and mineral degree is 0.14 g/l. It is a source-type underground water, the source of Xiangxi River.

The Xiangxi River near Muyu Town produces wooden fish stone, a kind of greyish-green tillite of Nanhua Group in wood grain shape, containing clay sandstone and belt-shaped granulated mudstone, compact and exquisite. Wooden fish stone can be made into handicrafts. The widely-distributed red sandalwood color siltstone of Shicaohe Formation, Shennongjia Group has the wood grain shape horizontal bedding, also called wooden fish stone.

青天炮冰斗 In ice age, when the snow and ice in the ditch near the snow line were accumulated to a certain degree, they would flow and became the glacier. The moving glacier dig the valley gradually, and then formed a cirque whose three sides were surrounded by mountains, just like a rattan chair. The elevation of the Blue Sky Gown Cirque base is 1,400 meters, with some residual ice ridges. The following part is a straight glacier-carved valley, with the elevation of 1,400 - 1,300 meters, and the bottom width of 40 - 60 meters, extending to south west. The Blue Sky Gown Glacier-carved Valley has about 50 meters elevation difference compared with the Wooden Fish Ground glacier-carved valley. The converging place of glacier-carved valleys has an obviously steep ridge, connecting with the hanging valleys. The mountain peak between The Blue Sky Gown Cirque and Muyuping Cradle Ditch Cirque assumes the edge spine.

Chapter 5 Hongping Scenic Spot 红坪景区

红坪海拔 1677 米，东距松柏镇 70 公里，处神农架林区中部偏北，气候温凉，水量充沛，是国营红坪林场所在地。该风景区包括燕子洞、燕子垭、天门垭、红坪画廊、古犀牛洞等。209 国道及其支线贯通其间，是神农架的旅游热点。

红坪 Hongping, the locating place of state-run Hongping Forest Farm, is situated in the central part of Shennongjia Forest Region, 70km away from Songbai Town, 1,677m above the sea level. The weather here is warn and cool, abounding in rainwater. The scenic spot includes Hongping Picturesque Gallery, Yanzi/ Swallow Cave, Yanzi Cliff/ Swallow Pass, Tiamnen Cliff/

Heaven Gate Pass, Ancient Xiniu/ Dicerorhinus Cave, Picturesque Gallery Valley, Liuxiang Mountain Village, Shennong Palace etc. The No.109 national highway passes through the region. It is one of the widely liked scenic spots in Shennongjia Forest Region.

燕子洞 Yanzi/ Swallow Cave is 17m high and 20m wide, whose elevation is 2,343m. The cave mouth faces north. There are well dissoluble dolomitic limestone and calcareous dolomite of Tianheban Formation and Shilongdong Formation and badly dissoluble dolomitic sandstone and carbonaceous limestone of Shipai Formation and Shuijingtuo Formation of Cambrian System. Along the interfaces between different formations of Cambrian System, the Cave extends 3,700m long from north to south and varies greatly from 0.3m to 4m in width and from 0.3m to 20m in height. There are many branch caves developed along the joints and fractures. The Golden Swallows with short mouth often nest in pairs in the dry cave wall, which is the mutated kind of golden swallow coming from ancient sea with fine discernment and without the characteristics of the migrating birds.

燕子垭 Yanzi Cliff/ Swallow Pass is a narrow mountain pass and the elevation is 2,200m. As there is a famous cave nearby named Yanzi Cave with many swallows, it is called Yanzi Cliff. It is an artificial ravine that is the result of artificial explosion when the No.209 national highway was building in the past years. Feiyun/ Flying Cloud Bridge is building over Yanzi Cliff, which is the highest sightseeing bridge of steel structure in Asia. Huixian/ Meeting Gods Platform stands on the precipitous cliff besides the bridge, which is surrounded with green trees and white clouds.

Tianheban Formation is composed of gray thin-bedded argillaceous striped limestone and nips with oolitic and fabaceous limestone. Oolite is the globular carbonate grain with core and concentric layer structure, whose shape and size looks like fish egg. The tidal power barrage and delta developed as the tidal action of shores supporting an ideal environment for the form of oolite. The concentric layer structure of oolite can show the times that it was agitated by the seawater into suspended state and the form and its thickness can show the time when it had been in the suspended state.

Liuxiang Mountain Village/ Fastness is located on the stratum of Tianheban Formation and Shilongdong Formation of the Lower Cambrian System, which is composed of dolomite and marlite. Liuxiang Mountain Village is built along the mountain range where there are many towering mountains, ridges and peaks, precipitous cliffs, ravines, stone peaks and columns propped up the sky, such as One-Line Sky and Touching Nose Cliff. Here you will feel enigmatic and seems to enter an ancient castle.

天门垭 Tianmen Cliff/ Pass is a narrow mountain pass whose elevation is 2,328m. Here strange peaks stand out on the both sides, the middle Pass just looks like a door up to the Sky, hence the name. When it becomes sunny initially after the rain, many clouds will gather into the sea of clouds over Yanzi Cliff, Tianmen Cliff, Huanglong Dam and Taiping Cliff. As the clouds refract the sunshine, a multicoloured aureola will hang over the sea of clouds. When the man or things are surrounded by the aureola, the golden ray called Foguang or Buddhist Light will cover the man's head.

The river in this scenic spot originates from the area of Tianmen Cliff and Liuxiang Mountain Village. The low-lying area from Tianmen Cliff to Taping is cirque vestige of the Quaternary Ice Age. The Zizhu River traces to the source and makes erosion ceaselessly that the cirque walls become more and more precipitous. The same phenomenon occurs at the south of this area because of the headward erosion of the Zhichang River. In the gradient places of rivers or ravines, the river banks become more and more precipitous, the part scoured by the stream will move upward to the upper reaches with the erosion of substances when the scouring action becomes stronger, which is called Headward Erosion.

The south and north areas of Tianmen Cliff and Liuxiang Mountain Village become more precipitous respectively because of the headward erosion of the Zhichang River and the Zizhu River, which made the Tianmen Cliff Ridge. As Tianmen Cliff Ridge is composed of dolomite and marlite with developed joints and fractures, physical weathering and karst effect make the Ridge become sawtooth-like as a picture curtain seen from far away. Here are karst peaks, Bianpi/ Whip Cut Stone cleaved by two groups of erecting joints, a column named Shennong Medical Dictionary composed of horizontal thin-bedded limestone and Chuanxin/ Crossing Heart Cave, a karst crack and the like.

Shipai Formation is mainly composed of shale and siltstone with many fossils of trilobite. Trilobite was a kind of extinct arthropoda, which emerged with some small-shell animals of low mollusk such as hyolithes and gastropods in the early period of Cambrian Era. As the whole Cambrian Era is the world of trilobites, these small-shell animals are the rich foods of trilobites and they also left their traces of activity called relic fossil.

Niutitang Formation is mainly composed of black carbonaceous shale and marlite with abundant rare element. There are axiolitic, caky and lentoid nodules, which root in the calc growing from a point of pressed filtration during the deep diagenetic process.

红坪画廊 When you stand on the highway and look to the north from the exit of Picturesque Gallery Valley to Hongping, you will find that the peak cluster of Hongqi/ Red Flag Cliff Ridge extends out just like a flying flag, which are composed of the dolomite of Dushantuo Formation and Dengying Formation of Sinian System. The dolomite is rigid, brickle, dissoluble and easy to form precipitous cliff. When you look to the south, you will find that the ridges composed of the same stratums are watching the door of Xianglong/ Taming Dragon Gate like two huge dragons.

Hongping Picturesque Gallery is located at the foot of the South Mountain of Tianmen Cliff and it's a 7,500m-long basin gorge, whose underlying stratum is silicious striped dolomite of Shicaohe Formation, Shennongjia Group. Here are bony and sheer peaks on both sides. This scenic spot consists of one river, two rivulets, three falls, four brides, five ponds, six cavities, seven towers, eight mountain villages, nine stones and thirty-six peaks connected with thirty-six beautiful legends.

Hongping Scenic Spot ranges from the Changshan Dam with many big and green China firs to the Hongqi Cliff with precipitous stones and strange peaks. Picturesque Gallery Valley is composed of the dolomite of Dushantuo Formation and Dengying Formation of Sinian System. Tianfeng/ Sky Crack Canyon, actually One-Line Sky is a long slit formed by the erosion and falling of the rock along the joints. The vertical depth is over 200 meters with steep cliffs on both sides, seen from the canyon bottom, just one line sky can be found. Zhaowang Sword, the corroded stone column stands in the slit.

In Picturesque Gallery Valley, two rivulets flow from east and west ravines and bypasses Baojian Cliff and Tianfeng Canyon, then join together into one rivulet, which rushes down into a small pond from 20m high precipitous cliffs like a silk or voile. There is respectively one strange stone like trumpet shell on the both sides of the pond, on which large pines look like an umbrella and reflects in the pond, so the pond is named Yingsan Pond or Umbrella- Reflecting Pond.

The spring is a tectonic and descending one with karst fissure, which emerges in the interface between the moraine breccia of Nantuo Formation of Nanhua System and Dushantuo Formation of Sinian System. The aquifer of the spring is Dushantuo Formation of Sinian System with the flux of 60L/s and the water is clear and clean, no color, no taste and no smell, and insipid calcium bicarbonate.

古犀牛洞 The mouth of Ancient Xiniu/ Dicerorhinus Cave in Hongping is 19m high and 15m wide like a door. This Cave extends to the northwest. The characteristics of the mouth and body of the Cave are determined by a group dense fractures with the strike direction of northwest 65°and the dip angle of 80°. There are well-developed stalactites, stone columns, stone curtains and stalagmites in the Cave.

Ancient Xiniu/ Dicerorhinus Cave is the Paleolithic site of alpine-zone people in the remote antiquity. Here are five cavities with 3m to 5m high mouth that are different from other ancient people's site just with a single cavity. More than one thousand of animal fossils and Paleolithic artifacts were excavated from the Cave. As the places of dwelling and living were different, the artifacts and animal fossils were relatively collected in the different cavities. There are 20 kinds of fossils of rhinoceros and stegodons. The rhinoceros have more than eight individuals and the stegodons have more than 6 individuals. Ancient animals were the food of ancient humans of Shennongjia Forest Region. There are more than 20 artifacts including scrapers, choppers, burin, flakes, and the like. Paleolithic artifacts are mainly made of black firestone and quartz sandstone by hammer hitting, which are evidently different from the ones made of the gravel in the Hanjiang River reaches and the south reaches ofthe Changjiang River.

通天洞 Tongtian/ Reaching Sky Cave, a karst cave, has a karst funnel up to the sky like a courtyard in the Cave. The wall is nearly perpendicular and even vertical. When the sun falls, multicoloured rays shines on the hidden rivulets in the cave through the funnel so that golden ray twinkles there. When it is raining outside, the surface water rushes into the Cave along the wall, full of breath-taking image, which is because the cave wall is corroded and collapses continually when the surface water flows into the Cave through the cracks.

经络石 When the hot liquid originated from the upper tectonic movement filled into the tensile fractures and joints of dolomite, breccia, dolomitic sandstone contained with gravel and siliceous and streaky dolomite, the calcite and quartz veins like comb came into being. Veins become very slippery because of the scouring of the flowing water and look like the veins of human body. Therefore they are called Jingluo/ Veins Stone and have a higher value in viewing and admiration.

There are dissoluble dolomitic limestone and dolomite of Shilongdong Formation and Tianheban Formation of Cambrian System and Dushantuo Formation and Dengying Formation of Sinian System. The stratum has a low dip angle and has had multi-group large-size fractures with high dip angle that made the rock fragmented, together with the erosion and karst effect of surface water and underground water, the beautiful karst geomorphic landscape in high mountains came into being. Longji/ Dragon BackPeak looks like a rolling long dragon and Fengchi/ Phoenix Wing Peak looks like a singing phoenix. Jiuhu/ Wine Pot Peak is located between the two peaks and looks like a wine pot with thin neck and round bottom.

鱼泉河 The Yema /Wild Horse River and the Zhichang River join together here and become the Yuquan/ Fish Spring River. The dolomite of Shicaohe Formation of Shennongjia Group cropped out here and the oldest stratum in Shennongjia Region, Zhengjiaya Formation cropped out in the joining part of the river valley bottom. The Karst effect has made the dolomite become into peak cluster, strange and multi-layered. The Yuquan River valley is very deep, steep and dangerous. The waterfall here is 3m wide and 48m high. The waterfall rushes rapidly into the green pond of surging water.

The oldest stratum in Shennongjia Forest Region, Zhengjiaya Formation Pt2z of Mesoproterozoic Changchengian era formed in the basin of the continental rift and is made of terrigenous chipping-volcanic rock. The deep-gray and medium and thin-bedded carbonaceous siltstone and packs and of upper Zhengjiaya Formation cropped out here, distributed fragmentarily in the east part of Xinhua fault, Guanmen/ Closing Door Mountain, the Xiangjiang River and Taizi/ Platform and often formed into the anticlinal core cropped out of the deep valleys and the upper plate of reverse thrust.

Anticline is a kind of structural feature that the stratum is extruded and distorted into bends. The Yema River's anticline is wide and level and looks like a arched roof, is an anticline with short axes. It is the stratum of Zhengjiaya Formation in the core and the stratum of Shicaohe Formation on the both sides. It cropped out of the surface with a clear feature as the incision of the river current. The soft black silicious mudstone formed into the physiognomy sight of the valley, which is called the inversion of relief.

野马河 The dolomite of Shicaohe Formation, Shennongjia Group is outcropped in the Yema River and the rock is rigid and brisk. There are two perpendicular groups of vertical fractures and the Yema River flows along one group of the fracture. Precipitous cliffs on both sides are facing tightly and the river channel is very narrow. Superimposed valley came into being as this kind of flat bottom valley with same width from top to bottom cutin the early wide valley, which is the result of crustal intermittent uplifting since the terminal Tertiary. The wide valley is formed because of early slow uplifting and the flat bottom valley with same width from top to bottom is formed because of later rapid uplifting. So the sight is grand, strange, beautiful, secret, and high-abrupt.

The Yema River is 10,000m long. The peaks on the both sides are incised and eroded by the current, and then formed perpendicular cliff, peak forest and flat bottom valley with same width from top to bottom formed because of water erosion, landslip and karst effect. The river current is very fast and strong and the waterfalls layer upon layer have come into being when the fast water falls on the rock, which is grand. This place is the important production area of giant salamander. Here you can find some stones with different color, veins and pictures.

Hot springs outcrop from the interface between the fractured zones of dolomite of east Shicaohe Formation to Huangbaoping Fault and the slope layer, which are tectonic ascending springs and can be divided into two groups along northwest direction. Gaojiawu Formation consists of 5 springs and Miaogou Formation consists of 19 springs. The total water yield of the two groups is more than 0.01m^3/s. The temperature of the water is 16.8℃~20℃ and it will decrease with the infiltration of cold water of the caves nearby.

It is a torsional fault in a northwest direction and it controls the distribution of two groups of springs in Gaojiawu Formation and Miaogou Formation. There is a 20m wide fractured stratum zone of Dushantuo Formation and Dengying Formation of Sinian System in the Wenshui/ Warm Water River and an escarpment came into being in Wuchi/ Five-Lake Mountain. Dawokeng Formation is incised by Huoshi Valley dyke, where there are abundant claret siltstones. Wuchi Mountain is the fifth order planation surface in Shennongjia Region and the elevation of its peak is 1,711m.

The full name of tillite of Nantuo Formation is Moraine-mudstone mainly consisting of glaucous massive moraine breccia, sand slime and sandstone contained with gravel and mud and nipped with arenaceous mudstone. This rock is one of the rare rocks in the world. The component of gravel is intrusive rock, dolomite, siliceous rock, slate and diabase, etc. “Snow - Ball Event” of Global Icecap Climate happened 600-700 million years ago and “Warm-house Event” happened after the ice age. This alternation of cold and warm made moraine and interglacial sediments formed.

Chapter 6 Dajiuhu/ Big Nine Lakes Scenic Spot 大九湖景区

大九湖景区包括大九湖、小九湖、落羊河等。大九湖是九湖乡所在地，距松柏镇 165 公里，处大巴山脉东麓，是神农架山脉西端的起点。景区西南与四川省巫溪县双阳镇、青龙乡及巫山县当阳镇、庙堂乡接壤，是林区通向小三峡的必经之地；东南面和板桥河乡相连，是通向神农溪、大三峡的要冲；西北和竹山县洪坪乡、房县九道乡毗邻，东面和东溪乡交界。有连接 209 国道的九酒公路线和通向四川省巫溪县双阳镇的九（湖坪）双（阳镇）公路。

大九湖自古号称“巴山前哨”，是“薛刚反唐”的基地和“刘体纯联明抗清”的盟誓地。有大九湖、国公坪等景点。大九湖景区有保存较好的冰川地貌，其现象主要有冰斗、冰窖、角峰、刃脊、槽谷、基岩鼓丘等。冰斗和冰窑是大九湖景区冰蚀地貌中较普通的一种形态，分布于大九湖盆地周围的山坡上。本区还有高山湿地、岩溶漏斗、落水孔、暗河等景观。深邃难测的落水孔，青秀多姿的红海棠、高山杜鹃，水清如镜的黑水河，望而生畏的五等子垭，川鄂连边的自生桥，形象逼真的鲤鱼岩、卧佛岭，五彩缤纷的山花，一望无垠的蓝天绿地，构成了一幅绚丽多姿的图景。

Dajiuhu/ Big Nine Lake Scenic Spot includes Dajiuhu/ Big Nine Lake, Xiaojiuhu/ Little Nine Lake, Luoyang River and so on. Dajiuhu is located at the eastern foot of Daba Mountain, which is the location of Jiuhu Town, 165km far away from Songbai Town. It is the west beginning point of Shennongjia Mountain, connecting with Wuxi County and Wushan County of Sichuan Province in the southwest direction, as the only way to the Small Three Gorges of the Changjiang River. It connects with Banqiaohe Town in the southeast direction as the main way to Shennong Stream and the Big Three Gorges of the Changjiang River. And it connects with Zhushan County and Fangxian County in the northwest direction. There is No. 209 national highway connecting with Wuxi County, Sichuan Province.

Dajiuhu has been the first pass of Bashan Mountain in the history and the base of Xue Gang fighting against the Tang Dynasty and the location for Liu Tichun to ally with the Ming Dynasty to fight against the Qing Dynasty. Dajiuhu has well preserved glacial landscape, such as glacial amphitheater, ice-scour notch, horn peak, cuchilla, trough valley, bedrock and drum-like hills. Glacial amphitheater and ice-scour notch are commonly distributed over the slope around Dajiuhu Basin, which is one of most common type. And here are alpine wetland, karst funnel, sinkhole and hidden river.

Here, deep sinkholes, charming red malus spectabilis and mountain rhododendra, clear and clean Heishui/ Black Water River, gorgeous Wudengzi Cliff, Zisheng/ Self-Made Bridge connecting with Sichuan Province and Hubei Province, lively Fish Cliff and Sleeping Buddha Ridge, colorful mountains flowers and long and wide blue sky and green land consist a picturesque view.

干沟干谷 Gangou/ Dry Valley extends from northeast to southwest and is flat in valley bottom, 1,000m long and 40~60m wide. Two stages of terrace are developed here and 2m thick moraine is covered on the second terrace, which is 2,000m far away from the west Gangou. The stream originates from Chaoshui/ Tide Water Pool and enters into subsurface near Gangou, then outcrops at west Gangou and converges into Pingqian River valley. Gangou is formed by the crust movement, the surface water infiltrating into subsurface along karst fractures which make the surface river dry. The stream is intermittent during the flood period.

大九湖岩溶盆地 Dajiuhu Karst Basin is a polje valley which is the result of combined action of karst and glacier of Quaternary, 15,000m long from south to north and 3,000m wide from east to west. The basin bottom area is 18km^2 and the elevation is 1,700m. The surface water and groundwater in the polje valley and the peak forests nearby converge into the Heishui River. The river water enters into subsurface from the sinkhole at the north and then crops out of the surface at the headstream of the Guandu River, Zhushan County. Many times of mountain glaciers have taken place since the Quaternary that changed the polje valley. Dajiuhu Lake was ever an ice lake.

黑水河 The Heishui River is the main surface river in Dajiuhu area and it flows through the full area like an intestine. The average flux is about 1.5m^3/s. Many years ago, this river connected with nine swamps and lakes like a piece of silver wire, flowing from the southeast to the northwest mountain foot and disappeared in the sinkhole and entered into the subsurface. Nowadays, when the sun rises up and falls down, the Heishui River is flowing in the grassland like a piece of greenish-black ribbon, which is very interesting too.

Sinkholes are the main discharging passages of surface water and groundwater with different shapes. The sinkholes of Dajiuhu are a row of holes developed along the bedding planes. When the surface water enters into the subsurface, it flows to the north along the interbedded fractures and is connected with many underground caves. The sinkholes with a low elevation always have water the whole year and ones with a high elevation only discharge water at the flood period. At rainy season or during the rainstorm, when the sinkholes here have no adequate ability to discharge water quickly, large area of Dajiuhu Basin will be flooded, forming a wide and brilliant lake view.

Open and wide Dajiuhu Lake, surrounded by many mountains is the largest alpine basin in the Central China. Here are rich in rainwater and water weeds, 70 percentage of the area is covered by aquatic plants. There is a peat bed with the thickness of 3~4m and the mollic is 120cm thick in average. Dajiuhu Lake is a karst basin formed at the end of Oligocene (25~40 million years ago), was ever a karst lake because of the clogging of groundwater passages and the lake water was drained up and lake's bottom appeared, and then current physiognomic sights have come into being. This swamp is the typical representation of semitropical upland wet lands and swamps in China.

Dajiuhu Basin is located in the west end of Shennongjia Forest Region, whose area is 16km^2 and the elevation is 1,700m. under the combined influence of glaciation, karst effect and stream action this basin has changed into a unique and close alpine basin. Since the Holocene Epoch, stable and consecutive peat deposit is formed, which is more than 2m thick. As it almost has not been disturbed by human beings, the reserved environmental information in peat can show the original features of the change of natural environment.

Liyu/ Carp Stone is a relic body of denudated dolomite of Qinjiamiao Formation of the upper Cambrian System, isolated and 80m long. As it covers on a steep incline and looks like a carp, so it is called Liyu/ Carp Stone. At the northeast, there is a cirque formed by the exaration of glacier and corrosion of flowing water's current.

There is a ridge on the back of Yangjia Bay of Dajiuhu Lake and three steep mountain ridges 30m-high formed at the north end, just like three big steps. The ridge looks like a huge dragon sleep there seen from the side and the mountain top looks like the mouth of a dragon, called Longzui. The stratum is composed of limestone nipped with mudstone of upper Ordovician System and the weak interbeds have formed physiognomic ridges because of weathering and denudation.

One horseshoe-shaped depression is located on the hillside of the head-stream of Xiejiatao Valley and the northwest slope of Laolongji watershed. There is only one exit at the northeast and there are all cliffs at the other three directions, hanging highly on the Xiejiatao Trough Valley with an elevation of 2,100m. The grade of the ice ridge joining the bottom of cirque and trough valley is 40°~45°.

Many monumental peaks are developed at the upper part of Dajiuhu cirque and the depression of ice erosion, which are the relics of cirque in different direction after glacier erosion. The hillside is very steep and the peaks are rising up to the sky. The main peak in Bawang/ Eight King Mountain Village with an elevation of 2,624m is a typical horn. Glacial trough valleys on both sides of the watershed developed and became edge peaks.

上坝槽谷 It is 600m long ranging from the southwest hillside of Bawang Mountain Village to Shangba Trough Valley, the upper part of the latter is called Fangniu/ Feeding Cattle Bay and the lower part is called No. Three. The trough valley is 60-80m wide. Glacial flank moraine banks are remained at the north side of Fangniu Bay, distributed like a ladder. There is a hanging valley at the north hillside.

Shangba Trough Valley is the largest glacial one in Dajiuhu Lake which extends in northwest-to-southeast direction, whose upper part is connected with No. Three Valley. There are many branches of glacial trough valleys on both sides and at the headstream. Besides No. Three valley at the headstream, two branch valleys, No. Two and Miaowan are at the north hillside. Six branch valleys, No.4, No.5, No.6, No.7, No.8, and No.9 are all at the south side from east to west. The valleys of Miaowan and No.3 are small in scale, the other ones are all wide and long, 250-300m in width and 700-800m in length. The two slopes and the upper source of glacial trough valley are connected with cirques.

Two elliptic residual hills are arranged in parallel along the Jiudeng/ Nine Lamp River Valley and the hilltops are 10m high and 20-30m long, whose extending directions are same to the extending direction of the Valley. The hills are composed of the limestone of Cambrian System. The hilltops are mainly composed of some primrose deposit like sand and mild clay nipped with gravel as the result of glaciation. There are also some bedrock drum-like hills in front of No. Two and Miaowan Trough Valleys and in the Padi/ Crawling Bay Trough Valley. The closer to Dajiuhu Basin, the lower is the grade between the peak and bottom of drumlins, and the thicker is the deposit over the hilltops. There are more than 20 drumlins in Dajiuhu Basin.

小九湖冰川 U 形谷 Xiaojiuhu Glacial U-Valley originates from Bawang Mountain Village cirque and extends in south-to-north direction and ends at the upper part of Tongdong Valley, which is 4,000m long and 200m wide at the widest part. A glacial branch valley originated from Luogu Cliff converges into it at Beiping/ Stele Ground and the trough valley's body is round. The grade of the valley bottom is 5°~7°and the slope grade is 45°~50°. There are well-preserved hanging valleys and cirques at the east slope. Hanging valleys are 50m higher than valley bottom. The typical cirque is located at the upper part of Yangliu Bay and its bottom elevation is

2,100m.

There is a flanking moraine bank remained at the west side of Xiaojiuhu Trough Valley, which is well preserved from Beiping/ Stele Ground to Tongdong Valley, whose bank is 10m wide and 2m high from the top to bottom. The flanking moraine bank consists of three layers: the upper layer is 30cm thick quick soil; the middle layer is 1.7m thick grit with coarse deposited bedding; and the lower layer is moraine consisting of different-scale gravels nipped with sand and clay. There are huge boulders in the glacial moraine that is the result of glacial transport.

The glacial U-shaped valley is also called trough valley. As it is eroded by the glacier, the valley bottom is wide and flat and the slope is very precipitous, whose cross profile looks like the letter U and the longitudinal section looks like a trough. The valley's source reaches the mouth of Dapo Cliff and its south arrives at Pingqian Town, 2,000m long from south to north and 500m wide from east to west, with an elevation of 1,520m. There is a drumlin of bedrock at the valley bottom like a steamed bread and the peak is 12m higher than the valley bottom.

响水河瀑布 The waterfall develops in the middle of the Xiangshui River valley. The grade of the valley slope is as big as 40°~50° and the stratum is rigid tillite so that it is easy to form a waterfall. The voice of the water falling is very resounding, hence the name Water-Resounding River Waterfall. Th waterfall consists of two parts: the upper part is 10m high and a shallow pond is below it; the lower drop can be further divided into three stages and the water flows through stone riprap.

落羊河 The Luoyang/ Falling Goat River belongs to Duhe River System, whose upper branch is the Gaoqiao River and then the Pingqian River. The river originates from Jieling Region. As the rainwater here is abundant and the grade of the river is big, the river erosion is very strong. The cross profile of the upper part of the Luoyang River valley looks like the capital letter U and that of the lower part looks like V, called sheathed valley in physiognomy, which is the result of later strong downcut of the river on the trough valley base. Some river ravines are called flat bottom valley with same width from top to bottom, whose lower both walls are steep.

There are lots of big and small sundry gravels that are called cobble on the flood plain of the Luoyang River. They consist of three colors of gravels: yellow gravels with red stripes, cyaneous gravels with emerald stripes or lens-shaped stripes and gravels contained agate. The stratum can be called meta-sandstone or conglomerate that is developed in the Shennongjia Group of upper Cambrian System. They are conveyed here from the upper reaches by the river. When these cobbles are placed in the river water, their colors are more vivid so that they are called Color-changing stone.

Chapter 7 Banqiao Scenic Spot 板桥景区

板桥景区位于神农架山脉南麓，神农溪上游，神农架林区西南部的下谷坪乡。地势北高南低，最高处大窝坑海拔 3032 米，最低处石柱河口海拔 398 米，高差 2634 米。是具备亚热带、暖温带、温带、寒温带景观的风景区。区内雨量充沛，水源丰盛，山高坡陡而俊秀。景区位于神农架—神农溪—长江三峡旅游线（“双神”线）的中段，出露地层以震旦系—三叠系为主，断裂构造发育，河流、泉瀑、石林、岩溶景观比较丰富，有擎天石柱、闹水河、莺嘴岩、金猴石等景点。

这里是土家族聚居地，土家族人占 40%以上，民风淳朴，民族团结。当地的堂戏、皮影戏独具特色。明末清初是长峰地区重要的历史发展时期，大顺朝右果毅将军、南明永历帝册封的皖国公刘体纯驻兵于此，与“夔东十三家”农军一道联明抗清达 11 年之久，动人的历史故事广泛流传。

大（界岭）下（谷坪）公路北联九（大九湖）酒（酒壶坪）公路抵神农架腹地，南接巴东县与 209 国道公路连接。景区南端的石柱河至巴东港仅 70 公里，是神农架通向长江三峡的捷径。

Banqiao Scenic Spot is located in Xiaguping Town, at the southern foot of Shennongjia Mountains, and the upper reaches of Shennong Brook. The landform is high in the north and low in the south, the highest place in Dawokeng of 3,032m above the sea level and the lowest place in the Shizhu River of 398m above the sea level, a height difference of 2,634m between them. Here are the sub-tropic, warm-temperate and cold-temperate views in the same place, which is rich in rainfall and water, and the mountains are high and the slopes steep and attractive. The scenic spot is located at the middle part of the travel line, Shennongjia—Shennong Brook—the Three Gorges of the Changjiang River, dominated by Sinian System and Trasic System and developed by the fault structure, which is rich in river, spring, waterfall, stone forest, karst cave and other views, such as, Stone Pillar, the Naoshui River, Yingzui Cliff, and Golden Monkey Stone.

Here is the inhabiting place of Tujia ethnic minority which is more than 40% of the population, who live together happily and harmoniously. The local Hall Opera and shadow play are distinctive. During the late years of the Ming Dynasty (1368—1644) and the early years of the Qing Dynasty (1644—1912), General You Guoyi and Duke of Wanguo Liu Tichun had troops there for 11 years, left many moving stories.

Daxia Highway (Dajieling-Xiaguping) connects Jiujiu Highway (Dajiuhu-Jiuhuping) in the north to the central region of Shennongjia Forest Region, and connects Badong County and No. 209 national highway in the south. The highway connecting the Shizhu River and Badong Port is the shortcut between Shennongjia Forest Region and the Three Gorges of the Changjiang River.

板桥断裂带 Banqiao Fault Zone extends in the north-west direction through the Banqiao River, the Gaoqiao River and Mochi/ Ink Pool Cliff, which is about 40 km long, with an upward fault movement and and a dip angle of 70° ~ 80°towards the south-west. There is splaying out and compounding of fault near Banqiao, with intensive compressed shatter belt in fault walls. The fault zone cuts through the west foot of the main peak in Shennongjia Forest Region, and the cutting depth is over 1,000m. Along the fault zone, there are fault cliff, fault trough-valley, which is the negative landform. Here also developed some rockfall avalanche, landslide and earth flow.

石柱河 The Shizhu/ Rock Pillar River is originated from Dachong Ground, which is 10 km long and pours into the Yandu River at Bailin Cliff from southwest to northeast. There is a rock pillar at the river center of the lower reaches, which looks like a dragon rushing out of water surface, hence the name the Shizhu River. The river mouth is located at the place of 398m above the sea level, which is the lowest point in Shennongjia Forest Region.

擎天石柱 Gigantic Stone Pillar also called Little Wudang or Taihe Mountain, is situated at the lower reaches of the Shizhu River, which consists of the limestone of Cambrian System and Ordorvician System and whose top surface is 1,300m^2. Climbing onto the steep mountain and looking to the far away, you will find that there are 36 peaks to the northeast which look like as 36 people are welcoming the bride, a lively cattle sleeping at the southwest, and Shennong Brook/ the Yandu River is flowing to the Three Gorges of the Changjiang River like a jade belt at the south. Xiao (Little) Wudang was the Holy Land of Taoism in Shennong Brook Reaches.

There is a narrow stone crack called One-Line Sky, which is 80m long, 3-5m wide and 50m high. The Shizhu River flows through the crack bottom. The highway is cut in the crack wall. There is a complete anticline which is made of the limestone of Baota Formation, Ordovician System.

There are six rock caves in a row near the bank of the Banqiao River in the upper reaches of Shennong Brook and at foot of Zaizibao Mountain in the west side. The water flows out of the six rock caves with an interval of six hours in normal conditions, the time of flowing continued about 15 minutes. When the water is flowing, fast in speed and large in volume, which will make the river water rise by 10cm, so that it was called Fashui/ Water-Dividing Cave, for it is an intermittent spring, one kind of hydro-power type discharging water collectively by siphon pulsating flow. The intermittent period closely connected with its own siphon pulsating flow character and the season change. The interval in normal conditions is six hour per cycle, which be longer when the weather is fine for a long time and which will be shorter when it meets a long-time rain.

闹水河 The Naoshui/ Water-Resounding River is one of the sources of Shennong Brook (the Yandu River), which has three sources, and the other two are Yinmen/ Silver Door Cave under Xiaojieling Mountain and Majia Valley under Red Cliff. Seeing from the volume, the Naoshui River is the biggest one as the main source. The River flows down from the cliff with a flow of 0.6m^3/second in the whole year. The river water is increased abruptly at about 12 and 24 o'clock, which makes a big resounding voice, hen the river name. The water raising at regular intervals results from the siphon pulsating flow.

莺嘴岩 Yingzui/ Beak Cliff is located in Baiqiaohe Village of Xiaogu Town, with an elevation of 1,678m above the sea level. There is a hidden river about 1.2km far away from Yingzui Cliff in the northeast and in the east bank of the Naoshui River, which comes out of the siliceous banded dolomitite of Dengying Fomation, Sinian System. The underground river is 1,440m above the sea level, with a flow of 417m^3/second, which belongs to valley-side type.

板桥河 The Banqiao River is situated in the upper reaches of the Shennong Brook (the Yandu River), which is famed for the plank bridge built over the river for people to pass. Here are many big or small streams and rivers which originate from the south side of Dajieling Mountain and the southwest side of Small Shennongjia Mountain, such as the Naoshui River, the Yinmen

Cave and the Majia Valley, flowing through Banqiaohe Village and Xiaguping Ground from north to south and then into Badong County and the Changjiang River. There are many huge rolling stones in the River and on the two side slopes, which are mainly made by the cliff's collapsing and some of which are moved here by the flood from the upper reaches.

Majiagou Valley Collapse is situated in the upper part of the left bank of the Banqiao River near Xinglong Temple Village, Xiaguping Town, which is under the impact of Banqiao fault belt, composed of light-gray thick-layer white cloud stone of Dengying Formation, Sinian System, and whose collapsing source is 860-900m above the sea level, 250m long and 40m high. The collapsing pile is 680-860m above the sea level, 400m long, 300m wide and 5m thick, composed of stone and soil in a ratio of 3:7, and the main component is white cloud stone with the diameter of 20-40cm, the biggest one is about 200cm and the soil is powder clay with a coarse structure and fine water permeability. The collapse is influenced by Banqiao fault belt, the moving water, cliff unloading and earthquake.

金猴石 Golden Monkey Stone is located at the east side of the highway opposite to Xiaguping Administrative Office of Shennongjia Nature Reserve Administration, formed on a huge stone of black limestone of Cambrian System. This isolated stone looks like father and son monkeys standing together on duty to keep guard, hence the name. Now the stone is the remained part after long time weathering and erosion.

Chapter 8 Laojunshan Mountain Scenic Spot 老君山景区

老君山景区位于神农架自然保护区东片，它东起毛家河，南抵五指山，北至宋洛河冰洞山，西达乌龟峡，主峰海拔2936米。老君山气候寒凉，8月降霜，10月飞雪，雨量充沛，山泉广布，北麓是里叉河发源地，注入关门河入南河，南麓是九冲河源头注入湘坪河入香溪。这里山势雄伟，层峦叠嶂，景色秀丽。

老君山生物资源丰富，有成片的华山松、桦树、青冈树、白杨、箭竹和珍贵的腊梅、稀有的珙桐。产有党参、天麻、延龄草、江边一碗水、七叶一枝花、文王一支笔等野生珍稀药材。金丝猴、猕猴、金钱豹、青羊、野猪、黑熊、白熊、白獐、白蛇以及被称为“奇异动物”之一的驴头狼等在山林洞穴中繁衍生息。老君山人迹罕至，堪称“生物乐园”，是旅游探奇、科研考察的理想天地，景点有九冲大断裂、五指山、关门岩、宋洛河等。

Laojunshan/ Old Taoist Priest Mountain Scenic Spot is situated in the east of Shennongjia National Nature Reserve Region, beginning from the Maojia River in the east, to Wuzhi/ Five Finger Mountain in the south, to Bingdong/ Ice Cave Mountain in the north, and Wugui/ Tortoise Gorge in the west, whose main peak is 2,936m above the sea level. Here are with cool weather, having frost in August and snow in October, rich in rainfall and mountain stream. The Licha River originates here in the north and converges in the Guanmen River and then in the South River. The Jiuchong River originates here in the south and converges in the Xiangping River and then in the Xiang/ Honey Stream. The mountains here are precipitous and marvelous, forming a charming view.

The zoology and botany resources here are extremely rich, including lots of Mount Hua pine, birch, white poplar, arrow bamboo, wintersweet, dangshen, gastrodia tuer, birthroot and other rare herbs, and golden monkey, macaque, leopard, green sheep, wild pig, black bear, white bear, white snake, donkey-headed wolf and other rare animals. The Scenic Spot is densely forest and few travelled by human beings, just a Biological Paradise and the ideal place of travelling, exploring and scientific research. Here are Jiuchong Large Fault, Five-Finger Mountain, Guanmen/ Closing-Door Cliff, the Songluo River and so on.

九冲大断裂 Jiuchong Large Fault extends in the northwest direction in Laojun Mountain and the Jiuchong River, 28km long, in a slight wave bend shape. The fault section is steep and almost vertical, rising up in the southwest, with some convergence of the branches at the two ends. Some of the landform is negative relief with some spring groups. The two sides of the Fault are of Shennongjia Groups and Sinian System, with a steep dip of fault surface. The Fault was strongly silicated, which formed a belt of 50-60m wide.

The Jiuchong River Fault Scarp of 60m in height was caused by the structural movement of the fault and strong trenching of the river, along which are high mountains, deep canyons and pools, winding streams and flying waterfalls. The narrow valley cut deeply underground and formed a stream with roaring water.

五指山 Wuzhi /Five-Finger Mountain is located on the west side of Wanchao Mountain, facing Laojunshan/ Old Taoist Priest Mountain in the north, looking like a huge palm with five uprising fingers. There are deep streams with resounding flowing water in the mountains. There is a pool of 10m in length on the east dome in Thumb Peak, whose water is black. The legend says that the old Taoist Priest cleaned his writing brush in the pool and made the water black now, so named it Yanwo/ Inkstone Pool.

关门岩 Guanmen/ Closing Door Cliff is composed of dolomitite breccia, silicic-banded dolomitite, and carbonaceous-muddy siltite of Dayanping Formation, Shennongjia Group. The Jiuchong Fault stroke across here and formed a steep cliff. Guanmen Cliff is a karst peak protecting Laojunshan Original Forest like a dutiful guard.

宋洛河 The Songluo River originates from the north slope of Motian/ Toughing Sky Ridge with the source of which starting from the deep Yingwo/ Eagle Nest Cave, 30km long and 1,200m above the sea level, formed high steep cliffs. There are eight scenic spots long the riverway, such as Panlong/ Twisting Dragon Bridge, Fanlong/ Dragon Cliff, Ice-Cave Mountain, Songluo Water, Jiadao Canyon, Inverted Golden Clock, Shanshu/ Fir Ground, and Motian Ridge. The Jiadao River is the key section that is most dangerously steep, hence known as The gate to Devil Hall.

The upper part of Shichaohe Formation of Shennongjia Group is composed of varicolored siliceous conglomerate of seashore sedimentation. Among them, ellipsoid gravel as cryptocrystalline aggregate of quartz, is of shining colors, sufficient hardness and smooth surface, with high value in viewing, hence the name Agate Stone.

Chapter 9 Tourguide Words of Shennongjia Forest Region 神农架林区导游词

1. Shennongjia Museums 神农架博物馆

游客中心 Tourist Reception Center

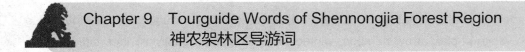

Ladies and gentlemen, welcome to Shennongjia Nature Museum. We are now in the Tourist Reception Center, and here is a topographic model of Shennongjia Nature Reserve, from which you can have an overview of its topography and location.

The green lights indicate the boundary of Shennongjia. Covering a total area of 3,253 square kilometers, Shennongjia has a population of 83 thousand. Here is where we are now, Guanmenshan/ Closing Door Mountain Subarea. The peak with the red name plate is Shennong Peak, the highest peak of central China, and its height is 3,106.2 meters above the sea level.

Now the lights indicate the boundary of Shennongjia Geopark. With a total area of 1,022 square kilometers, Shennongjia Geopark consists of five subareas. We'll learn more about the Geopark in the Geo-museum.

That is the Shennongjia Airport under construction and will be finished in this October. You can fly here next time.

The blue lights indicate 317 rivers in Shennongjia. The yellow lights indicate highways, and this is a national highway that connects Yichang City and Shennongjia Forest Region. OK, please enjoy yourself.

The museum has a Chinese and English bilingual interpretation system. Please get the audio interpreters at the reception desk. When you use it, you can choose English first, and then enter the number of the item on which you are interested. For example, you can enter 002 if you want to know about the reception center. Auto-sensors are installed in key informative parts. You can have the information without selecting the number. If you need to go to the rest room, please go this way.

OK, let us go to the Geo-Museum. Please look at that statue, it tells us a true story of a heroine in 1970s. The girl's name was Chen Chuanxiang, who killed a leopard with her bare hands in order to save a kid. Let's move on.

地质博物馆 Geo-Museum

The Geo-museum mainly introduces Shennongjia Geopark, the ancient strata of Shennongjia Group, the geological evolution history, rich mineral resources and magnificent geological landscape of Shennongjia.

That is the Geo-Museum, let's go and see. This is a map of Shennongjia Geopark. With a total area of 1,022 square kilometers, Shennongjia Geopark consists of five subareas, namely ShennongTop, Guanmenshan/ Closing Door Mountain, Laojunshan /Old Taoist Priest Mountain, Dajiuhu Lake/ Big Nine Lake and Tianyan Cliff.

Please look at this map. The pink part is Shennongjia Group, which was formed 1.9 to 1 billion years ago. Most of the rocks of Shennongjia belong to Shennongjia Group.

From the bottom to the top, Shennongjia Group can be divided into four formations: Zhengjiaya Formation, Shicaohe Formation, Dawokeng Formation and Kuangshishan Formation. All the cabinets display the rocks from Shennongjia area.

This section is mainly about the geological development history of the earth and Shennongjia area. The geological history of Shennongjia can be divided into 4 stages. After repeated change between ocean and continental environment, the landform of Shennongjia gradually took shape. This cabinet displays the three rock types of the earth's lithosphere. These are magmatic rocks and sedimentary rocks collected in Shennongjia. And this one is a metamorphic rock.

Shennongjia is one of China's important mineral resource bases. According to survey, there are 15 useful minerals in Shennongjia. Some minerals and wonder stones are displayed here. This section mainly introduces glacial events and glacial relics. These are glacial rocks.

The video is displaying the magnificent geological landscape of Shennongjia, including alpine landform, fluvial landform and karst landform. This section introduces the 5 subareas of Shennongjia Geopark. OK, please use the Audio Guide and enjoy yourself, and ask me if you have any questions.

The wonder-stone section is downstairs, let's go and have a look.

奇石馆 Wonder Stone Gallery

Most of the rocks displayed in the Wonder Stone Gallery were collected from Shennongjia area. With various colors and shapes, these rocks are of high ornamental value. This agate stone belongs to Dawokeng Formation. Let's go to watch a movie about Shennongjia.

4D 影院 4D Cinema

In this 4D cinema tourists can personally experience the natural scenery of Shennongjia. Please take the seats of the first five rows in the middle. The film will begin in a minute, please be seated and put on your glasses. Let's enjoy.

生物博物馆 Bio-museum

There are over 4,000 species of higher plants, and over 500 species of vertebrates. We will know more in the bio-museum. The first floor is the plant section, and the second floor the animal section. Here are some fossils of different geological times. The biological cladogram demonstrates the history of biological evolution.

植物馆 Plants Section

The next section is about the 6 vegetation types of Shennongjia, including broad-leaf forest, coniferous forest, bamboo forest, mash, meadow and bush. These are the plant specimens collected from Shennongjia Area. Now let's enjoy the charm of Chinese Dove Tree, a first-class national protected species. When the flowers are blown by the wind, they look like flying doves.

This section is a gene bank of Shennongjia area. Shennongjia is the largest seeds bank of the northern subtropical zone. Some types of seeds are displayed here, including walnut, chestnut, acorn, peanut, wild soybean, Chinese dove tree, azalea, impatiens, etc. Besides, the rare plants and Chinese medicinal herbs are also introduced here. Shennongjia has more than 2,000 species of wild flowers, and more than 300 are displayed here. There are over 2,000 species of Chinese medicinal herbs.

You can use the audio interpreters to learn about them.

动物馆 Animal Section

This is a true representation of the scene of various animals in the subalpine wetland of Shennongjia. There are white stork, white spoonbill, mandarin duck, wild duck, etc. There are 308 species of birds in Shennongjia. You can hear many of them in this Bird Singing Gallery.

These are some animals that live in the primitive forests in Shennongjia. This place mainly displays the specimens of birds and mammal. This is the national treasure, Golden Snub-nosed Monkey. You can enter No.58 in your audio interpreter to know more about it.

There are 47 species of fishes, 40 species of reptilians, and 23 species of amphibians in Shennongjia. The next section mainly displays amphibian, reptilian, fishes and insecta. These are specimens of snakes. These are fishes, Asiatic salamander and frogs. There are over 4,000 species of insects in Shennongjia, and over 700 specimens of beautiful insects are displayed here.

科学探索馆 Scientific Exploration Museum

The Scientific Exploration Museum mainly introduces the history and achievements of the scientific explorations in Shennongjia. This section introduces the significant inventions and contributions made by Shennong. The eight great inventions made by Shennong are cattle ploughing, the five-string instrument, hemp clothing, wooden, stone and pottery housewares, primitive agriculture, Chinese medicine, market trade and well irrigation.

American botanist Henry Wilson was the first foreigner to investigate on Chinese plants. This is a projector, we can use it to read Wilson’s exploration journal. This is a comparison of Shennongjia between now and 100 years ago.

Lots of animal fossils and Paleolithic tools used by ancient people have been excavated from the Rhino Cave, which are key material evidence for the study on geology, animal and ancient people’s activities here. Here is the introduction of some major geological expeditions and discoveries. This video is about the albino animals, including bear, Golden Snub-nosed Monkey, snake, toad and so on. No scientific answer has been found.

The next section is about the history of explorations on animals and plants. If you want to know more, please use your audio interpreter. The mystery of Wildman of Shennongjia is world-famous and arouses curiosity of many people. These are Wildman witness events, and these are the photos of the witnesses, mainly including government officials, local peasants and tourists.

Let’s see an animation about one of the witness events. Wildman, or Big Foot, have been seen in many places around the world. This is the distribution map of the witness events. Whether wildman exists is still a mystery.

野人洞 Wildman cave

A Wildman living scene is simulated for tourists' exploration.

茶艺馆 Tea gallery

This is a tea gallery, we can take a rest and have some tea here. This way, please. Please have a seat and wait a minute. We have learned about the geology, animals and plants of Shennongjia. Now let's go to the folkway museum to experience the local life style. The Folkway Museum displays various local articles for daily use.

2. Charming Bushes and the "Yinyuhe Canyon" 迷人垱与阴峪河大峡谷

Mirentang/ Charming Bushes or "Natural Labyrinth" actually is a tract of arrow-bamboo bushes. The arrow-bamboo is the most important alpine vegetation type in Shennongjia area. People sometimes will get lost within the bushes here, especially in foggy weather, so this place is called the "Natural Labyrinth".

When passing the dense arrow-bamboo bushes, you can enjoy the alpine fir forest and rock blocks with strange shapes. We are now on a viewing deck. Here is the best place to view the "Yinyuhe Canyon", which is the deepest valley in central China. The strong cutting and deeply weathered valleys in the area were caused by regional extension faults and vertical joints derived from uplift of Shennongjia area. The "Yinyuhe Canyon" is one of the best representatives. With 40 km in length and 2,200 meters of altitude difference, the "Yinyuhe Canyon" is grand and magnificent. The "Yinyuhe Canyon" is a vast steep-walled gorge. The whole valley is covered by thick vegetation. Clear vertical plant zonation reflects that the terrain and topography control the distribution of vegetation.

As one of the most well-preserved primitive forests, the "Yinyuhe Canyon" is an ideal habitat for Golden Snub-nosed Monkey and Giant Salamander, because of its dense trees and vines, as well as riptide and rapid. The forest coverage here is over 80%, so it is called "The Green Labyrinth" and "The Paradise of Giant Salamander".

Standing here you can get a sweeping view of the precipitous sight of the "Yinyuhe Canyon", especially in clear days. Inside the canyon, the living condition is so tough that only golden eagle can nest on the cliffs. That is why the "Yinyuhe Canyon" is also called the "Eagle-Fish-River Valley". It is almost impassable for people except for professional expeditions.

3. Jinhouling/ Golden Monkey Ridge 金猴岭

With an altitude of 3,019m, Jinhouling/ Golden Monkey Ridge is one of the habitats of the famous Golden Snub-nosed Monkeys, which is a first class national protected animal. The thick primitive forest and Jinhou/ Golden Monkey Stream that flows all the year round are the most attractive. Two separated footpaths have been set within the scenic area: walking up, you can enjoy the natural scenery of thick primitive forest along a circular footpath; walking down you can appreciate riptide and beautiful waterfalls.

This thick forest is with lots of typical primitive forest characteristics; such as the quite thick layers of humus formed from putrid branches and leaves, which indicates that the forest has already been here for many many years; the concomitance of ancient species, such as orchid and fern; lots of adnascent fungus and moss, which prefer dark and humid environment; and naturally rotten wood that indicates there is no any human intervention in the forest. There is even the phenomenon of "vine strangling" in this forest, which usually can only be seen in tropical primitive forests. This reveals the bio-diversity in Shennong Top subarea.

Here in Jinhouling, the Jinhou/ Golden Monkey Stream flows all the year round, and forms lots of riptide and beautiful waterfalls especially after rainfalls. It is quite interesting that in some area with weak runoff, you can still hear rumble of running water. It is because the streams become underground river.

The primitive forest not only conserves moisture, but also generates oxygen, it is actually a huge generator of negative oxygen ions. The Jinhou Top primitive forest can be praised as a "Natural Oxygen Bar", because the average content of negative oxygen ions reaches up to 160 thousands per-cubic centimeter.

Walking down along the steps, we can enjoy a string of torrents and waterfalls. Several bridges and pavilions are scattered along the footpath providing comfort and safety for tourists. At dull tourist season, you may see pheasants or other birds go around here foraging. It implicates rich bio-diversity in Shennongjia Geopark, as well as the harmonious coexistence between human and animals.

4. The Guanmenshan Mountain Park 官门山

Near the parking lot there is a well-preserved outcrop of glacial deposits named as Nantuo Formation by B. Willis in 1907. Stratigraphically, the Nantuo Formation lies at the top of the Neoproterozoic Nanhua System. Although the rock of Nantuo Formation mainly comprises grayish-green mass muddy and sandy breccias with poor sorting, and the gravels are of bad roundness, it provides good evidence to the research about the Neoproterozoic glacial period.

The design of the gate of the Guanmenshan/ Closing Door Mountain Park is quite unique. It is a statue of a mother with her son of the mysterious Shennongjia Wildman in local legend. The image of mother and son is a symbol of the great mother love and the humanitarian spirit. It represents an idea in man's respect for Mother Nature and also the wish for a harmonious coexistence with it.

With the theme of "Exploration and Discovery", the Guanmenshan Park is a special zone established for the purpose of scientific research and explorations, science popularization and ecotourism experiences. The scenic spots spread along the Shicaohe River. Roaring waters rush now on the ground, but then disappear into complicated underground river channels. What a spectacular scene! Here you can see over 2,500 species of plants that range from the subtropics to the cool temperate. An 8-km hiking trail has been built along the river bank for visitors to take a close look at such a rich diversity of rocks, animals and plants.

The Guanmenshan Park possesses several gardens of floral plants and fruit trees, such as the Wintersweet Garden, the Orchid Garden, the Azalea Garden and the All-kinds-of-fruit Garden. You can also see centers and breeding or growing grounds for the research of rare animal and plants, such as the Giant Salamander Breeding and Research Center, the Spotted Deer Breeding Base, and the Bee House. The Nature Museum is built here to meet up any possible interest in geology, biology, scientific explorations or folk cultures: they are all in one here! With all these great things, plus a brand-new 4-D cinema and many other cultural sites, the Guanmenshan Park makes a couldn't-be-better teaching ground for scientific studies, explorations and science popularization.

Built in August, 2007 at 1,280 meters above sea level, the Orchid Garden covers an area of nearly 17,000 m^2. It plants over 10,000 corms of orchids including 36 genera and over 90 species. Walking through the garden you can appreciate not only the orchids, but also a great deal of beautifully shaped fossil stromatolite in the rocks at the roadside and on the pavement slabs under your feet. Fossil stromatolite was primitive unicellular algae that grew on the surface of rocks in the sea. Generation after generation, the algae adsorbed tiny sedimentary particles in the sea water while they grew, and meanwhile a concentric fossil structure took its shape bit by bit one layer on top of another. From the variations of the thickness of annual layers and other characteristics of stromatolite, a lot can be discovered about how climate changed over time in that period. Stramotolite's algae played a critically important role in emerging life and their reproduction on the Earth: photosynthesis by the algae produced oxygen, which is indispensable for all of other lives that were to appear later.

The Shicaohe Formation of the Shennongjia Group takes its name from the outcrops beside this bridge. As the second lithostratigraphic unit in the Shennongjia Group, the Shicaohe Formation comprises mainly of dolomitic rocks and dolomites with siliceous bands and abundant fossil stromatolite. The lithological characteristics of this formation can be clearly observed here from the profiles along the riverbank and roadside.

For the purpose of science popularization, the Shennongjia Nature Museum has been built in Guanmenshan subarea to demonstrate the local rich biodiversity and human history. The Museum is made up of a variety of specialized sections: the Geo-museum, the Eco-museum, the Folkway Museum, the Wonder Stone Gallery, the Calligraphy & Painting Gallery, and so on. It also includes other resources and facilities such as the "Wildman Cave" for expeditions, the "Reception Lobby", the "Lecture Hall", and an arc screen cinema. The facilities in this museum have proven to be a good support to the scientific research and science popularization， as well as tourism promotion of the Shennongjia Resort by extending her communications with the outside. The facilities of museum also clearly demonstrate the efforts of administrators of the Geopark in the protection of natural resources. It will certainly elevate the connotation of scientific-cultural tourism, and satisfy visitors' quest for explorations into the unknown.

Here is the research and viewing area for protected Chinese Giant Salamanders. As a rare, ancient relic species, the Giant Salamanders are commonly believed to have originated in the late Devonian period, which dates back to 350 million years ago. The giant salamanders are nocturnal animals. They prefer undisturbed habitats and are most often found in mountain rocky streams or karst caves. They make yell just like the cry of infant, so they are also called the Infant Fish by the locals. There are 35 giant salamander breeding pools that cover more than 1,000 square meters area. They are built for breeding and researching into this unique and rare species of amphibians. Besides giant salamanders, we also built snake and spotted deer breeding and researching yards in Guanmenshan subarea.

The Bee House in Guanmenshan subarea was built in May, 2011 and has more than 1,100 bee hives, each of them produces up to 6 kg of honey a year. The mountains in Shennongjia are a huge treasure-house of plants. Over 2,000 plant species were discovered in the Guanmenshan Valley, 84% of which rely on honey bees for pollination. This abundant reservoir of bee plants is clear of contamination from chemical fertilizers and pesticides, provides an excellent natural source of nectar, and greatly contributes to the extraordinary medical and healthcare properties of the honey production here.

5. Shennong Valley 神农谷

神农谷 As one of the most attractive scenic spots of Shennong Top Subarea, with a maximum sea-level elevation of 2,820m, Shennong Valley has a height difference of over 400 meters from the bottom to this viewing platform. To allow the tourists to fully enjoy the miraculous scenery, a 4.4km long hiking trail was specially designed and built. Here is a stone lion, called the "Sitting Golden Lion"; it guards this entrance.

With quite complete facilities, such as hiking trail, safety devices and interpretation system, Shennong Top Subarea passed the quality certification of ISO9000 and ISO14000, and was approved by China National Tourism Administration as a National "Five-A" Tourist Scenic Area in January 2012.

We will walk down here to the bottom of the valley, and then climb up to another entrance along this winding hiking trail. During the walking we will enjoy not only mythic pretty scenery, but also beautiful alpine vegetation, for example the bamboo bushes, alpine fir and meadow, alpine azalea and procumbent juniper. There are lots of geological phenomena in the valley, such as the rocks that make up the valley-wall, including siliceous striped dolomite, slate, basal conglomerate, etc. and various sedimentary structures, for example, fine beddings and interlayered folds; and the contact relationship between the strata. It is worth to be mentioned that there is an outcrop of diabase intrusion which is of great significance to the global geological correlation for the event of the Rodinia super-continent splitting.

According to stratigraphic division, the rocks exposed in the valley belong to "Shicaohe Formation" and "Dawokeng Formation" of "Shennongjia Group", which are mainly made up of dolomite. The formation of this valley was caused by long term of weathering, frost splitting, collapsing and karst corrosion on the basis of extension faults and vertical joints. The topography of the valley is characterized by steep cliffs and swarm of stalagmites and peak forest. With high aesthetic value, it is a typical landscape formed by exogenous geologic agents.

Rambling on the hiking trail, you can see gorgeous natural scenery. You may have already noticed that just as a big dragon that twines among the peak forest and cliffs, this hiking trail itself makes a beautiful Chinese painting. Along the hiking trail 26 geological and geomorphologic landscape interpretation boards have been built for science popularization and education.

The clouds of Shennong Valley is one of scenic highlights. The floating clouds increase the charm of the valley, and make it more worth viewing. Against the cliffs, tall and straight peaks and stalagmites arranged upwards from the bottom of the valley; they are flickering in the floating clouds, and changing their shapes all the time. This scenery really brings strong visual impact and soul shock.

In this gully, piles of rock blocks with different sizes and lithologic features can be seen. The weathered and collapsed rock debris is moved by intermittent floods. Each single block of the rocks in this gully tells a story about its formation, its change, and how it came here.

辉绿岩 Please look at this rock; it is diabase, a mafic intrusive igneous rock. Look at this xenolith of dolomite surrounded by the intrusive body; it provides good evidence to the relationship between these two rock types. About 7 hundred million years ago, in Shennongjia area, the mafic igneous rocks, mainly as diabase, intruded into different mesoproterozoic sedimentary strata, including the Shennongjia Group. According to geochemical analysis, tectonically the diabase has most characters of the continental extension environment. So, it may provide evidence to the splitting of “Rodinia Supercontinent”. It is an important geological event and can be correlated globally.

Here you can see a parallel unconformity: the purplish red siltstone with interlayered dolomite of “Shicaohe Formation” lies below, and above it is the “Dawokeng Formation”, which is made up of basal conglomerate, thin-bedded sandy mudstone and medium to thick bedded dolomite. The appearance of basal conglomerate and the gradual change of sedimentary grains ascendingly from coarse to fine indicates a new marine sedimentary cycle.

This sequence of medium-thick bedded pale fine-crystalline dolomite with siliceous bands, which was formed 13 hundred million years ago, belongs to “Shicaohe Formation” of “Shennongjia Group”. The formation of siliceous striped dolomite reflects a rhythmic alternation between carbonate and silica deposit sediments, as well as the different sedimentary conditions. Since dolomite is more subject to weathering, differential weathering made siliceous bands protrude from the rock surface and forming this beautiful appearance.

Tiny bedding structures can be seen in the siliceous silty dolomite of “Dawokeng Formation”, which was formed 13-12 hundred million years ago. With 3-8 millimetre thickness, these very thin bedding show regular light-dark color changes. It may imply seasonal change during its deposition.

This interesting sedimentary structure is called boudinage. Actually, these separated rock blocks with line array once belonged to a same layer. During the compaction and diagenesis, weak sediment layers formed plastic flows, meanwhile the rigid layers broke into pieces surrounded by the plastic flow of weak sediments and resulted in the boudinage.

There are quite lots of the box trees in this valley. Box tree is one of the evergreen tree species, which can grow up to 8-10 meters high. These trees often grow in areas below 2,500 meters above the sea level. Box tree has a graceful posture with small but thick glossy leaves. They always keep beautiful green color in any season. Since box tree is of fine wood character, it is an ideal material for wood carving. But it is strictly protected here by the Geopark.

6. Shennong Alter 神农坛

Ladies and Gentleman, please be seated, now we are going to Shennong Alter. The Shennong Altar, six kilometers away from Muyu Town, is the south entrance to the Geopark, which tells you what Shennong, or Emperor Yan, really means to China by a lot of miracles he made. He was virtually one of the founders of the great, long-lasting Chinese Civilization. In order to worship him, people across the country come here every year to pay their highest tribute to him. Now, we have arrived in the scenic area. Please follow me to get off the bus. Ladies and Gentleman, here is the park for remembering the Emperor Yan.

Please look back there, the gate of this area, it takes the form of a pair of buffalo horns made of brass and coated with gold. You may feel it strange. According to the legend, Emperor Yan had a buffalo head and human body. They are the logo of the resort. As the buffalo horns were the totem of the Shennong's prehistoric agrarian tribe, they show the local people's reflection on the past of an amazing agricultural civilization, as well as their wish to pass this agrarian tradition down.

Shennong Alter Scenic Spot is a place to celebrate the great achievements of Shennong. This big board gives the main information about this area. You can take a closer look at it. The main attractions include the 24 Solar Terms Garden, Shennong Altar, the 1,000-year-old King of David Keteleeria, the Shennong Tea Farm, and the Shennong Merit & Virtue Woods, etc. Now we are at the first grade square. Please follow me to move on.

Shennongtan, or the Shennong Altar, is built on a relic of old rocky landslide. Surrounded by mountains on the three sides, the block of the landslide inclines step by step to the river gully. According to Fengshui, the Chinese traditional geomatics, the topography of Shennongtan is perfect, so, it is really a treasure ground. Major buildings and various gardens are laid out on the slope one step after another up to the top, which constitute a magnificent and harmonious view in the park.

Now we are at the second grade square. Look at this big stone which is covered by the green plants, doesn't it look like a frog? This pictographic rock was naturally formed by dolomite. If you like it, you can take a photo here.

Now, let's move on. Our next stop is the 24 Solar Terms Garden. Please be careful and watch your steps. Here you can see 24 round-roof buildings decorated with relevant style; each of them represents a solar term. In the Chinese calendar, a year falls into 24 equal solar terms, including 12 major and 12 minor solar terms interlaced with each other. Believed to have been first created by Shennong and other ancestors of Chinese people, the 24 solar terms system is the result of the ancient people's constant observation and exploration on astronomy, weather and phenology.

This house represents Slight Heat. It means that weather starts to getting hot, but not very hot. Great heat is the hottest period of a year. All of these houses are for tourists to live in. This is a stone disc demonstrating the locations and names of the 24 solar terms.

We are now in the Grain in Ear. In June, there are two solar terms. One is called Mangzhong or Grain in Ear, and the other is named Xiazhi or the Summer Solstice. Mangzhong is the busiest time of a year for agricultural production and it means the harvest is coming. Xiazhi is the date with longest daytime and it means the summer has arrived.

OK, now let's head to the Shennong Altar, it is the core of the site. Built in 1997, this altar is where the descendants of Shennong pay tribute to their ancestor, worship their gods and pray for blessings. Solemn rituals are held here every year in honor of Shennong. Here you can see several men in the dress of ethnic minorities, they are the folk band in this scenic area.

That big tree is the King of David Keteleeria. It's over 1,200 years old and is the biggest tree in Shennongjia Region. We will take a closer look at it later. And here is the best position to take a photo with the whole tree, you can take photos if you like. This tree is Henry Emmenopterys, a Chinese peculiar rare species that has been listed as a class 2 national protected plant. English botanist EH. Wilson praised it as the Glory of the Chinese Forests.

Now we've arrived at the Shennong Altar. The giant statue on top is Shennong, one of the forefathers of the Chinese people. 21m tall, 35m wide, together the total is 56, a symbol of great unity of the 56 ethnic groups in China. The Shennong Altar is built precisely in Chinese royal garden style. In front of Shennong's statue is the Heaven Altar reserved specially for emperors in rituals; below it here is an Earth Altar, which is the place, by a strict hierarchy, for ordinary people in rituals.

The Earth Altar is designed according to Yinyang and Wuxing in the paradigm of "a square earth under spherical heavens", the typical Taoist arrangement of the universe, accurate and thought-provoking. Ancient Chinese people believed that everything in the world was made of five elements: metal, wood, water, fire and earth, which are called Wuxing in Chinese language. The mutual promotion and restraint between the five elements can explain the interrelation of all different things. Such rules summarized by ancient people from life practices have always been respected.

Shennong made many great achievements in history, the eight main great inventions made by Shennong are cattle ploughing, the five-string instrument, hemp clothing, wooden, stone and pottery housewares, primitive agriculture, Chinese medicine, market trade and well irrigation. Shennong is indeed the great forefather of Chinese agricultural civilization.

There is a ritual today. We will watch it and you can learn something about the folk culture in Shennongjia. OK, the ritual has finished. Let's move on to take a close look at the King of David Keteleeria. It's 48 meters tall and 2.8 meters in diameter; it takes 5 or 6 men to hug it hand in hand.

Now, you can still see many root of it. It is said that, long time ago, most of tree's root was exposed outside. The scene was very spectacular. In order to protect this tree, the local people buried its root with soil, that's why this tree is a lot higher than the area around. It was found that the underground water kept seeping out. The fact that this tree grows so flourishingly that must have something to do with the underground water. This tree is a symbol of health and long life, so it has become a wishing tree. The red cloth is hung there by local people and tourists to express their gratitude for their wishes made here became true.

Next we will go to see the most important miracle that Shennong made in the ancient time—the Chinese herbs. Here is the Shennong Herbal Garden. Here grow over 100 species of herbs which are peculiar to Shennongjia. They can not only cure but also prevent many diseases. The Shennong Herbal Garden is established for the purpose of cultivating precious herbs and studying their usage in Chinese medicine.

This is the Shennong Tea Farm, and here grows alpine tea. Due to the high elevation, the tea trees are well moisturized by the mist and clouds all year round, so their leaves can be made into high quality natural organic tea. OK, Let's have a taste in the tea house over there.

OK, ladies and gentlemen, let's continue our walk through the Shennong Herbal Garden, and enjoy the beauty of flowers as well. Many medicinal herbs found in Shennongjia are included in Shennong's Herbal Classic. Shennong's Herbal Classic is China's earliest pharmaceutical book. The book records 365 medicines, including 252 botanical medicines, 67 animal medicines and 46 mineral medicines. According to the properties and functions these medicines are divided into three different levels. Compiled by many medical scientists in Eastern Han Dynasty on the basis of previous pharmaceutical experiences, this book made the first systematic summarization in history on Chinese traditional medicines.

Here on the platform, you can see a magnificent Chinese painting on the cliff. Actually, people have different opinions about it, some think that is a galloping horse, and others believe there is a young girl. I saw a horse and also a girl in the right side. It is really an amazing gift from the great nature.

Now, we have arrived at Shennong Merit & Virtue Woods. In this place grow over 2,000 trees of more than 40 ancient, rare and endangered species. By allowing people to subscribe them, it will promote love devotion and afforestation, establish environment protection and low-carbon life, and encourage common effort to build an ecological civilization.

You could see many rocks under the trees, the names on the rocks are the subscribers' names. There are many davidia involucrate trees here. This plant is also called Chinese dove tree, because its flowers look like flying doves. As a first-class national protected species, it is a world-famous rare relic species survived the Tertiary Ice Age. This species is well worth research and protection and is of high ornamental value.

After we walk down, we will go to another scenic area. Now you can enjoy the natural beauties. Stromatolites, formed 1.2-1.1 billion years ago, contain the oldest fossils on the earth.

During the growth of the lower unicellular blue-green algae, they bound lime mud and lime sand, and thus formed alternating dark and bright layers. And this is the interpretation board for stromatolite. You could take a close look at it.

7. The Tiansheng Bridge 天生桥

Ladies and gentlemen, now we are heading to the Tiansheng/ Nature-Made Bridge Scenic Spot. It will take us about 10 minutes to get there. Tiansheng Bridge Scenic Spot is an Eco-culture tourist area that integrates natural landscape, the culture of Ba tribe, folkways, recreation and sight-seeing. The beautiful natural scenery and the folk buildings make up a magnificent landscape scroll.

On the way, you can see green mountains, colorful flowers and waterfalls. May you have a nice day! Now you can enjoy the scenery outside.

Here we have arrived at the Tiansheng Bridge Scenic Spot. The toilet is over there, if you need to wash your hands, please go ahead.

Tiansheng Bridge scenic spot is a 5A national tourist attraction. 5A is the top class. That is the geological protection station of this area.

OK, please follow me to begin our sightseeing.

Now we are standing on the Square of Raw Stones. And there is a pebble thatched cottage. They are both characteristic because they were built with local building materials. If you observe carefully, you will find many fossils in the stones.

Tiansheng Bridge Scenic Spot has an altitude of 1,800 meters and an area of 20 km^2. The three high peaks, Caomao/ Straw Cap Peak, Yingzi Cliff, and Gaodeng Peak, form a natural barrier.

Here, you can see a big board, it gives the main information about this area. If you are interested, you may take a close look at it.

Tiansheng Bridge, is a natural formation of an arc. Viewed from afar, that 17m high penetrating rock cave looks like a bridge, and that's why the area in and around is called Tiansheng/ Nature-Made Bridge.

The rocks that make up this natural bridge were formed in the Mesoproterozoic and belong to the Shicaohe Formation, Shennongjia Group, whose main content is medium-bedded dolomite.

The Shennongjia Group is the most exposed of all stratigraphic units in this Geopark, a set of strata in continental margin rift basin at the northern margin of the Changjiang Craton, which was formed by extensional structure.

Shennongjia Group can be divided into four formations, named accordingly as Zhengjiaya Formation, Shicaohe Formation, Dawokeng Formation and Kuangshishan Formation. Exposed here in the Tiansheng Bridge area is the dolomite of the Shicaohe Formation. The stratotype sections of all the four formations are established in the Shennongjia Region.

Now let's start our trip today. Please be careful and watch your step. In order to make the best use of the abundant natural resources, and to create perfect tourist conditions, the Geopark has built a 2.6 km circle hiking trail in the valley. The trail will take you to many wonderful view sites, such as the Yishui Bridge, Flying Waterfall through Rock Fissure, Eagle Pool, Moss-covered Stream and so on.

Here we are at the Yishui Bridge, the first bridge of this scenic area.

Please look up. The underground water flows through the rock fissure and forms a waterfall. In sunny days, you can see very beautiful rainbows here. That is the interpretation board for Flying Waterfall through Rock Fissure. If you are interested, you may take a closer look at it. Let's move on, and our next stop is Eagle Pool.

This pool is called the Eagle Pool, because we can often see the reflection of flying eagle in the water. The pool is about 8 meters deep, and in this pool lives Giant Salamander, a class 2 national protected animal.

This cave is about 17m high, a stream flows through it into The Yellow Rock River. Travelling up the stream, you will arrive at the Orchid Mountain. This huge karst cave is a masterpiece of wonders created by erosion and weathering. Crystal clear stream water rushes out of the cave and forms overlapping waterfalls. This place is a feast of amazing karst beauty to the eyes, but it also provides cool, refreshing refuge from the heat of summer. It has been one of the most visited tourist sites. We are going through the cave, please take care and watch your step. Here we can see the whole cave, you could take photos, if you like.

This is the Moss-Covered Stream. The rocks here are covered with aquatic moss, which can be made into delicious food by the local people.

There are many lianas here, please take care and mind your head. In the front, we will arrive at the Zhuisi Bridge or Bridge of Rethinking. This is the Bridge of Rethinking. Sometimes people should slow down and rethink to avoid mistakes and make better progress. Few steps further, there is an ascending spring named Heaven Well, the water is very clean, which can be drank directly.

Tianquan Spring, or the Heaven Well, is an ascending spring. Here underground water is forced out of the ground surface by hydrostatic pressure to form a spring. The spring works pretty much the same way as a connecting vessel does. You fill in water through the upper end (in this case just as the rain or underground water), and it flows out from the lower end (just as this spring).

This pool is called the Goat Pool, because wild goats and other animals often come here to drink water.

This is the fourth bridge over the stream, Guanyin Bridge. During the wet seasons the stream makes loud sound, which can be as enchanting as symphonic music. In Chinese, Guanyin means to hear the sound, it is also the name of a female Buddha, or Goddess.

This is the Tiger Pool. Once there were tigers drinking here. Besides, under weathering and leaching, zigzag groove marks of different depths and colors appear on the cliff across the stream, seeming like tiger stripes. That's way the pool is called Tiger Pool.

This bridge is called the Mountain Connecting Bridge, for it connects the two sides of the valley. It symbolizes the link between two hearts in love.

This hovel built with scabblings is called Yansha; it represents a typical style of the residence of ancient Ba people.

Here is actually a souvenir shop, you can take a close look.

The high mountains, green forests and crystal clear streams here make Tiansheng Bridge a perfect destination for tourists.

Please follow me to move on, and you can enjoy the fresh air and natural beauty now.

This is the Woods on Rocks. Many trees take their roots in the fissures of this mountain. That is Laojun Post. According to the legend, Laojun, a Taoist god, once lived here. His two servants Qingfeng and Mingyue were so loyal to him that they respectively became a pool and a bridge to accompany Laojun forever. That's why the bridge and the pool are called Qingfeng Bridge and Mingyue Pool. The water in Mingyue Pool comes from Laojun Mountain covered by the primitive forest.

Now we are walking in the quiet natural secondary forest. This forest is a subtropical evergreen broad-leaved forest. We can hear various birds singing from time to time and appreciate the wonderful sounds of the forest. Please enjoy the beauty here.

This is the Boat-Shaped Rock.

On this platform, we can have an overview of the natural bridge. With abundant stromatolite fossils and over 4,000m in the thickness, the Shennongjia Group, which is mainly made up of dolomite, is the world's most complete stratigraphic unit of the late Precambrian. Stratigraphically, the Shennongjia Group formed the oldest fold basement at the northern margin of the Changjiang River.

Now, you can see several houses ahead, all of these houses were reconstructed with the Ba style. Along the trail you will also see Villages of the Ba People, which reconstruct the life of the ancient Ba Tribe, as well as various production workshops that show the local arts, crafts, and production methods for daily foods in the past.

This building is called Baman Thatched House. According to the hierarchy of Ba people, it should be a residence of ordinary people. Now it's a souvenir shop.

This building is called Wuyi Grass House. It's reconstructed according to the residence style of mid-class Ba people. Now it's a holiday villa.

This house is called Linjun Hall, it is the place where the head of Ba tribe receives his guests. Now it is used as a recreational place for calligraphy, painting, tea-tasting and musical instrument playing.

Here is Tusi Palace. Tusi is an administrative unit set by the central government in the Ming and the Qing dynasties to reinforce the control of remote ethnic groups. This is where the head of Tusi lives. Now it is a holiday villa. Maybe you've heard someone singing here. Yes, our next stop is the Tang Opera Theater. Please follow me to move on, and watch your step.

Tang Opera is a local opera of Shennongjia Region. Tang means the central room or sitting room of a house. Because the performance requires relatively small space, it was usually performed in the central rooms of farmers' houses. The singing styles are full of local background and rustic flavor. We will have lunch here and while we are eating, we can experience the folk music in Shennongjia area.

Now let's visit the workshops of Ba Tribe. There are several reconstructed ancient production workshops along the hiking trail, such as sugar refinery, wine distillery, bean mill, flour mill and the like. They bring back into practice the methods in which local people once prepared their daily food in the past. Please be careful and watch you step.

The first is the workshop of cooked wheaten food. This is bride-cake. Making bride-cake is one of the endemic customs in Shennongjia Region, and also one of the important activities in wedding ceremonies. Bride-cake is a traditional handmade cake made of high-quality wheat powder, oil and sugar, etc. Bride-cake is crispy outside and soft inside, and of agreeable sweetness, so it is one of local people's favorite foods.

This snack is called crispy noodle. The crispy noodle is made with traditional techniques of Ba People. Fried with natural rapeseed oil, the noodle is golden yellow, fragrant, and crispy, and can be stored for a long time. It's a very popular snack.

This is deep-fried dough sticks. Deep-fried dough sticks made here are golden yellow, crispy outside, and soft inside. Let's move on, and our next stop is Soy Bean Workshop. This is the Soy Bean Workshop. The soy milk and soy pudding made here are completely natural and healthy; they are milky white and full of protein. The local soybeans are soaked in natural spring water, and then are ground, with a grindstone driven by a waterwheel, into yellow slurry, which is filtered and boiled into soy milk. Soy milk is mixed with some natural gypsum powder, into soy pudding. Waterwheel was invented in the Eastern Han Dynasty over 2,000 years ago. As a tool for irrigation or production, it is a fruit of ancient Chinese people's wisdom. OK, let's move on.

This is the Candy Workshop. The local people use corn or sweet potato to make candy, and further process the candy into various snacks. This candy's name is Sesame Candy. Sesame candy is a local traditional snack made of corn syrup and high quality sesame seeds. The local people make sesame candy several days before the spring festival, to offer sacrifice to the Kitchen God. Otherwise, the Kitchen God may speak ill of people to the Jade Emperor in the Heaven. Please have a taste.

Now we are at the Oil Mill. Like Chinese weaving machine, it has a long history and is a best example of ancient workshops. This is a truly primitive way of oil production. This mill sells various fresh edible oils, especially pollution-free rapeseed oil. The oil made here is very popular with the tourists. Please follow me to move on.

This workshop is a wine distillery. White wine is made here with the most traditional technique. Wine distillery is the technical foundation of Chinese wine culture. This workshop can produce pure corn wine with 45% to 80% alcohol content, which has been one of the tourists' favorite beverages.

The cured meat here is produced with secret recipe. Normally they don't allow other people to observe their production process, but their products are really delicious. This is the jiusi or restaurant. It was the place for drinking and entertainment of Ba people in the ancient time.

These primitive ways of preparing food may have been replaced by modern means, but the traditional wisdom and delicate skills in making a smart use of nature are still well worth learning and passing down. The reconstruction of these ancient workshops really offers a perfect opportunity to look back on the life we once had and learn from it.

This is the Magpie Bridge, the last bridge of the scenic spot. Its name comes from an old Chinese love story. Two lovers, a fairy lady from the heaven and a cowherd, were separated by the Milky Way. On the seventh day of the seventh month every year, the Chinese Valentine's Day, many magpies would build a bridge with their bodies over the Milky Way for the two lovers to meet each other. This story praises faithful love, so this bridge is a good place for young lovers.

Ok, please follow me to move on and watch your step. Our tour in Tiansheng Bridge Scenic Spot ends here. Have a nice day. Goodbye.

8. Taizi Cliff—Watchtower 太子垭——瞭望塔

太子垭 We have now arrived in the west part of Shennong Top Subarea. This place is called Taizi Cliff or the Prince Gap because Li Xian, a prince of the Tang Dynasty, once visited here. The house back there by the road is the Monkey Stone Protection Station. Its main functions include monitoring of the area, preventing forest fire, and protecting the geological relics. There are more than 30 such viewing decks in Shennong Top Subarea. It is convenient for tourists to enjoy the magnificent and beautiful mountain scenery of Shennongjia.

Located in the southwestern part of Shennongjia Region and with an average altitude of 2,400 meters, Shennong Top is the highest among the five subareas of the Geopark. Standing here and looking afar, you can see grand and magnificent mountains in the south. Doesn't this make you relaxed and joyful?

You can see vast primitive alpine fir forest in front and in the southwest of this deck. Many of the trees are hundreds of years old. They constitute a unique forest vegetation landscape here. The 1.6km long hiking trail built in the forest allows tourists to closely enjoy the fragrance of flowers, the bird singing and the fresh air in this quiet primitive forest. In warm spring, the hiking trail will be decorated by flourishing fargesia and various flowers (such as alpine azalea and malus spectabilis), making tourists reluctant to leave.

Looking to the east, you can see the vast alpine meadow and fargesia that we have seen on the way here. These plants often grow together. In addition to alpine fir, they are the most important plants here, forming a vegetation landscape commonly seen at the high altitude and constituting very unique alpine vegetation scenery.

Now let's look to the northeast. We can clearly see the weathered bed rocks exposed on the top of the ridge. Lithologically, they are sandstone and colomite respectively belonging to Liantuo Formation of the Nanhua System and Kuangshishan Formation of the Shennongjia

Group. Corrosion and frost weathering along the joint fissures made this special landform of swarming rocky crests, or called Clints. They look like a group of playing monkeys, so they are called the Monkey Rocks.

On our way here, you may notice the living condition of the fargesia: on the bedrock of the slope there is only a very thin layer of soil for the plants. The growing environment of the fargesia here is very fragile: once the soil is lost, it will not survive anymore, and then, this place will become an area of bare rocks like the Monkey Rocks.

This place was once a station on the ancient Sichuan-Hubei Salt Road. Entering the hiking trail here, you can enjoy the quiet and comfortable environment and fresh air in the primitive fir forest when walking around. It's a natural oxygen bar rich in negative oxygen ions.

板壁岩 Banbi/ Board Wall Cliff or the Cliff Rocks, is one of the tourists' favorite scenic areas. The dolomite exposed here was formed 1.2 billion years ago. After millions of years of weathering and leaching, the rock-outcrops gradually formed this beautiful stone forest. Stratigraphically, these rocks belong to Kuangshishan Formation at the top of Shennongjia Group.

Like limestone, dolomite is also subject to chemical weathering. Long term of tectonic activity resulted in many fissures and joints in various directions in these rocks. They facilitate the weathering, leaching and denudation, which made these clints in different shapes.

These clints of various shapes constitute many interesting pictographic rocks, for example, The Rock from the Sky, The Rooster Announcing Dawn, the Baby Phoenix Crying for Feeding, The Stone Column, the Beauty Looking into the Mirror, the Peacock-Shaped Rock, the Galloping Horses, and Sun Wukong Guarding Xuanzang, etc. These amazing works and generous gifts of the great nature attract large number of tourists every year.

Passing through this alpine meadow, we are now standing on the other side of the Cliff Rocks. Looking back at this meadow, we can see the swaying grass waves in the wind surround the scattered clints, which are just like the reefs in the sea. The different shapes of the clints can arouse limitless imagination.

In the narrow tourist path, you can see some regular concentric arc lines in the rocks. They are stromatolite, the fossil of the earth's most ancient life. Generation after generation, these primitive unicellular algae that grew on rock surface constructed such beautiful concentric fossil structure by continuously adsorbing tiny sediment particles in sea water. Stromatolite has great significance to the emergence and multiplying of various living beings: as the pioneer of life on earth, continuous photosynthesis by the algae that formed stromatolite produced essential oxygen for all the subsequent living beings.

This is the Tourist Service Center. It integrates multiple functions, such as catering, shopping, medical care, lounge, and waiting, and provides thoughtful services to the tourists in need.

凉风垭 With an altitude of 2,770m, this mountain pass receives cold wind all year round, so it is called Liangfeng Cliff or the Cold Wind Pass. It is a very important geological observation spot: from the slope beside the road we can see two distinct kinds of rocks: the crouching beasts at the top are dark gray conglomerate, and the fresh outcrop beneath the vegetation is greyish-green sandstone. The significant lithological contrast represents big difference in the environments and ages in which the rocks were formed.

Here we can learn an important geological term: unconformity. Unconformity represents a gap of sedimentation in rock forming process. That's to say, after an older rock stratum is formed, the sedimentation stops for a period; or the older stratum goes through weathering and denudation or folding and faulting in tectonic movement, then the sedimentation starts again and forms a new stratum. The contact relation between the two different sedimentary sequences is called unconformity.

In the stratigraphic section in front of us, we can see two different rock formations. They differ greatly in rock type and their attitude, the contact surface between them is rough and uneven, which implies remarkable erosion. It indicates there was a sedimentation gap here. It is typical unconformity: the lower grayish-green sandstone belongs to Liangfengya Formation, which is the first lithostratigraphic unit directly covering mesoproterozoic Shennongjia Group. Here is the place giving the name to the formation, Liangfengya Formation. The dark conglomerate up there belongs to Liantuo Formation of Nanhua System.

Conglomerate is usually considered as the earliest sediments of a sedimentary cycle, so it is called basal conglomerate geologically. The conglomerate in Liantuo Formation we are seeing right now is a kind of basal conglomerate; it represents the beginning of a new sedimentary cycle, which is called Nanhua System in geology. The period of Nanhua System was controlled by cold climate of ice age. The famous moraine conglomerate in Nantuo Formation is a typical representative of it, and we will see its outcrop in Guanmenshan/ Closing Door Mountain Subarea.

With the open visual field here, when we are walking on this hiking trail, we can not only overlook the magnificent mountains, but also enjoy the typical alpine vegetation landscape around consisting of alpine meadow, fargesia, pine and fir. With a total length of about 13.4 kilometers, such hiking trails have been built in almost all the most beautiful and interesting scenic spots of Shennong Top Subarea, allowing the hikers to enjoy the view safely. This is another reason why the tourists love Shennongjia Geopark so much.

From this viewing deck at the end of the hiking trail, we can see many big rock blocks on the opposite slope and in the valley forming a Glacial Rock Sea. According to investigation, the rocks are mainly diabase, and they are glacial erratic boulders, a product of Quaternary glaciation. It is direct evidence of the Quaternary glacial activity in Shennongjia area.

瞭望塔 Shennong Top Subarea is the highest in Shennongjia Geopark, and the Watchtower occupies the commanding height of this open area of mountain ridge and pass. Due to its superiority in position, this watchtower has always been a stationary monitoring station at the boundary line of forest fire prevention in Shennongjia area. With the telescope, in clear days we can even see the border region between Shennongjia and Chongqing from here. So, this watchtower is the most important monitoring spot for forest protection and fire prevention in this area.

Here is also the best position to overlook Shennong Peak, the highest mountain of Shennongjia. With an altitude of 3,106.2m, it is known as the highest peak in central China. So here is one of the viewing spots that tourists must go and take pictures.

Facing Shennong Peak, the highest one in central China, we can see the outlines of a series of high mountains. All the six mountains with altitudes over 3,000m gather here, constituting the famous "Roof of Central China": in the east there are Shanmujian and Jinhouling/ Golden Mountain Ridge, in the west there are Dashennongjia/ Big Shennongjia and Xiaoshennongjia/ Little/ Small Shennongjia, and beyond Shennong Valley, there is Dawokeng.

The "Roof of the Central China" is a very important geographic separator and watershed in Shennongjia area. It separates the Changjiang River from its most important tributary–the Hanjiang River: The north of the mountain ridge is the Hanjiang River basin, and the south is the Changjiang River basin.

Along these mountain ridges, we can see many valleys and corresponding vegetation landscapes. According to survey, many of these valleys are glacial gullies, cirques and horns shaped by Quaternary glacial scour. Although most of them have been reshaped by later weathering, denudation, landslide and collapse and failed to keep their original typical shapes of U valley and cirque, they indeed provide reliable Geo-morphic proof of Quaternary glacial activity in Shennongjia area.

The rocks exposed here are fine-crystal dolomite with siliceous beds belonging to Shicaohe Formation of Shennongjia Group, which can be closely observed beside the hiking trail, and purple red laminated micro-fine-crystal dolomite at the top of the same formation, which can be seen around the watchtower.

9. Shennong Valley—the Great Dragon Pool 神农谷——大龙潭

神农谷（上入口） As one of the most attractive scenic spots of Shennong Top Subarea, with a maximum sea-level elevation of 2,820m, Shennong Valley has a height difference of over 400 meters from the bottom to this viewing platform. To allow the tourists to fully enjoy the miraculous scenery, a 4.4km long hiking trail was specially designed and built. Hiding here and reappearing there, the winding hiking trail perfectly integrates with the green valley, making itself a perfect scene.

Along the hiking trail you can walk down to the bottom of the valley while rambling among the primitive forest; then you can circle up and return to the ridge from another entrance. Along the hiking trail 26 geological and geomorphologic landscape interpretation boards have been built for science popularization and education.

Please look at this magnificent cliff; it is actually a fault scarp. Shennong Valley is located at the core of Shennongjia Anticline. Many extension fractures and vertical joints developed well on the top of the anticline. They facilitate rock weathering, erosion and collapsing, which formed the magnificent landscape of this valley.

Since Shennong Valley occupies the north-south airflow pass, rich moisture brings rain and thick clouds frequently. So, here is a perfect place to view the sea of clouds. The climate here not only forms a beautiful dynamic and mysterious scene, but also results in the special karst topography with variously shaped swarm of peaks.

神农谷（下入口） With quite complete facilities, such as hiking trail, safety devices and interpretation system, Shennong Top Subarea passed the quality certification of ISO9000 and ISO14000, and was approved by China National Tourism Administration as a National “Five-A” Tourist Scenic Area in January 2012.

As one of the most classic and the tourists’ most favorite scenic spots of the Geopark, Shennong Valley is characterized by typical dolomite karst landscape and topography. Deep-cutting valley, towering cuesta, steep cliff, graceful peak forest, and floating clouds form a dynamic picture scroll.

Here is a perfect place for mountaineering. A 4.4-kilometer-long circular hiking trail travels 400 meter high from the valley bottom to the top. Walking along this trail, you can not only enjoy the beautiful natural scenery, but also have a physical exercise for your body. That is why Shennong Valley is so popular with most tourists.

神农营 Shennongying, or Shennong Campground, has an altitude of 2,620m. The name came from a legend: the forefather Shennong once camped here for herb collecting. Here is the campground for the tourists hoping to climb the highest peak in Shennongjia – Shennong Peak. The Geopark provides here various related services to the tourists who are interested in climbing.

For example, tourists can rest here and get prepared for climbing; they can get climbing equipment such as climbing shoes, sunhat, sun glasses, sun cream, and climbing stick, etc., as well as drinking water, oxygen bottle and snack; they can also change clothes and deposit personal stuff here (lighters and matches are forbidden in the field); we also provide first-aid service.

Most tourists consider it a great honor to climb onto the highest peak in Shennongjia. In order to guarantee the safety of the climbers, the Geopark built 2,999 steps with a total length of 1.6km across the slope, meadow and forest. Along the steps there are many interpretation boards explaining the geological and geographic landscapes and giving tips about proper climbing, so that the tourists can learn while they are climbing and feel less tired. Before starting to climb, all tourists must register at the wooden booth at the entrance. This is mainly for safety purpose, and also helps us collect information of the tourists.

Those tourists who are physically strong and climb onto the peak within shortest time may get their names listed in the Honor Board of Fastest Climbers. This can incite and promote climbing activities and help build up people’s health. However, since participation and experience are the most important, the Geopark emphasizes the tenet of healthy tourism: Safety and fun first.

For those tourists of poorer physical condition who are not appropriate to climb, the camp provides them a comfortable environment for resting and touring. They can have tea and wait for the climbers to return, they can also enjoy the geological and geomorphological spots around:

The gray outcrop near the parking lot is thick-bedded dolomite in Dawokeng Formation, Shennongjia Group, in which stromatolite can be found;

On the far slope there are a few outcrops of karst clints and stalagmites; beside the driveway to the campground there is a thin bed of siliceous conglomerate called gemstone conglomerate, because the gravels in it consist of chert with various colors and fine roundness;

The far slope is covered by alpine meadow, fargesia and a few pine trees and alpine fir, making a beautiful scenery of soul-calming peace and beauty.

酒壶坪 With an altitude of 1,900m, Jiuhuping/ Wine Pot Ground is the entrance and tourist transfer center of Shennong Top Subarea. It combines a parking lot, a transfer lobby, a restaurant, a lounge, a hotel, an office building, a dispatch center, a gas station, a repair plant and a car wash, with a total area of over 54,000 square meters.

In the Tourist Transfer Center there is a sign system with four languages: Chinese, English, Japanese and Korean, so tourists can get services in a convenient, friendly and fast manner. The whole place of the tourist service center is an environment-friendly park with 90% green coverage. Tourists can get information about the Geopark, book hotel, choose tour guide (including English-speaking tour guide), find medical care and receive convenient and comfortable transportation service.

To protect precious geological resources and tourists' safety, all tourists have to take the environment-friendly bus provided by the Geopark to enter Shennong Top Subarea. Without special permission, private vehicles are not allowed to enter this subarea. With one ticket a tourist can go to all scenic spots within the Geopark. The transfer center has 65 environment-friendly buses with 1,935 seats. All the buses are equipped with GPS system for real-time monitoring of their operation conditions.

The main purpose of the Tourist Transfer Center is to protect geological resources and achieve sustainable development of it, meantime to guarantee tourist activities (especially in peak seasons) are in order and provide the tourists with convenient, comfortable and friendly services.

According to survey, this open valley was once a Quaternary glacial valley. The Quaternary glaciation relics in Shennongjia area can be divided into three phases: the earliest phase was 900 thousand to 750 thousand years ago in the middle period of Mid-Pleistocene, which is called Muyu Ice Age in Shennongjia; the second phase was 200 thousand to 100 thousand years ago in the early period of Late Pleistocene, which is called Jiuhu Ice Age. The glaciation relics found around the tourist center belong to this phase. The third phase was 70 thousand to 10 thousand years ago in the late period of Late Pleistocene.

小龙潭 Xiaolongtan, or the Small Dragon Pool, has an altitude of 2,120 meters. According to the geological survey, this place was once a glacial erosion lake. As a tourist service center of

Shennong Top Subarea, there are all supporting facilities here, including restaurant, shopping center, recreation facility and etc.

This place is also an animal shelter and scientific research base, including a wildlife aid station, and a real time video center of Golden Snub-nosed Monkey open free to tourists, etc. So we can say that Xiaolongtan is an Eco-environment science popularization and research center.

Xiaolongtan possesses quiet and peaceful environment, flourishing trees and a babbling creek. There are three small bridges over the creek: Henry Bridge, Wilson Bridge and Wang Zhan Bridge. In honor of three scientists who made great contributions to the scientific research of Shennongjia, the three bridges encourage people to learn from the predecessors, and follow their paths to respect, learn about and protect the great nature.

Augustine Henry was an Irish botanist. In 1888 he collected over 50,000 dry plant specimens and seeds in Shennongjia, including many newly recorded species. Many of his specimens are still collected by the British Museum.

Ernest Henry Wilson, a famous English naturalist, botanist, explorer and writer, came to Shennongjia area to collect plant specimens in 1900. He travelled to west China for three times and made great achievements in China, so he was nicknamed “Chinese Wilson”.

Wang Zhan was a famous Chinese forestry scientist and ecologist. In 1943 he led a team to explore Shennongjia area, collected hundreds of specimens, and wrote a related report about Shennongjia, providing important scientific basis for later development of Shennongjia.

The restaurant here will serve us with a delicious and healthy lunch. The food materials are mostly local specialties such as fresh vegetable and mushrooms. They are loved by many tourists.

大龙潭 Dalongtan, or the Great Dragon Pool, lies at the foot of Dragon Head Hill at an elevation of 2,100 meters above sea level. It is a glacial valley formed by Quaternary glaciation. The Great Dragon Pool is the relic of a glacial erosion lake. Now, this place has been built into a Golden Snub-nosed Monkey conservation and research base.

The unique geographic location and good Eco-environment of Shennongjia make it an ideal habitat for Golden Snub-nosed Monkey. Like Giant Panda, Golden Snub-nosed Monkey is peculiar to China.

Although this species has been there for over 1.5 million years, its existence hadn’t been recognized by the international zoological society until 1880s. Only 20 years ago it was confirmed that Golden Snub-nosed Monkey does exist in Shennongjia.

There are three snub-nosed monkey species in China: Sichuan Snub-nosed Monkey, Guizhou Snub-nosed Monkey, and Yunnan Snub-nosed Monkey. The Golden Snub-nosed Monkey in Shennongjia was originally identified as a subspecies of Sichuan Snub-nosed Monkey, but it has been confirmed a species peculiar to Shennongjia by some experts.

With strong body, long golden hair and shiny eyes, the Golden Snub-nosed Monkey in Shennongjia is the most beautiful species. Living in the alpine area at 1,600 to 3,000 meters above sea level, a Golden Snub-nosed Monkey colony normally has a population of 50-200 including one all-male unit and several families.

In 1980s, due to poaching and forest destruction, the population of Golden Snub-nosed Monkey fiercely dropped to 500. This drew great attention by the Nature Reserve, who immediately took relevant protective actions. In addition, after years of continuous tracking and study, we finally learned their habits and lifestyle. With scientific methods, the Golden Snub-nosed Monkey population has been conserved and expanded.

Currently there is a colony with a population of about 80 monkeys in this area. Through regular feeding, the research center has established mutual trust with them. Now researchers can closely observe their habits and lifestyle, providing scientific basis for further protection.

To guarantee the health and safety of the monkeys, before entering this area to have a close contact with these beautiful creatures, tourists have to contact the research center for approval, put on sterilized coat and accept disinfection by ultraviolet light.

10. The Tiansheng Bridge to Shennong Altar 天生桥——神农坛

天生桥 Tiansheng Bridge, is a natural formation of an arc. Viewed from afar, this 17m high penetrating rock cave looks like a bridge, and that's why the area in and around is called Tiansheng/ Nature-Made Bridge. A stream flows through it into The Yellow Rock River. Travelling up the stream, you will arrive at the Orchid Mountain.

The rocks that make up this natural bridge were formed in the Mesoproterozoic (1.9 -1.0 billion years ago) and belong to the Shicaohe Formation, Shennongjia Group. Its main contents are medium-bedded dolomite. The Shennongjia Group is the most exposed of all stratigraphic units in this Geopark. It is a set of strata in continental margin rift basin at the northern margin of the Changjiang Craton, which was formed by extensional structure.

With abundant stromatolite fossils and over 4,000 meters in thickness, the Shennongjia Group, which is mainly made up of dolomite, is the world's most complete stratigraphic unit of the late Precambrian. Stratigraphically, the Shennongjia Group formed the oldest fold basement at the northern margin of the Changjiang Craton.

The Shennongjia Group can be divided into four formations, named as Zhengjiaya Formation, Shicaohe Formation, Dawokeng Formation, and Kuangshishan Formation accordingly. The stratotype sections of all the four formations are established in the Shennongjia region. Exposed here in the Tiansheng Bridge area is the dolomite of the Shicaohe Formation.

The high mountains, green forests and crystal clear streams here make Tiansheng Bridge a perfect destination for tourists. The huge karst cave is a masterpiece of wonders created by water erosion and weathering. Crystal clear stream water rushes out of the cave and forms overlapping waterfalls. This place is a feast of amazing karst beauty to the eyes, but it also provides cool, refreshing refuge from the heat of summer. It has been one of the most visited tourist sites.

In order to make the best use of the abundant natural resources, and to create perfect tourist conditions, the Geopark has built a 2.6 km circle hiking trail in the valley. The trail will take you to many wonderful view sites, such as the Yingtan (Eagle Pool), Hutan (Tiger Pool), Yangtan (Goat Pool), Yishui Bridge (One Water Bridge), Yanxifeipu (Flying Waterfall through Crack), Taiman Stream (Moss-Covered Stream), Tianquan (Heaven Well) and Qianshan Bridge (Mountain-Connecting Bridge).

Along the trail you will also see "Villages of the Ba People", which reconstruct the life of the ancient Ba Tribe, as well as various production workshops that show the local arts, crafts, and production methods for daily foods in the past.

"Tianquan", or the "Heaven Well", is an ascending spring. Here underground water is forced out of the ground surface by hydrostatic pressure to form a spring. The spring works pretty much the same way as a connecting vessel does—You fill in water through the upper end (in this case just as the rain or underground water), and it flows out from the lower end (just as this spring).

There are several reconstructed ancient production workshops along the hiking trail, such as "sugar refinery" "wine distillery" "bean mill" "flour mill" etc. They bring back into practice the methods in which local people once prepared their daily food in the past. These primitive ways of preparing food may have been replaced by modern means, but the traditional wisdom and delicate skills in making a smart use of nature are still well worth learning and passing down. The reconstruction of these ancient workshops really offers a perfect opportunity to look back on the life we once had and learn from it.

神农坛 The Shennongtan, or the Shennong Altar, lies six kilometers away from Muyu Town, it is the south entrance of the Geopark. Shennongtan tries to tell what Shennong, also known as Emperor Yan, really means to China by showing a lot of miracles he made. He was virtually one of the founders of the great, long-lasting Chinese civilization. In order to worship him, people across the country come here every year to pay their highest tribute to this earliest forefather.

The gate takes the form of a pair of buffalo horns made of brass and coated with gold. They are the logo of the resort. As buffalo horns were the totem of Shennong's prehistoric agrarian tribe, it rests the local people's reflection on the past of an amazing agricultural civilization, as well as their wish to carry this agrarian tradition.

Shennongtan, or the Shennong Altar, is built on a relic of old rocky landslide. Surrounded by mountains on three sides, the block of the landslide inclines step by step to the river gully. According to Fengshui, the Chinese traditional geomatics, the topography of Shennongtan is perfect, so, it really is a treasure ground. Major buildings and various gardens are laid out on the slope one step after another up to the top. Mighty and yet harmonious, the view is as magnificent as it is mesmerizing.

Here is the core of the site—the Shennong Altar. Built in 1997, it is where the descendants of Shennong pay tribute to their ancestor, worship their gods, and pray for blessings. Solemn rituals are held here every year in honor of Shennong. The giant statue on top is Shennong, one of the forefathers of the Chinese people. 21 meters tall, 35 meters across, together the total is 56, a symbol of great unity of the 56 ethnic groups in China.

The Shennong Altar is built precisely in Chinese royal garden style. In front of Shennong's statue is the Heaven Altar reserved specially for emperors in rituals; below it there is an Earth Altar, which is the place, by a strict hierarchy, for ordinary people in rituals. The Earth Altar is designed according to Yinyang and Wuxing in the paradigm of "a square earth under spherical heavens", the typical Taoist arrangement of the universe, accurate and thought-provoking.

We are here in the 24 Solar Terms Park. In Chinese calendar, a year falls into 24 equal solar terms, including 12 major and 12 minor solar terms interlaced with each other. Believed to have been first created by Shennong and other ancestors of Chinese people, the 24 solar terms system is the result of the ancient Chinese people's constant observation and exploration on astronomy, weather and phenology.

The Shennong Farming Culture Park consists of three theme subareas: the Farming Culture Park, the Tea Picking and Processing Park, and the Farm Fun Park. Each has several exhibition sections with distinctive features and purposes. In the House–and–living stuff section you'll see the primitive forms of a variety of items such as lamps and lanterns, beds and bedding, and fishing tools, while in the Workshops section you'll witness the procedures in which traditional oil and bean-curd mills work.

The Shennong Herbs Garden is established for the purpose of cultivating precious herbs and studying their usage in Chinese medicine. In this garden grow over 100 species of herbs, some of which are proved to be of anticancer effects. This garden has been an important place for the revival and promotion of Chinese traditional medicine.

Part 04 十堰周边

Shiyan Suburbs

Chapter 1 Yunxi County and the Main Tourist Resources 郧西旅游

Yunxi County is located in the northwest of Shiyan City, Hubei Province, whose geographical location is superior, lying between the natural regions of North China and Central China, which is a transitional zone, which belongs to the subtropical northern boundary continent with a pleasant climate. Human beings have lived here since the ancient time, with a long history and culture. There are rich historical, cultural and natural tourism resources. Among them, natural tourism resources have Daliang Nature Reserve, Yunxi Tianhe Cherry Valley Scenic Spot and so on. Historical and cultural tourism resources include Wang Ancestral Hall, Liu House and so on.

Yunxi Tianhe Tourist Area 郧西天河景区

Yunxi Tianhe Tourist Area, one of the national AAAA-level tourist attractions and national water scenic spots, is located in Yunxi County proper, elaborately built by the County Committee and the County Government. The core scenic spot, Yunxi Xuangu Mountain is built by taking "China Marriage City" and "Qixi Date Town" as the core and "human love river", the unique Tianhe River as the link. The "Fu-Yin/ Fuzhou-Yinchuan" high-speed crosses through scenic spots and urban areas, here are convenient transportation, colorful folk customs, beautiful mountains and rivers, worthy of your coming and visiting.

The planned area of the scenic area is about 12,000 mu, from the Jinchai Stone in Tumen Town in the north, to the Tianheping Estuary in the south, to the Yushu Cliff in the west and to the Dajian Mountain in the east, including the Qixi Festival Cultural District and Taoist Cultural District. The Qixi Festival Cultural District is characterized by "Yunxi ancient scenery, mysterious Tianhe, and Qixi festival folklore (the love story about the Cowherd and the Weaver Maiden)". In a Chinese legend, the Cowherd and the Weaving Maid, once a happy couple, become stars separated by the Milky Way. They can meet only once in a year when magpies fly together to form a bridge over the Milky Way. Nowadays, the Romantic Qixi Festival has become a theme tourism of many main functions including sightseeing, marriage, vacation, leisure recuperation, and ecological protection.

Shangjin Ancient Town 上津古镇

Shangjin Ancient Town also named as Liuzhou/ Willow Town, is located in the northwestern of Hubei Province, and is one of the national AAAA tourist attraction and a key cultural relic protection unit in China, the only one well-protected ancient county-level wall in Hubei Province and one of the four existing county-level walls in China, the center of the circle made by the three cities of Shiyan, Shangluo and Ankang, bordering Manchuan Ancient Town of Shaanxi Province bounded by the Jinqian /Gold Coin River Basin in the south and the Qinling Mountains in the North. The ancient town is located on the east bank of the lower reaches of the Jinqian River, a tributary of the Hanjiang River, and Fuzhou-Yinchuan Expressway running through the town. It is an important historical town in political, cultural, commercial, military fields as the threshold of Qin Kingdom and Chu Kingdom and the Port of Imperial Families, known as the famous town "Serving Qin Kingdom in the morning and Chu Kingdom in the evening".

In accordance with the literature and archaeological analysis, the town construction covered 2-3 years (1523—1524), and the re-repaired work lasted 7 years. Now, the Town walls are complete, and the majority of the town building is in the original appearance. The ancient City Wall made of black bricks is 1,236-meter long, 7-meter high and covering 80,000 m^2, in ladder shape. The existing city wall was built in the seventh year of Emperor Jiaqing of the Qing Dynasty, located in the north of the ruins of the Ming Dynasty city wall. The City Wall has four gates in the south, the north, the west and the southwest. Since the establishment of Pingyang County in Shangjin in the fourth year of Emperor Wen of the Wei Kingdom, the Three Kingdoms Period (223), Shangjin has had a history of over 1,800 years. The weathered Shangjin Ancient City Wall, ancient-style Shanxi-Shaanxi Guild Hall, the ancient streets of the Ming and Qing Dynasties, unique and elegant catholic church, the port of the royal families, and others have shown the ancient history of Shangjin Town.

The special and important geographical location has made Shangjin significant in the wars of all generations where General Yue Fei (the national hero in the Northern Song Dynasty, 1103—1142), Li Zicheng (the leader of farmer uprising troops who broke down the Ming Dynasty) and Wang Cong'er (the leader of White Lotus Uprising Troops) had settled their troops here. During the years of Democratic Revolution, many proletariat revolutionists came here, including Li Xiannian, Xu Xiangqian, He Long, Liu Huaqing and Cheng Zihua. In November, 1947, the first county-level democratic political power, Shangguan County Democratic Government came into being in Shangjin Town.

In 1998, Shangjin Town was approved as one of the Key Border Trade Towns of Hubei Province. In 2007, Shangjin Town was awarded China Historical Culture Town by the State Ministry of Construction and the Administration for Cultural Relics. In 2013, Shangjin Town as included in the Seventh List of Key Cultural Relics under the National Protection. In the same year, Shangjin Culture Tourism Zone was approved as the AAAA-Level Scenic Spot.

Shangjin Town is rich in tourist resources, such as, the Ancient City Wall, the Jinqian River, Tianpeng/ Sky Cover Mountain, Yuhuang/ Jade Emperor Bay, Huanglong/ Yellow Dragon Bay,

Tianqiao Ancient Cave, Long Band with Willows. Here are many fine and famous local products, including fermented soya beans, walnut, Tung oil and tu-chung. To build Shangjin Town into a showcase of Hubei Province tourism to Xi'an City of Shaanxi Province, and the important resting post in the golden travel line of Wudang Mountains—Xi'an City, Shiyan City and Yunxi County have decided to invest more programs and capitals to promote the tourist industry development in Shangjin Town.

Wulong/ Five Dragon River Scenic Spot 五龙河景区

Wulong River Scenic Spot, one of the national AAAA-level tourist attractions and provincial nature reserves, is 18 km away from Yunxi Exit of Shi-Man (Shiyan-Manchuan) Expressway. It is auspicious because of sacred dragons, elegant and clean because of quiet water and valley. Wulong River valley is deep, the river is clean, the mountains are beautiful, giving the tourists an enjoyable, detached and well-deserved adventure. Wulong River is old and magical, composed of 4 scenic spots, which are "Wulong Valley, Xiandao Health-preserving Recreation Area" "Wulong River Enthusiasm Drifting Area" "Searching for Roots and Ancestors in Shenwuling Mountain" and "Sanguandong Camping and Hunting Area", known as China's "Lesser Jiuzhaigou Valley" and "A Natural Oxygen Bar".

The Longtan River 龙潭河

The Longtan River Scenic Spot, on the banks of the Hanjiang River, belongs to Yangwei Town, Yunxi County. Totally, it is 2.5 km in length, about 52 km away from the highway exits. It is a forest park and Geo-park as well as an AAAA-level scenic spot. In a sense, this river has become a corridor decorated with appealing landscape, no wonder it is hailed as The First Scenic Spot on the Hanjiang River.

The Longtan River manifests how the mountains, waters, falls, caves and streams are well combined. The trees and slender bamboos are crystal and green. The picturesque precipices, deep and serene valleys, tumbling streams and waterfalls go well with the ancient constructions. Here the houses have black roofs and yellow blazing tiles. The well retained handicrafts represented by paper-making reflects the wisdom of the locals. A lot of people swarm into this place for painting, photographing, relaxing and sightseeing.

The legend has it that the Dragon King of the Western Sea was responsible for the weather once had a bet with a fortune-teller named Tan in a village. In order to win, the King defied the order from the Jade Emperor and hold back the rain. In order to evade the punishment from the Emperor, the King hid himself in the river with the help of Tan. After having escaped from the arrest of the Heavenly Soldiers, the Dragon King behaved himself and brought along the rain timely, thus guaranteeing the locals to have good harvests every year. The locals, in return, built temples and enshrined the Statue of the Dragon King. Gradually, this place has become a place of interest attracting many tourists.

Generally speaking, this scenic spot consists of four sections, Local Customs Experiencing Section, Waterfall Exploring Section, Taoist Worshiping Section and Dragon Origin Tracing Section. There are more than 80 small scenic spots, such as the former residence of the

Gongye, Paper-making by Cai Lun, Winding of the Purple Clouds, Moon Reflected in the Pond, Immortals' Temple, Dragon King Temple and Dragon Spring and so on. The plants here are also varied and amount to more than 1,700 kinds, including over 400 kinds of rare and precious Chinese medical ingredients. The animals here have more than 100 kinds.

The residences on the banks of the Longtan River are hardworking and economical. The bygone days have left abundant traditional custom and conventions. A popular local snack is called Baiqiao Dried Tofu. It used to be a kind of food that was for royal family. Almost every family can make wines and they have special manners for toasting. Their buildings have gabled walls and are constructed according to the variation of the topography so as to make the best of the mountainous surroundings. The making of touch paper is a specialty that the locals take pride in. This kind of handicraft has a year over 2,000 years. It is said that Cai Lun was almost drown before he was saved by the fishermen from the nearby villages. In order to repay them, Cai Lun taught how to make paper in person.

龙潭 Dragon Pool is the first destination. Look to the rest, this is the very place we are to visit. Legend has it that there used to be a dragon living inside, but now it is gone and only fishes swarm in the pool.

金蟾观银杏 Now what you can see is called Golden Frog Watching Gingko. Please be careful and do not watch the scenery while walking. Now we can stop here and watch the Gingko tree closely. It has been here for thousands of years and the frog-shaped rock is just in front of it. Some people say the frog is lifting its head and gazing passionately at the tree. The legend also tells that the Prince of Western China Sea was deeply attracted by the beauty of the Gingko, however, it is the Golden Frog whom the Gingko had a crush on. Lastly, the Prince was fury at this and make Gingko become a tree standing here. The Golden Frog, crying his heart out, kept her company at her foot. The Prince regret his misdoing and had a pit on the couple. He made the Gold Frog become a stone, sitting under the tree.

相会桥 After hearing the touching story, we must have a deeper understanding about their true love for each other. The bridge is built for their reunion. Standing on the bridge, we can imagine how excited they would be after a long departure.

珠帘瀑布 This scene is called Pearl Curtain, for the spring dribbles down the trees in the forests and falls on the stones, the reflections sometimes become a rainbow, like a necklace decorated with beard pearls. It is said that not only ladies but also gentlemen can become appealing after taking photos.

双狮护龙门 Now you can find two stone lions squatting at a gate. The one on the left is male named Golden Lion, the one on the right is female with the name Silver Lion. The Prince of Western China Sea made a couple become a tree and a stone, for which he himself was punished by his benevolent father, the Dragon King. The supreme God in Chinese culture, Jade Emperor, ordered the Golden and Silver Lions to arrest the Prince. The two warriors had a fierce battle with the Prince and finally caught him. The story ended with the detention of the Prince, the two warriors being the guards on duty.

天鹅湖瀑布 Each scenic spot has its own feature and so does the Longtan River. As you can see, its biggest feature goes to its mountains and waters and waterfalls. There are dozens of waterfalls here, some of them are abrupt and some of them are calm. The first waterfall before us is called Swan Paddling. It is said that one of the Eight Immortals, Lü Dongbin had his cultivation here and made the river become a flying swan. If you look at the waterfall carefully, you might find its shape resembling a paddling swan.

连心桥 Heart Connecting Bridge. This is a multi-step waterfall. You can see the stream flows out of the gaps and gurgling waves wind along the slopes. The white ripples are like clouds in the sky hovering around the waist of the mountains.

龙太子洞 Now we have arrived at the cave of Dragon Prince, you can see it on your right. Though not big in size, you never know there is a mysterious story about it. Just now, we learned the Golden and Silver Lions were ordered to arrest the rebellious Dragon Prince and they fought against the Prince day and night. An adviser of the Dragon King, by the name of Nine-Head Tortoise was asked to persuade the Prince to surrender. Turning a deaf ear to the persuasion, the Dragon Prince returned to his cave and even suddenly attacked the tortoise by ejecting two streams. You can see the two streams still running in front of us.

公主沐浴 Now you can see a big waterfall before us called Princess Bathing. Judging from this name, you can figure out the romantic connotation in it. The waterfall gushes down out of the crack and nobody knows the how deep it can be. The water supply seems endless and boundless. The lower part of the waterfall is wider and just like the showering in our life. In the legend, the Princess, daughter of the Dragon King, worried about her brother and father. She often stayed here alone, dreaming to marry a beloved husband and live a real life. Too preoccupied with this daydreaming, she missed the deadline for returning to the Dragon Palace and became a stone. What a pity it is.

龙宫 Move on and then we will take a rest in another cave. This is the most spectacular part of the whole scenic area, the Dragon Palace. In the myth, Dragon King of Western China Sea used to live in it while fleeing from calamity. There is a saying that it is easy to stay home and hard to go outside. The feeling of the Dragon King is very complicated during the two warriors' fight with his son. On the one hand, he was indignant about his son's misdoings and hoped he can repent and reform; on the other hand, he felt upset for fearing that his son be killed by Jade Emperor, if so he would have no offspring to carry on the family line. Because of this, he fidgeted and continually asked his prime minister to see the fights. He walked to and fro in the cave and that's why we find the ground uneven. The dents, in fact, are said to be footprints of the King.

Move upwards, you can see the peach flowers are in full blossom. The bamboos lining on the sides are luxurious and pine trees green. There is a great poet named Zheng Banqiao in the late Qing Dynasty. He once wrote a poem praising such beautiful circumstances. Plant Bamboo and Pine for Phoenix and Crane, Protect Mountain and Water for Tiger and Dragon. These two lines are best examples for describing the beauty of such natural environment.

Standing on the ridge, you can have a bird's eye of the Longtan River. There seems nothing special outwardly, and it is for this reason the Dragon King chose to hide here. Tourists have to reach its depth if they want to appreciate this scenic spot. Though not as grand as other world-renowned mountains and rivers, it is characterized by uniqueness and beauty. Nobody will say it is not worth visiting after they take a trip in it.

八仙观 The Dragon King brought benefits to the locals for thanking their kindness by rendering wind and rain come on time. The local villagers, in return, built this temple to worship the Dragon King. The current temple was renovated on the old sites. After that, Jade Emperor Hall and Three Purity Hall were built in succession and their statues were enshrined. Whenever there are important occasions and festivals, the locals burn incenses and set off firecrackers for the blessing of the gods. Their praying reflect the simple wishes of the pious and earthy wishes.

月老庙 In Chinese culture, a matchmaker is called Yuelao, which means the god under the moon. He is believed to be responsible for matchmaking for men and women with a red thread. If the young man and women are destined to be a couple, Yuelao will do his best to let them marry each other, regardless of their social status, prejudice and distance.

Jiahe Pass 夹河关

Jiahe Town was approved as one of the three Famous Cultural Towns by Shiyan City in 2008, Jiahe Pass Tourist Spot is located in the side of the Hanjiang River where there are Jinlan Mountain also named Small Wudang and other Taoist tourism cultural resources and convenient transportation, 100 km away to Shiyan City proper, 70 km away to Yunxi County proper, Xiangyang-Sichuan Railway and No. 316 national highway running in the other side of the Hanjiang River and connecting the Wulong River and the Longtan River. There are 40m-long Hanjiang River Wall, 200m-long uphill walkway, ancient city wall, observation pavilion, dragon-head incense, Jinlan Avenue, ancient buildings of the Ming and Qing dynasties, Sunjiatan Reservoir and Hui People Folk Culture Zone, which was appraised as one of the AAA-level scenic spots in 2011.

Wudang Red Wine Eco-industrial Tourism Area 武当红葡萄酒酒庄

Wudang Red Wine Eco-industrial Tourism Area is one of national AAA-level tourist attractions. Wudang Red Eco-industrial Tourism area is located in the central and western region of the largest pure European Winery-Yunxi Maynoch Winery, covering an area of 40,000 square meters, with an annual production capacity of 3,000 tons of high-grade wine. The scenic spot is comprehensive which mainly develops, produces and manages high-grade wild wine, and integrates the research and development, production and distribution of wild wine. It is the first wine manufacturer to obtain double certification of organic products and AA grade green products in China.

Huanglong/ Yellow Dragon Cave 黄龙洞

Yellow Dragon Cave, one of the key cultural relics under state protection, is located at the northwest of Xiangkou Town, 30 km away from Yunxi County proper. The Cave is located on the southern part of the eastern slope of the Qinling Mountains and is a Paleolithic cave site. There is a river in front of the cave. The mouth of the cave is about 7 meters above the river. Behind the cave is Huanglong Mountain.

Hanging Drum Temple 悬鼓观

Hanging Drum Temple is located at the southwest, 2 km away from Yunxi County proper, with a total area of 5 square km, and 440 meters above sea level. There are Taoist gods and buildings in the Temple, with red gravel cliffs near the top. During the lunar festivals, many people come here to offer incense and pray for better health and fortune.

Tianhe Cherry Blossom Valley 天河樱花谷

Cherry Blossom Valley is a newly developed scenic spot, the small and bright cherry trees leaning against the valley, increasing much fresh and charming.

Chapter 2 Fangxian County and the Main Tourist Resources 房县旅游

Fangxian County, named Fangling Prefecture in the history, is located in the northwest of Hubei Province, the south of Shiyan City, neighbouring Baokang County and Gucheng County in the east, Danjiangkou City in the northeast, Shennongjia Forest Region in the south, and Zhushan County in the west. Here are cultural relics of the Paleolithic Period and the Neolithic Age, which is one of the cradles of Chu Culture.

Now, Fangxian County has been honored as Home of Black Fungus, Home of Yellow Wine, National Model County of Forestation, and the Heart of China's Ecology. Here are exuberant forests in the whole county with a coverage of over 70%. The Qinba Ecology Function Region with Fangxian County as the key part is the ecological regulator to prevent sand storm southwards and acid rain northwards. Here are rich grasslands with over 28.7 million mu pasture, the first one in Hubei Province and one of the million commercial sheep bases.

Fangxian County is rich in mineral resources, such as, lead, zinc, copper, magnesium, iron, manganese vanadium, dimension stone and mineral water and so on. The mineral water has been certified as the Best Mineral Water in China for its contents of radon and pylon.

In the magical land, there are long and profound Shijing Culture, Shennong Culture, Faith and Piety Culture, Exile Culture and the exploration for Wild Man, which have formed the unique folk customs. Here are over 50 kinds of green foods, such as green tea, mushroom, black fungus, Fangling yellow wine, and Chinese traditional herbs.

Shijing Culture in Fangxian County 房县诗经文化

Fangxian County used to be named Fangling and it's the source of the Duhe River, the biggest branch of the Hanjiang River reaches. Many poets have taken their field trips here and wrote down many poems eulogizing the natural beauty, hence the poetry book *Shijing Zhounan /The Book of Songs (Zhounan)*. This book had a deep influence on the local culture. There are many words that are still spoken in the local dialect which can be traced to the poetry. Besides this, there are many sites and buildings scattered among the green fields and mountains, such as the former residence of Yin Jifu (the King of Yin Kingdom, the collector and compiler of *The Book of Songs*, also one of the important poets, thinkers, and educators, musicians, and statesmen), ancestral hall, temples and tomb, added by his descendants.

For thousands of years' accumulation and development, Fangxian County has stood out for its profound ancient cultures. *Shijing* /*The Book of Songs* in its inheritance, contributed to the growth of a unique literary form, Fangxian Folk Songs. Characterized by wide diversity, variable intonation and rich contents, the rhythmic lyrics reflect such customs and conventions as the local production, life, love and marriage. Well combined with Chu Diao, Ba Yin and Qin Yun, Fangxian Folk Songs are hailed as the living fossils of pre-Qin Dynasty cultures.

The locals still have an intense and pure love for poems. A great majority of the elderly local residents can recite and interpret the ancient poems in *The Book of Songs*. Their sound knowledge proves its intrinsic link to this classic poetry. It is no exaggeration to say poetry has shaped their makeup and is playing an indispensable role in their routine life. Fangxian County has inherited the essence of Shijing. Therefore its thousand-year-long history of culture and literature is well retained and passed on from generation to generation.

The Legends of Yi Jifu has been inscribed on the Hubei Provincial Intangible Cultural Heritage List. Various forms of activities are held by the media to claim the public's attention, such as folklore contests, tourism award-giving meetings and so on. CCTV music channel also made a TV program specially entitled *Poetry Born in Fangling* and won the applause from audiences all over China.

Currently, the Fangxian County Government has invested RMB 500 million yuan to build a 99-acre Shijing Cultural Garden whose theme include three major contents of Shijing, i.e. Feng, Ya and Song. The Garden is able to receive 600,000 visitors every year. The construction and the efforts will definitely contribute to the spreading of Shijing Culture.

Shijingyuan/ *The Book of Songs* Source National Forest Park 诗经源国家森林公园

There is a green land located in the magical north altitude 30℃—Shijingyuan National Forest Park — 33 km away from the County Proper in the southeast, which connects Shennongjia Forest Region and Wudang Mountains, where there are original secondary forest, exuberant plants and bushes, full of vitality and oxygen. When in thick fog, the park is more charming, you will feel the cloud flowing around you and you are just in the wonderland.

There are great vertical changes of climate in the park which has formed different kinds of plants and flowers. Here are mountains and peaks, valleys and canyons, streams and waterfalls, pines and firs, with a forest coverage of over 91% and a high connotation of anions, 80 thousand pieces per cm^3, a pure and natural oxygen.

Here are full of low and medium mountainous forest landscapes, special karst landforms, caves, water, pagota, forest, and gorge which has formed the magnificent, unique, charming, deep and wild features. Many plants and animals are under state protection.

The park has integrated sightseeing, educating, appreciating, entertaining and participating functions and realized a coordinated development of ecology tourism, science education, cultural entertainment, exploration, environmental protection and economy production, which is a best choice for you to regulate the body and mind, relax the pressure and enjoy the happy life.

Xiansheng/ Emperor Zhenwu Appearing Hall 显圣殿

Xiansheng Hall, one of the key culture units under provincial protection, is located in the Ancient Street of Xiadianzi Village, one of traditional villages in China, Jundian Town, 10km away from the County Proper in the west. Here are many ancient buildings, including Wushen Palace, Scriptures-Collecting Tower, Zhenwu Pavilion, as one of the ten wonders in Fangxian history and the outside Taoist buildings of Wudang Mountains, also called Medium Wudang.

The Ancient Street has two parts in the style of small courtyard Siheyuan, with blue stone as the base, brick and earth as the wall, fir wood as the structure and earthen tiles as the roof cover, and the joints and conjunctions of pillars and beams fixed by mortice and tenon. The street was paved by cobbles and built in accordance with the landform, free and extending. As early as in the Tang Dynasty, here were shops, stores and stands, many merchants from Sichuan, Shaanxi, Hubei and Hunan provinces came here for business, full of vitality and prosperity. During the Temple Fair days, lots of pious incense-burners and visitors came here, especially on the day of March Three Temple Fair in Xiansheng Hall of Jundian Town, colorful culture events were held here.

Shennong Gorge Yanwugou Scenic Area 神农峡岩屋沟风景区

Shennong Gorge Yanwugou Scenic Area is located in Duchuan Village, Yerengu Town, Fangxian County, one of the must place from Wudang Mountains to Shennongjia Forest Region, which begins from Guanmen/ Closing Door Mountain in the east, extending to the Gaoqiao/ High Bridge River in the west, beginning from Dujia Plain, extending to Suozi/ Shuttle Mountain and Tanpa/ Charcoal Rabble Mountain.

The mountains in the Scenic Area are relatively low in the surrounding but high-rising in the central place, mainly composed of Paleozoic phyllite and callys and some granite. The stone layers develop in accordance with the joint structure and rise with the fault line, forming many steep cliffs, with many dropping basins in the two sides of the mountains.

Here are unique stones and peaks, streams and waterfalls, rare trees and flowers, high mountains and low lawns, stone caves and grottoes. The trees here are mainly pines, firs, birches, and oaks, forming a charm of nature and harmony, and chosen as the summer resort of the royal families.

Guanyin/ Kwan-yin Cave Scenic Area 观音洞风景区

Guanyin/ Kwan-yin Cave Scenic Area is located in Fenghuang/ Phoenix Mountain and near the state highway No. 209, 3km away from the County Proper in the south. The Scenic Area, lying between Phoenix Ridge and Dragon Hill, is characterized by flowing mountain ridges, birds and flowers.

Built in the Tang Dynasty after many times of renovations and extending, the Cave has had the current status and been approves as the key culture unit under the provincial protection. The main scene is a natural cave in the steep cliff, which divided into South Cave, Guangong Cave deep in 8m, wide in 6m and high in 4m and North Cave, Guanyin Cave, deep in 9m, wide in 13m and high in 5m, where a Guanyin Statue is worshiped in the center. In front of the Cave there stands a one-thousand-year Cinnamon Tree, full of fragrant flowers in spring.

In the Scenic Area, there are exuberant plants, high ancient trees, Fenghuang/ Phoenix Villa, Shari-la Valley, Qingren Valley, Taichi Square, Jingxin/ Cleaning Heart Pavilion, Kuixing Pavilion, Guanyin Corridor and Xuanwu Palace. When you climb onto the mountain top, you can have a bird-eye view of the County Proper.

Going into the Cave for about half a km, you will find two coordinating natural caves with a distance of about 15 meters. In the bigger cave Guanyin Statue is worshiped and in the smaller cave Guangong worshiped. Three auxiliary halls were built outside of the two caves which formed an ancient and elegant mountain Taoist temple with the living houses for the Taoists. The Cave has been prosperous in incenses and followers for several hundred years. In front of the Cave, there are high slim bamboos and ancient trees and a stone-made path winding downwards to the valley bottom with about 633 steps.

Yeren/ Wild Man Valley and Yeren/ Wild Man Cave Scenic Area 房县野人谷、野人洞景区

Fangxian County has two AAAA-level national scenic spots named by Yeren or Wild Man, Yeren/ Wild Man Valley and Yeren/ Wild Man Cave, which is near the tourist highway between Wudang Mountains and Shennongjia Forest Region, connecting Wudang Mountains in the north and Shennongjia Forest Region in the South, where there are moist climate, charming landscapes, well-developed karst caves, exuberant plantations, high mountains and deep waters, approved as provincial-level scenic spot, nature reserve and Geo-park.

Yeren Valley was formed by the geological changes of sky hole, karst cave and underground river 0.5 billion years ago, well-known for the appearance of wild man in the Valley and the first man who fought against wild man is living the back part of the Valley. The natural five-km-long valley is characterized by water, waterfalls and streams surrounded by green mountains, original and ancient, such as Senior Dragon Beard Waterfall, Wild Bath Pool, Sky Root, Yeren/ Wild Man Hall and exuberant plantations, which have formed an innovative and imaginative landscape scroll where you can appreciate flowers in spring, experience cool summer, enjoy golden autumn and white snow in winter.

Yeren Cave is located very near to Yeren Valley and famous for the footprints of Wild Man in the Cave, which is deep in 1,980m and has two parts with a 45-m drop between the upper cave and the lower cave. There is a huge sky hole between the two caves, dangerous and exciting. There are four halls, five palaces and 59 wonders in the Cave, such as stone pillars, forest, gods and animals, gates, paths, shoots, flowers, screen, and the like, vivid and interesting. Especially, the scenes as Wild Man Hitting Drum, Wild Man's Bed Room, Wild Man and Beauty, Wild Man's Footprints, lively in forms and form a natural art gallery with Wild Man as the theme.

Chapter 3 Zhushan County and the Main Tourist Resources 竹山旅游

Zhushan County, named Shangyong County in the ancient times, under the control of Shiyan City, is located in Qinba Mountainous Region, northwest of Hubei Province, lying between Wudang Mountains and Daba Mountain. Zhushan County is bordering Fangxian County in the east, Yunyang District in the north, Baihe County of Shaanxi Province in the northwest, Zhuxi County and Xunyang County of Shaanxi Province in the west, and Shennongjia Forest Region and Wuxi County of Chongqing City in the south.

The County Proper is 158km away from Shiyan City proper in the northeast, 638km away from Wuhan City in the southeast, covering a total area of 3,587.8km^2, of which 80% is mountainous area. The southern mountains are most over 1,500m above the sea level. In the middle river valley there are some narrow and long flat lands and dams. Here are eight ethnic groups, including Han, Hui, Zhuang Mongolian, Man and others. Here planted many bamboos in the Western Wei Dynasty and were full of green mountains and clean waters, so the County was renamed Zhushan, meaning Bamboo Mountain.

The whole County is declining from south and and west to northeast, characterized by big drop, steep slope and deep valley. The southern part is mountain and the middle and west are low hill and basin with an altitude difference of 2,520 meters. The highest peak is Congping Mountain with an altitude of 2,740.4 meters, while the lowest is the Mouth of the Nigu River with an altitude of 220 meters.

There are 646 rivers, big or small, long or short, among which 98 are long rivers and 548 are seasonal ones. The river banks are stable, made of coarse sand and cobbles. The Duhe River, starting from Zhengping County of Shaanxi Province and Shennongjia Forest Region of Hubei Province, is flowing across the Sihe River in Zhuxi County and the Jiudaoliang River in Fangxian County from southwest to northeast with three main branches, the Shenhe River, the Huohe River and the Kutao River, working as the main transportation channel.

Zhushan County is in subtropical monsoon continental climate and the north temperate zone, but it is located in Hanjiang and Duhe Basin, therefore it is also in the high temperate zone, having plentiful warmth, whose annual temperature is between 10.2℃ and 15.6℃, influenced by southwest wind.

Zhushan County is of outstanding tourist resources, such as the Duhe River Source, Lvtou/ Donkey Head Gorge Gallery, Jiuhua Mountain Forest Park, and the Huohe Reservoir. Here are colorful folk arts, including drama, songs, stories, paper-cutting, clay sculpture and handwriting. Located in the middle line of the Three Gorges of the Changjiang River, Shennongjia Forest Region, Wudang Mountains, Xi'an City, Xiangyang, Zhushan County has had a special location advantage.

Wuling Gorge Scenic Area 武陵峡风景区

Wuling Gorge Scenic Area, composed of Taohua/ Peach Flower Source Scenic Spot,

Gorge Original Ecology Park and Geo-park, located in Guandu Town, is long in 33km, high in 1,000m, and wide in 5m, approved as the longest, deepest and narrowest gorge in the Central China, and named Qingfeng Fault Zone by the famous geologist Li Siguang. The mountains and peaks in the Gorge are steep and charming, with many big karst caves, streams and waterfalls, sky holes, and original forests standing on the cliffs and peaks, such as Taohua Source Ancient Village, Monkey-Jumping Canyon, One-Line Sky, Middle Pillar Peak and Five-Dragon Cave.

The Duhe Source Scenic Area　堵河源风景区

The Duhe Source Scenic Area is made up of Jiuhua Mountain Forest Park, Liulin Mochi Lake and Lu Ban Canyon. The Duhe River, originated from the overflowing of Dajiuhu Lake of Shennongjia Forest Region, is clean and clear, flowing downwards through mountains and formed a 4km-long waterfall group of 108 pieces, grand and majestic, full of changes and charms. Here are some karst caves, such as, Wild Man Cave, Nature-made Bridge, White Tiger Stream. As one of the main sources of the middle-line project of South-to-North Water Diversion, the Scenic Area has many attractive spots, including Lingpai/ Token Mountain Village, Gun-Knife Mountain, Peach Flower Ridge, Leopard Cliff, original forest, and Swan Lake.

Nüwa Mountain Scenic Area　女娲山风景区

Nüwa Mountain Scenic Area is in Baofeng Town, 180km away from Shiyan City Proper, with No. 305 provincial highway and Xiangyang-Tianshui Expressway running across. Here are 22 peaks, among which the main peak is over 900 meters and on which Nüwa Sacrifice Altar is built with other smaller peaks guarding and looking up. In accordance with the textual studies, the ancestors Fuxi and Nüwa made man and fixed the sky in Nüwa Mountain of Zhushan County. The Altar is built in accordance with original Eight Diagrams with the statue of 16 meters in height, the highest one in China. The main spots are Nüwa Sacrifice Altar, Double-Dragon Cave, and Man-making Place where Nüwa made man from earth.

Stone Buddha Temple　石佛寺

Stone Buddha Temple is in Shuangtai Town, 35km away from the County Proper in the northwest, originally built in the Ming Dynasty. In accordance with *Zhushan County Annals*, a monk sit here and died whose body kept fresh and sound after many years winds and rains, so that the village residents called him Buddha, hence the name of Stone Buddha Temple. People said that it is very effective for the followers to come here and ask for fortunes, therefore many people come here from the neighbouring Sichuan and Shaanxi provinces, including Yunyang District and Zhushan County. It was destroyed in the Great Cultural Revolution (1966—1976) and rebuilt again.

Gao Family's Former Residence　高家花屋

Gao Family's Former Residence is a folk house in Xiejiagou Village of Zhuping Town, built in the years of Emperor Jiaqing and Daoguang of the Qing Dynasty. The Residence is in a style of palace with three-layer courtyards, decorated with lots of stone-carved wall paintings and wood-cut thresholds, colorful and vivid after many years' weathering. The original coverage is 1,218m^2, now 48 pieces of rooms and halls remained.

Nanshui/ South Water Source Scenic Area 南水源风景区

Nanshui/ South Water Source Scenic Area is made of Muyu Lake/ Huohe Reservoir Scenic Spot, Guojiashan Yong Culture Theme Park, Longbei/ Dragon Back Mountain and Lianhua/ Lotus Temple. Muyu Lake is in the east of the County Proper, named after the form of a wooden fish with an altitude of 440 meters, under which is Huohe Reservoir, the first earthen dam reservoir in Asia. The Reservoir has 7,000-mu water coverage, 20,000-mu mountain field, eight valleys, seven peaks, one pagoda, two temples, one mountain village, two caves, one islet, and one tea garden, full of charming scenes. Guojiashan Yong Culture Theme Park has copied the cultural relics in Zhushan County, such as, Dengshuang Pavilion, Tiyun Pavilion, Dacheng Hall of Wen Temple, and Wang Sansheng's Big House.

Guanyin Valley Ecology Culture Tourism Zone 观音沟生态文化旅游区

Guanyin Valley Ecology Culture Tourism Zone is in Santai Village of Loutai Town, 12km away from the County proper and 127km away from Shiyan City Proper, with the national high No. 242 running across. Here are clean waters and green mountains, flowers and birds, ancient trees and unique peaks, which was the sacred place for Guanyin/ Kwan-yin to help the people and drive out sufferings. The Zone has four functional units, the martyr of the Revolution of 1911, Zhang Zhenwu's Graveyard, used as Honest Lecture Hall, Eco-agriculture Sightseeing and Picking Zone including grape, strawberry, watermelon, peach, tea and vegetables, religious worshiping zone including Guanyin Valley, Zhenwu Temple, Fortune God Temple, Huatuo Temple and Thousand-year Hanging Coffin Group, and comprehensive service center for visitors to park their cars, have meals and buy souvenirs.

Wang Sansheng's Former Residence 三盛院

Wang Sansheng's Former Residence is in Shangyong Town and the joining part of the Duhe River and the Sihe River, as the important and influential courtyard in the late years of the Qing Dynasty, named from the family clan' shop founded by Wang Yingkui born in 1785 and in Macheng County, Hubei Province. Wang's mother died early when he was very young. He left home when he found out his stepmother wanted to poison him to death. After travelling a lot, he came to Zhushan County and began his business in copper making and beancurd shopping in Nanguan Street. After one-year's hard working, he obtained some money and then transferred to Tianjia Dam, now called Shangyong Town where he continued his business and expanded to salt dealings and became richer and richer. Two years later, he ran many general stores here and did barter trade so as to make lots of money and found the big houses.

Lütou/ Donkey Head Gorge 驴头峡

Lvtou/ Donkey Head Gorge is in the joining zone of Guandu Town and Liangjia Town, 70km away from the County Proper, formed by Lvtou/ Donkey Head Mountain and Songshu/ Pine Ridge. Lvtou/ Donkey Head Mountain, the former is 1,470-meter high and the latter 1,250-meter high. The Gorge is 5km long and with an average width of 30 meters, zigzagging forward with steep cliffs and strange-formed stones on the two banks where there are red and green cirrus, exuberant trees and bushes. The river water is flowing forward, now silently, then violently.

There are many charming natural scenes in the Gorge, such as Donkey Head Mountain, Double Fish Cave, Monkey Jumping Canyon, One-Line Sky, Sky Dog Watching the Moon, Black Dragon Ridge, and Taichi Picture. Now here river drifting is provided and you can have a relaxed and exciting time in the serene gorge.

Qinba Folk Customs Garden 秦巴民众风情苑

Qinba Folk Customs Garden, one of the national AAA-level tourist spots, is located in Guandu Town, a very good place to know about Qinba culture evolution and migrating people's new life. Here collected folk cultural relics which covered folk songs, tales, paper-cuttings, farming, marriage, craftsmanship, construction, costumes, religion and sacrifice of about 2,000 years.

Chapter 4 Zhuxi County and the Main Tourist Resources 竹溪旅游

Zhuxi County is located in the north slope of Daba Mountains and the southwest of Shiyan City and the border region of northwest of Hubei Province, connecting Hubei Province and Shaanxi Province and Chongqing City. Zhuxi County, the source of the Duhe River, the biggest branch of the Hanjiang River, is connecting Pingli, Zhengping and Xunyang counties of Shaanxi Province in the west, Wuxi County of Chongqing City in the south, and Zhushan County in the east. Zhuxi County is the important linking point to connecting the Central China, the northwest and southwest with a unique location advantage. Starting from Zhuxi County, you can easily get to the neighbouring major cities, such as Chongqing, Xi'an, Shiyan and Ankang. Zhuxi is famous for its abundant plant and mineral resources, local products and delicious foods, especially green tea and Zhuxi Steamed Pot.

Daba Mountains is the source of all the mountains in Zhuxi County, which demonstrate a form of wrinkle and extend forward from southwest to northeast. Therefore, Zhuxi County is higher in the southwest and lower in the northeast, with an altitude difference of 2,464 meters. The mountains develop with the stratum, river valley, canyon and basin, forming small hills, basins, medium hills and high mountains.

Zhuxi County is in northern tropical monsoon climate with four distinctive seasons, big temperature difference, plenty sunshine and suitable rainfall.

Zhuxi County has abundant mineral resources, such as copper, iron, manganese, aluminium, zinc, coal, stone materials and the like. Here are three main rivers, the Zhuxi River, the Huiwan River and the Wanjiang River, all belonging to the Duhe River system.

Longhu/ Dragon Lake National Wetland Lotus 龙湖国家湿地千亩荷花

Longhu/ Dragon Lake National Wetland has taken many effective measures to turn farmlands, river and lake, valley and channel into lotus pond, such returning the farmlands for wetland, returning lake for wetlands and the like, which grow into vast areas of lotus as to reduce the pollutants, improve water quality and maintain water ecology and popularize wetland ecological system construction and drinking water source protection among the nearby residents and visitors for a purpose to guide them to love and care environment and wetland, and achieve the wetlands' complete function and sustainable development. Now, many visitors come here for a sightseeing or relaxation which also provide a good business opportunity for the nearby residents so that they can make more money, improve their living standards and strengthen the sense of protecting environment and wetlands.

Eighteen-Li Long Gorge 十八里长峡

Eighteen-Li Long Gorge begins from the Chahe River in Xiangba Town and extends to Shuangqiao Town, covering 46.8km^2, whose altitudes are different from 1,000m to 2,800m, and total length is eighteen li (nine km), hence the name. The Long Gorge is located in the very center of China mainland geographically, whose tourism development can serve the tourist markets in China.

As one of the national nature reserves, Eighteen-Li Long Gorge is a scenic spot of interesting stories, special landscapes, many kinds of rare plants and animals, and ecology-protecting local residents, which make the visitors moved and remember it in deep impression.

The Long Gorge Nature Reserve, full of mountains and peaks, valleys and canyons, wild plants and animals, is an encyclopedic of rare plants and animals in China.

Here are 49 peaks higher than 2,000 meters among which the highest one is 2,740 meters, covered by clouds and fogs the whole year, seem as high-rising long sword, charming lady, Buddha watching the sky and the like. Here are exuberant grasslands and ancient trees, whose coverage is over 96.5%, recognized as the rare natural Oxygen Bar in Central China for its original plantation and fine ecology. It is an ideal place for all tourists to return to, approach and experience the Nature.

Eping Reservoir 鄂坪水库风光

Eping Reservoir is in Eping Town, the nearest one to the County Proper in the south direction, about 28 km distance (nearly 40 minutes' drive), with Ehong highway running across and the Huiwan River flowing through the Town, lying between mountains and waters, quiet and elegant. In the years of Emperor Jiaqing of the Ming Dynasty, the Emperor wanted to build the Imperial Palace and traveled many places to look for nanmu and found it here, so he was very happy and excited to write a poem to memorize it. Now Eping Town is devoted to developing tourism so that the charming scenery has attracted my visitors and cameramen to be here, especially Eping Reservoir.

Traditional Village 穿越时空的传统村落

Wangjiaping Village is a high-mountain village in Longba Town, whose folk houses can be divided into five categories in accordance with their plane layout, 一-form, T-form, 凹-form, free courtyard and countryside house form, which are simple and decent, completely suitable to the mountainous areas in Hubei Province, for they are less influenced by the neighbouring restrictions, harmoniously integrated with the nearby landscapes. The layouts are changing with the landform and demonstrating colorful house styles.

一-form: the commonest one, three or five rooms standing together. The middle one is the main hall used to worship the ancestors, perform the daily life and meet friends, the right and left one used to be restaurant or bedroom, which are divided into the front part and the back part usually.

T-form:a layout developed from the 一-form, bigger than the former. Two or three smaller rooms are built besides the main room to be bed rooms, or restaurant or storing room, also called zigzag shape.

凹-form: also called U-form, two or three smaller rooms are built in the two sides of the main room, hence a relatively complete front courtyard, which is very important for farmers in the countryside to harvest grains and store some crops. The family of more person and better economy conditions often apply this form.

The traditional residence in Wangjiaping Village is well protected and has been designed to develop rural culture tourism, which is supported by the County government.

Gan Clan Hall in Zhongfeng Town 中峰镇甘宗祠

Gan Clan Hall in Zhongfeng Town is in Ganjialing Village, Zhongfeng Town, used as the place for the local Gan Family people to worship and sacrifice their ancestors and discuss important things. The Hall was built in the thirteen year of Emperor Kangxi of the Qing Dynasty (1674) in the memory of Gan Jifang, an important official who died for protecting the country. The Government of the Qing Dynasty gave three boards and ordered to build a memorial hall, then one of his offspring Gan Kaigong built the Main Hall and the Back Hall in the thirteen and nineteen years of Emperor Qianlong of the Qing Dynasty (1748—1754), another grandsons named Gan Jingzhi and Gan Jingchun offered money and built side rooms, dinning hall, bounding wall, playground and gateway during the years of Emperor Guangxi of the Qing Dynasty (1888—1889). The Official Hall in the east side was built in 1914.

Gan Clan Hall, covering an area of 3.5mu and of a construction area of 400m^2, is in a brick-wood structure and closed courtyard form of two layers, composed of the Main Hall, the Back Hall, side room, dinning hall, bounding wall and gateway. On the gateway there inscribed a board and two couplets telling Gan Jifang's outstanding contributions. As one of the bigger clan halls in the northwest of Hubei Province, the Hall is of great significance to the study of the clan buildings, the clan system and regional patriarchal clan system of the Qing Dynasty.

Longwangya Regiment Villa 龙王垭养生山庄

Longwangya Regiment Villa is a AAAA-level tourist hotel co-supported by Hubei Longwangya Tea Company Limited, the Key Leading Enterprise of National Agriculture Industrialization and Wuhan Gewei Hotel Manament Company Limited.

The Villa is one of the key projects of Zhuxi County's effort to build a county of energy, ecology, culture, livability and tourism, a comprehensive tourist holiday hotel which integrates summer resort, tourist sightseeing, tea culture experience, local dishes, accommodation, conference, fishing, entertainment, fitness and leisure. The Villa is far away from urban clamour and has green tea trees and colorful flowers in spring, clouds, fogs and green plantations in summer, cool air, blue sky and charming sunset glow in autumn, and white snow world in winter. There are pavilion, corridor, observation tower and artificial scenes in the villa where you can meet with relatives and friends, hold conference, business reception, and have a tour, cool summer, regiment and leisure time here. The Villa also provides a good platform to show the tea industry of Zhuxi County and expand the developing space for the county's leisure tourism and improve its new image, too.

Tea Culture Walking on the fitness & sightseeing road in the tea garden, you will be nurtured by a thick and profound tea culture atmosphere as well as appreciating the tea pavilion, tea information, tea culture gallery and boards in the two sides and experience the wide and profound Chinese tea culture. If you are interested in making a tea by yourself, you can pick tea leaves and produce tea in the operation room.

Leisure gathering If you are tired of the noisy and busy life in cities, you will think of having a leisure gathering with your relatives or friends, then you are advised to come here, Longwangya Regiment Villa, far away from the noisy city and convenient in transportation, only about 15-minutes' drive from county proper to be here. Here is a comprehensive reception center which will meet all your requirements in gathering, meeting, summer resorting and leisure regiment.

Ecological tourism Here is no high buildings, no wide lake, no strange stone or cultural relics, just an ideal place of ecological tourism. Here you can enjoy green tea trees and colorful flowers in spring, clouds, fogs and green plantations in summer, cool air, blue sky and charming sunset glow in autumn, and white snow world in winter, and also you can taste fragrant tea and local dishes, visit ecological tea garden and experience tea culture.

Chapter 5 Danjiangkou City and the Main Tourist Resources 丹江口旅游

Danjiangkou City, the Water Capital of China, one of the name brands of China tourism and China Tourist Cities, is located in the middle of China, the middle and upper reaches of the Hanjiang River. Danjiangkou Reservoir is the core water source of the mid-line project of South-to-North Water Diversion, also called the biggest man-made lake in Asia. And the Heightening Project of Danjiangkou Reservoir is the key control project of the mid-line project of South-to-North Water Diversion.

Here are many tourist resources connecting water and mountain, such as, Danjiangkou Reservoir, Danjiangkou Dam, Danjiangkou National Forest Part, Jingle/ Clean and Happy Palace, Taichi Gorge and Jinchan/ Golden Frog Gorge and other scenic spots.

Danjiangkou City is the biggest production place of Wudang Orange in North China, also rich aquatic products and Wudang Taoist Tea. The industrial competence is also excellent, especiallynitrogen-oxygen sensor and auto transmission shaft.

Danjiangkou Dam 丹江口大坝

Danjiangkou Dam, located in the joining area of the Hanjiang River and its branch Danjiang River, is composed by concrete dam, power plant, ship-lifting system and two division canals, which was wholly designed, built and managed by Chinese after 1949. Danjiangkou Dam is a huge water control project mainly on flood prevention and on power producing, irrigating, shipping and fish breeding at the same time. As the key project of controlling and developing the Hanjiang River and of providing clean water for South-to-North Water Diversion, the Dam is 2.5km long, 162m high, with six generator units and an annual power production of four billion kw.

When the control project of the mid-line project of South-to-North Water Diversion, the Heightening Project of Danjiangkou Dam finished, Danjiangkou Reservoir has become the water source of the Mid-line Project and the Dam is high in 176.6m and the water level is 175m and water storage is 29.05 billion m^3. Recently, the annual water diversion is 9.7 billion m^3, and the future water diversion will be 13 billion m^3. The northward water is providing for over twenty metropolitan cities' living, producing, agriculture and ecology in Henan Province, Hebei Province, Beijing City and Tianjin City.

When climbing onto the top of the Dam, you will have a bird-eye view of Danjiangkou City proper, high buildings and ample parks, blue water and green mountains, which is the best choice for you to have a tour and relax your mind.

Danjiangkou Reservoir 丹江口水库

The beautiful Danjiang River originates from the high mountains in Shaanxi Province and runs across Danjiangkou and Xichuan County, Henan Province, both of two cities border Henan Province, Hubei Province and Shaanxi Province.

The whole Reservoir is located on the borders of Henan and Hubei provinces. There are lots of mountains surrounding it, so the climate is rather pleasant and tourists enjoy the fresh air and mild sunshine. The water in the Reservoir is crystal clear and there are no great waves. Of all the reservoirs in China, this is the most multifunctional and cost-effective one. It is a super huge reservoir and brings numerous benefits to us, including flood-prevention, power generation, navigation, irrigation, aquaculture and tourism. Started in the 1950s, this water conservancy project was aimed for overall development and administering the Hanjiang River. It consists of two river sections, the Hanjiang River and Danjiang River. The gross storage capacity amounts to 17.4 billion cubic meters. It is the largest man-made fresh lake in Asia.

If you are a fan of natural beauty, then you'd better not miss this chance. There are sailing route reaching different directions and the land transportation within the reservoir is also very systematic. Go westwards and you can get to Sichuan and Shaanxi provinces. The very center of Hubei Province is to the south. The flatland in Central China is to the east. The vast waters of Danjiangkou Reservoir blends with the color of the sky and they constitute a harmonious picture in tourists' minds. What is more appealing also include the oddly-shaped rock formations. If you rent a yacht and drive it on the waters, you will feel you are moving in a picturesque dreamland. The river becomes rather narrow at Yankou which ranges for several dozen miles. There are precipices on both sides and vines enlaced. This area of cliffs and watery is named Xiaosanxia, or Lesser Three Gorges, for they are composed of Yunling Gorge, Dazi Gorge and Yankou Gorge. On the cliffs of Lion Mountain, there is a naturally shaped Stone Statue of Buddha, 15 meters in height. He faces the rivers and seems rather calm and composed, resembling the Buddha statues in Leshan, Sichuan Province. The kind and smiling face, as well as the crisscross hands on his bosom, seems chanting and praying for the bliss of every tourist on the yacht.

Beneath the river, there are lots of cultural relics, adding more flavor to the appeal of the Reservoir. The cultural treasures of Western Henan Corridor were all well reserved. If you head for Yangchuan and on the 45-kilometer journey, you may have an eyeful of the places of historical interests. They are of the ancient Chu State, and also bear the features of Central China.

The heartland submerged used to the capital of ancient Chu State. The renowned patriotic poet, Qu Yuan, on his exile trip, wrote down many poems. On the banks of the Reservoir, there are tomb complexes of the Autumn and Spring Periods and the Warring State Periods. More than 7,000 relics have been unearthed. The chimes dug out of a Prince's tomb prove the best in quality all over China, reflecting the long history and high civilization of this place. All of these relics and natural scenery make Danjiang River an extremely charming scenic spot.

Now come to the top of the Dam. Overlook the flowing water of the Hanjiang River, you must be deeply impressed by its grandeur. Now I'd like to say something about the history of Danjiang Dam. The construction began in 1958 and was completed in 1973. In those hard times, it was unimaginable to have such a huge project completed. At the beginning, the construction of cofferdam involved about 100,000 local workers. They worked day and night consecutively in three shifts. The construction site is not more than two square kilometers, but tens of thousands of workers gathered around. The working conditions were even worse, for there is no electricity before, accordingly, workers had to resort to torches and lights on trucks. In 1968, the first 15 mw power units were put into use. It is until 1974 the first stage of construction was brought to an end. By then, the huge Dam is about 2.5km in length and 162 meters high. The total power volume amounts to 90 mw. Since its completion, more than 40 years has passed and the Dam remained sound and safe even in the face of unprecedented floods.

Looking from afar, we can find Danjiangkou Dam is just like a sleeping lion on the Hanjiang River, guarding the thousands of local residents. With the completion of South-to-North Water Diversion Project, the Hanjiang River now can make a greater contribution by providing water to cities like Beijing, Tianjin and so on.

Jingle/ Clean- Happy Palace 净乐宫

Jingle/ Clean- Happy Palace, the first one of the Nine Palaces in Wudang Mountains, is located in Danzhao Road, Danjiangkou City, now as the national AAAA - level tourist spot and key cultural unit under national protection. In the history, Jingle Palace was located in the north side of Wudang Mountains. In accordance with *Taihe Mountains Annals*, the father of Emperor

Zhenwu was the king of Jingle Kingdom which governed Junzhou Prefecture/ currently Danjiangou City.

The Palace was built in the sixteenth year of Emperor Yongle of the Ming Dynasty (1418) and destroyed by a big fire in the twenty-eight year of Emperor Kangxi of the Qing Dynasty (1689), and then rebuilt in the thirty year of Emperor Kangxi (1691) and finished six years later, but destroyed again by a big fire in the first year of Emperor Qianlong (1736). There were halls, gateways, pavilions, and Taoist dorms which totaled over 520 pieces, composed of west, middle and east courtyards in the Palace. The main buildings were Memorial Gateway, First Palace Gate, Second Palace Gate, the Main Hall, Parents' Hall, Zhenwu's Hall, Abbot's Hall, Dinning Hall, bathroom, kitchen, storage and other rooms with red walls and blue tiles, deep, quiet and complex, as the main Taoist building in Wudang Mountains.

Much of the remained Palace was drowned in the water when Danjiangkou Reservoir was built in 1958, so that the main cultural relics such as memorial gateway, tortoise carrying stele were transferred to Danjiangkou city. In 2002, Danjiangkou City attracted 70 million Yuan to comprehensively rebuild Jingle Palace. After two-year construction, the square, mountain gate, Imperial Stele Pavilion, three main halls and side halls were finished which made Jingle Palace have the former grandeur and has been the fine example of transferring and rebuilding cultural relics in South-to-North Water Diversion Project.

Danjiangkou National Forest Park 丹江口国家森林公园

Danjiangkou National Forest Park is characterized by rich wild animal and plant resources, unique landscape resource and fine ecological environment, high planning, complete auxiliaries and effective control and protection measures.

After upgraded as national forest park, Danjiangkou City has centered on Water Source of South-to-North Water Diversion, waters and mountains in Danjiangkou and decided to build national forest part, protect the plant and cultivate the water source as to provide clean and clear water to Beijing, invested more capital, completed the mechanism and strengthened management with a purpose to build Danjiangkou Forest Park into the only, different and special national forest park and first-class and world famous ecology tourism destination and the genuine key ecology protect let of Danjiangkou Reservoir.

Danjiangkou National Forest Park is surrounding with Danjiangkou Reservoir and divided into two part by the Hanjiang River, Niuhe Core Area and Taichi Gorge Core Area.

Niuhe Forest Park has 33 main scenes, such as Green Mountains and Blue Water—A Gallery of Thousand Islets, Home of Cattle Boy and Weaver Maiden—God Valley—Core Area, Natural Waterfall Valley—Devil's Nose Gorge, Ancient Junzhou Port—Qingshan Port, and so on. Here are exuberant trees and grasses, many trees over one thousand years, such as, pines, willows, ginkos. Here are abut 363 kinds of wild birds and animals, most of which are under state protection, such as, giant eagle, deer, wolf, monkey and wild pigs and so on. Here are lakes and streams, green mountains and blue waters, recognized as the natural oxygen bar of Danjiangkou City proper.

The Taichi Gorge in Danjiangkou City 丹江太极峡

Here comes The Taichi Gorge. It goes without saying that there must be a close relation with Taichi, or Shadow Boxing to some extent. This scenic spot is located in Shigu/ Stone Drum Town, about 45km away from the downtown area of Danjiangkou City. The Hanjiang River runs across this area. It borders Asian largest man-made lake—Danjiangkou Reservoir, where the splendid project South-to-North Water Diversion originates. The Taichi Gorge is also very close to the holy land of China Taoism, Wudang Mountains that is famous at home and abroad for its gorgeous scenery, majestic ancient building complex, rich and valuable cultural relics, prominent martial arts and affecting folklore. We have talked much about its location and I guess you can't wait to see the charming scenery. What await us includes the precipices, peaks, greenery, fresh air and water.

九龙湖 Now please look to the right and you will find the White Stone Reservoir. A legend has it that there used to be an abyss occupying several acres. Though not big in size, at the bottom, it connected with the East China Sea and South China Sea. The sons of the masters of the two seas often took this shortcut to visit their relatives and friends. In 1968, the pool was submerged because of the construction of the Reservoir. In fact, the locals now have given the reservoir another name, Nine-Dragon Lake. The mountains surrounded by the lake also have interesting names. The exterior peak is called Taoist Mountain, and the interior peak Monk Mountain. Some people say the two names are related to the typography of the two peaks, for they look like the heads of Taoist and monk respectively, while others argue that the mountains are places where wise Taoist and senior monks have a discussion about self-cultivation. None of the legends can be supported by any virtual records. In spite of this, the Danxia landform proves incomparably typical here.

盘龙洞 At the western end of the Taichi Gorge lies a cave named Panlong/ Twisting Dragon Cave, which means a dragon nestles in it. The main cave consists of several parts, including Panlong Cave, Empress Cave, Princess Cave, and Moon Cave and so on. Panlong Cave, as the biggest one, is about 40 meters wide, 50 meters tall and 120 meters high. On the walls inside there are oddly-shaped stone formations, blazing with colors. The legend hast it that there used to be the place where the empress of Chu State retired after falling into disfavor. Empress Cave, the steepest one, lies in the cliff that is about 100 meters high. It is said to be the residence of Princess of Chu State who paid visits to her mother. The naturally formed Taichi Diagram is acclaimed as the most mysterious scenic spot.

二龙山 The story tells that in the unwritten history of mankind from time unrecorded, Nanyang Basin was a vast sea watery and the Taichi Gorge was on the western bank. The charming mountains and waters, with the pleasant climate and lively animals, attracted dozens of the offspring of the Sea Gods. The Jade Dragon, a son of South China Sea God, met the Yellow Dragon, a daughter of East China Sea God by accident. They fell in love with each other and soon got married. Finding here a livable place, they settled down here and refused to return to the Dragon Palace. Their parents got fury at their choice and decided to get them back by force. By then, the new couple had given birth to nine sons and thought it impossible to make them apart. On the other hand, they dared not defy their parents' order and consequently, they turned into two mountains so that they could keep company to each other. So, we can see the mountains on the southern and northern banks, i.e. Yellow Dragon Mountain and Jade Dragon Mountain. The Gorge runs between the two mountains. If you look at them closely, you may find the two peaks, resembling the heads of two dragons, linked with each other and presented a wonderful design of the Diagram. What is also well kept in this area include other scenic spots, such as, Nigh-Dragon Bridge, Two-Dragon Village, Flying-Dragon Mountain. They have become indispensable parts that well stand for cultures of Taoism, Emperor and Celestial Dragon.

玉龙潭 Now come to Jade Dragon Pool, the very beginning of the Gorge. It is about 100m in length and 1 meter deep. The first part of the Gorge is Dragon Lifting Head, the quintessential component of the whole scenic spot. Look up and then you may see the lofty peak, which is said by the locals A Male Dragon Is Lifting Head. The roaring waterfall adds more appeal to it. A master of Fengshui once pointed out that this is a best place for praying promotion, good luck and wealth.

蟾观北斗 Now come to Frog Watching Big Dipper. Look ahead, the rock is shaped like a frog sitting at the bottom of well and watching the sky. What is more amazing is that it can stand unharmed in the face of natural disasters. For thousands of years, countless floods flew over it and a lot of larger stones had been washed away, but it remained perfect in the right place.

西施梳妆池 Now what you can see in front of you is called Xi Shi Dressing-up Pond. Xi Shi was an incomparably charming lady in Chinese history. The pond is rare in that it is a natural round pond. About 3 meters deep, 10 meters in diameter, it looks like a large mirror for dressing up. People say that the empresses of Chu State used to come here for sightseeing and pleasure. Xi Shi, on her journey back to his husband's hometown, once stopped by and put up her cosmetics.

Here is the Xi Shi Temple, or Goddess Temple, once for Xi Shi stayed here for a rest. There used to be three tile-roofed houses and the statue of Xi Shi was enshrined. The wing rooms were places for guests and prayers. It is said that no matter what the locals pray for, the Goddess will help them realize their dreams. A lot of pregnant women swarmed here and prayed for the safety of their babies. In the period of the Great Cultural Revolution in China (1966—1976), the temple was demolished.

The last scenic spot is Re-worshiping Platform. Since it is sandwiched by the two mountains, it is also called Dragon Platform. There is also a legend behind it. Emperor Liu Xiu, after conquering the head of rebels Wang Mang, seized the throne and ordered soldiers to offer sacrifices here. He believed that here was a lucky place for him, for he was saved three times in times of adversity. He even climbed the mountains and kowtowed to show his gratitude. In the feudal society, the Emperors were said to be sons of Dragons, hence the name Dragon Mountain. To prove his sincerity, Emperor Liu Xiu knelt again before he left this place and this is the reason why it is named Re-worshiping Platform.

Jinchan/ Golden Frog Gorge Scenic Spot 金蟾峡景区

Jinchan/ Golden Frog Gorge Scenic Spot is 500m away from Baiyangping Town with a length of twenty km and the fine travel line open to the visitors is 5km. The Gorge has had fine and diverse tourist resources and has been appraised as the First Gorge in Central China for its excellent tourist resource characteristics. Taking Frog Culture as the main theme, special mountain, cliff, stone, water and abundant wild plants and animals as the main body, the Gorge is famous for its charming landscapes, such as, Golden Frog Welcoming Guests, Golden Frog Looking the Moon, Golden Frogs Enjoying Happiness, Jade Girl Welcoming Spring, and natural cliff complex. The Gorge is also a good choice for you to carry out exploration, scientific expedition, painting and drawing.

Here has Jianghe River Drifting, 3.5km long, safe and exciting, with rich and special landscapes on the both banks, which will give the tourists a special happy and exciting experience. Here is Jiangshan Mountain, one of the seventy-two mountains and peaks in Wudang Mountains. The Jiangshan Park is centered on the experience of Jiang/ unbending or unyielding Culture, that is, keeping on exploration, being brave to innovate and never giving up until obtaining success, with a purpose to help the tourists understand and appreciate Jiang Culture and have a special experience so as to have a self-cultivation or self-sublimation through tourism outside of Taoist palaces and halls.

The former People's Commune was well protected and can provide many experiences in the former commune life, such as, having dinner at the commune canteen, living in the commune's rest house, shopping in the commune's supply and marketing cooperative, and appreciating the commune songs and dances. What's more the visitors also can have many farming experience here, such as, extracting oil, striking iron, making wine, spinning thread, making flour by use of stone mill and waterwheel.

Chapter 6 Tourist Resources in Yunyang District 郧阳旅游

Yunyang, China, home of mankind. Yunyang District is located near the magic 30°north latitude of the Earth and in the "Chicken heart" of Chinese geography. Here are world-sensational skull fossils of "Yunxian Man", old Meipu apeman, Bailongdong apeman, Huanglongdong apeman, and Longshan dinosaur fossils. Yunyang District covers an area of 3,863 square kilometers with a total population of 630,000 people, including 19 townships (farms) and 1 economic development zone. After the liberation, the county was set up first and then the administrative system was set up. On September 9, 2014, the State Council approved Yunxian County to withdraw the county title, the whole changed into Yunyang District of Shiyan City. Yunyang is the first area of Danjiangkou Reservoir Base. Due to its unique geographical location and fresh natural environment, Yunyang District has become the place with the most tourism potential. Here are many charming natural landscapes and human scenery.

The Jiulong/ Nine-DragonWaterfall Tourist Area 九龙瀑

The Jiulong Waterfall Tourism Area is one of the national AAAA level tourist attractions, located in Zhaohe Grand Canyon between Nanhuatang Town and Daliu Township, a junction part connecting with Hubei, Shaanxi and Henan provinces which is very near to the Qinling Mountains, the Hanjiang River, and Wudang Mountains. It is a waterfall landscape and the largest waterfall group in Central China. Here are steep cliffs, deep streams, gorgeous gorges and flying waterfalls, and other karst landscapes demonstrating the wonders of the Great Nature. The working and living traces of ancient people thirty thousand years ago formed the unique features of Qinba folk culture.

The scenic spot covering 48km^2, takes "Chinese Dragon Culture" as the main line to connect with all the relevant tourist resources about seven km long. Here are nine waterfalls named by the nine sons of the Dragon, just like nine small dragons jumping and flying, different to each other with its own characteristics. In *The Book of Change*, there is a sentence writing When the sky is healthy, the gentleman will keep on improving himself; on earth, a gentleman carries things by virtue, which is a good praise to the Nine Dragon Waterfall. With a pious heart and walk into the main hall of the Dragon Palace on the steep cliff, appreciate the homes of the ancient people, sense the devotion of the Dragon King teaching his sons and the nine small dragons' excellent performances and strike the Dragon Clock, which will make your best wished come true that your sons and daughters will be powerful and successful.

Confucius said, the wise man loves the water, the benevolent man loves the mountain. The scenic spot is building the tourist programs in accordance with the landscape and demonstrating the principles of Taoism following the Nature and man being an integral part of Nature, such as, sightseeing railway on the cliff, bamboo raft in the lake, flying bike by steel thread, sliding strop in high sky, Jurassic dream river drifting. Here are Shaking Bridge, Alphabetic Bridge, Heart-Linking Bridge and other nine outward bound programs which will make happy and excited. There maybe some wild animals in the deep valleys and canyons, so you are strongly advised to come with partners for the sake of your safety and happiness.

In the Jiulong Waterfall Tourism Area, there are mountains, streams and lakes, and dragons and phoenix where you will be happy, relaxed and motivated to work harder and further in your life and career.

Tiger-Roaring Shoal 虎啸滩

Tiger-Roaring Shoal is in Daliu Town, over 30km away from the District Proper, very near to the unearthing place of Yunyang Ape Man, made by the conjoining of the big streams in the upper reaches of the Quyuan River, one of the branches of the Hanjiang River. The Shoal is about 3km long, with over 30 scenic spots, including Tiger-Jumping Cliff, Drunken Tiger's Painting Screen, Three-Layer Waterfall, Thousand-Layer Waterfall, Jiutian/ Nine-Sky Waterfall, Tiger-Roaring Gorges, Tiger-Jumping Gorge and so on, charming and amazing. Here are small paths in the green and dense forests, strange stones and echoing waterfalls, which is a good place to do an expedition, have a cool summer and happy leisure time.

Dragon-Singing Gorge Tourist Area　龙吟峡旅游风景区

Dragon-Singing Gorge Tourist Area is in Gumu Village of Huangshi Town, 35km away from the District Proper and 70km away from Shiyan City Proper. The green and dense forests has formed a complete landscape belt, providing a sense of wonder and charm. There are nearly 20 big and small karst caves and other 30 scenic spots, such as Goddess Cave, Huaxi/ Flower Stream Valley and Dragon Singing Gorge.

The Goddess Cave is a natural karst cave group with the main scenic spots such as, Lion Peak, Thunder Cave, Wind Cave, Hot Spring, Goddess Cave, Guanyin/ Kwan-yin Cave, Moon Cave and some relevant interesting stories.

Huaxi/ Flower Stream Valley is full of strange mountains and fresh waters, closely connected with Dragon Singing Gorge, an ideal place to do a spring walking, have a cool summer, enjoy a golden autumn and snow-white winder. Here are also exuberant plantations, big trees and colorful flowers, just like the Shangri-La in the novel of John Milton.

Dragon-Singing Gorge is a good place to do expedition and play with waters, including Swing Cliff, Water-Dropping Cliff, Dragon Head Cliff, Cold Water Platform, and Elephant Trunk Pond, full of wonders and terrible experiences.

Yingtaogou Village/ Cherry Valley　樱桃沟

Yingtaogou Village/ Cherry Valley is located in the junction of Shiyan City proper and Yunyang District, 4 kilometers north of Yunyang District, and 10 kilometers south of Shiyan City downtown, very convenient for both residents to have a relaxation here. Cherry Village is named after the wild cherry trees scattered all over the mountainous areas and the villages scattered among the luxuriant cherry trees, forming a very beautiful rustic picture. The village mainly distributes in the valley bottom. Every year after March, the weather is warm, the cherry flowers around family houses begin to be in full profusion. The best shooting point of cherry flower in the village is mainly located in the high-lying area east of the village. Here are beautiful mountain flowers in spring, delicious cherry, strawberry and peach full of the mountains in summer, and sweet orange full of garden in autumn. Every year, from mid-March to May, you can enjoy cherry flowers, plum flowers, peach flowers, mountain peach flowers, Persian chrysanthemums, golden chrysanthemums and wild flowers all over the mountains and valleys. When the mountain flowers fall down, cherry and strawberry fruits will soon mature in May, and visitors can enjoy the double feast of scenery and taste. Cherry trees begin to mature a month after flowering and visitors may appreciate fresh sweet cherries around May Day. The picking period of cherry is lasting about 2 weeks. Then the whole Village becomes a world of cherries and strawberries. The scarlet cherries hung on the branches and bent the branches down. The industrious people put the branches up, and the bright red fruits passed through the trees.

Yunxian Hanjiang River Bridge　郧县汉江大桥

The Bridge was completed and opened to traffic on January 28, 1994. It is an anchor reinforced concrete cable-stayed bridge with a main span of 414 meters (14 meters longer than the 400-meter main span of Wuhan Changjiang River Bridge built in 1995). Adopting the gem type hollow cable tower, double space-inclined cable, the cable tower height is 108.5 meters. The Bridge was advanced in design, novel in design, and compact and beautiful in shape at that time as the first bridge in China and in Asia.

The National Geopark of the Dinosaur Egg Group 恐龙蛋国家地址公园

The National Geopark of the Dinosaur Egg Group is located in the Qinba Mountain area in the middle and upper reaches of the Hanjiang River. It is based on the precious geological relics of the Chilongshan Dinosaur Egg Group and integrates other geological relics in the county, forming the Qinglongshan Dinosaur Egg Fossil Park.

Skull Fossil of Yunyang Ape Man "郧阳人"猿人头骨化石

Skull Fossil of Yunyang Ape Man was unearthed in Mituoshi Village of Qingqu Town by the archeologist in May, 1989 and confirmed by Jia Lanpo and other ten experts and scholars in archeology and paleoanthropology, which has been the first discovery in China and Asia and acknowledged as the National Treasure. The discovery has broken the theory that all human beings have come from the same source. Skull Fossil of Yunyang Ape Man was collected in Yunyang Museum and open to the public.

Yunxian Geopark 郧县地质公园

Yunxian National Geopark is located in the Qinba Mountain area and in the middle and upper reaches of the Hanjiang River. Relying on the precious geological relics of the Chillongshan dinosaur egg group, it integrates other geological relics resources in the District and forms the Qinglongshan Dinosaur Egg Fossil Park.

Yunyang Jinsha Bay 郧阳金沙湾

Yunyang Jinsha Bay, one of the national AAA-level tourist attractions, established in 2001, is a tourist resort with natural scenery and cultural landscape in northwest of Hubei Province, close to Qinglongshan National Geopark, 209 national highway and Shiyan City proper, convenient in transportation, known as Beidaihe in Shiyan.

Yunayang Lake National Wetland Park 郧阳湖国家湿地公园

Shiyan Yunyang Lake National Wetland Park is located in Yunyang District, Shiyan City, Hubei Province, covering a total area of 1,743.6 hectares.

Chapter 7 Zhangwan District and the Main Tourist Resources 张湾旅游

Zhangwan District, administrated directly by Shiyan Municipal Government, bordering the Duhe River and the Hanjiang River, is the core water source of the Middle Project of South-to-North Water Diversion, the cradle of China Second Auto Plant, the headquarter location of Dongfeng Commercial Vehicle Company, called the Home of China Truck, and the biggest economy entity in Shiyan City.

Zhangwan District administrates four towns, four street offices and one provincial-level economic development zone, covering an area of 657km^2, having very convenient transportation and better location advantages, with Xiangyang-Chongqing railway, national highways No. 316 and 209, and Yinchuan-Wuhan Expressway running through. Here are rich tourist resources, such as Dongfeng Auto Industrial Tourism Zone, Sifangshan Mountain Ecology Park, and Huanglongtan/ Yellow Dragon Bay Industrial Ecology Tourism Zone.

Dongfeng Auto Industrial Tourism Zone 东风汽车工业旅游区

The General Assembling Plant of Commercial Vehicle, Dongfeng Auto Company has have three automatic productions of vehicle assembly controlled by the computers and with the competence of producing many kinds and different sizes of vehicles. The Line 1 is mainly on many kinds and mixed production, the Line 2 mainly on heavy vehicles and new types' trial assembling, and the Line 3 on heavy vehicles. Here are four automatic examining lines of commercial vehicles. In 1998, the General Assembling Plant of Commercial Vehicle, Dongfeng Auto Company has made indications and labels, equipped safety facilities, beautified the environment and an air sightseeing corridor of the automatic production in accordance with national AAA-level scenic spots' standard and open to the public, hence the coming of Dongfeng Auto Industrial Tourism Zone. Many state leaders have come here for a visit and inspection, including Li Xiannian, Deng Xiaoping, Hu Yaobang, Zhu Rongji, Li Lanqing, Jiang Zemin, Wu Bangguo, Wen Jiabao and so on.

Huanglongtan/ Yellow Dragon Bay Industrial Ecology Tourism Zone 黄龙滩工业生态旅游区

Huanglongtan Industrial Ecology Tourism Zone was built in 2001 and completed and open to the public in 2003, with Huanglongtan Hydraulic Power Plant as the core, composed of two parts, Industrial Production Zone and Gardening Zone. The total installed power is 0.51 million kw. The former waterway of the Duhe River over the dam of Huanglongtan Reservoir has formed a water gallery of over 20km. The Gardening Zone is divided into three parts, Ecology Tourism Part, Humanities Exhibition Part and Sporting Part. In the Living Tourism Zone, holiday hotels, villas service center, conference rooms are built and open to the public. Now Huanglongtan Industrial Ecology Tourism Zone has been approved as national AAAA-Level Scenic Spot in 2011.

Sifangshan Mountain Ecology Park 四方山生态公园

Sifangshan Mountain, also named Siwang Mountain, meaning overlooking faraway in all direction when you climb onto the mountain top where there was a Siwang Temple which was destroyed in the Great Cultural Revolution. In 1969, Shiyan Television Sending Station was built on the site of Siwang Temple. Because Siwang is homophone to Die in Chinese pronunciation, so it changed to Sifang/ Four-Direction Mountain. In 1992, Shiyan City, Yunyang Prefecture and Dongfeng Auto Company jointly built Sifangshan Botanical Garden, covering 15,000mu, composed of sightseeing orchard, botanical garden, comprehensive zone, water park, deer park, camping zone, hunting zone, and national defense base. The Park was approved as AAA-level scenic spot in 2012. A 25-km-long fitness walkway connecting the South Part and the North Part,

South Gate Plaza, ecology parking lot, signals and directions and other infrastructure were finished in 2014.

Niutoushan/ Ox Head Mountain National Forest Park 牛头山国家森林公园

Niutoushan/ Ox Head Mountain National Forest Park was named by its two outstanding peaks, just like the two horns of the oxes. In 1987, Niutoushan state tree farm was built and renamed Niutoushan/ Ox Head Mountain National Forest Park in 1995, covering 18km^2 and of a forest coverage of 93%, which is composed of Niutoushan Mountain, Yanhu Park and Charming Garden. It was approved as national AAA-Level Scenic Spot in 2010.

The Park is full of green mountains, fresh water, exuberant plantations, clouds-covered peaks. Many scenic spots have been developed, such as, Bonsai Pot Garden, Cliff Stone Park, Cliff House Valley, Tiger Mountain Village, Shennong Picking Herbs, Ox Head worshiping Generals, Plum Garden, Mirror Pond, Gaofeng/ High Peak Temple, Sigu/ Missing Ancient Pavilion and so on. The Tiger Mountain Village has had a very long history with many cultural relics including White Tiger Temple, Taishan/ Mount Tai Temple, Caishen/ Fortune God Temple, White Tiger Stone and the like, which is an ideal place to explore the ancient culture and serene experience.

Baima/ White Horse Mountain Tourist Zone 白马山旅游区

Baima/ White Horse Mountain Tourist Zone, also called Horse-Shouting Mountain, is located in the south of Bailin Town and Huanglong Town, extending from south to north, as one of the seventy-two mountains in Wudang Mountains, whose main peak is 1,088-meter high and covering an area of 10km^2. The landform is like a horse, the mountain top like a high-up horse head, the middle part wide and level like the saddle, and the west part like a horse tail and the mountain top is always covered by white clouds, so the name White Horse Mountain came into being. The main buildings in Jin’an/ Golden Saddle Mountain Village are Five-Immortal Temple, Horse Saddle Stone, Horse Saddle Cave, Zushi/ the Founder’s Hall, Sky Well, Lute-Performing Pavilion, Sacred Tortoise Stone and Flower Cliff. When you climb onto the mountain top, you can enjoy the wonders of phoenix, dragon, sunrise, waterfall and white snow capped mountain in different places and seasons. In 1996, the Five-Immortal Temple in White Horse Mountain was approved as key culture unit under the provincial protection.

Longquan Temple Tourist Zone 龙泉寺旅游区

Longquan Temple Tourist Zone was approved to be built by Shiyan Municipal Government in 2005, covering an area of 1,030mu and of a forest coverage of 90%, among which the temple is covering 30mu, composed of the Great Buddha’s Hall, Sansheng Hall, Tianwang Hall, Captive-Fish-Free Lake, Jiulong/ Nine-Dragon Spring, Guanyin Waterfall, Dragon King Palace, Match-making Bridge, Promising Lake, Mind-Cleaning Spring, One-Hundred-Year Ladder, Happy Forest, Birds Guard, Observation Pavilion and Fortune Gate. The supporting facilities are Longquan Hotel, Longquan Catering Center, Longquan Tea House, Shopping Precinct, Barbecue Zone, Camping Zone, and outdoor development base. The Zone was approved as National AAA-Level Scenic Spot in 2007.

Shiyan Renmin/ People's Park 十堰市人民公园

The former name of Shiyan Renmin/ People's Park was Yangu Park, built in 1975 and extended by adding a zoo in 1976, Zhuanma/ Horse-turning Pavilion, Guanwu/ Watching Boxing Pavilion, Song/ Pine Pavilion and classical entrance hall, hothouse and bonsai pot zone in 1978, forming the primary structure of the Park. The Park was open to the public in 1981. In 1998, an ancient-style great wall of 600 meters and a mountain skidway were built. Chongyang Pagoda of the Tang Dynasty style, 72-meter-high and of nine floors and nine eaves was built on the top of Meihua/ Plum Blossom Mountain. The Park was approved as National AAAA-Level Scenic Spot in 2013.

Daxigou Valley Ecology Tourism Zone 大西沟生态旅游区

Daxigou Valley Ecology Tourism Zone, or Xigou Town, is located in the south of Zhangwan District, covering 113km^2, and of a forest coverage of 94%. Here are Tingzhou/ Boat-Stopping Temple, Hongmeng/ Romantic Dream Temple, Shigu/ Stone Drum Temple, Jiuquan/ Nine-Stream Temple, Hongyan/ Red Cliff Mountain Village, Shouba/ Hand-Picking Cliff, One Line Sky, Three Immortals Guarding Jade Seal, Chongtian/ Washing Sky Channel, Tianzhu/ Heavenly Pillar Peak, Longtou/ Dragon Head Cliff, stone gate, stone window, Guanling Waterfall, and Changping Charming Lake, Changping Reservoir, Sanfeng Village Revolution Site, Education Base of The Three Represents of Shiyan City, Rural Tradition Education Practice Base for Young People, and ecology agriculture and sightseeing trees, grasses, flowers, fruits and herbs, and many rare wild birds and animals, including kiwi fruit, grape, musk deer, golden pheasant, Mongolian gazelle, and masked civet.

Bailong/ Hundred-Dragon Pool Tourist Zone 百龙潭旅游区

Bailong/ Hundred-Dragon Pool Tourist Zone is located in Taozi/ Peach Valley Village, Huaguo Street Office, connecting with Niutoushan/ Ox Head Mountain National Forest Park and the Touyan Reservoir, covering 6 km^2. The Zone is 8-km long and with a vertical altitude difference of over 800 meters. Here are 374 kinds of plants and over 200 ancient trees, including love pea tree, ginko and other rare plants under the national protection, and 20 water ponds and waterfalls.

Fulong/ Taming Dragon Mountain Tourist Zone 伏龙山旅游区

Fulong/ Taming Dragon Mountain Tourist Zone is located in Majiahe Village, 30km away from the City Proper, having 640,000-mu natural forest and 40,000-mu original forest of Bashan Mountain Pines. It's famous for its main peak, 1,730m, higher than the main peak of Wudang Mountains, Tianzhu/ Heavenly Pillar Peak, and acknowledged as a good place to return to the nature.

Huanglong Ancient Buildings Complex 黄龙古建筑群

Huanglong Ancient Buildings Complex, built in the Qing Dynasty, located in Huanglong Town, Zhangwan District, is made up of Shanxi-Shaanxi Guild Hall, Huangzhou Guild Hall, Jiangxi Guild Hall, Wuchang Guild Hall, No. 64 traditional folk house and other folk residences, covering an area of 27,640 m^2, most of which are backing the north and facing the south and the others extending from east to west. Most of the ancient buildings are high and hard gables, whose beam-frame structure includes post and lintel construction, column and tie construction, and mixed type, whose building materials include brick, wood and stone, all having grey tile roofing. Stone gate and window have many types, Chi head and eave have rich decorations, and gables have three main types. Side-rooms and pavilions are different in decoration forms. The Ancient Buildings Complex, the witness of communication and integration of politics, economy, culture and commerce in the northwest of Hubei Province, large in scope, compact in layout and rational in organization, is the typical remains of Shiyan building culture of the Qing Dynasty, has very important value in studying the ancient folk house and construction in the Hangjiang River reaches.

Huanglong Ecology Agriculture Demonstration Garden 黄龙生态农业示范园

Huanglong Ecology Agriculture Demonstration Garden is in Jinping Village of Huanglong Town, covering an area of 30,000m^2, composed of High-tech Agriculture Exhibition Hall, Vegetable & Flower Hall, Green Life Hall, Tropical Plants Hall and Ecology Dinning Hall. Here are 800 big trees and flowers including peach flower and the like, a lawn of 4,000m^2, 200,000 pieces of tulips and ornamental sunflowers. Since the opening in May, 2014, the Garden has hold five sessions of Tulip Tourist Festival consecutively and chose Tulip Goddess and image speakers as to promote the tourist development.

Moon Lake Villa 月亮湖山庄

Moon Lake Villa, located in Fangtan Town, based on clean river water and charming landscapes of the Duhe River, has developed into a comprehensive tourism center including dinning, accommodation, traveling, entertaining and shopping from the former drafting sport. Moon Lake, 30 km away from Shiyan City Proper, is surrounded by green mountains and clean waters, fitted with Thailand-style bamboo tower, bamboo pavilion and corridor and tropical flowers and trees, where the visitors can have a complete relaxation here.

Moon Lake Villa, covering an area of 35km^2, provided with Golden Bamboo Forest, Hanging Tower, Pearl Pond, Lovers' Cliff, Lion Playing with Water, Golden Water Pond, Horse-Returning Stone, the Graveyard of Han Xin's Mother (Han Xin, one of the important generals and strategists of the Western Han Dynasty, same as Xiao He and Zhang Liang) and other scenic spots.

Now the Villa is providing swimming pool, bamboo raft drafting, sand beach volleyball, speedboat, sky bike, sliding surfing, Wuyishan Tea tasting, field existence training and other leisure programs, which can hold small and medium conference and training courses, with a competence of entertaining 1,000 visitors' tour, 300 people's dining, and 120 people's accommodation.

Taohua/ Peach Flower Lake Villa 桃花湖度假村

Taohua/ Peach Flower Lake Villa is located in Majiahe Village, 15km away from the City Proper, among original forest and god-made lakes. Here you can walk in the path upwards the mountain, pick strange and colorful stones, wild crabs in the small streams, and taste the local dishes in the farm stays near the lake while enjoying the water scenery.

Maojian District is special in natural conditions and rich in tourist resources and has been awarded as the back garden of Shiyan City Proper. Here are ecology tourism, revolution tourism, farm stay leisure tour scattered in Saiwudang/ Surpassing Wudang Mountains Nature Reserve, Maota Town and Dachuan Town, such as Ziwei Islet, Peach Flower Islet, Nanshan/ South Mountain Park, Yuanyuan Park, Culture Square, Railway Station Square, Baierhe River Banks and Huilong/ Returning Dragon Temple.

Checheng/ Motor City Plaza 车城广场

Checheng/ Motor City Plaza is located in the intersection of Dongfeng Avenue and East Ring Road opposite to Shiyan (East) Toll Station of Wuhan-Shiyan Expressway, which is a culture plaza recording Dongfeng Motor Company's development history from 1969 to 2010 by way of some significant events. The Plaza has inherited Hanjiang Culture and Wudang Culture to demonstrate the brilliant history of Shiyan City in internationally-applied simple line language and with the combination of nature and ecology gardening skills, forming the landmark plaza of Shiyan City. The plaza space is of a rational layout with stretching force, full of rhythm and metre, embracing Shiyan people's hope and wishes for speed life and bright future.

With the music sound of the Plaza, the fountains and other ornamental water systems will start and create a dreamlike water world in the East Entrance of Shiyan Expressway. Many local residents come here to enjoy their leisure time.

Saiwudang/ Surpassing Wudang Mountains Nature Reserve 赛武当自然风景区

Saiwudang/ Surpassing Wudang Mountains Nature Reserve, also called Fulong/ Taming Dragon Mountain, is located in Xiaochuan Village, 30km away from Shiyan City Proper, named by its main peak of 1,740m, 118m higher than that of Wudang Mountains. Saiwudang Nature Reserve, a provincial-level nature reserve approved by the Hubei People's Government in 2002, has an area of 38,667 hectares and a forest coverage of over 95.1%.

It is neighboring Maota Town in the east, Fangxian County in the south, Dachuan Town in the east and Wudang Road Street Office in the north, 32km away from the City Proper, and facing Wudang Mountains, the holy land of China Taoism in the distance. Here are Master's Temple, Jade Emperor's Hall and other Taoist culture spots, Putuo Peak, Tortoise Head Cliff, Peach Flower Lake, Missing Ridge and other twenty natural wonders, vivid and attractive.

The Nature Reserve is rich in plants and animals, about 1,316 kinds of plants, some of which are under the state protection or the province protection, such as Ginko and Chinese Yew, and 204 kinds of animals, some of which are under the state protection or the province protection, such as leopard, forest musk deer, golden eagle and Aquila heliaca. Here are many high and big pines in a diameter of one meter and a height of over 30 meters.

Standing on the main peak and looking to the southeast, you will see the Golden Top of Wudang Mountains. Here, you can appreciate cloud sea after rains, sunrise in the morning, huge ancient trees, deep and steep cliffs, running animals, and fragrant flowers in spring, snow capped mountains in winter, full of charm and changes, which is an ideal place for Shiyan residents to have a travel, sightseeing, holiday, scientific research and expedition. The Reserve was approved as AAA-level Tourist Spot in 2003 by Hubei Provincial Quality Degree Evaluating Committee of Tourist Spots.

Huilong/ Returning Dragon Temple 回龙寺

Huilong Temple, located in Qujia Bay, Xiping Village of Dongcheng/ East City Economy Development Zone, was first built in the late years of the Yuan Dynasty and rebuilt in the second year of Emperor Hongzhi of the Ming Dynasty (1489) as the place to spread Buddhism. The Temple was built on a small hill with the form of a twisting dragon sleeping there, two well of clean water are near the temple gate just like two eyes of the dragon. The Temple is backing the east and facing the west and Xiping/ West Field and the Majiahe River winding through in front of the Temple, hence the name Huilong Temple, Returning Dragon Temple.

In the left front of the Temple, there stands a brick-wood-structure Zhaobei/ Facing North Pogada, built in the seventh year of Emperor Chenghua of the Ming Dynasty (1471), and completely destroyed in the early years of the Republic of China. A Taishan/ Mount Tai Temple stands in the right and Grandma Temple of three rooms in the left, which was destroyed and only wall bases left there. Huilong Temple was divided into five parts, front, middle and back halls, right and left side rooms, 42 pieces of rooms in total, covering 1,094m^2. There are four stone statues in the Front Hall, the Great Bodhisattva Wei Tuo in the Middle Hall and a tortoise carrying a stele standing in front of the Hall, which is 226cm high and 92cm wide, inscribed the records of rebuilding the Temple in 1489—1494. Now, the tortoise and stele inscription are well kept. A copper chime put in the Hall and the Taoist will hit it when they recite the scriptures, clear and crisp. There are colorful and vivid wall paintings in the Back Hall.

Shiyan Ancient-style Street 十堰老街

Shiyan Ancient-style Street is in Eryan Street Office, built in the Ming and Qing dynasties, formerly named Zhangjia Street, then Chenjia Street in the late years of the Ming Dynasty. In the middle years of the Qing Dynasty, for the purpose of watering the farmlands, the people here built ten weirs in the Bai'er River and the Jianghe River and the administration controlling the ten weirs was located in the Street, therefore the residents were accustomed to call Chenjia Street Shiyan meaning ten weirs. The buildings in the Ancient Street are in North-South symmetry, earth-wood structure, and full of shops and stores, which was the shopping center of Shiyan and the distributing center of local products. The Ancient Street was rebuilt in 2003 and some of the old houses were dismantled and now only some ancient buildings remained in the East Street.

Ziwei Islet Villa 紫薇岛度假村

Ziwei Islet Villa is located in the southwest bay of the Majiahe Reservoir, 7 km away from the City Proper, covering an area of 160,000 m^2. The Villa center is surrounded by water and planted many trees and flowers and equipped with many leisure and entertainment facilities, such as, fishing, basketball, tennis ball, swimming pool, water skidway, billiard ball, playing cards and chess, catering, boarding and meeting. It is an ideal place for you to hold meetings, have dinner, and enjoy leisure time and holidays.

Peach Flower Islet 桃花岛

Peach Flower Islet is located in Liaojia Village of Maota Town. Here is a man-made reservoir with a 18-meter-high dam and 2,561,000 m^3 water storage. The narrow and steep river valley has formed a water coverage of 6.6 hectares, surrounded by high mountains and green plants. In the center of the reservoir an islet made by cutting the mountain stands there. There is a tourist center near the lake where the visitors can do boating, have dinner and appreciate the surrounding landscapes.

Ancient Tree Complex 千年古树群

Ancient Tree Complex is in Langxi Village of Dachuan Town, formed by seven big and ancient trees whose total age is over one thousand years, whose diameter is over one meter and the tree shade is as big as a basketball playground.

Zushi/ Founder's Hall/ Lesser Golden Top 祖师殿（小金顶）

Zushi/ Founder's Hall/ Lesser Golden Top is located in the peak top of Saiwudang Mountain, originally built in the years of Emperor Jiajing (1522—1566) of the Ming Dynasty and rebuilt in the Qing Dynasty and the Republic of China. The scenic spot is composed of Zushi Hall and Clock Tower, in brick and wood structure and backing west and facing east. The original temple had twelve pieces of rooms and Zushi Statue and two stone steles of the Ming Dynasty, now just Clock Tower built in the Republic of China remained. The Statue and the two steles were destroyed in the Great Cultural Revolution (1966—1976).

Yuanyang/ Mandarin Duck Temple 鸳鸯寺

Yuanyang/ Mandarin Duck Temple is in Yuanyang Village of Dongcheng/ East City Economy Development Zone, originally built in the eighth year of Emperor Daoguang of the Qing Dynasty (1828), destroyed in 1987 for the reason of building Yuanyang Primary School. Now there are two complete stone Buddhas and many broken ones. Three stone steles were buried in the bounding walls as the base. There hanged a iron pot in the tree in the campus used as the clock to tell students to begin or stop a class several years ago.

Tianyuan Temple 天元观

Tianyuan Temple is in Zhujia Valley of Xiaochuan Village, built in the Ming Dynasty and destroyed in the following dynasties. Now here only Stone Stele inscribing Imperial's Dragon Gate and construction site left.

Ke Family's Courtyard 柯家大院

Ke Family's Courtyard, also the Folk Customs Museum of Saiwudang Mountains, located in Xiaochuan Village of Saiwudang Nature Reserve, was built in the years of Emperor Jiaqing of the Qing Dynasty (1796—1821), with a coverage of 1,200m^2 and a construction area of 450m^2. Ke Family's Courtyard is a Chinese-style Siheyuan made up of front and back halls and left and right siderooms, whose main building is in brick-wood structure, built by Ke Zhengdong and lasted for about nine years. After the construction, Ke Family's Courtyard became the key hotel on the way from Shiyan to Fangxian County, full of visitors.

Maojian Lutang/ Hall 茅箭陆塘

Majian Lutang/ Hall is located in Maojiantang Village of Dongcheng Economy Development Zone, built in the Qing Dynasty. Tang/ Hall was the unit or organization of the feudal ruling class to maintain law and order, transmit official letters and station troops. The former Maojian Lutang was a Siheyuan of sixteen rooms, among which the main halls were 10 and three side rooms in each side. In the years of Emperor Guangxi of the Qing Dynasty, Maojian Lutang had one official, one horse, and twenty-four armed servicemen. In the early years of the Republic of China, Maojian Lutang was canceled and changed into Maojiantang Primary School. In 2000, the original building was dismantled.

Shiyan-Fangxian Old Road 十堰通房县古道

Shiyan-Fangxian Old Roads had two, one was the ancient salt way from Kazi Village of Dachuan Town to Longtan Village of Damu Town, Fangxian County, 7.5km long and 1.2 meter wide, used as the key road to connect Shiyan and Fangxian before 1967. Now the Third Group of Kazi Village of Dachuan Town remained over-80-steps stone ladder besides which a tower was built for the passengers to have a rest here. The other road is from Ke Family's Courtyard of Xiaochuan Village to Fangxian County, formed in the Qing Dynasty. Just through the two roads the passengers and goods were transported from Henan Province, Xiangyang City and Yunxian County to Fangxian County.

Appendix

问道十堰 逐梦茅箭

Appreciate Taoism in Shiyan and Realize Dreams in Maojian

无数次的旅程，总是期待再一次来到这里，阳光下的城市，车轮上的精彩，这里有更多的激情和诗意。

Though having travelled many times, I am looking forward to visiting Shiyan once again, a city in the sun, on the moving wheels and full of passion and poem.

地处“几何国心”，位居中国十大魅力城市——湖北省十堰市中心城区，武当滋养，汉水润泽。新时代，新茅箭，正以大气开放、兼容并蓄的胸怀向世界张开热情的臂膀。

Located in the center of China geometrically, Maojian District is the core area of Shiyan City, one of the Ten Charming Cities in China, nourished by Wudang Mountains and the Hanjiang River. In the new era, Maojian is open, warm and active to welcome the world.

Auto Industry, the Cornerstone of China 汽车产业 国之中枢

40 多年前，中国汽车工业从这里涅槃新生，40 多年后，东风汽车誉满全球，东风商用车、东风实业、中正、驰田、海龙、汇斯诚展开造车竞速赛；大洋、正奥、通达、同创、康明斯屡次增资扩产，向世界输送高端汽车智能制造装备……

Forty years ago, China auto industry was born here, and now, Dongfeng Auto is famous in the world, such as Dongfeng Commercial Vehicle, Dongfeng Industrial Company, Zhongzheng Auto, Chitian Motor, Hailong Motor, and Huisicheng Special Auto are working hard in making cars and vehicles; Dayang Vehicle, ZhengAo Automotive Accessories, Tongda Motor, Tongchuang Shaft and Dongfeng Cummings are increasing capital and expanding production, providing high-end auto and intelligent equipment...

“茅箭造”驰骋世界，沙漠冲浪车、房车、罐式车、文化演艺车、环卫车、洒水车等 200 多个专用车品种热销国内外。

All kinds of cars and vehicles Made in Maojian are driving fast in the world, such as desert surfer, touring car, tank car, theatrical performance car, sanitation truck, watering cart, and other 200 kinds, widely welcomed home and abroad.

世界 500 强 2 家，上市企业 1 家，新三板、新四板挂牌企业 58 家，茅箭区全域开放硕果累累。

There are two World Top 500 enterprises, one listed enterprise, and 58 New Three/ Four Boards listed enterprises in Maojian District, open and fruitful.

沐浴“东风”，百业兴盛。植根于中国汽车工业的“东方底特律”，茅箭区形成了以汽车及零部件产业为主导的高端装备制造、电子信息、商贸物流、新材料、新工艺等多元化产业体系。截至 2017 年底，全区规模以上工业企业 135 家，实现产值 309 亿元。茅箭被授予“国家商用车零部件高新技术产业化基地”“湖北省重点产业集群”等殊荣。

Supported by Dongfeng Auto, all industries are flourishing. Developed from Shiyan, the East Detroit of China Auto Industry, Maojian District has formed multi-element industry system of high-end manufacturing, electronic information, commercial logistics, new material and new process with auto and accessories as the mainbody. By the end of 2017, there are 135 enterprises above designed size, with a total value of RMB 30.9 billion Yuan. Maojian District has been awarded as The High-tech Industrialization Base of State Commercial Vehicle Accessories, Key Industries Cluster of Hubei Province, and so on.

绿色化现代山水之城，涌动着创新驱动的喷薄活力，彰显着十堰人追赶时代潮流的风范和勇于革故鼎新的精神纬度。

A green, modern city of mountains and waters, is full of vitality of innovation, demonstrating Shiyan people striving for fashion and creation.

Innovation Driven, Industries Prosperous　创新驱动　业之天元

敢为人先、勇于逐梦，茅箭创造了“向山要地”，建设“工业梯田”的集约用地模式，率先探索出高科技、高附加值的产业革新道路，孕育 2 家国家级众创空间、1 家国家级中小企业公共服务示范平台、6 家省级众创空间、13 家省级技术中心，成为茅箭人道和天下、创新筑梦的精神标识。

Brave enough to be No. One to realize our dreams, Maojian District has created intensive land use models of obtaining land from mountain and establishing industrial terrace, has explored industry reform ways of high technology and high value. There are two state-level Maker Spaces, one state-level Public Service Demonstration Platform for Medium and Small Enterprises, six province-level Maker Spaces, thirteen province-level technological centers, which are the symbol of Maojian people striving for harmony and innovation.

创新驱动打造“智慧引擎”，茅箭区国家知识产权强县（区）通过验收，共建成省级院士专家工作站 7 家，全区每年引进、培养、输出成熟的产业工人达 10 万人次。

Making Intelligent Engine by innovation, Maojian District has been The State Intellectual Property County, and set up seven provincial workstations of academician and expert, having introduced, cultivated and output skillful industrial worker 100,000 person-times.

坚持与国际接轨，茅箭区开通“大企业”服务直通车，创新政府投资重资产、企业投资轻资产的“拎包入住”模式，提供量身打造的标准厂房、生产设备，纯熟的技术人才，有效激活投资，搭建起产业集聚发展平台。

Acting on international convention, Maojian District has provided Mega-enterprise through-platform, innovated move-in model where the government invests on heavy assets and enterprises invest on light assets, provided customized plant, production equipment, and skilled technician, as to effectively stimulate investment and establish industry cluster development centers.

“企业家第一”理念深入民心。区政府加大财政、税收、金融支持，设立政府发展基金，建立银企对接为主，贴息贷款担保，区领导担任重点企业“首席服务官”，明确专班提供“全程式”“保姆式”服务。有效补充融资机制，推广运用 PPP 运作模式，改革跨境交易管理，实行意愿结汇，企业融资更加方便快捷。

Adhering to Entrepreneur-first principle, Maojian District has increased supports in financing, tax and banking, established bank-enterprise connections to offer soft loan and government officials work as the senior clerk of key enterprises and provide whole-process-style and nanny-style services. Improving financing mechanism and practicing PPP operation model, reforming cross-border transaction management, practicing willingness exchange settlement system, enterprises are easy and quick to finance.

用青春之手触摸诗意梦境，在这座春意盎然的城市里，每一个茅箭人都享受着绿色诗意的生活，品味着自然与人文之美。

Touch the poetic dreamland with youth hand, Maojian people are enjoying the green life and the harmonious charm of nature, people and culture.

A Poetic City of Harmony 诗意之都 张弛有道

移民城市，亲善包容。商场超市，星罗棋布。城在山中，林在城中，人在画中。

A city of immigrants, warm, kind and inclusive. Supermarkets and department stores are here and there. Shiyan sits in mountains, forests in city proper and people in picturesque gardens.

成功创建“省级生态区”的茅箭，繁华尽收眼底，现代都市气息扑面而来。建有双语幼儿园、省级重点高中，3 所高等院校，2 家三甲医院，科教医疗资源傲视全国。

Maojian District, Provincial Ecological District, is full of fashion and modern city life. There are bilingual kindergartens, provincial key high schools, three universities and college, two First-class Hospitals at Grade 3, rich of scientific, educational and medical resources.

登武当山悟道，品味悠闲慢生活随东风车驰骋，感受现代快生活。快慢之间，张弛有道。

Climb Wudang Mountains to experience Taoism and enjoy leisure life, drive Dongfeng Auto to enjoy modern speed. Between leisure and speed, here is harmony.

新时代、新征程。宏图大业，你我同行！邀约世界，集结茅箭，让我们携手共建这座旖旎繁华的现代化汽车城。

A new era, a new journey. You and I are making great progress. Friends from home and abroad, welcome to Maojian District, work together for a better future.

十堰茅箭欢迎您！

Welcome to Maojian District, Shiyan City!

A Poetic City of Harmony

Welcome to Maojian District, Shiyan City!